Advanced Topics in Information Resources Management
Volume 5

Mehdi Khosrow-Pour, D.B.A.
Information Resources Management Association, USA

IDEA GROUP PUBLISHING
Hershey • London • Melbourne • Singapore

Acquisitions Editor:	Renée Davies
Development Editor:	Kristin Roth
Senior Managing Editor:	Amanda Appicello
Managing Editor:	Jennifer Neidig
Copy Editor:	April Schmidt
Typesetter:	Diane Huskinson
Cover Design:	Integrated Book Technology
Printed at:	Integrated Book Technology

Published in the United States of America by
     Idea Group Publishing (an imprint of Idea Group Inc.)
     701 E. Chocolate Avenue, Suite 200
     Hershey PA 17033
     Tel: 717-533-8845
     Fax: 717-533-8661
     E-mail: cust@idea-group.com
     Web site: http://www.idea-group.com

and in the United Kingdom by
     Idea Group Publishing (an imprint of Idea Group Inc.)
     3 Henrietta Street
     Covent Garden
     London WC2E 8LU
     Tel: 44 20 7240 0856
     Fax: 44 20 7379 3313
     Web site: http://www.eurospan.co.uk

Advanced Topics in Information Resources Management, Volume 5 is part of the Idea Group Publishing series named *Advanced Topics in Information Resources Management Series* (ISSN 1536-9329).

ISBN 1-59140-929-2
Paperback ISBN 1-59140-930-6
eISBN 1-59140-931-4

British Cataloguing in Publication Data
A Cataloguing in Publication record for this book is available from the British Library.

All work contributed to this book is new, previously-unpublished material. The views expressed in this book are those of the authors, but not necessarily of the publisher.

Advanced Topics in Information Resources Management

Volume 5

Table of Contents

Preface

Modern organizations are constantly in search of more effective and efficient technologies and managerial techniques to manage their ever-evolving information resources. While researchers and educators study various critical factors effecting strategies and technologies utilized by organizations, practicing managers apply emerging technologies and methodologies to increase the firm's returns made in information resources and technologies infrastructure. *Advanced Topics in Information Resources Management, Volume 5*, provides information technology researchers, scholars, educators, and practicing managers with the latest research on managing the technological, organizational, and human aspects of information utilization and management. This volume presents current trends and challenges in implementing and strengthening information resources strategies in organizations worldwide.

Chapter I, "Multimedia Impact on Human Cognition," by Hayward P. Andres, North Carolina A&T State University (USA), discusses the increasing costs organizations need to train employees in today's high technology environment. This study suggests that trainee/learner cognitive processing capacity, information presentation format and complexity, and multimedia technology should be leveraged in order to minimize training duration and costs and maximize knowledge transfer. It presents a causal model of how multimedia and information complexity interact to influence sustained attention, mental effort and information processing quality, all of which subsequently impact comprehension and learner confidence and satisfaction outcomes.

Chapter II, "IT Project Managers' Perceptions and Use of Virtual Team Technologies," by Catherine M. Beise, Salisbury University (USA), Fred

Niederman, Saint Louis University (USA), and Herb Mattord, Kennesaw State University (USA), presents the results of a case study pertaining to the use of information and communication media to support a range of project management tasks. In this study, "virtual" describes the extent to which communication is electronic rather than the extent to which team members are geographically separated. Although the number of respondents was limited, the richness of the data collected leads to the conclusion that successful project managers and teams become skilled at adapting a variety of existing communication technologies to match the project task or process, the receiver, their own role as sender, and the content of the message. This study suggests that groupware designers and developers need to better understand project management methods and best practices in order to provide better tools for practitioners, particularly as organizations expand globally and increasingly outsource various functions of their IT development and operations.

Chapter III, "Information Sharing in Supply Chain Management with Demand Uncertainty," by Zhensen Huang and Aryya Gangopadhyay, University of Maryland, Baltimore County (USA), presents information sharing as a major strategy to counteract the amplification of demand fluctuation going up the supply chain known as the bullwhip effect. However, sharing information through inter-organizational channels can raise concerns for business management from both technical and commercial perspectives. The existing literature focuses on examining the value of information sharing in specific problem environments with somewhat simplified supply chain models. The present study takes a simulation approach in investigating the impact of information sharing among trading partners on supply chain performance in a comprehensive supply chain model that consists of multiple stages of trading partners and multiple players at each stage.

Chapter IV, "The Impact of IT Personnel Skills on IS Infrastructure and Competitive IS," by Terry Anthony Byrd, Auburn University (USA) Bruce R. Lewis, Wake Forest University (USA) and Douglas E. Turner, State University of West Georgia (USA) describes the critical importance of the knowledge and skills of information technology (IT) personnel as the strategic value of IT in modern organizations has become apparent. In addition to technical skills traditionally expected of IT personnel, organizational, functional, and managerial skills have been increasingly cited as mandatory for these employees. This chapter uses a well-accepted typology of IT personnel knowledge and skills, and investigates its relationship to desirable technological traits in organizations and to technological variables that have been closely aligned to competitive advantage in organizations. Implications of these findings and a call for further research into the strategic value of IT personnel knowledge and skills are discussed.

Chapter V, "A Socio-Technical Heuristic for Analysis of IT Investments: Results from Two Case Studies," by Grover S. Kearns, University of South

Florida (USA), states that a majority of CEOs have experienced failed information technology (IT) investments. While such investments have the potential for providing competitive advantage, actual returns have varied widely. Numerous methods exist for investment evaluation, but traditional methods do not adequately account for the intangible benefits that characterize strategic investments and lack other features of portfolio selection. This chapter presents a framework based upon the analytic hierarchy process, combined with integer programming, to overcome the deficiencies associated with traditional approaches to economic evaluation of IT investments. Based on socio-technical theory and observations from two case studies in which the framework was applied successfully, a heuristic is developed for the investment process. Findings and implications are discussed.

Chapter VI, "Global Service Provider Strategies and Networking Alternatives," by Rob Landi, WorldCom (USA) and Mahesh S. Raisinghani, University of Dallas (USA) discusses how deregulation and liberalization of the telecommunications markets have led to tough international competition. This chapter presents well-established approaches used by large telecom service providers in assessing the technical and market forces impacting their network planning and strategies. This chapter, in the form of a tutorial, takes the reader through the assessment and analysis processes dealing with the requirements, design, and implementation issues facing global communications carriers today. Four generic telecommunication network models (varying based on the degree of capital intensity required) are presented to demonstrate that a strategy of employing these generic models to appropriate settings generates cost savings and network efficiencies. A specific case analysis conducted by the global communications carrier for a regional network in Italy is included that discusses strategic planning for the provision of new data and Internet services, and assesses alternative network designs and technologies to provide optimized solutions and service delivery.

Chapter VII, "Toward a Greater Understanding of End-Users' Acceptance of ERP Systems," by Fiona Fui-Hoon Nah, Xin Tan, and Soon Hing Teh, University of Nebraska-Lincoln (USA), states that despite huge investments made by organizations in ERP implementation, maintenance, and user training, ERP implementation failures and less than expected productivity improvements are not uncommon. End users' reluctance or unwillingness to adopt or use newly implemented ERP systems is often cited as one of the main reasons for ERP failures. To understand the lack of end-user acceptance of ERP systems, we examined end users' attitude toward system use and symbolic adoption; the latter refers to users' voluntary mental acceptance of a system. Four instrumental beliefs — perceived usefulness, perceived ease of use, perceived compatibility, and perceived fit — were modeled as the antecedents. The research model was tested using a survey on end users' perceptions in adopting and using a newly implemented ERP system. The study provides managerial implications for organizations in engendering positive user acceptance of enterprise systems and applications.

Chapter VIII, "Inclusion of Social Subsystem Issues in IT Investment Decisions: An Empirical Assessment," by Sherry D. Ryan and Michael S. Gates, University of North Texas (USA), describes how researchers have attempted to augment the traditional cost/benefit analysis model used in the IT decision process. However, frequently social subsystem issues are inadequately considered. Survey data, collected from a U.S. sample of 200 executives, provides an empirical assessment of how these issues compare with other IT decision criteria given differing decision types. The social subsystem issues considered most important by decision makers are also identified, and the manner by which they consider these issues is investigated.

Chapter IX, "Effect of Tasks, Salaries, and Shocks on Job Satisfaction Among MIS Professionals," by Fred Niederman, Saint Louis University (USA) and Mary Sumner, Southern Illinois University, Edwardsville (USA), contrasts attitudes and attributes of current and former positions of IT professionals who have changed jobs within the IT field. It also examines relationships among key variables of tasks performed, salary, job satisfaction, and external influences or "shocks" that may have precipitated turnover. Survey data were collected from 169 MIS professionals. A number of significant relationships among variables between some tasks and salary, some tasks and job satisfaction, and low former job satisfaction and response to particular "shocks" relative to turnover emerged from the data.

Chapter X, "Empirical Evaluation of an Integrated Supply Chain Model for Small and Medium Sized Firms," by Toru Sakaguchi, Northern Kentucky University (USA) Stefan G. Nicovich, University of New Hampshire (USA) and C. Clay Dibrell, Oregon State University (USA) explains that, with increased global competitive pressures, companies operating in these competitive environments are not only looking to their distribution division to save money, but also to generate competitive advantages. One technique is the integrated supply chain. This chapter draws on resource dependency theory and the realities of ever-increasing information technology sophistication as enablers of successful supply chain integration, resulting in the creation of our model to guide managers throughout this process. Through a Web-based survey, 329 responses were collected and analyzed through a structural equation modeling technique using LISREL to confirm the relationships in the model.

Chapter XI, "Identifying and Managing the Enablers of Knowledge Sharing: An Exploration in the UK Healthcare Sector," by W. A. Taylor, University of Bradford (UK) and G. H. Wright, Manchester Metropolitan University Business School (UK), presents the idea that knowledge sharing in public services has not yet received much attention in the research literature. This chapter investigates knowledge sharing in one public service context, the UK National Health Service (NHS), and identifies factors that influence the readiness of an organization to share knowledge effectively. Using participant observation, document analysis, interviews and a survey of managers, data are presented to highlight enablers of effective knowledge sharing in health care service delivery.

Chapter XII, "Tranquilizing the Werewolf that Attacks Information Systems Quality," by Evan W. Duggan, University of Alabama (USA), discusses a variety of available user-centered and process-oriented systems delivery methods, philosophies, and techniques, which may be used in innovative permutations to tranquilize the dragon beyond its capacity to generate terror. The application context for these approaches, their strengths and weaknesses as indicated by the research literature, and reported practitioner experiences are also discussed.

Chapter XIII, "Testing and Extending Theory in Strategic Information Systems Planning Through Literature Analysis," by Irwin T. J. Brown, University of Cape Town (South Africa), states that strategic information systems planning (SISP) has been, and continues to be, a key concern to information systems managers, and much research effort has been devoted to studying it. SISP has been theorized in terms of an input-process-output model, with well-defined categories, and a set of hypotheses to be tested. Based on this theoretical framework, a comprehensive analysis of academic literature published since 1991 is undertaken. The analysis reveals the extent to which the various categories and hypotheses within this framework have been researched, as well as identifying additional hypotheses that are suggested from the literature.

Chapter XIV, "Business Process Reengineering: The Role of Organizational Enablers and the Impact of Information Technology," by Hamid Reza Ahadi, Iran University of Science and Technology in Tehran (Iran), examines organizational factors that affect the implementation of business process reengineering (BPR) when applying two specific information technologies (i.e., Electronic Data Interchange and/or Internet technology). This research uses a survey methodology to gather information about how organizational enablers and information technology affect BPR implementation. By determining the factors that affect BPR implementation, these factors can be managed in the best interest of customers, employees, and organizations. From the nine hypotheses tested in this study, six factors were found to be positively associated with successful implementation of BPR: top management supports, change management, centralization of decision making, formalization of procedure, organizational culture, and customer involvement. By determining the factors that affect BPR implementation, these factors can be managed in the best interest of customers, employees, and organizations.

In today's information society, organizations more then ever revolve around information resources management to improve their strategic posture and to stay competitive. From organizing data to providing effective communication, technology facilitates impressive growth and success for both organizations and their stakeholders. Effective management of information resources has become a necessity, and learning from the latest research and advances of practitioners, researchers, and educators within the information resources management and information technology field provides others with the opportunity to learn from the success and pitfalls of other organizations. An outstanding collection of the latest research associated with the effective utilization of information technology, *Advanced Topics in Information Resources Management, Volume 5*, provides insight on how to successfully implement and expand information resources and technology in modern organizations globally.

Mehdi Khosrow-Pour, D.B.A.
Editor-in-Chief
Information Resources Management Association, USA

Chapter I

Multimedia Impact on Human Cognition

Hayward P. Andres
North Carolina A&T State University, USA

ABSTRACT

Organizations are faced with increasing costs needed to train employees in today's high technology environment. Educators are also striving to develop new training and teaching methods that will yield optimal learning transfer and complex skill acquisition. This study suggests that trainee/ learner cognitive processing capacity, information presentation format and complexity, and multimedia technology should be leveraged in order to minimize training duration and costs and maximize knowledge transfer. It presents a causal model of how multimedia and information complexity interact to influence sustained attention, mental effort, and information processing quality, all of which subsequently impact comprehension and learner confidence and satisfaction outcomes. Subjects read a text script, viewed an acetate overhead slide presentation containing text-with-graphics, or viewed a multimedia presentation depicting the greenhouse effect (low complexity) or photocopier operation (high complexity). Causal path analysis results indicated that presentation media (or format) had a direct impact on sustained attention, mental effort, information processing quality, comprehension, and learner confidence and satisfaction. Information complexity had direct effects on sustained attention, mental effort, and information processing quality. Finally, comprehension and learner confidence and satisfaction were both influenced through an intervening sequence of sustained attention, mental effort, and information processing quality.

INTRODUCTION

During information presentation, the target audience must construct a mental representation of situations or scenarios conveyed by the verbal content and images contained in the presentation. Cognitive psychologists refer to these representations as situation models (Friedman & Miyake, 2000; Kaup & Zwaan, 2003). During situation model construction, increases in the number of alternative order of events, number of interconnections among objects and events, and factors that give rise to specific events will lead to a decline in the accuracy and capacity in cognitive processing utilized to construct a situation model (Zwaan & Madden, 2004; Zwaan, Magliano & Graesser, 1995).

During multimedia presentation, subjects are presented with information in verbal and pictorial form, and both the verbal and visual processing channels of memory are used to translate the information into the appropriate situation model (Hegarty, Narayanan, & Freitas, 2002; Mayer & Moreno, 2002). In instructional settings, animation and other types of graphics that depict the behavior of various phenomena such as meteorology, physics, or chemistry have been used to reduce information complexity, augment cognitive processing, and facilitate comprehension (Moreno & Mayer, 2002; Moreno & Mayer, 2004; Rieber, 1991). Multimedia can also reduce the perceived equivocality of a low-analyzable decision-making task (Lim & Benbasat, 2000) and promote computer self-efficacy that leads to increased performance in computer-based training situations (Christoph, Schoenfeld & Tansky, 1998).

The goal of this study is to investigate the impact of multimedia information representation on cognitive processing activities (e.g., information encoding, situation model construction, and comprehension) typical to problem solving, training, and decision-making contexts. A capacity theory of comprehension (Just & Carpenter, 1992), dual processing theory of working memory (Mayer & Moreno, 2002, 2004; Paivio, 1986), theory of attentional inertia (Burns & Anderson, 1993; Lavie et al., 2004), and the PASS (Planning, Attention, Simultaneous, and Successive) cognitive processing theory (Naglieri & Das, 1997; Naglieri & Rojhan, 2004) are used to provide a framework for this investigation.

The following section presents a review of empirical research on information presentation mode (i.e., format), information complexity, and cognitive processing. Next, using relevant research findings, a causal path model that presents hypothesized linkages among information presentation mode, information complexity, sustained attention and mental effort, information processing quality, comprehension, and learner confidence and satisfaction is presented. This is followed by a discussion of the findings, implications of results, and suggestions for future research on assessing multimedia-based information presentation on cognitive processing in learning, training, and decision-making settings.

BACKGROUND AND
THEORETICAL FRAMEWORK

Information Presentation Media

Visual imagery depicts spatial arrangement, relative size, physical appearance, and the configuration of subcomponents (Lloyd-Jones & Vernon, 2003). Levin, Anglin, and Carney (1987) noted that pictures have the following effects: (1) minimize explanatory content by summarizing distinctive features or procedures; (2) facilitate interpretation by clarifying abstract concepts; (3) facilitate comprehension by eliminating the need to translate text into imagery; and (4) facilitate long-term memory by creating a memorable mnemonic. Mayer and Moreno (1998) noted that verbal (text or auditory) and visual information are each processed through distinct cognitive processing channels (i.e., verbal and visual) that compliment each other.

Multimedia utilizes computer and audiovisual technology to present information verbally (text or auditory), as static pictures or diagrams, and as animated graphics or video (Kozma, 1991). Attentional inertia (i.e., sustained attention and applied mental effort) results when a presentation medium induces perceptual arousal that sustains attention to the medium, and when learner confidence and satisfaction is promoted through enhanced cognitive processing (Burns & Anderson, 1993).

Information Complexity

Inferential complexity associated with information is a function of the number of causal links in a chain of actions, physical states, or mental states. Causal links between units of information are typically defined through the use of temporal (e.g., before then after), causal (e.g., which caused, which enabled, because, if-then), or intentional (e.g., in order that, so that, to allow) connectives (Gennari, 2004; Millis, Golding, & Baker, 1995). As the number of causal links needed to convey an idea or concept increases (i.e., causal chain length), working memory becomes overloaded because it is limited in the number of related ideas that can be simultaneously stored and processed (Halford, Wilson, & Philips, 1998). Halford et al. (1998) noted that when working memory capacity is exceeded, subjects begin to condense the situation model to reduce cognitive load but at the expense of making some relational information, that may be needed in subsequent processing, inaccessible. Information complexity is also a function of the extent to which one clause is related to more than one other clause-connective span (Millis, Graesser, & Haberlandt, 1993; Wolfe, 2005). Cognitive complexity or managing information complexity reduces the number of simultaneous concepts processed by working memory (Lien et al., 2005; Oberauer & Kliegl, 2004).

Cognitive Processing

The dual-coding theory of working memory suggests that information encoding and processing can take place in a verbal working memory and/or in a visual working memory workspace (Paivio, 1986). Comprehension is enhanced as a result of a reduction in cognitive load because the visual working memory workspace immediately encodes spatial information and does not require any translation of verbal information into imagery (Mayer & Moreno, 2002; Moreno & Mayer, 2002, 2004). According to PASS cognitive processing theory, effective cognitive processing is controlled by an executive function responsible for selective attention, sustained attention, attentional switching, and mental effort, while encoding incoming verbal and/or spatial information and constructing the situation model (Naglieri & Das, 1997; Naglieri & Rojhan, 2004). Recent studies have suggested that greater human information processing and comprehension outcomes in complex sequential cognitive tasks are associated with increased mental effort or focused and directed concentration (Brumback et al., 2005; Oberauer & Kliegl, 2004; Rende, Ramsberger, & Miyake, 2002; van Merrienboer et al., 2002; Washburn & Putney, 2001).

Comprehension

The main contention of the capacity theory of comprehension is that cognitive capacity (e.g., short-term and long-term memory) facilitates or constrains computational (i.e., causal analysis of noun-verb clauses) and storage demands imposed in the construction of situation models (Cain, Oakhill, & Lemmon, 2004; Just & Carpenter, 1992). Gordon, Hendrick, and Levine (2002) observed lower comprehension when subjects attempted to remember a short set of words while reading syntactically complex sentences. McElree (2000) suggested that information is maintained in working memory via a content addressable mechanism, and this information is periodically accessed to fill in gaps existing in the current situation model. Some studies have also shown that comprehension is also enhanced when information presentation takes place in multimodal form (i.e., verbal, images, animation) thereby enhancing information processing by making use of the additive and synergistic properties of the verbal and visual working memory systems (Carlson, Chandler, & Sweller, 2003; Mayer & Chandler, 2001; Mayer & Moreno, 2002; Park, 1998).

Learning Satisfaction

Learning satisfaction has been described as a sense of accomplishment that learners feel at the conclusion of a learning event when the learning environment facilitated information processing that led to successful comprehension outcomes (Keller, 1987; Song & Keller, 2001). In Keller's (1987) ARCS Model of Motivational Design, effective learning contexts exhibit four essential conditions—attention, relevance, confidence, and satisfaction. Learning satisfaction is highest when the information presentation arouses and maintains attention, curiosity, and interest throughout the entire duration of the presentation. Further, attention is maintained when the instructional content is coherent and conveys relevant importance and meaningfulness to the learner. Finally, learning satisfaction arises from learner confidence that understanding of the content has been achieved, and there is a positive correlation between learner mental effort and the extent of learning achievement (Keller, 1987; Small & Gluck, 1994). Self-reported learning satisfaction has also been associated with evaluations of the learning time and effort efficiency (Cole, 1992), willingness to learn more about the topic (Maki et al., 2000), and perceived ease at learning (Hackman & Walker, 1990).

Research Hypotheses Development

Figure 1. Impact of media and information complexity on information processing and comprehension outcomes

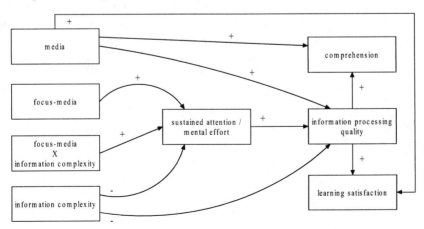

Figure 1 graphically depicts the theoretical framework used in the formulation of the research hypotheses. In this study, the causal model presented suggests that information presentation media (i.e., text-only, graphics-and-text, and multimedia) and information complexity will each directly impact information processing quality (i.e., understandable, informative, interesting) and will interact to exert influences on the amount of sustained attention and mental effort applied in cognitive processing (i.e., situation model construction) of the information presented. Sustained attention and mental effort would then have an intervening influence on information processing quality. Finally, information processing quality would then impact comprehension and learning satisfaction outcomes.

Mental Effort

Cognitive processing of text-based information imposes a required involuntary demand for applied mental effort and sustained attention because sentences must be parsed to identify and extract noun-verb linkages representing concepts or ideas. Mental effort is then further extended when these concepts are placed into a situation model that is then mentally simulated for comprehension, verification, and self-correction (Lavie et al., 2004). Alternatively, Burns and Anderson (1993) noted that increased sustained attention was associated with presentation media with the greatest sensory stimulation and appeal (i.e., dynamic visual and auditory stimuli). Sensory appeal and sustained attention were associated with the subjects' anticipation of forthcoming content. Therefore,

H1: Text-based and multimedia information presentations, when compared to graphics with text information presentations, will lead to greater applied sustained attention and mental effort.

Information complexity has also been associated with sustained attention and applied mental effort (Burns & Anderson, 1993). Content that is very difficult to encode and place into an appropriate situation model lowers sustained attention because the complex content is lower in intellective appeal, and the subject determines that applying continued attention and mental effort to forthcoming information will not be beneficial (Wolfe, 2005). Further, sustained attention and mental effort are inhibited when the subject's ability to understand the information presented is lowered by complex information (Christoph, Schoenfeld, & Tansky, 1998). Therefore,

H2: As information content increases in complexity, subjects will expend less sustained attention and mental effort.

Information presentation media and information complexity can interact to influence applied mental effort and sustained attention. As information complexity increased or the task required greater imagery or visualization, visual presentation reduced cognitive load through immediate encoding (Burns & Anderson, 1993). In addition, the sensory features of multimedia such as visual complexity, movement, and sound effects created an "audiovisual momentum" that led to perceptual arousal, which subsequently induced sustained attention and mental effort (Burns & Anderson, 1993). The audiovisual momentum reduces the tendency to withdraw attention and mental effort typically associated with the presentation of complex information. Therefore,

H3: As information complexity increases (decreases), text-only and multimedia information presentations will lead to greater (lesser) sustained attention and mental effort when compared to graphics-with-text information presentations.

Information Processing Quality

Mayer and Moreno (1998) noted that when using multimedia, subjects were able to integrate words and pictorial animation of lightening formation more easily when the words supplementing the animation were presented auditorily as opposed to written text. The encoding of the auditory/animation information presentation was more efficient because the subjects were able to maintain complete visual attention on the animation while simultaneously attending to the narration content. In contrast, the animation/text group experienced diminished cognitive processing due to a "split-attention" effect (i.e., required alternating shifts of visual focus between text processing and visual imagery processing). Mayer et al. (2004) also noted that, consistent with a cognitive theory of multimedia learning, multimedia audio can also induce a feeling of personalization which promotes active processing of incoming material. Therefore,

H4: As information presentation format increases in modality (i.e., from text-only to graphics-with-text to multimedia), subjects will experience greater information processing quality.

Rieber's (1991) study comparing static graphics vs. animated graphics observed better knowledge extraction with animated graphics and, when given a choice to return to either presentation format, subjects overwhelmingly preferred the animated graphics presentation. The subjects in Rieber's (1991) study exhibited attentional inertia (i.e., sustained attention and applied mental effort) when viewing the animated graphic presentation. The subjects found the multimedia presentation intellectually appealing, easier to understand, and more interesting. In addition, increased information processing quality was evidenced by the fact that the subjects viewing animation were able to acquire incidental knowledge when making inferences from imagery than with text-based propo-sitions constructed from static graphics. Lavie et al. (2004) noted that subjects utilize selective attentiveness in order to minimize interference from distractions thereby maintaining concentration and focus on specific incoming material. Otherwise, switching attention between desired incoming material and any distractions leads to working memory overload and lower information processing quality (Oberauer, 2003). Therefore,

H5: An increase in sustained attention and mental effort will lead to greater information processing quality.

Information complexity can directly influence information processing qual-ity through an imposed increase in cognitive load. Long causal chain length can create difficulty in acquiring local coherence within a situation model and extensive hierarchical connections, and high connective spans among related concepts can create difficulty in acquiring global coherence. Friedman and Miyake (2000) noted that casual connectives with long causal chains or high connective span temporarily suspended purging of the working memory in attempts to construct a complete and coherent situation model. Failure to purge working memory caused working memory overload. Consequently,

H6: As information complexity increases, subjects will experience lower information processing quality.

Comprehension and Learning Satisfaction

Information processing quality mediates comprehension because multime-dia can lead to a reduction of complexity and increased cognitive processing capacity by targeting both verbal and visual working memory channels, thereby making the information presented more understandable, interesting, and informa-tive. Alternatively, because of its linear structure, a text presentation that is structurally equivalent (i.e., equality in the setting, characters and/or objects, conceptual content, and episodic structure) to a static image with supporting verbal information or multimedia presentation will require more cognitive processing capacity to process (Mayer & Moreno, 1998, 2002). This suggests the following hypothesis.

H7: As information processing quality increases, subjects will experience greater comprehension.

In the comparison of text, narration, and graphics with text, Mousavi, Low, and Sweller (1995) found that a combined text and graphics presentation reduced the cognitive load in solving geometry problems resulting in superior learning.

The graphics depicting the geometric problem space clarified the abstract equation representation; this enabled timely solution to the problem. Cassady (1998) noted that, compared to traditional lecture presentations, students found multimedia-based presentations to be superior in the following areas: (1) flow, organization, and understandability of the information presented; (2) ease in following the presentation; (3) ability to pay attention to the presentation; and (4) interest in the information presented. Enhanced visualization associated with multimedia presentation lead to greater comprehension of geological concepts (Mayer, Mautone, & Prothero, 2002). Therefore,

H8: As information presentation format increases in modality (i.e., from text-only to graphics-with-text to multimedia), subjects will experience greater comprehension.

Towler and Dipboye (2001) observed superior training outcomes when the training presentation was characterized as higher in coherent organization and trainer expressiveness. Effective training presentations provided clarifying and elaborative content and commanded sustained attention through appropriate vocal intonations that acted as cues that made the presentation easy to follow. The trainees also displayed greater positive affect, information recall and comprehension, and perceptions that they could apply what they learned to actual task execution and problem solving. After 12 weeks of study and practice in an introductory programming class, Ramalingam and Wiedenbeck (1998) observed an increase in subject-perceived computer-programming learning achievement. The multimodal aspects of multimedia also facilitate accommodating learners of varied learning styles thereby promoting greater comprehension and satisfaction with the learning process (Mayer & Massa, 2003). Consequently,

H9: As information processing quality increases, subjects will experience greater learning satisfaction.

H10: As information presentation format increases in modality (i.e., from text-only to graphics-with-text to multimedia), subjects will experience greater learning satisfaction.

RESEARCH METHODOLOGY

Participants

Seventy-eight male and female undergraduate students voluntarily partici-pated in the experiment. Each subject was eligible to participate in a lottery of five drawings of fifty dollars. The average age was 25 years ($SD = 5.39$).

Materials

Two text passages, Photocopier Operation (high information complexity) and Greenhouse Effect (low information complexity), with relatively equal readability scores were utilized. Every attempt was made to keep the following factors as constant as possible between the passages: text length, Flesch Reading ease, and Flesch-Kincaid Reading Grade Level (Wagenaar, Schreuder, & Wijlhuizen, 1987). The Flesch Reading ease statistic is calculated by multiplying the average sentence length by 1.015, multiplying the number of syllables per 100 words by .846, and then the sum of these products is subtracted from 206.835. The Flesch-Kincaid Reading Grade level statistic is calculated by adding the average sentence length to the percentage of long words (i.e., more than two syllables), and the sum is then multiplied with 0.4. Table 1 details specific readability scores.

For complexity, the passages differed in causal chain lengths and the extent to which one clause was causally related to other clauses throughout other parts of the scenario (i.e., connective span). Connective span was computed as the number of causal relationships each idea unit had with other idea units within the same sentence and across sentences throughout the text. The Greenhouse Effect and Photocopier Operation, respectively, had 9 and 18 idea units with a connective span of 3 and 10 and 29 sentences with direct contiguous causal links greater than 1. The connective span and direct causal links values indicated that the Photocopier Operation passage was higher in information complexity than the Greenhouse Effect passage.

The overhead slides and multimedia presentations were both equivalent in overall content (i.e., idea units expressed) and episodic structure (i.e., sequence of events) to the text passages (Baggett, 1979). The overhead-slides presentation utilized static diagrams that illustrated components involved in photocopier operation or elements involved in greenhouse gas generation. The multimedia presentation animated the elements contained in the static diagrams used in the overhead presentation.

Procedure

Path analysis was chosen as the data analysis procedure because analysis of variance is not particularly well suited for testing direct mediating and intervening relationships among a set of variables. Each subject was randomly

Table 1. Passage readability measures

Readability Measure	Photocopier Operation	GreenHouse Effect
Paragraphs	14	12
Sentences (words/sentence)	86 (19.6)	85 (16.8)
Flesch Reading Ease	44.8	40.7
Flesch-Kincaid Grade Level	11.8	11.7

assigned to one of the media (i.e., text-only, text-with-graphics, or multimedia) and complexity conditions (i.e., high or low information complexity). The overhead slides sessions presented the same conceptual content using static overheads composed of graphs and pictures supplemented with text. Subjects in the computer-based multimedia presentation sessions watched a series of PowerPoint slides that contained animated graphs and images along with supporting text. All sessions (text-only, text-with-graphics overhead slides, and multimedia) were executed for a duration of 12 minutes. After each session, the subjects completed a Likert-type questionnaire that elicited perceptions of the amount of sustained attention/mental effort, information processing quality, and learning satisfaction. Following this, they were administered a timed comprehension test composed of short essay questions.

Measures

Information Presentation Media. Presentation media (i.e., text-only, text-with-graphics, or multimedia) was coded using two contrast code variables (Pedhazur, 1997). The first contrast code variable, *media*, contrasted group mean outcomes of each of the three presentation modes (i.e., text-only, text-with-graphics, and multimedia). The second contrast code variable, *focus-media*, contrasted the group means of text-only and multimedia combined against the mean of the text-with-graphics group.

Information Complexity. Information complexity was operationalized as a function of connective span (i.e., the number of causal relationships each idea unit had with other idea units within the same sentence and across sentences throughout the text) and causal chain length (i.e., number of contiguous causal connections). The Photocopier Operation content was greater in information complexity than the Greenhouse Effect content. Information complexity was contrast coded. Grade Reading Level scores for both passages were similar in value in order to restrict complexity to connective span and causal chain length (see Table 1) and minimize confounding from differences in domain content.

Sustained Attention/Mental Effort. The sustained attention/mental effort scale (Likert-type; see Appendix B) was developed using Burns and Anderson's (1993) theory of attentional inertia. The sustained attention scale elicited self perceptions regarding sustained looks at and concentration on the presentation. The scale reliability (Cronbach's alpha) for the sustained attention/mental effort scale was 0.78.

Information Processing Quality. Perceived information processing quality was assessed using questionnaire items (semantic differential and Likert-type items; see Appendix B) adapted from Buchheit (1996). The perceived information processing quality elicited an assessment of the perceived interestingness, understandability, and informativeness of the presentation. The scale reliability (Cronbach's alpha) for the information processing quality scale was 0.90.

Comprehension. In order to facilitate objective scoring, the short essay questions were constructed and scored according to the analytic approach of essay assessment (Jacobs & Chase, 1992; Linn & Gronlund, 2000). In the analytic approach to essay assessment, each question has a predefined list of items that make up a correct response. A research assistant used the predefined list of correct responses to score the essay questions by assigning one point for each correct item response. The Photocopier Operation and Greenhouse Effect comprehension tests each required 13 correct responses. In order to normalize the test scores across text passages of different content, the percentage of correctly specified responses was utilized as a measure of comprehension. Sample comprehension questions are: "How is the electrostatic image formed on a photoconductor's drum surface?" and "How does livestock production lead to an increase in global warming?"

Learning Satisfaction. The learning satisfaction scale (Likert-type; see Appendix B) was developed using Keller's (1987) ARCS Model of Motivational Design of effective learning environments. The learning satisfaction scale elicited self perceptions regarding extent of comprehension and understanding of the information presented, sense of mastery to use the information presented, usefulness of the information presented, and desire to learn more about the information topic. The scale reliability (Cronbach's alpha) for the learning satisfaction scale was 0.84.

RESULTS

A series of regression analyses was chosen as the data-analytic strategy for testing the proposed causal path model depicted in Figure 1 (Pedhazur, 1997). The variables were entered into the equation based on their temporal ordering in the model. In each regression analysis, all variables occurring prior to and at the same point in the conceptual model were included in order to test for both direct and indirect effects. Problem solving ability (i.e., grade point average) was considered as a covariate to comprehension but there was no significant

Table 2.   Means, standard deviations, and correlations

Variables	M	SD	1.	2.	3.	4.	5.	6.	7.	8.
1. media	♦	♦	·					(.18)	(.30)	(.29)
2. focus-media	♦	♦	.02	·			(.26)	(.16)	(.06)	(.12)
3. information complexity	♦	♦	.00	.00	·		(-.23)	(-.48)	(-.19)	(-.38)
4. focus-media x information complexity	♦	♦	.00	.16	-.06	·	(.23)	(.14)	(.06)	(.26)
5. sustained attention	18.95	5.70	-.08	.22	-.22	.18	·	(.70)	(.24)	(.51)
6. information processing quality	41.14	9.06	.13	.09	-.48**	.11	.68**	·	(.43)	(.83)
7. comprehension	3.90	2.33	.23*	.06	-.60**	.02	.24*	.43**	·	
8. learning satisfaction	16.60	4.46	.25*	.15	-.33**	.23*	.64**	.81**	.32**	·
9. problem solving ability	3.32	.35	-.22	.04	-.10	.16	.15	.04	.20	-.07

Notes $N = 78$ $* p < .05$ $** p < .01$ ♦ media, focus-media, and information complexity are contrast coded variables
The original correlations are reported in the lower half of the matrix. The reproduced correlations of relevant variables are reported in the upper half of the matrix.

bivariate correlation. The overall results from the series of regression analyses used to test the fit of the causal model to the data are summarized in Figure 2. Table 2 presents the means, standard deviations, original correlations, and reproduced correlations of the variables in the study.

The path coefficients (see Figure 2) were used to compute the reproduced correlation of variables (see upper half of matrix in Table 2) that are interconnected through direct and indirect causal paths (Pedhazur, 1997). The total variance explained by the causal path model was 0.927. A root mean squared residual (RMR) of 0.076 and a normed fit index (NFI) of 0.822 suggest that the model provides a good fit to the data (Gerbing & Anderson, 1993; Pedhazur, 1997).

Sustained Attention and Mental Effort

As posited in Hypothesis 1, the text-only and multimedia groups (i.e., focus-media) did exhibit a positive increase in sustained attention and mental effort (standardized beta = .26, $p < .05$). Increases in information complexity lowered the motivation to maintain sustained and effortful processing of the information presented (standardized beta = -.23, $p < .01$) thereby supporting Hypothesis 2. Hypothesis 3 predicted that text-only and multimedia presentations would positively moderate the tendency for increases in information complexity to lead to withdrawal of sustained attention and mental effort as compared to text-with-graphics presentations. The results indicated that Hypothesis 3 was supported (standardized beta = .23, $p < .05$).

Information Processing Quality

The results indicated support for Hypothesis 4 and suggest that presentations that target both the verbal and visual working memory channels are perceived to be more understandable, informative, and interesting (standardized beta = .18, $p < .05$). The results for Hypothesis 5 indicated that sustained attention and applied mental effort are positively correlated with information processing quality (standardized beta = .62, $p < .01$). For Hypothesis 6, the results indicated that information complexity was negatively related to information processing quality (standardized beta = -.34, $p < .01$).

Comprehension and Learning Satisfaction

For Hypothesis 7, the results indicated that information processing quality was positively related to comprehension (standardized beta = .39, $p < .01$). As suggested in Hypothesis 8, increased comprehension was associated with increased presentation modality (standardized beta = .23, $p < .05$). The results also indicated that increased information processing quality was positively related to learning satisfaction (i.e., perceived understanding and mastery of the topic). Consequently, Hypothesis 9 was supported (standardized beta = .81, $p <$

Figure 2. Model results: Standardized regression weights

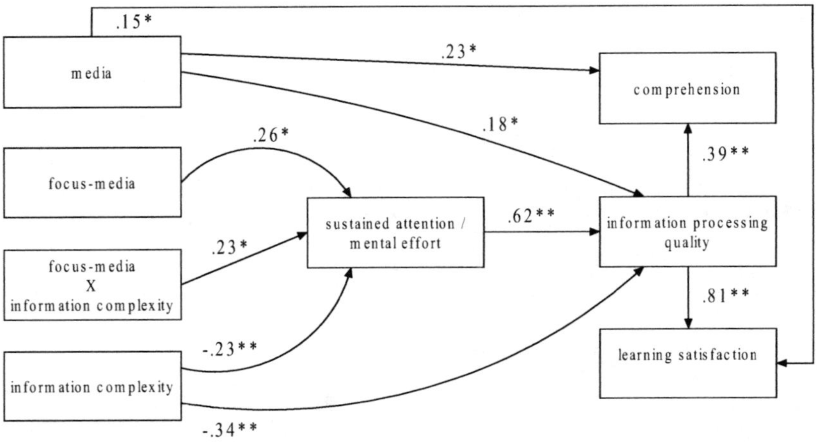

Note: $*p < .05$ $**p < .01$

.01). Finally, hypothesis 10 predicted that increases in media modality would be positively related to greater sense of mastery of use of the information acquired (i.e., learning satisfaction). The results indicated support for Hypothesis 10 (standardized beta = .15, p < .05).

DISCUSSION

The path coefficient between sustained attention and focus-media interaction with information complexity (beta = .23) was only slightly lower than the path coefficient between sustained attention and focus-media alone (beta = .26). These results suggest that adverse effects on sustained attention (Burns & Anderson, 1993) typically associated with information complexity (beta = -.23) were moderated by increased media modality. Apparently, the multimedia group subjects recalled more accurate details regarding sequence of operation and dependency among photocopier components or the process of greenhouse gas generation. Further, the results suggest that multimedia did not create a split attention situation (i.e., cognitive load due to switching attention between text and visual content) typically observed in text-with-graphics presentations. This supports the major tenet of dual coding theory (Paivio, 1986); the verbal/auditory and visual memory channels actually augmented each other.

The direct effect of media on comprehension (beta = .23) supported the contention that verbal and visual working memory effects are additive and synergistic. Sustained attention exhibited a greater association with information processing quality (beta = .62) as compared to media (beta = .23). Apparently, media's role in inducing and maintaining attention was more important to information processing quality than its role in targeting both the verbal and working memory channels. Media modality was related to learning satisfaction (beta = .15), but information processing quality imposed greater relative variation (beta = .81). It is clear that sustained attention, associated with focus media, was essential for positive information processing quality needed to enhance both comprehension and learning satisfaction.

The positive relationship between focus-media (i.e., text-only and multimedia) and sustained attention and mental effort support previous findings that text-only presentations impose a required cognitive processing effort while multimedia induced voluntary attention and mental effort (Andres, 2001; Kozma, 1991). Sustained attention and mental effort were highest for the text-only group (mean = 20.25), followed by multimedia (mean = 19.27), followed by text-with-graphics (mean = 17.08). The text-only group reported higher levels of attention and mental effort, which was likely expended to encode the information (i.e., identify noun-verb linkages and to establish local and global coherence among related clauses). Here, focus and considerable mental effort are needed to translate text into a visual simulation. There is less potential to be distracted from external stimuli under such periods of high concentration. In contrast, multimedia appeared to generate higher sustained attention through the sensory appeal of its multimodal content (i.e., text, images, narration, and animation).

The results indicate that high information complexity was second to sustained attention in its magnitude of explained variation in information processing quality (beta = -.34). The negative association of information complexity with information processing quality is evidence that there were considerable information processing errors in identifying idea units (noun-verb linkages) and establishing causal connections among idea units to create a situation model. This result supports the "cognitive resource allocation" perspective proposed by Millis et al. (1993). According to the resource allocation perspective, the presence of excessive causal connectives and high connective spans creates ambiguities in the encoding and interpretation of incoming information. This overloaded working memory and diminished information processing quality and, subsequently, comprehension and learning satisfaction. The results also indicate that the magnitude of relationship between information complexity (beta = -.23) and focus-media (beta = .26) are fairly equal but opposite in direction. This suggests that competing external stimuli or disinterest can possibly distract a subject when comprehensibility of information is difficult. In addition, high local and global connections among concepts result in minimal situation model simulation accuracy, greater sense of confusion, and greater disinterest in presentation content.

A review of relevant literature suggested that the interaction term, focus media x information complexity, should be included in the model. As stated earlier, focus-media (i.e., text-only and multimedia) has a tendency to command greater required (e.g., text parsing) or voluntary (e.g., perceptual arousal) sustained attention and mental effort. In contrast, increased complexity has the potential to lead to withdrawal of sustained attention and mental effort through incomprehensibility and disinterest in the information presented. The results for Hypothesis 3 suggest that both the encoding process (e.g., verbal vs. verbal and visual) and semantic structure of information (i.e., causal chain length and connective span) interact in the determination of effort to encode incoming information. Apparently, the semantic structure of information should drive information presentation format decisions.

IMPLICATIONS AND CONCLUSIONS

The results indicated implications for the use of computer-based instruction, meeting presentations, and computer-supported decision-making contexts. It is clear that multimedia provides a unique opportunity to examine the nature of human information processing (i.e., encoding, situation model construction, and situation model simulation) and how information processing interacts with information format and information complexity. The ability of multimedia to target both the verbal and visual working memory channels affords the opportunity to create experimental tasks that can be used to assess cognitive processing limitations. Apparently, increasing presentation modality can minimize the occurrence of excessive cognitive load when processing complex information. Multimedia-based visuals supported by text and/or narration can convey a maximum amount of information that is processed more efficiently than static images and text.

Information content should be organized so as to minimize local and global causal dependencies among concepts. Instructional and training presentations should be examined to identify what content is best suited for a specific presentation modality. Such decisions would be driven by the complexity of the topic, the extent of mental model construction and simulation required to understand the topic (i.e., abstract level), and the extent to which information processing requires greater short-term memory capacity and/or long-term memory capacity. In decision-making contexts, subjects must often analyze data, construct mental models of alternative solutions, simulate these alternative models as potential scenarios, and finally compare the outcomes of each simulation against a set of decision-making criteria. In engineering contexts (e.g., mechanical or chemical), multimedia can be used to depict physical models that represent abstract models defined by mathematical equations. It is clear that multimedia can be applied in such contexts with the aim of reducing cognitive load through the provision of graphs, imagery, and animation that summarize data physical form and motion.

Past research on multimedia use has noted that there can be negative outcomes during multimedia use. Split-attention effect (i.e., the need to integrate information from two different sources—text and diagrams) has been observed in some multimedia studies. Split-attention was not observed in this study, and it is believed that split-attention can be avoided through careful embedding of text onto or nearby the related images. Further, some research studies on presentation mode and cognitive processing outcomes have observed mixed results regarding effectiveness of increased presentation modality. These mixed results could possibly be attributed to inconsistencies in the experimental task used (e.g., word recognition, word-image associations, short passages, minimal information complexity). In an attempt to isolate presentation/instructional media effects, presentation content across media (i.e., text-only, overhead slides, multimedia) was structurally equivalent in idea units expressed and sequence of events. Information complexity was limited to the causal chain lengths, and local and global connections of idea units (i.e., connective span) needed to describe the Greenhouse Effect or Photocopier Operation. Readability scores were essentially equivalent.

A limitation of the current study is the use of self-reported measures for sustained attention and mental effort and information processing quality. Objective measures of sustained attention would offer greater internal validity. Future studies should attempt the use of objective measures of attention and applied mental effort. Although larger and more realistic than tasks previously utilized, this study's task can be viewed as a limitation to the study. Future studies should extend the length and complexity of the tasks in order to afford greater generalizability. Finally, the use of a laboratory study offers greater internal validity, but its use can be viewed as a limitation because field studies offer more external validity. The ability to take advantage of the power of computer-based technologies such as multimedia will depend on continued research aimed at understanding the relationship between the capabilities of the technology and information processing requirements of the task to be supported with the technology.

REFERENCES

Andres, H. P. (2001). Presentation media, information complexity, and comprehension. *Journal of Educational Technology Systems, 30*(3), 225-246.

Baggett, P. (1979). Structurally equivalent stories in movie and text and the effect of medium on recall. *Journal of Verbal Learning and Behavior, 18*(3), 333-356.

Brumback, C. R, Low, K. A., Gratton, G., & Fabiani, M. (2005). Putting things into perspective: Individual differences in working-memory span and the integration of information, *Experimental Psychology, 52*(1), 21-30.

Buchheit, N. A. (1996). *Multimedia: A persuasion tool for affecting decision outcome.* Unpublished PhD dissertation, Texas A&M University College of Business, College Station.

Burns, J. J., & Anderson, R. A. (1993). Attentional inertia and recognition memory in adult television viewing. *Communication Research, 20*(6), 777-799.

Cain, K., Oakhill, J., & Lemmon, K. (2004). Individual differences in the inference of word meanings from context: The influence of reading comprehension, vocabulary knowledge, and memory capacity. *Journal of Educational Psychology, 96*(4), 671-681.

Carlson, R., Chandler, P., & Sweller, J. (2003). Learning and understanding science instructional material. *Journal of Educational Psychology, 95*(3), 629-640.

Cassady, J. (1998). Student and instructor perceptions of the efficacy of computer-aided lectures in undergraduate university courses. *Journal of Educational Computing Research, 19*(2), 175-189.

Christoph, R. T., Schoenfeld, G. A., & Tansky, J. W. (1998). Overcoming barriers to training utilizing technology: The influence of self-efficacy factors on multimedia-based training receptiveness. *Human Resource Development Quarterly, 9*(1), 25-38.

Cole, P. (1992). Constructivism revisited: A search for common ground. *Educational Technology, 32*(2), 27-34.

Friedman, N. P., & Miyake, A. (2000). Differential roles for visuospatial and verbal working memory in situation model construction. *Journal of Experimental Psychology: General, 129*(1), 61-83.

Gennari, S. P. (2004). Temporal references and temporal relations in sentence comprehension. *Journal of Experimental Psychology: Learning, Memory, and Cognition, 30*(4), 877-890.

Gerbing, D., & Anderson, J. (1993). A Monte Carlo evaluations of goodness-of-fit indices for structural equation models. In K. A. Bollen & J. S. Long (Eds.), *Testing structural equation models* (pp. 40-65). Newbury Park, CA: Sage.

Gordon, P. C., Hendrick, R., & Levine, W. H. (2002). Memory-load interference in syntactic processing. *Psychological Science, 13*(5), 425-430.

Hackman, M. Z., & Walker, K. B. (1990). Instructional communication in the televised classroom: The effects of system design and teacher immediacy on student learning and satisfaction. *Communication Education, 39*(3), 196-206.

Halford, G., Wilson, W. H., & Phillips, S. (1998). Processing capacity defined by relational complexity: Implications for comparative, developmental, and cognitive psychology. *Behavioral & Brain Sciences, 21*(6), 803-864.

Hegarty, M., Narayanan, N., & Freitas, P. (2002). Understanding machines from multimedia and hypermedia presentations. In J. Otero & J. A. Leon (Eds.), *The psychology of science text comprehension* (pp. 357-384). Mahwah, NJ: Lawrence Erlbaum Associates.

Jacobs, L. C., & Chase, C. I. (1992). *Developing and using tests effectively: A guide for faculty.* San Francisco: Jossey-Bass.

Just, M. A., & Carpenter, P. A. (1992). A capacity theory of comprehension: Individual differences in working memory. *Psychological Review, 99*(1), 122-149.

Kaup, B., & Zwaan, R. A. (2003). Effects of negation and situational presence on the accessibility of text information. *Journal of Experimental Psychology: Learning, Memory, and Cognition, 29*(3), 439-446.

Keller, J. M. (1987). Strategies for stimulating the motivation to learn. *Performance and Instruction, 26*(8), 1-7.

Kozma, R. B. (1991). Learning with media. *Review of Educational Research, 61*(2), 179-212.

Lavie, N., Hirst, A., de-Fockert, J. W., & Viding, E. (2004). Load theory of selective attention and cognitive control. *Journal of Experimental Psychology: General, 133*(3), 339-354.

Levin, J., Anglin, G., & Carney, R. (1987). On empirically validating functions of pictures in prose. In D. Willows & H. Houghton (Eds.), *Psychology of illustration: Vol. 2 instructional issues* (pp. 51-85). New York: Springer-Verlag.

Lien, M. C., McCann, R. S., Ruthruff, E., & Proctor, R. W. (2005). Dual-task performance with ideomotor-compatible tasks: Is the central processing bottleneck intact, bypassed, or shifted in locus? *Journal of Experimental Psychology: Human Perception and Performance, 31*(1), 122-144.

Lim, K. H., & Benbasat, I. (2000). The effect of multimedia on perceived equivocality and perceived usefulness of information systems. *MIS Quarterly, 24*(3), 449-471.

Linn, R. L., & Gronlund, N. E. (2000). *Measurement and assessment in teaching* (8th ed.). Upper Saddle River, NJ: Prentice Hall.

Lloyd-Jones, T. J., & Vernon, D. (2003). Semantic interference from visual object recognition on visual imagery. *Journal of Experimental Psychology: Learning, Memory, and Cognition, 29*(4), 563-580.

Maki, R. H., Maki, W. S., Patterson, M., & Whittaker, D. (2000). Evaluation of a Web-based introductory psychology course: Learning and satisfaction in on-line versus lecture courses. *Behavior Research Methods, Instruments, & Computers, 32*(2), 230-239.

Mason, R. A., Just, M. A., Keller, T. A., & Carpenter, P. A. (2003). Ambiguity in the brain: What brain imaging reveals about the processing of syntactically ambiguous sentences. *Journal of Experimental Psychology: Learning, Memory, and Cognition, 29*(6), 1319-1338.

Mayer, R. E., & Chandler, P. (2001). When learning is just a click away: Does simple user interaction foster deeper understanding of multimedia messages? *Journal of Educational Psychology, 93*(2), 390-397.

Mayer, R. E., Fennell, S., Farmer, L., & Campbell, J. (2004). A personalization effect in multimedia learning: Students learn better when words are in conversational style rather than formal style. *Journal of Educational Psychology, 96*(2), 389-395

Mayer, R. E., & Massa, L. J. (2003). Three facets of visual and verbal learners: Cognitive ability, cognitive style, and learning preference. *Journal of Educational Psychology, 95*(4), 833-846.

Mayer, R. E., Mautone, P., & Prothero, W. (2002). Pictorial aids for learning by doing in a multimedia geology simulation game. *Journal of Educational Psychology, 94*(1), 171-185.

Mayer, R. E., & Moreno, R. (1998). A split-attention effect in multimedia learning: Evidence for dual processing systems in working memory. *Journal of Educational Psychology, 90*(2), 312-320.

Mayer, R. E., & Moreno, R. (2002). Aids to computer-based multimedia learning. *Learning & Instruction, 12*(1), 107-119.

McElree, B. (2000). Sentence comprehension is mediated by content-addressable memory structures. *Journal of Psycholinguistic Research, 29*(2), 111-123.

Millis, K. K., Golding, J. M., & Baker, G. (1995). Causal connectives increase inference generation. *Discourse Processes, 20*(1), 29-49.

Millis, K. K., Graesser, A. C., & Haberlandt, K. (1993). The impact of connectives on the memory for expository texts. *Applied Cognitive Psychology, 7*(4), 317-339.

Moreno, R., & Mayer, R. E. (2002). Verbal redundancy in multimedia learning: When reading helps listening. *Journal of Educational Psychology, 94*(1), 156-163.

Moreno, R., & Mayer, R. E. (2004). Personalized messages that promote science learning in virtual environments. *Journal of Educational Psychology, 96*(1), 165-173.

Naglieri, J. A., & Das, J. P. (1997). Intelligence revised: The planning, attention, simultaneous, successive (PASS) cognitive processing theory. In R. F. Dillon (Ed.), *Handbook on testing* (pp. 136-163). Westport, CT: Greenwood Press.

Naglieri, J. A., & Rojhan, J. (2004). Construct validity of the PASS T\theory and CAS: Correlations with achievement. *Journal of Educational Psychology, 96*(1), 174-181.

Oberauer, K. (2003). Selective attention to elements in working memory. *Experimental Psychology, 50*(4), 257-269.

Oberauer, K., & Kliegl, R. (2004). Simultaneous cognitive operations in working memory after dual-task practice. *Journal of Experimental Psychology: Human Perception and Performance, 30*(4), 689-707.

Paivio, A. (1986). *Mental representations: A dual coding approach.* Oxford, UK: Oxford University Press.

Park, O. (1998). Visual display and contextual presentations in computer-based instruction. *Educational Technology Research and Development, 46*(3), 37-50.

Pedhazur, E. J. (1997). *Multiple regression in behavioral research* (3rd ed.). Fort Worth, TX: Harcourt Brace.

Ramalingam, V., & Wiedenbeck, S. (1998). Development and validation of scores on a computer programming self-efficacy scale and group analyses of novice programmer self-efficacy. *Journal of Educational Computing Research, 19*(4), 367-381.

Rende, B., Ramsberger, G., & Miyake, A. (2002). Commonalities and differences in the working memory components underlying letter and category fluency tasks: A dual-task investigation. *Neuropsychology, 16*(3), 309-321.

Rieber, L. P. (1991). Animation, incidental learning, and continuing motivation. *Journal of Educational Psychology, 83*(3), 318-328.

Small, R. V., & Gluck, M. (1994). The relationship of motivational conditions to effective instructional attributes: A magnitude scaling approach. *Educational Technology, 34*(10), 33-40.

Song, S. H., & Keller, J. M. (2001). Effectiveness of motivationally adaptive computer-assisted instruction on the dynamic aspects of motivation. *Educational Technology Research & Development, 49*(2), 5-22.

Towler, A. J., & Dipboye, R. L. (2001). Effects of trainer expressiveness, organization, and trainee goal orientation on training outcomes. *Journal of Applied Psychology, 86*(4), 664-673.

van Merrienboer, J. J., Schuurman, J. G., de Croock, M. B., & Paas, F. G. (2002). Redirecting learners' attention during training: Effects on cognitive load, transfer test performance and training efficiency. *Learning & Instruction, 12*(1), 11-37.

Wagenaar, W. A., Schreuder, R., & Wijlhuizen, G. J. (1987). Readability of instructional text, written for the general public. *Applied Cognitive Psychology, 1*(3), 155-167.

Washburn, D. A., & Putney, R. T. (2001). Attention and task difficulty: When is performance facilitated? *Learning & Motivation, 32*(1), 36-47.

Wolfe, M. (2005). Memory for narrative and expository text: Independent influences of semantic associations and text organization. *Journal of Experimental Psychology: Learning, Memory, and Cognition, 31*(2), 359-364.

Zwaan, R. A., & Madden, C. J. (2004). Updating situation models. *Journal of Experimental Psychology: Learning, Memory, and Cognition, 30*(1), 283-288.

Zwaan, R. A., Magliano, J. P., & Graesser, A. C. (1995). Dimensions of situation model construction in narrative comprehension. *Journal of Experimental Psychology: Learning, Memory, and Cognition, 21*(2), 386-397.

APPENDIX A

Photocopier Operation (Excerpt)
(high causal chains and connective spans among concepts)

Development occurs when a visible image is created on the drum's surface with toner ink. Toner ink is feed into the toner reservoir by a toner transport roller. A friction roller rotating inside of the toner reservoir applies a positive charge to the toner ink. A developer magnetic roller, with a negative charge (-200 volts) carries the toner ink (positively charged) near the photoconductor's drum surface. As the developer magnetic roller and drum rotate, charged areas on the drum's surface attract toner ink to create the visible image on the drum's surface.

The transfer section's role is to transfer the drum's visible image onto the copy paper. A corona wire is also utilized in this step. A negative charge (-150 volts) is applied to the transfer corona wire creating a corona at the rear side of the copy paper. This allows the positively charged toner ink to be attracted from the drum onto the copy paper. As the toner ink is attracted to the copy paper, the greater negative charge on the drum also attracts the copy paper to its surface.

During the transfer process, the copy paper is attracted to the photoconducting drum. Separation of the paper from the drum occurs by applying a voltage level equal to that of the drum (-700 volts) to a separation corona. This eliminates the attraction force between the copy paper and the drum. If electrical separation fails, a separation pawl (or blade) mechanically separates the copy paper from the drum.

Greenhouse Effect (Excerpt)
(low causal chains and connective spans among concepts)

Nitrous oxide (N_2O) is composed of two nitrogen molecules and one oxygen molecule. It is also released by nitrogen-based fertilizers that are frequently used in agriculture. Nitrous oxide is also produced by the exhaust from cars. Nitrous oxide reacts with ozone molecules leading to a reduction in the ozone layer of the earth's atmosphere. Nitrous oxide absorbs 250 times as much heat as carbon dioxide. Fortunately, nitrous oxide accounts for only 10% of the enhancement to the greenhouse effect. The atmospheric lifetime of nitrous oxide is 120 years.

Methane (CH_4), also called marsh gas, is composed of one carbon molecule and four hydrogen molecules. It is lighter than air, colorless, odorless and flammable. Methane is released from swamps and garbage in landfills. It is also produced by animals such as cows during the digestive process. Methane also escapes from natural gas production processes. Methane gas accounts for 22%

of the enhancement to the greenhouse effect. As population increases, more garbage is generated and more livestock production is required for food. Since methane has 25 times the heat trapping capability of carbon dioxide, and since methane production is directly related to population growth, methane is a serious contributor to the greenhouse effect. The atmospheric lifetime of methane gas is 15 years.

Sample of slide transitions in the multimedia presentation on photocopier operation.

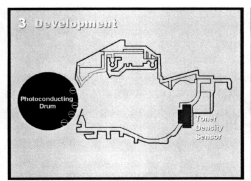

State #1

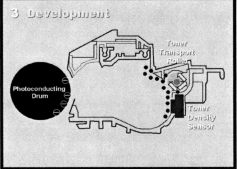

State #2

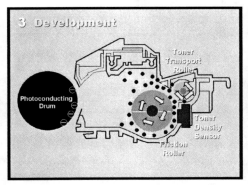

State #3

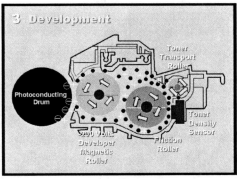

State #4

* Only the State #4 diagram was used in the overhead presentation (no animated transitions were shown)

APPENDIX B

Sustained Attention/Mental Effort

- I became bored and lost interest while viewing the presentation.
- I maintained complete attention throughout the entire presentation.
- There were moments when I was thinking about something other than the presentation.
- There were moments when I looked away from the presentation.

The *sustained attention/mental effort* items were rated on a seven-point Likert scale from strongly disagree to strongly agree.

Information Processing Quality

The following items were seven-point Likert scale items:

- Overall, I liked viewing the presentation (not at all—to a great extent)
- Overall, the presentation captured my attention (not at all—to a great extent)
- The overall format of the presentation was (poor—excellent)
- I would recommend this presentation to an interested friend (strongly disagree—strongly agree)

The following items were seven-point semantic differential scale items:

- The information in the presentation was (confusing—understandable)
- The information presented was (boring—interesting)
- The information presented was (uninformative—informative)
- The information presented was (unconvincing—convincing)
- Watching the presentation was (unenjoyable—enjoyable)

Learning Satisfaction

- I gained a significantly better understanding of photocopier operation (or the greenhouse effect).
- The knowledge I gained from this presentation will be very useful.
- The presentation format made learning about photocopier operation (or the greenhouse effect) easy.
- I would like to learn more about a similar topic under the same presentation format.

The *learning satisfaction* items were rated on a seven-point Likert scale from "not at all" to "to a great extent."

Chapter II

IT Project Managers' Perceptions and Use of Virtual Team Technologies

Catherine M. Beise
Salisbury University, USA

Fred Niederman
Saint Louis University, USA

Herb Mattord
Kennesaw State University, USA

ABSTRACT

This chapter presents the results of a case study pertaining to the use of information and communication media to support a range of project management tasks. A variety of electronic communication tools have evolved to support collaborative work and virtual teams. Few of these tools have focused specifically on the needs of project managers. In an effort to learn how practicing IT project managers employ these tools, data were collected at a North American Fortune 500 industrial company via interviews with IT project managers regarding their use and perceptions of electronic media within the context of their work on project teams. In this study, "virtual" describes the extent to which communication is electronic rather than the extent to which team members are geographically separated. Although the number of respondents was limited, the richness of the data collected leads to the conclusion that successful project managers and teams become skilled at adapting a variety of existing communication technologies to match the project task or process, the receiver, their own role as sender, and the content of the message. Groupware designers and developers need to better understand project management methods and best practices in order to provide better tools for practitioners, particularly as organizations expand globally and increasingly outsource various functions of their IT development and operations.

INTRODUCTION

Electronically supported communication media, ranging from telephone connections to Internet Websites to low-earth orbital satellite cellular technologies, have become increasingly available to organizations and individuals throughout the world. In addition to the straightforward opportunity to link individuals across time and geography, these technologies provide opportunities for organizations to develop new patterns of work-related interaction, even when groups are co-located.

A large number of organizations are becoming increasingly "projectized" in structure, accomplishing their strategic and tactical goals through bringing together for a fixed period of time cross-functional groups of people, whose knowledge, skills, and experiences are complementary and focused on a time-dependent set of deliverables. This approach is widely used in information technology (IT) areas, where much work is structured as a set of distinct, sometimes overlapping projects. Designing work as a set of projects allows the use of organizational learning through the application of accumulated knowledge regarding the organization of project work. It also emphasizes the creation of particular deliverables, whether computer applications, configurations of hardware, software or integrated systems, or technology-supported business processes. Project management provides a rich framework for the study of team use of communication media for performing project tasks, yet few researchers or groupware designers have focused specifically on supporting project management.

At present, many individuals use computer-mediated communication (CMC) tools, such as e-mail, on a self-directed, ad-hoc basis to support various types of work including participation on project teams. Many firms expect advances in electronically mediated communications to enable a more formal structured use of CMC tools to support the goals of project management. In addition they expect electronically mediated communications to allow for teams to coordinate work at different geographical sites. With the continued expansion of multinational operations and global IT work outsourcing (Arnold & Niederman, 2001), more IT design and programming are being conducted in projects involving individuals of multiple cultures resident at multiple locations (Carmel, 1999). These trends illustrate the continually growing importance of and critical role for technologies that enable and enhance communication in the context of project management and execution.

Modern organizations have the challenge of simultaneously understanding the dynamics of project management and the intricacies in the changes to communication as those technologies evolve. For example, learning the social along with the technical use of these new telecommunication devices is important for successful collaboration (Knoll & Jarvenpaa, 1995). In order for technology designers to better support co-located as well as distributed project work, it is important to have a better understanding of the characteristics and needs of real project teams working on real projects using commercially available CMC tools and technologies.

The objectives of this study were to identify, observe, and analyze the use of electronically mediated tools and technologies by practicing project teams. The goals were to gain a deeper understanding of the link between tools and tasks, for the purposes of:

- contributing to development of a more useful framework for researchers;
- identifying best practices for practitioners;
- providing useful insights and direction for groupware designers.

The paper begins by reviewing background literature relevant to virtual teamwork and technology tools that potentially support project management, resulting in several research questions. Following that is an explanation of methods and analysis of the results of interviews with project managers (PMs) in an industry work setting. The paper concludes with a discussion of the findings and their implications for practitioners, groupware designers, and academic researchers.

BACKGROUND

Technology Support for Teams

Studies focusing on organizational and technical challenges and opportunities for these communication media in support of work groups come from numerous research streams, including computer-mediated communication (CMC) (Hiltz, 1985), group support systems (GSS) (Jessup & Valacich, 1993), computer-supported cooperative work (CSCW), and telework (Solomon, 2001). A wide range of results from all these areas include effects and comparisons of specific technologies (audio, video, e-mail) (Fowler, 1980), comparisons of technologies to FTF communication (Ocker, 2001), and case studies of organizational usage of a single technology in context (Orlikowski, 1992; Zack and McKenney, 1995). Methodologies have included experiments (Fjermestad and Hiltz, 2000), field studies, and case studies (Fjermestad and Hiltz, 2000). Results from experimental studies have been ambiguous (McLeod, 1992); Dennis and Wixom, 2001-2002), leading to the conclusion that it is difficult if not impossible to understand technology use apart from task, group, and organizational context (DeSanctis, 1993).

E-Mail

Because it is now ubiquitous in most organizations, a number of studies have focused on e-mail as a common surrogate for understanding CMC. Benefits of e-mail which have been found include speed, changing patterns of distribution (Sproull & Kiesler, 1988), the ability to cut across traditional hierarchical channels (Hinds & Kiesler, 1995), and support for changing organizational forms, particularly virtual organizations (Ahuja & Carley, 1998). In spite of its early characterization as a "lean" medium, e-mail is often preferred by managers depending upon task and organizational context (Markus, 1994a, 1994b).

The first research question is: *How do successful PMs utilize electronic communication technologies such as e-mail to manage projects and teams?*

Defining Project Management

Increasingly, organizations are adopting and adapting the formalized best practices embodied in the Project Management Body of Knowledge (PMBOK), developed and distributed by the Project Management Institute (1996). This body of knowledge structures project management into five groups of interrelated processes that occur throughout the project lifecycle. These are Initiating, Planning, Executing, Controlling, and Closing processes. The PMBOK is also categorized into nine knowledge areas: project integration, scope management, cost management, time management, human resources, communication, quality, risk, and procurement. Each area has formally prescribed inputs, processes, outputs, and tools. The prescriptions are intended to be generic and adaptable to different application areas, such as manufacturing, banking, or IT, and also adaptable to the particular organizational context in which they are applied.

The PMBOK provides a potential framework for studying project team-related use of CMC tools. Effective communication is a central theme that runs throughout the PMBOK as essential to successful project management. Collection, storage, retrieval, updating, and presentation of information in appropriate forms are key to each of the PMBOK knowledge areas. Numerous forms of information and communication technologies (ICTs) continue to offer support for the various communication needs of project team members and stakeholders.

The most effective project managers (PMs) may be those who most effectively select and employ the right technologies for the right purposes at the right time, regardless of where team members are located.

A second research question is: *How well do current technologies such as e-mail support the needs of project management?*

Defining "Virtual"

The term "virtual" has been applied to groups, teams (Chudoba & Maznevski, 1996), and meetings (Hiltz & Turoff, 1992), as well as to work (Nilles, 1995) and organizations (Ahuja and Carley, 1998). Although much has been proposed regarding new "virtual" communication methods and organizational forms, the terminology surrounding these remains ill-defined. In this paper, the meaning of the term is discussed and defined for the purpose of this study.

According to *Webster's New World Dictionary*, there are two definitions for the term "virtual". The more general definition means "being such practically or in effect, although not in actual fact or name." This definition implies that *virtual* groups, meetings, organizations, etc., are not *actual* groups, meetings, or organizations, which is clearly not the case. The second definition pertains to the extension of computer memory by developing "virtual storage" such that the computer acts as if it had more available memory. This definition is more applicable to groups and organizations, though perhaps still somewhat murky in terms of strict boundary conditions (definition of membership). For example, a work team might call on non-members to provide input, comment, and advice in such a way that they operate as if they were part of the team, but without necessarily having a formal membership designation.

A better definition recognizes that *virtual* groups, teams, and meetings represent subsets or extensions of all examples of groups, teams, and meetings. The *virtual group*, like all groups, consists of a set of members that may evolve over time, where membership rules may be crisp or fuzzy, and where there is some degree of interaction or commonality among the members. The *virtual team* still consists of a set of individuals who through common purpose are distinguished from being merely a group. The *virtual meeting* is still a meeting in terms of having a purpose, a limited scope of interactions, some explicit or implicit agenda, one or more task foci, and some level of accomplishment (or regression in the worst case). The virtual group, team, and/or meeting are distinguished by the use of CMC supplementing or substituting for traditional face-to-face (FTF) forms of communication. In the present discussion, the focus will be on "virtual" teams working on specific projects and conducting face-to-face or computer-mediated meetings, where meetings can include as few as two people. With this definition, actual geographic distance or co-location (or lack thereof) is less important than how the group uses CMC tools to enhance or substitute for FTF meetings.

RESEARCH FRAMEWORK

A Framework for Virtual Teams

Considering group type as a function of both face-to-face (FTF) and electronically mediated communication, and given the above discussion, the amount of *virtualness* for a particular project team should be related to the amount of ICT use. However, this is likely to be moderated by the amount of continued traditional or FTF activity of the group. A group that communicates solely through electronic media differs from one with an equal amount of communication through electronic media but with additional communication in FTF mode. This suggests measurement on two dimensions: amount of FTF group interaction (from 0 to very high) and amount of electronically mediated communication (from 0 to very high) over a period of time. This view has the added benefit that each dimension is observable and measurable (although, perhaps, with some subtleties and difficulties in practice).

Splitting these measures into high and low levels leads to the categories shown in Table 1.

The low-low combination refers to a group that meets infrequently, either electronically or FTF. Groups in this quadrant can be labeled as *inactive*. It may either be a productive or non-productive group. If it is productive, it is likely a group that delegates work to individuals and meets only rarely to review/coordinate outcomes, or it is a group that settles policy (e.g., a school board, a corporate board of directors, or IT project selection committee). If it is an unproductive group, it may have a function that is (or is viewed as) relatively unimportant. Alternatively, it may display other group dysfunction such as lack of leadership, inability to provide meeting discipline, or inability to schedule at a mutually convenient time.

The low FTF and high electronic would be considered a *highly virtual* group. Regardless of where the group members are physically located, they choose to communicate predominantly through electronic mediation. If they are widely dispersed, of course, this may be the only mechanism by which they can operate as a team. Another example could be where a group is formed in an FTF

Table 1. Categories of virtualness

| | | Face-To-Face | |
		Low	High
Electronically-Mediated	Low	**Inactive**	**Traditional**
	High	**Highly-Virtual**	**Fully-Supported**

environment, but then uses electronic coordination and exchange of documents to integrate and coordinate individual or subgroup work products.

The low electronic and high FTF group would be the *traditional* group bound by geographic proximity (which may or may not include significant travel for members). The bulk of past group-oriented research targets this quadrant but provides rich material for speculation about other formats.

The high electronic and high FTF group is termed *fully supported*. A workgroup with complex tasks that require high volumes of individual contribution and coordination of contributions probably requires both frequent FTF meetings and much electronic communication for additional communication.

The third research question is: *How are successful project teams distributed in terms of FTF and electronic media usage?*

METHODS

Recognizing the importance of studying technology use in context, the researchers focused on a single organization and solicited data from practicing project teams within that organization. An internal contact at a Fortune 500 firm headquartered in the southeastern US identified a convenience sample of about a dozen practicing PMs based on their willingness to participate and their reputations as successful PMs, based on peer and management evaluations within the organization. Ultimately, eight completed their participation in the study. All came from a large IT subdivision and all were involved in IT-related projects.

The participants were informed about the purpose of the study and asked to select up to five projects in which they were currently involved. They were asked to log a series of communication events for a total of four hours over a period of two weeks regarding those projects. The purpose of the logging process was to stimulate their thinking about their uses of technology to perform project-related tasks. After the logging period, each of the participants was interviewed for approximately an hour using semi-structured interview questions. The interviews were audiotaped (with the participants' permission) and professionally transcribed. Finally, a vice-president with ultimate responsibility for all the participants and their projects was also interviewed, and provided open-ended comments regarding the broader organizational context in which the study was undertaken.

The interviewers asked a number of different questions to discover insights into the participants' use of tools on projects:

•   Tools they used for project tasks, frequency of use, and experience with the tools.

- Types of project tasks for which they used the tools, and the strengths and limitations of particular tools.
- The most frequent problems they had working on teams, how they were resolved, and specifically using which tools.
- How they measured project success.
- In which of the four quadrants in Table 1 each project fell.

The list of tools included one-on-one meetings, FTF group meetings, phone calls, voicemail, e-mail, Excel, MS Project, audioconferencing, videoconferencing, and intranet. Several of the participants added "pagers" to the provided list. Participants were asked what tools they most frequently used for a list of common project management tasks: allocating resources, calling meetings, scheduling tasks, getting signatures or authorization, making group decisions, preparing group documents or spreadsheets, submitting status reports, team-building, and general discussion.

Analysis of the data include compilation of simple descriptive statistics, shown in Table 2, and qualitative review of transcribed interview data, aggregated into themes that emerged from the analysis. The researchers separately reviewed and then together discussed and analyzed the interview results.

RESULTS

Table 2 displays basic information about the study participants.

Table 3 shows the participants' analysis of where in the 2×2 described above each of their projects fell. Clearly the majority of projects were active and highly supported by electronic communication, and about half were frequently supported by FTF communication as well.

Table 2: Description of Respondents

Demographic Variable	Values
Total participants	8 (6 f, 2 M)
Average Age	41
Average years in IT	18
Average Years as PM	10
Average # of Projects Led	18
Total Number of Projects	30
Total Log Entries	91
Average Group (Project Size)	10
Job Titles	Lead Analyst (2)
	Information Resource Senior Manager
	Corporate Security Manager
	Director IRSS
	Network Projects Manager
	Technical Consultant
	Administrative Secretary

Table 3. Number of projects per grid quadrant

		Face-To-Face	
		Low	High
Electronically-Mediated	Low	Inactive 2	Traditional 4
	High	Highly-Virtual 11	Fully-Supported 13

Table 4. Media use (logs)

Media	Log Entries	Percent of Total
E-mail	35	38%
One-on-One	17	19%
Meeting	11	12%
Voice Mail	8	9%
Phone Live	7	8%
Audio Conference	3	3%
Pager	1	1%
Videoteleconferencing (VTC)	0	0%
Other	9	10%
TOTAL	91	100%

Table 4 shows aggregated log entries based on media used. These log entries described a sampling of project-related communication interactions that included task, purpose, medium, and with whom. Nearly 40% of the logged entries used e-mail, twice as many as used face-to-face one-on-one communication, and four times as many as used voicemail messages.

The next section first provides an overview of the organizational context, based on the interviews. This is followed by a summary of what the participants used to measure project success, and then a list of the most common project problems they encountered. This provides a foundation for analyzing and integrating the participants' answers to interview questions, aimed at addressing the research questions.

Organization Context

The organization was described as decentralized, with an entrepreneurial culture, that has grown through acquisition. The organization was termed by more than one participant as "extremely collaborative ... the actual work we do is much flatter than our organization chart suggests." The current business goals mentioned included searching for synergies and leverage points, including with external business partners. The organization is heavily *projectized*. Many current projects deal with cross-cultural teams and changes to business processes due to acquisitions and mergers.

One respondent described projects in this organization as "a seeming continuous set of deliverables. You're typically driven around meetings that provide information to other people who make decisions and provide information...I always use the next meeting to try to get the tools that I need for that decision plan. In theory I have this overall plan ... All I worked on was getting that briefing ready ... in the process I ... accomplished a lot of other deliverables ...that fed into it."

One interesting comment was a categorization of organizational projects into three types for funding prioritization purposes: "oil change", traditional ROI, and venture capital. The oil change projects are those needed just to stay in business, thus must be funded. The traditional ROI type must demonstrate benefits exceeding costs, with a life cycle described as "analyze, commit, do." The venture capital type was more risky, more of an R&D type project. This approach would include a portfolio of experiments, some of which would be expected to fail, which should not have to demonstrate ROI up front, but which are needed for innovation, and which should be funded from a separate source than traditional projects.

Many employees in this organization had had formal training in a version of the PMBOK adapted to fit the company, and this was reflected in many of their comments. At the time of the study, the standard collaborative tools were MS Exchange for e-mail, MS Schedule, and MS Project. Few respondents appeared to fully utilize the features of the tools available for interactive collaboration, however. Intranet use for collaboration was growing, but there was little evidence of cultural adoption of chat or instant messaging as a regular tool for collaboration. Several of the interviewees sounded intrigued by the possibilities, however. A few people mentioned pagers as growing in usefulness but not yet widespread.

Project Success Measures and Obstacles to Success

In order to understand the use of CMC tools by practicing PMs, it was important to understand their measures of project success. Based on what they mentioned in the interviews, the following list maps clearly to generally accepted success measures for project status. As one participant stated, you "add value to your project by accomplishing a deliverable by a deadline."

Project success measures included:

- deliverables (if the project meets its objective) (3);
- employee satisfaction (if they like each other at the end of the project, turn over) (3);
- schedule (2);
- budget (2);
- client satisfaction (2);

- political perception/high level excitement (2);
- lack of disaster (1).

(Note that the number indicates how many times each was specifically mentioned by a participant in the interviews.)

Additional indicators mentioned by the participants regarding ongoing projects that they would use themselves informally to assess how well the project was going included quality of plan; direction & focus; clear priorities; clear deliverables; scope definition; user sponsor; communication; "close project management"; frequent status reports; team rapport and trust; and follow-up.

The most common problems encountered by these practicing PMs included: coordination of time (2); priority conflicts (2); resources (2); coordination of objectives (1); keeping them focused (1); a clear definition of deliverables and accountability (1); miscommunication and misinterpretation (1).

Tool Use and Preferences

The following discussion of tool use reflects analysis of the participants' descriptions of critical incidents reflecting this list of problems, and how the respondents used the tools to address a specific problem they had encountered as a PM.

It is clear from both the logs and the interview data that the participants overwhelmingly use e-mail most frequently, regardless of project task. As one participant said: "You can get a lot done in e-mail." However, most of the participants used e-mail in conjunction with various other tools to accomplish their tasks. They also discussed limitations of e-mail in various situations.

Nearly all the participants, when asked, stated e-mail would be the one tool they'd miss the most. They viewed e-mail as essential for scheduling. They liked receiving project communications via e-mail versus via voicemail, because they could review it and better understand the implications. E-mail was called "concise and to the point ... don't have to waste time with pleasantries and chit-chat." One participant referred to e-mail "like an addictive disease ... you can't function any more without keeping up with it." One person mentioned that e-mail "makes it easier to extend the work day ... can get ... project status from individuals without calling a meeting." Several liked e-mail due to the ability to quickly distribute and share project information via attachments, such as Word and Excel, with which many of them said they get a lot of project work done.

One participant said that when they urgently needed to get in touch with someone, they would use the phone first, because if the person was not there, they could usually find someone else in the office to find out where they were and how to get in touch with them.

A formal scheduling tool was apparently more often used passively rather than actively. A standard procedure would be to look in others' schedules for possible times, then send out e-mails to confirm, rather than actually scheduling meetings for each other. Even though MS Project was also available to everyone, it appeared to be used primarily for initial planning by PMs. Most preferred Excel for communicating schedule and budget information.

Intranets were frequently mentioned as an increasingly useful way to share project information, and appeared to be somewhat replacing shared e-mail folders. The corporate intranet was described as an informal Knowledge Management tool.

Videotelecommunication (VTC) was viewed as the least useful or essential tool. Participants said they could achieve everything in an audioconference (conference call) that could be achieved in a VTC. "If you're effective in your communications, you don't really have to put a face to a voice." However, a limitation of audioconferencing was someone not showing up (dialing in), or someone not knowing when they are rambling on too long, because they can't see others' faces, which would be giving them signals.

When asked what tools they did not have that would be useful, most often mentioned was a whiteboard or presentation-sharing tool. Traveling, or using VTC, to give a presentation was viewed as too complicated, expensive, and overkill. Desktop conferencing would be preferred. The current culture was not averse to new synchronous tools such as NetMeeting, but just not as familiar with them as they were with e-mail. Also, technical support for such tools was still lagging.

E-Tools vs. Face Time

The majority of participants agreed that, although they most frequently used e-mail for most project tasks, FTF interaction "could quickly become first" if problems arose in a project. Interestingly, "face time" was considered more formal than e-mail and voicemail, and was often described as needed to gain commitment or re-order priorities.

One of the most common project-related problems mentioned by participants was getting their own projects higher on others' priority lists, especially external partners and high-level sponsors. One person mentioned: "I do phone calls, but they don't do any good." Another described how he used e-mail, unsuccessfully, to get a boss to agree to get some employees trained in what they needed to proceed with their part of a project. The PM also used e-mails, unsuccessfully, to remind the trainees to get it. Apparently, they weren't being given enough time to do the training. Finally, he dropped by the boss' office for a face-to-face visit to finally gain the commitment. Face time is sometimes needed to "increase the perception of accountability." Physical presence can also gain commitment from team members through peer pressure.

Another participant described an incident where he kept sending e-mails and even calling meetings, but the ultimate project sponsor wouldn't come to the meetings and wouldn't write up the plan. He used phone calls to increase urgency, then dropped in FTF to increase urgency even more. At the same time, he felt he had to hold back a bit, trying to balance his own style with the different style of the sponsor, who had to own the project himself, rather than have it imposed on him.

It's "easy to say no" in an e-mail or not to answer a voicemail. E-mails and phone calls, especially to external team members, often get ignored. In one case, even an FTF with a peer level partner didn't work, so the PM had to do an FTF with a higher-level contact to get some issues prioritized and resolved. In another case, a team split geographically appeared to be on track whenever they were together, but lost focus as soon as they all returned to their respective offices. The PM had to fly out every couple of weeks to keep them on track, and finally instituted a regular daily phone call, to keep the project in the priority forefront.

Limitations of E-Mail

When asked to describe a specific instance of a problem caused by a tool, one of the most frequent issues mentioned was inappropriately copying messages to others besides the original recipient, because it's so easy to add "cc's". One type of outcome of this described by participants is that some people misinterpret, ask for explanations, others offer opinions, the misunderstanding gets escalated, and lots of time is wasted following up and explaining. Another outcome is that some people begin to ignore e-mails that have long lists in the "cc:" field. A third outcome is that the recipient may wonder or misinterpret (or correctly interpret and react negatively) as to why certain people, especially at higher levels, have been included in the "cc:" list.

The interviewees emphasized, in this situation, the need to pick up the phone right away to prevent escalation or find out the real issue, or to call a meeting to clarify misunderstandings before too many people continue to offer opinions. Of course, if the intended people don't show up at the meeting, the escalation may continue.

One participant described receipt of "E-missiles," which "are OK if you know the person," but otherwise may come across as more hostile than intended. Another participant mentioned one colleague whose messages often appeared dyslexic, which again was OK if one knew him, and another discussed a colleague who had to receive counseling in developing greater awareness of appropriate e-mail communication. People in organizations often are more likely to have developed verbal political etiquette before they learn to do it via e-mail.

Finally, respondents mentioned the legal ramifications of putting things in writing via e-mail. "Something this sensitive you don't put in an e-mail." Organizational policy now directs employees to delete all e-mails over seven days old, and does not backup e-mail over 30 days old.

DISCUSSION AND IMPLICATIONS

The main purpose of the study was to improve understanding of electronic tool usage within a project management framework, by discerning patterns and themes in the respondents' answers to interview questions. In addressing the first two research questions, their responses reveal a pattern of adapting a combination of familiar technologies to fit the particular situation, and acknowledging that FTF interaction still plays an important role, even among those who primarily communicate via electronic tools. They placed the bulk of their projects into the two highly electronically supported quadrants of the virtualness grid (Table 3), with about half of those also including frequent FTF interaction (addressing the third research question). The implication is that regardless of geographic distance, e-tools are heavily used because they support the way project teams work rather than simply because they bridge geographic distance.

On the surface, e-mail appears to be the most popular tool. The interviews reveal, however, that it is only effective in accomplishing project tasks when used appropriately and in conjunction with other tools. For example, one respondent stated that cell phones and e-mail complement each other, if used correctly. "Anybody who thinks you're replacing a phone call with an e-mail ... [or vice-versa] ... doesn't understand how to use them." The tools do not replace each other; they enhance each other. Their usage is context dependent, based on the objectives, the tasks, the recipients, and the urgency and content of the message.

Another recipient stated that, before e-mail was widespread, "I guess we were a lot more localized on our projects." There was more one-on-one interaction, more travel, more conference calling. Some participants stated that the electronic tools have made it much easier to work with remote team members. This implies that the e-tools have indeed increased the ability of the organization to bring in outside resources from remote locations, and thus establish distributed project teams and partnerships with external stakeholders.

One interesting outcome of the study was an almost complete lack of any reports on misuse of e-mail for personal purposes. It is true that in many organizations today, there are likely to be organizational policies that guide appropriate e-mail use (Schafer, 2001). More likely, at least in this case, there is an organizational culture that views e-mail as a work tool. The practicing PMs in this study demonstrated little time or patience for flaming or strictly social interaction; they are simply always trying to accomplish their tasks and goals.

Groupware designers should take note that in this large successful Fortune 500 company, there appears to be little use of formal groupware (MS Project, MS Exchange/Outlook), such as for interactive calendaring and scheduling, beyond as a static planning tool, or beyond the few early adopters. Instead these PMs integrate a variety of more familiar tools into a personalized toolset that matches their project management style and practices. They use intranets and bulletin boards to some extent, but much more often use e-mail and spreadsheets for sharing documents, schedules, status reports, and other project artifacts. When the going gets tough, they rely on traditional FTF interactions to resolve problems and re-order priorities.

Finally, if these results are considered within the PMBOK framework, the respondents' demonstrated their use of e-tools across most of the main PMBOK processes, namely, Project Initiation, Planning, Execution, and Controlling. Probably the least discussed of the five main processes was that of Closure, which incorporates formally storing project information and outcomes, including perceptions of problems, solutions, and learning, for future reference on future projects. Ideally this should contribute to organizational learning. If so much goes on via e-mail, and if e-mails are encouraged to be deleted, is there project information and learning that is lost?

Implications for Researchers

This study offers a simple framework for measuring virtualness, which provides a rich array of potential opportunities to investigate many traditional communications and small-group research questions as they apply to varying degrees of virtualness in a group. This framework has the advantage over "same-different time/place" frameworks in that each of the dimensions is directly measurable and covers a wider range of potential group communication situations. The study also introduces a useful new approach to researching, understanding, and designing tools for teams, that of the project management framework, which reflects how collaborative work gets done in many of today's organizations.

The study highlights complexities in studying project management and communication support, and suggests directions for future research. Why do project teams fall into one or the other quadrant in the model? This likely depends upon a variety of factors, including task type, group history, available and acceptable media, as well as group, organizational, and possibly national culture, as globalization increases. The entire set of media options should be viewed as a portfolio, which continually changes as new technologies are introduced and adopted. The findings of this study need to be examined in other organizations, with other portfolios of communications technologies available, and for other sorts of project tasks.

Implications for Practitioners

The results of this particular study are based on best practices of experienced project managers in a successful project-oriented organization. Table 5 summarizes their collective wisdom.

Firms could likely profit from accelerating the learning curve for assimilating new communications technologies by: encouraging experimentation with new tools (such as personal data assistants linked to the Web or Instant Messaging),

Table 5: Summary of Best Practices

- To monitor and control a project, a PM often uses a weekly one-on-one (FTF or e-mail) for individuals, a weekly staff meeting (by conference call for distributed teams), and lots of interim e-mails.
- A successful project team needs a common toolset, the knowledge of how to use them, and a standard approach and style.
- Successful PM's are those who are more inclined to use e-mail and who carefully select targeted recipients, but who are comfortable with switching to different media as the occasion demands.
- When sending an e-mail to someone outside that you don't know, also call and leave a message to expect the e-mail with the information.
- When scheduling, offer specific options, not just "When are you available?"
- Successful PM's pro-actively seek out new project opportunities.
- Executive managers still prefer phone vs. e-mail, and need more face time.
- Obstacles to project success are much more often due to resistance to organizational change than resistance to technology.

actively monitoring best practices among skillful users, distributing information about effective techniques, and providing sufficient technical support. Trainers should emphasize social as well as technical operation of the tools, and sensitivity to contextual clues, thus describing not only the technique, but something about the situation in which it was successfully applied (and others where its success has not been tested) for maximum organizational learning.

Implications for Groupware Designers

These practicing PMs specifically mentioned that they want and need: "... the information to be readily available as soon as we finish whatever meeting we're at. I don't want to wait two days or a week for the minutes"; to overcome geographic time difference delays; more filtering and prioritizing of e-mail; the ability to "automatically capture what I'm working on when... I'm working on it." They clearly need the ability to flexibly integrate and adapt their preferred and familiar tools, such as e-mail, spreadsheets, and documents, with shared presentation tools, intranets, and desktop video. Certainly, standard platforms and interfaces are critical if end-users are to be able to pick and choose to build a personalized toolset. More importantly, they need this flexible toolset in a framework that presents, stores, retrieves, and shares the information in a manner consistent with the PMBOK and project management practices. To date, much of the technical groupware research has focused on supporting more complex problem-solving situations by attempting to simulate realistic FTF interaction. It would be helpful if groupware designers additionally addressed the need for a flexible, simple, easy-to-use, integrated toolset that offers day-to-day operational capabilities necessary for effective project management, which, if done well, might help to reduce the need for some of those FTF showdowns.

Limitations

This study consists of a qualitative analysis of a small number of practitioners in a single, large organization, consisting of both localized and distributed project teams. As such, it controls for differences in organization context variables, by investigating practitioners within a fairly homogeneous structure and culture. However, the small number of subjects and the single organization clearly limits the general application of the results. The methodology did not attempt to distinguish variability, but instead sought to uncover common patterns and themes. Although not a subject of this study, the fact that three-fourths of the respondents were female leads to an interesting direction for future research: Might gender or other dimensions of diversity be factors in the use of these tools for project management?

CONCLUSION

This study provides a rich picture of practicing project managers' use of electronic tools for communication and collaboration in an IT project context. In summary, the findings of this study suggest that communication technologies can and do play a role in supporting project work activities. The use of communication technologies does not appear to substitute for, but rather complements use of traditional face-to-face communication. The results should be useful for organizations faced with a growing collection of media alternatives and opportunities, and with the challenges of learning how to use each while organizing a sophisticated portfolio of options into productive work arrangements and communication choices. The results should also form a starting point for IT project managers considering cultural and international issues, in addition to content and technical issues with staff members working in diverse locations. The majority of IT project teams exhibit a high degree of electronic communication, regardless of whether or not the members are co-located. This suggests a smoother transition than might be expected, as teams become more distributed across time and geography.

ACKNOWLEDGMENT

Many thanks to Martha Arellano and to the project managers and organization VP who were willing to give up valuable time and energy out of their busy schedules to share their insight and experiences regarding the study. Thanks also to the anonymous associate editor and reviewers who contributed valuable suggestions.

REFERENCES

Ahuja, M. K., & Carley, K. M. (1998). Network structure in virtual organizations. *JCMC, 3*(4), 29.

Arnold, D. & Niederman, F. (2001). The Global IT Workforce. *Communications of the ACM, 44*(7), 30-34.

Chudoba, K. M., & Maznevski, M. L. (1996). *Virtual Transnational Teams and Their Use of Advanced Information Technology*. Paper presented at the International Conference on Information Sytems, Ohio.

Dennis, A. R., & Wixom, B. H. (2001-2002). Investigating the moderators of the group support systems use with meta-analysis. *Journal of MIS, 18*(3), 235-258.

DeSanctis, G., Poole, M.S., Dickson, G.W. & Jackson, B.M. (1993). Interpretive analysis of team use of group technologies. *Journal of Organizational Computing, 3*(1), 1-30.

Fjermestad, J., & Hiltz, S. R. (2000, January 4-7). *Case and field studies of group support systems: An empirical assessment.* Paper presented at the 33rd Hawaii International Conference on System Sciences, Maui, Hawaii.

Fowler, G. D. a. W., M.E. (1980). Audio teleconferencing versus face-to-face conferencing: A synthesis of the literature. *The Western Journal of Speech Communication, 44*(44), 236-252.

Hiltz, S. R., & Turoff, M. (1992). Virtual meetings: Computer conferencing and distributed group support. In R. P. Bostrom, R. T. Watson & S. T. Kinney (Eds.), *Computer augmented teamwork: A guided tour*. New York: Van Nostrand Reinhold.

Hiltz, S. R. T., M. (1985). Structuring CMC systems to avoid information overload. *CACM, 28*(7), 680-689.

Hinds, P., & Kiesler, S. (1995). Communication across boundaries: Work, structure, and use of communication technologies in a large organization. *Organization Science, 6*(4), 373-393.

Jessup, L. M., & Valacich, J. S. (1993). *Group Support Systems: New Perspectives*. New York: MacMillan Publishing.

Knoll, K., & Jarvenpaa, S. (1995). *Learning to work in distributed global teams*. Paper presented at the 28th Hawaii International Conference on Systems Sciences, Hawaii, January.

Markus, M. L. (1994). Electronic mail as the medium of managerial choice. *Organization Science, 5*(4), 502-537.

Markus, M. L. (1994). Finding a happy medium: Explaining the negative effects of electronic communication on social life at work. *ACM Transactions of Information Systems, 12*(2), 119-149.

McLeod, P. L. (1992). An assessment of the empirical literature on electronic support of group work: Results of a meta-analysis. *Human Computer Interaction, 7*(3), 257-280.

Nilles, J. (1995). *Making telecommuting happen.* Van Nostrand Reinhold.

Ocker, R. (2001, January 3-6). *The effects of face-to-face and computer-mediated communication: Results on group development, satisfaction and performance.* Paper presented at the 34th Annual Hawaii International Conference on System Sciences, Maui, Hawaii (Jan. 3-6).

Orlikowski, W. J. (1992, Oct 31-Nov 4). *Learning from NOTES: Organizational issues in groupware implementation.* Paper presented at the CSCW '92, Toronto, Canada.

Project Management Institute, T. (1996). *PMBOK — A guide to the project management body of knowledge.* Sylva, NC: The Project Management Institute.

Schafer, S. (2001, January 4). CA fires workers over e-mail. *Washington Post,* E05.

Solomon, C. M. (2001). Managing virtual teams. *Workforce, 80*(6), 60-65.

Sproull, L., & Kiesler, S. (1988). Reducing social context cues: Electronic mail in organizational communication. In I. Greif (Ed.), *Computer supported cooperative work: A book of readings* (pp. 683-712). San Mateo, CA: Morgan Kaufmann.

Zack, M. H., & McKenney, J. L. (1995). Social context and interaction in ongoing computer-supported management groups. *Organization Science, 6*(4), 394-422.

This chapter was previously published in the *Information Resources Management Journal, 17*(4), 73-88, October-December, Copyright © 2004.

Chapter III

Information Sharing in Supply Chain Management with Demand Uncertainty

Zhensen Huang
University of Maryland, Baltimore County, USA

Aryya Gangopadhyay
University of Maryland, Baltimore County, USA

ABSTRACT

Information sharing is a major strategy to counteract the amplification of demand fluctuation going up the supply chain, known as the bullwhip effect. However, sharing information through interorganizational channels can raise concerns for business management from both technical and commercial perspectives. The existing literature focuses on examining the value of information sharing in specific problem environments with somewhat simplified supply chain models. The present study takes a simulation approach in investigating the impact of information sharing among trading partners on supply chain performance in a comprehensive supply chain model that consists of multiple stages of trading partners and multiple players at each stage.

INTRODUCTION

During the last decade, supply chain management, collaboration, coordination, and integration have been a concern of the world of business as well as the academic community. It is generally accepted that supply chain collaboration has a major impact on an organization's ability to meet customer needs and reduce costs. A key step in supply chain collaboration is to share information among the supply chain partners.

While information sharing is also viewed as a major strategy to counter the bullwhip effect (Chen et al., 2000; Gavirneni 2002; Lee, Padmanabhan & Whang, 1997a, 1997b; Simchi-Levi, Kaminski & Simchi-Levi, 2000), the advances in information technologies make information sharing possible, and these advances actually become a key driver of supply chain integration. However, sharing information through interorganizational channels has brought about new concerns for business management. Due to the competitive and adversarial nature of the business itself, managers tend to overestimate the possible risks without seeing the potential benefits and thus are reluctant to share information with their trading partners (Lee & Whang, 1998; Whang, 1993). Under this context, evaluating the effectiveness or the value of the information sharing becomes prominent before the managers are willing to push for any IT investment on supply chain collaboration (Huang, 2004).

In this chapter, we focus on addressing the above issues by investigating the effectiveness of information sharing under several different scenarios within a comprehensive supply chain model where a supply chain is defined as follows:

multiple trading partners with suppliers/manufacturers and customers at the opposite ends with wholesalers and retailers located between them, and all entities are interconnected through the flow of materials and/or information. (Huang, 2004, p. 3)

The rest of the chapter is organized as follows. In the next section, we describe some of the relevant work, which is followed by our research methodology including the design of the simulation study, experimental results, and conclusion.

PREVIOUS WORK

In the supply chain management research literature, a phenomenon that has been observed for a long time is that the fluctuation of demand information is amplified throughout the supply chain from downstream to upstream. While Forrester (1958, 1961) and Sterman (1989) identify and study this phenomenon, Lee et al. (1997a) coined this "the bullwhip effect" using several case studies and mathematical models. One of the case studies used is the sales of Pampers diapers by Procter & Gamble. While the consumers (in this case, babies) consume diapers at a steady rate, the variability of demand grows as it progresses up the supply chain.

Several researchers attempt to quantify the demand amplification in order to better understand the specific causes of the bullwhip effect and the economic benefit of eliminating them. Fransoo and Wouters (2000) study the bullwhip effect in two convenience food supply chains. Empirical estimates of demand amplification in the food services supply chain for meals (salads) are 1.67 (2.09), 1.26 (2.73), and 1.75 (1.23) for the retailer, distribution center, and production facility, respectively. Taylor (1999) quantifies the bullwhip effect in an upstream automotive component supply chain and finds that demand variability moves up the supply chain with values of 0.88, 1.63, 2.17, 3.64, 3.05, and 13.76 at OEM demand, final assembly, pressing, blanking, service center, and steel mill, respectively. Chen et al. (2000) analytically quantify the bullwhip effect associated with demand forecasting and order lead-time in a two-stage system with a single retailer and a single manufacturer. The results indicate that the bullwhip effect can be reduced, but not completely eliminated, by centralizing demand information. Sahin and Robinson (2002) summarize, based on the review of over 100 studies, that the potential causes of the bullwhip effect are seasonal retail sales variations, random fluctuations in sales, advertising and price discount policies, factory capacity limitations, order cycle lead-time, and traditional purchasing and inventory policies.

Furthermore, other studies have been conducted to investigate the bullwhip effect under different scenarios. Empirical evidence of the bullwhip effect is provided in economic data analysis (Baganha & Cohen, 1998) and case studies (Fransoo & Wouters, 2000; Houlihan, 1987; Taylor, 1999). Bourland, Powell, and Pyke (1996) examine the case in which the review period of the manufacturer is not synchronized with the retailer. Chen (1998) studies the value of centralized demand information by comparing the cost difference between two inventory policies—one based on echelon stock and the other based on installation stock where the echelon stock focuses on the inventory position of the subsystem consisting of the stage itself as well as all the downstream stages, and the installation stock is only concerned with local inventory position. Thus, echelon stock policy requires centralized demand information, and installation stock does not. The extensive numerical results in this study reveal that the centralized information system's costs are on average 1.75% lower than that of the decentralized information system with a maximum 9% savings. Lee and Whang (1998) discuss how and why the information is shared using several industry examples. Cachon and Fisher (2000) analytically show how the manufacturer can benefit from using information about the retailer's inventory levels when the retailers use a batch ordering policy in a supply chain model with one supplier, N identical retailers, and stationary consumer demand. Gavirneni, Kapuscinski, and Tayur (1999) consider the scenario in which the manufacturer has limited capacity and evaluate the benefit of obtaining additional information about the retailer's inventory level. Chen (1999) examines the value of information sharing among the divisions within the same firm and concludes that it is important for the upstream member of the supply chain to have access to accurate customer demand information. Lee, So, and Tang (2000) quantify the benefits of information sharing for a simple two-level supply chain with nonstationary end demand and show that the value of demand information sharing can be quite high, especially when demands are significantly correlated over time.

Although information sharing is often considered a generic cure for the bullwhip effect, and it is generally accepted that information sharing can optimize the supply chain-wide performance (Chen et al., 2000; Forrester, 1958; Lee et al., 1997a, 1997b; Simchi-Levi et al., 2000), some literature shows that the value of information sharing varies under different scenarios. Baganha and Cohen (1998) find that, under certain conditions, the variance of demand faced by a manufacturer is less when filtered through a distribution center than when the retailers submit their orders directly to the manufacture. Bourland et al. (1996) reveal that when the order cycles of the suppliers and the assembly plant are of equal length and each channel member replenishes on the same day, information sharing has no effect on inventories. Lee et al. (2000) indicate that analysis assuming stationary demand may be insufficient to capture the benefits in high-tech, grocery, or other industries, where auto-correlated demand is prevalent. Haines, Hough, and Haines (2004) claim that supply chain performance is driven by decision style, environmental variability, and rational decision-making, but not information availability. Also, Chiang and Feng (2004) examine a two-level supply chain where the supply-side uncertainty coexists with the demand-side uncertainty and find that the impact of production yield variability on the value of information sharing for the retailers is not significant.

A review of the existing research of the bullwhip effect reveals several issues (Huang, Gangopadhyay, & Gupta, 2004). First, the magnitude of the impact of information sharing is highly dependent upon the specific problem environment including the retailer's ordering pattern (i.e., synchronized vs. balanced orders), the demand process (i.e., stationary vs. nonstationary), and the inventory policy applied by the channel members. Second, most existing research focuses on some simplified scenarios where trading partners share information with each other to some extent. However, a current literature review finds little work, if any, on investigating this issue in a complex supply chain model that introduces competition (Huang & Gangopadhyay, 2004). Third, existing literature looks at two extreme scenarios of information sharing, that is, no information sharing and/or full information sharing. However, in practice, information sharing is more than a Yes or No choice. A systematic approach to define the degrees of information sharing from the perspective of supply chain integration has been proposed and is utilized in this chapter to identify and address various issues related to the impact of information sharing on reducing the bullwhip effect (Huang, 2004).

METHODOLOGY

The disparate research findings in supply chain management suggest that it is necessary to expand research scope to consider a wider variety of problem environments with more comprehensive models (Sahin & Robinson, 2002). In this chapter, we first describe a four-level supply chain structure with multiple entities in each level. Based on the supply chain model, our approach is to identify the common factors that affect the value of information sharing in terms of reducing order fluctuations, and then to study the correlations among these factors and the value of information sharing without considering any product and industry characteristics. In this section, we describe how the various factors in the simulation study are designed. These factors include the supply chain structure, degree of information sharing, independent variables such as demand variability, capacity limitations, performance measurement, and simulation scenarios.

Supply Chain Model

Modeling a generalized supply chain is difficult because of the potentially unlimited number of combinations of the various entities, performance measures, and interaction effects (Swaminathan, Smith, & Sadeh, 1998). Little work has been done on studying distribution channel structure as a means to improve supply chain efficiency (Dong & Lee, 2003; Song & Yao, 2003). Our selection of the four-level supply chain is more generic than the two-level supply chain structure that is prevalent in most of the work in existing literature. The four levels also provide insights into the ability to generalize the results to multiple levels through extrapolation. We note, however, a limitation of this research is that it does not attempt to make such generalizations. At each level, we have multiple trading partners. As shown in Figure 1, there are 100 customers, eight retailers, four distributors, two wholesalers, and one manufacturer. While the ratio of the number of trading partners at each level varies from industry to industry, in general, the number of business entities increases as we move from upstream to downstream levels of a supply chain (Gupta, Marques, & Bianchi, 2001).

Defining the Degree of Information Sharing

We define the degree of information sharing as the volume/type of information shared among trading partners. Most of the existing research focuses on scenarios with the type of information shared, and most researchers agree that the more information is shared, the better the performance achieved in terms of reducing the bullwhip effect.

Another standpoint for defining the degree of information sharing is the amount of integration, which refers to the number of trading partners involved in supply chain integration for the purpose of information sharing. From this perspective, the degree of information sharing can be further divided into the following two scenarios. In the first scenario, only certain levels of the whole supply chain share information among each other, and others do not. Given the importance of customer demand information, the integration usually starts from downstream supply chain partners. In the second scenario, the number of trading partners involved in information sharing at each stage of the supply chain varies. From this perspective, this study defines three degrees of information sharing: no information sharing, partial information sharing, and full information sharing.

There are different degrees of partial information sharing. A simple model for partial information sharing is 50% information sharing, in which case, half of the trading partners at each stage are involved in information sharing while the other half does not participate. This study examines the partial information sharing scenario using a 50% information sharing model. We chose 50% because it is a midpoint between no information sharing and full information sharing which might enable interpolation for other degrees of information sharing.

In the scenario of 50% information sharing, the way that trading partners are connected can be different. One possibility is that all the trading partners are randomly connected. For example, it is possible that a retailer who participates in information sharing may deal with a distributor who does not participate in information sharing. The same situation can happen between the distributor and the wholesaler. The second possibility is that information sharing is well-organized, where if a retailer participates in information sharing, all of the next level trading partners they work with also participate in information sharing. No research shows evidence in favor of either random connections or well-organized integration. For simplicity of this research, we focus on the well-organized partial information sharing scenario as described above. The third type of information sharing is full information sharing. Obviously, in this scenario, all the trading partners are integrated together for the purpose of information sharing.

To summarize, this research examines three degrees of information sharing in studying the value of information sharing: no information sharing, 50% partial information sharing, and full information sharing.

Other Independent Variables

Information sharing is considered as one way to reduce the bullwhip effect, but it cannot eliminate the bullwhip effect completely. Other factors affecting the bullwhip effect include seasonal retail sales variations, random fluctuations in sales, advertising and price discount policies, factory capacity limitations, order cycle lead-time, and traditional purchasing and inventory policies (Sahin & Robinson, 2002). The value of information sharing should be examined with the combination of these factors to correctly reveal their interaction, if any. In these factors, seasonal retail sales variation, random fluctuations in sales, and advertising and price discount policies reflect the demand variability in the supply chain. Thus, demand variability, capacity limitations, lead-time, and inventory policies are discussed in this research.

Demand Variability

Customer demand variability is the nature of supply chains in almost all industries. There are long-term demand variations and short-term demand variations. Generally speaking, there are four basic demand patterns (Stevenson, 1982) in long-term demand variations, and these patterns can be normally identified using standard forecasting techniques in the different stages of product life cycles and are not the focus of this study. Short-term demand variations are normally concerned with seasonal changes and other variations from average and are particularly important in meeting customer service satisfaction. The seasonal changes are referred to as demand seasonality (Metters, 1997). For example, the sale of ice cream is possibly much higher in the summer than in the winter. Demand seasonality is generally predictable and can be normally discovered from historical sales data by applying data mining techniques, and it varies from one industry to another. Therefore, this study ignores demand seasonality. Other variations are normally caused by stochastic shopping behaviors and are referred to as "demand uncertainty" in this research. For example, it is almost impossible for a grocery store to forecast exactly how many bottles of milk will be sold the next day.

Demand uncertainty is affected by many unpredictable factors: weather, political unrest, or natural disasters. In addition, demand uncertainty is always amplified by retailers' promotions. When a retailer plans a promotion on a specific product, the retailer knows there will be a demand increase and can even forecast based on previous sales data how much the increase could be. Thus, from this retailer's perspective, this uncertainty can be predicted and prepared for. However, this demand increase has an impact on competitors' demand—a potential decrease in customer demand for the same product. Since the competitor typically has no idea of this promotion and therefore could face an unexpected demand decrease. Furthermore, even the retailer who provides such a promotion can face a potentially uncertain demand fluctuation due to customers' forward-buying on this product.

To summarize, this study focuses on stationary independent demand with demand uncertainty. In order to incorporate demand uncertainty, in this study, customer orders are generated by the computer program at random points in time and are of random sizes. Different parameters in random number generator are used to present two different levels of demand fluctuation: low and high. The detailed information, such as random number distributions, is presented in Appendix 1.

Capacity Limitations

In the efforts to study the bullwhip effect and to quantify the value of information sharing, existing literature handles supply capacity differently: some researchers examine the scenarios under limited capacity (Iyer & Bergen, 1997) while others study the situations with unlimited supply (Bourland et al., 1996; Gavirneni et al., 1999; Metters, 1997). In reality, the supply capacity is always limited due to production arrangement and resource limitation. Since this research takes a simulation approach and one of the principles in simulation study is to mimic the reality as closely as possible, this research only considers limited manufacturing capacity.

On the other hand, most of the capacity planning is designed with some flexibility considerations. The actual output is normally a fraction of effective capacity and/or design capacity determined by the efficiency and utilization ratios (Stevenson, 1982). In operations management, it is practical to adjust the production planning based on inventory level by utilizing strategies such as subcontracting, working overtime, and so forth (Stevenson, 1982). In this study, the manufacturer produces the product within a limited capacity with four levels of lot sizing based on the demand forecasting. The details on the production schedule that is implemented in this study are presented in Appendix 1.

Lead Time

Lead time refers to the period between the placing of an order and its receipt in the inventory system (Shim & Siegel, 1999). The issues related to order lead time include the length of lead time and lead time variability. Most of the researchers agree that the shorter the lead time, the better the performance because the shorter the lead time, the less the safety stock required to cover the demand during lead time. Apparently, the length and variability of lead time are determined by the inventory availability of the upstream trading partner and the product travel time (shipping time) between the upstream and downstream trading partners. For instance, when the upstream trading partner faces an out-of-stock situation, the downstream trading partner will experience a longer than normal lead time. From this perspective, lead time is not a separate independent variable. Thus, this research integrates lead time with the inventory status of the upstream trading partners while using a fixed product shipping time.

Specifically, a one-day shipping delay is introduced between two directly connected trading partners. For example, if a retailer places an order to the distributor at the end of Monday, the order is processed right away, and the shipment is arranged thereafter if the products are available at the distributor's inventory. At the end of Tuesday, the shipment arrives at the retailer's inventory and is ready for business on Wednesday.

In the industries in which products can be digitalized, the order lead-time can be reduced to a minimum. For example, most of the software vendors provide immediate download when customers make online purchases. In this scenario, it is very possible that the intermediate links in a supply chain can be eliminated, and the order cycle time can be reduced to close to zero.

Inventory Policies

The proper management of inventory systems has been a subject of investigation since the beginning of operations research. Different algorithms for inventory planning and control have been discussed in the supply chain literature (Axsater, 2000; Clark & Scarf, 1960; Collier, 1982; Gao & Robinson, 1994; Graves, 1996; Shim & Siegel, 1999; Silver, Pyke, & Peterson, 1998; Stevenson, 1982). Inventory models generally need to answer two questions: when to order and how much to order. Based on when to order, there are two types of inventory models used to manage independent demand: the fixed-quantity model and the fixed-order-interval models. In the fixed-quantity model, a fixed amount of order is placed at various time points. The often referenced model in the fixed-quantity variation is economic-order-quantity (EOQ) and reorder point (ROP). In this model, an optimum order size and reorder point that minimize the sum of the costs of holding inventory and the costs of ordering inventory are calculated so that when the amount of the on-hand inventory reaches a certain level (ROP), a quantity of EOQ amount is ordered to replenish the inventory. Clearly, the fixed-quantity model requires close monitoring of inventory levels in order to know when the amount on hand has reached the reorder point.

In the other model, the fixed-interval model, varying quantities are placed at fixed time intervals. The fixed-interval model requires a periodic review of inventory levels just prior to placing an order to determine how much is needed. The fixed-quantity model and the fixed-interval model react to the demand variations in different ways: in the fixed-quantity model, a higher than normal demand causes a shorter time between orders, while in the fixed-interval model, the result would be a larger order size.

Note that different models may be used for different situations. For example, the EOQ model needs to be adjusted when the inventories build up gradually over time instead of instantaneously (economic production run size) and when price discounts are available for large quantity purchases (quantity discounts model). Also, the fixed-interval model is a better option when a supplier encourages orders at fixed interval or when grouping orders for different items from the same supplier can yield savings in ordering, packing, and shipping costs.

Many retail operations use a fixed-order-interval model. In addition, for the industry that handles perishable goods, a single-period model can be used to balance the inventory costs and stock-out penalty. For more discussion on the inventory models and their variations under different scenarios, readers can refer to Stevenson (1982) and Handfield and Nichols (2002).

Due to the number of strategies in inventory control, it is impossible for this research to examine the effect of each inventory control on the bullwhip effect. Furthermore, each specific inventory model typically requires some industry-oriented parameters. However, the common point of various inventory control models is to provide a certain amount of inventory buffer to overcome potential demand uncertainty. Since this research attempts to take a generic approach toward examining the value of information sharing, different levels of inventory buffers instead of a specific inventory model are used. Based on discussion in Westland and Clark (1999), this study examines three different ranges of inventory buffer levels: 100%-150%, 150%-200%, and 200%-250%.

Performance Measurement

The existing literature presents a large variety of performance measures used to analyze supply chain performance (Beamon, 1998; Gunasekaran, Patel, & Tittiroglu, 2001; Liker & Wu, 2000). In their case study at Hewlett-Packard, Callioni and Billington (2001) mentioned three metrics: fill rate, sales/inventory ratio, and sales. Kleijnen and Smits (2003) presented five measures used by a large multinational company: fill rate, confirmed fill rate, response delay, stock, and delay. Based on these, they further proposed a balanced scorecard (BSC) including four dimensions of performance metrics: customers, internal processes, innovation, and finance. Also, the measures may be correlated, either positively or negatively. For example, higher stock inventories increase costs, so they decrease profits in the short run. However, higher stock definitely increases the fill rate, which increases goodwill, so market share may increase in the long term.

In general, for a given number of metrics n $(x_1, x_2, ..., x_n)$, there are two most commonly used functions for studying the combined effects of these metrics. One is the linear function:

$$u = a_1x_1 + ... + a_nx_n$$

The other is the logarithmic function:

$$\ln(u) = a_1\ln(x_1) + ... + a_n\ln(x_n)$$

In principle, the various supply chain performance metrics may be affected by many factors because of the large scale of the supply chain. As most of the existing literature does (Chen, 1999; Raghunathan, 1999), in this study, the inventory costs and backorder penalties are measured in evaluating the supply chain performance.

Let λ be the performance, μ the inventory costs, ν the backorder penalties, the relationship between supply chain performance, and inventory costs and backorder penalties can be expressed as:

$$\lambda = f(m,n) \tag{1}$$

In equation (1), a specific function between λ and μ and ν is determined by the product characteristics and generally varies from industry to industry. For example, the holding cost for a dozen eggs is obviously different from that of a computer system. Also, an inventory cost in the PC industry might be much higher than that in the automobile industry since the technologies advance fast in the PC industry, and any stock held more than 2 months could significantly depreciate in value. In these cases, different functions should be used to evaluate the performance.

This research intends to be a generic supply chain study instead of a specific industry-oriented study. Given the uncertainty of the weighting scheme in different industries, for generalization purposes, no specific values are set for two constants. As a result, both inventory costs (μ) and backorder penalties (ν) are examined separately, instead of using the single value for performance (λ). Furthermore, inventory costs and backorder penalties can be expressed as a function of inventory level and backorder quantities, respectively. As a result, instead of measuring the inventory costs and backorder penalties directly, this study measures the inventory level and the amount of backorder.

In the context of supply chain, these metrics can be measured at least at two different levels: independent entities or the entire supply chain. The system level is concerned about the overall performance enhancement of the entire supply chain (or the entire industry), while the individual level is concerned about what each trading partner can gain from information sharing. Hausman (2002) describes a number of metrics expressly designed to monitor performance across the whole supply chain.

Research demonstrates that system improvement may impact each channel member differently. In addition, information sharing does not solve the problem, especially when players are evaluated based on their individual performance vs. system performance (Sahin & Robinson, 2002). Hence, it is important to evaluate the impact of information sharing both at the system level and at the individual channel member (Sahin & Robinson, 2002). This research examines both measures at both system and individual levels.

Research Hypotheses

To summarize, the overall objective of this research is to study the value of information sharing by examining the combined effects of information sharing, demand variability, and inventory level on supply chain performance. Let Y be the supply chain performance, a be the degrees of information sharing, b be the demand variability, and c be the inventory buffer level. The relationship this study examines can be summarized as follows:

$$Y = f(a, b, c)$$

The potential hypotheses are $Y=f(a)$, $Y=f(b)$, $Y=f(c)$, $Y=f(ab)$, $Y=f(ac)$, $Y=f(bc)$, and $Y=f(abc)$. The focus of this study is to examine the effect of information sharing, thus the hypotheses which do not involve the degree of information sharing (a) will not be tested. In other words, the following hypotheses involving the degrees of information sharing (a) will be tested: $Y=f(a)$, $Y=f(ab)$, $Y=f(ac)$, and $Y=f(abc)$.

H_{01}: There is no relationship between the degrees of information sharing and the supply chain performance.

H_{A1}: There is a positive relationship between the degrees of information sharing and the supply chain performance. $(Y=f(a))$

H_{02}: There is no relationship between the demand variability and the effect of information sharing on the supply chain performance.

H_{A2}: There is a positive relation between the demand variability and the effect of information sharing on the supply chain performance. $(Y=f(ab))$

H_{03}: There is no relationship between inventory buffer level and the effect of information sharing on the supply chain performance.

H_{A3}: There is a positive relation between inventory buffer level and the effect of information sharing on the supply chain performance. $(Y=f(ac))$

H_{04}: There is no relationship between the demand variability, the inventory buffer level, and the effect of information sharing on the supply chain performance.

H_{A4}: There is a positive relation between the demand variability, the inventory buffer level, and the effect of information sharing on the supply chain performance. $(Y=f(abc))$

In this study, all of the above four hypotheses were statistically tested based on the simulation results.

Factorial Experimental Design

Based on all the independent variables discussed above, simulation scenarios for this study can be defined for each variable. Table 3 summarizes the possible scenarios of simulations. The numbers in the table indicate the individual simulation scenarios.

EXPERIMENTAL RESULTS

As discussed previously, this study measures the supply chain performance in the combination of inventory costs and backorder penalties. Multivariate analyses of variance (MANOVA) are conducted using SAS to test the statistical significance of the simulation results for each of the four hypotheses listed before. Specifically, the main effect of information sharing and its possible interactions with inventory buffer levels and order fluctuations are tested using the overall performance of the retailers, distributors, and wholesalers, respectively.

Since this study employs a 2X3X3 factorial design, each complete simulation run consists of 18 scenarios. In the 3-replication run, it generates 54 observations, and 180 observations in the 10-replication run. For each observation, 1080 data points are collected during the 60-day valid period for each trading partner. The average of each measure across all the replications are used in the final analyses including the MANOVA testing. This section presents the MANOVA testing results for each of the hypotheses proposed in a previous section.

H_{01}: There is no relationship between the degrees of information sharing and the supply chain performance.

Table 3. Simulation scenarios

	Degrees of Information Sharing					
	No Sharing		Partial Information Sharing		Full Information Sharing	
	Customer Order Fluctuation		Customer Order Fluctuation		Customer Order Fluctuation	
Inventory Buffer Level	Low	High	Low	High	Low	High
100%-150%	1	2	3	4	5	6
150%-200%	7	8	9	10	11	12
200%-250%	13	14	15	16	17	18

H_{A1}: There is a positive relationship between the degrees of information sharing and the supply chain performance.

In 3-replication results, the analysis of simple effect shows that the effect of the degrees of information sharing is significant for the distributors and the wholesalers, F(distributor, info_sharing) = 119.91, $p < 0.001$, F(wholesaler, info_sharing) = 304.74, $p < 0.001$, but not for the retailers, F(retailer, info_sharing) = 0.49, p = 0.74. The 10-replication simulation run shows similar results, specifically, F(distributor, info_sharing) = 290.58, $p < 0.001$, F(wholesaler, info_sharing) = 698.33, $p < 0.001$, and F(retailer, info_sharing) = 2.21, p = 0.07. Thus, the null hypothesis is rejected, and the alternative hypothesis is accepted for the distributors and the wholesalers.

H_{02}: There is no relationship between the demand variability and the effect of information sharing on the supply chain performance.

H_{A2}: There is a positive relation between the demand variability and the effect of information sharing on the supply chain performance.

The MANOVA results also show significant information sharing by demand fluctuation interaction for the distributors and the wholesalers, F(distributor, info_sharing x order_fluc) = 15.91, $p < 0.001$, F(wholesaler, info_sharing x order_fluc) = 31.89, $p < 0.001$, but not for the retailers, F(retailer, info_sharing x order_fluc) = 0.08, $p = 0.98$. The 10-replication simulation run shows similar results, specifically, F(distributor, info_sharing x order_fluc) = 26.76, $p < 0.001$, F(wholesaler, info_sharing x order_fluc) = 90.99, $p < 0.001$, and F(retailer, info_sharing x order_fluc) = 0.13, $p = 0.97$. Thus, the null hypothesis is rejected, and the alternative hypothesis is accepted for the distributors and the wholesalers.

H_{03}: There is no relationship between inventory buffer level and the effect of information sharing on the supply chain performance.

H_{A3}: There is a positive relation between inventory buffer level and the effect of information sharing on the supply chain performance.

A significant information sharing by inventory buffer level interaction for the distributors and the wholesalers is indicated in the MANOVA results, F(distributor, info_sharing x invt_buffer) = 54.47, $p < 0.001$, F(wholesaler, info_sharing x invt_buffer) = 92.82, $p < 0.001$, but not for the retailers, F(retailer, info_sharing x invt_buffer) = 0.54, $p = 0.82$. The 10-replication simulation run shows similar results, specifically, F(distributor, info_sharing x invt_buffer) =

149.54, $p < 0.001$, F(wholesaler, info_sharing x invt_buffer) = 216.25, $p < 0.001$, and F(retailer, info_sharing x invt_buffer) = 1.81, $p = 0.07$. Thus, the null hypothesis is rejected, and the alternative hypothesis is accepted for the distributors and the wholesalers.

H_{04}: There is no relationship between the demand variability, the inventory buffer level, and the effect of information sharing on the supply chain performance.

H_{A4}: There is a positive relation between the demand variability, the inventory buffer level, and the effect of information sharing on the supply chain performance.

In addition, the MANOVA results show a significant 3-way interaction (information sharing by demand fluctuation by inventory buffer level) for the distributors and the wholesalers, F(distributor, info_sharing × order_fluc × invt_buffer) = 4.89, $p < 0.001$, F(wholesaler, info_sharing × order_fluc × invt_buffer) = 11.46, $p < 0.001$, but not for the retailers, F(retailer, info_sharing x order_fluc x invt_buffer) = 0.03, $p = 1.00$. The 10-replication simulation run shows similar results, specifically, F(distributor, info_sharing × order_fluc × invt_buffer) = 9.43, $p < 0.001$, F(wholesaler, info_sharing × order_fluc × invt_buffer) = 23.78, $p < 0.001$, but not for the retailers, F(retailer, info_sharing x order_fluc x invt_buffer) = 0.10, $p = 1.00$. Thus, the null hypothesis is rejected, and the alternative hypothesis is accepted for the distributors and the wholesalers.

To summarize, the MANOVA testing results indicate that from the perspective of both inventory levels and backorder quantities, wholesalers and distributors benefit from sharing information, but retailers do not gain significantly from information sharing. One explanation for this is that retailers have access to the same information no matter what degree of information sharing is implemented in the supply chain while both distributors and wholesalers gain access to additional customer demand information that is provided in the partial or full information sharing scenarios.

CONCLUSION

In this chapter, we presented a simulation study that investigates the effectiveness of information sharing under several different scenarios within a comprehensive supply chain model. The experiments show that from the perspectives of both end inventory and backorder quantities, distributors and wholesalers gain significantly from information sharing. This research does not compare the end inventory of manufacturer in the simulation scenarios due to the uncertainty of production management for the manufacturer. However, the results indicate that the manufacturer actually benefits from having less back orders if they participate in information sharing. The experimental results indicate that for retailers, not much gain can be realized from information sharing in terms of end inventory and back orders. However, the gains from information sharing that the upstream trading partners enjoy could be potentially shared with retailers. For example, distributors, wholesalers, and manufacturers could provide price discount and/or higher fulfillment priorities for those retailers who participate in information sharing (Whang, 1993).

There are several limitations of the chapter which may impact the ability to generalize the results. Given the innumerable possible combinations of business entities, performance measures, and interaction effects, it is impossible to simulate a supply chain structure that will represent all industries. We have, however, attempted to model a nontrivial supply chain that has some semblance to reality. Our future research plans include studying the effect of information sharing in industry specific supply chains and building analytical models based on the simulation results.

REFERENCES

Axsater, S. (2000). *Inventory control*. Boston/Dordrecht/London: Kluwer Academic Publishers.

Bagahna, M. P., Cohen, M. A. (1998). The stabilizing effect of inventory in supply chains. *Operations Research, 46*(3), 72-83.

Beamon, B. M. (1998). Supply chain design and analysis: Models and methods. *International Journal of Production Economy, 55*, 281-294.

Bourland, K., Powell, S., & Pyke, D. (1996). Exploring timely demand information to reduce inventories. *European Journal of Operation Research, 92*, 239-253.

Cachon, G. P., & Fisher, M. (2000). *Supply chain inventory management and the value of shared information* (Working paper). University of Pennsylvania, Wharton School.

Callioni, G., & Billington, C. (2001). Effective collaboration. *Operational Research/Management Science Today, 28*, 34-39.

Chen, F. (1998, December). Echelon reorder points, installation reorder points, and the value of centralized demand information. *Management Science, 44*(2), S221-S234.

Chen, F. (1999). Decentralized supply chains subject to information delays. *Management Science, 45*(8), 1076-1090.

Chen, F., Drezner, Z., Ryan, J. K., & Simchi-Levi, D. (2000). Quantifying the bullwhip effect in a simple supply chain: The impact of forecasting, lead times, and information. *Management Science, 46*(3), 436-443.

Chiang, W. K., & Feng, Y. (2004). The impact of uncertain production yield on the value of information sharing in a two-level supply chain. *Proceedings of DSI Annual Meeting 2004* (6731-6736).

Clark, A. J., & Scarf, H. (1960). Optimal policies for a multi-echelon inventory problem. *Management Science, 6*(4), 475-490.

Collier, D. A. (1982). Research issues for multi-level lot sizing in MRP systems. *Journal of Operations Management, 2*(2), 113-123.

Dong, L., & Lee, H. L. (2003). Efficient supply chain structures for personal computers. In Song, J.-S. & Yao, D. (Eds.), *Supply chain structures, coordination, information and optimization*. Boston: Kluwer Academic Publishers.

Forrester, J. W. (1958, July-August). Industrial dynamics. *Harvard Business Review*, 37-66.

Forrester, J. W. (1961). *Industrial dynamics*. Cambridge, MA: MIT Press.

Fransoo, J. C., & Wouters, M. J. F. (2000). Measuring the bullwhip effect in the supply chain. *Supply Chain Management: An International Journal, 5*(2), 78-89.

Gao, L. L., & Robinson, E. P. (1994). An arborescent network formulation and dual ascent based procedure for the two-stage multi-item dynamic demand lotzide problem. *Decision Sciences, 25*(1), 103-121.

Gavirneni, S. (2002). Information flows in capacitated supply chains with fixed ordering costs. *Management Science, 48*(5), 644-651.

Gavirneni, S., Kapuscinski, R., & Tayur, S. (1999). Value of information in capacitated supply chains. *Management Science, 45*(1), 16-24.

Graves, S. C. (1996). A multiechelon inventory model with fixed replenishment intervals. *Management Science, 42*(1), 1-18.

Gunasekaran A., Patel, C., & Tittiroglu, E. (2001). Performance measures and metrics in a supply chain environment. *International Journal of Operations and Production Management, 21*, 71-87.

Gupta, J. N. D., Marques, A. C., & Bianchi, C. (2001). *Supply chain integration through e-collaboration tools* (Working paper). Ball State University.

Haines, R., Hough, J., & Haines, D. (2004). Decision style and information availability: Predicting individual performance in a supply chain simulation. *Proceedings of DSI Annual Meeting 2004* (3101-3106).

Handfield, R. B., & Nichols, E. L. (2002). *Supply chain redesign: Transforming supply chain into integrated value systems*. Upper Saddle River, NJ: Prentice Hall.

Hausman, W. H. (2002). Supply chain performance metrics. In Billington C., Harrison, T., Lee, H., & Neale, J. (Eds), *The practice of supply chain management*. Boston: Kluwer.

Houlihan, J. B. (1987). International supply chain management. *International Journal of Physical Distribution & Materials Management, 17*(2), 51-66.

Huang, Z. (2004, May). *The value of information sharing in supply chain management with demand uncertainty.* PhD dissertation, University of Maryland, Baltimore County.

Huang, Z., & Gangopadhyay, A. (2004). A simulation study of supply chain management to measure the impact of information sharing. *Information Resource Management Journal, Special Issue in Supply Chain Management, 17*(3), 20-31.

Huang, Z., Gangopadhyay, A., & Gupta, J. N. D. (2004). Sharing information among supply chain partners to counteract the bullwhip effect. *Proceedings of the DSI Annual Meeting 2004,* 2101-2106.

Iyer, A. V., & Bergen, M. E. (1997). Quick response in manufacturer-retailer channels. *Management Science, 43*(4), 559-570.

Kleijnen, J. P. C., & Smits, M. T. (2003). Performance metrics in supply chain management. *Journal of the Operational Research Society, 11*(11), 1-8.

Lee, H., Padmanabhan, V., & Whang, S. (1997a). The bull-whip effect in supply chains. *Sloan Management Review, 38*(3), 93-102.

Lee, H., Padmanabhan, V., & Whang, S. (1997b). Information distortion in a supply chain: The bullwhip effect. *Management Science, 43*(4), 546-558.

Lee, H., So, K. C., Tang, C. S. (2000). The value of information sharing in a two-level supply chain. *Management Science, 46*(5), 626-643.

Lee, H., & Whang, W. (1998). Information sharing in a supply chain. *International Journal of Technology Management, 20*(3/4), 373-387.

Liker, J. K., & Wu, Y. (2000). Japanese automakers. U.S. suppliers and supply-chain superiority. *Sloan Management Review, 42,* 81-93.

Metters, R. (1997). Quantifying the bullwhip effect in supply chains. *Journal of Operations Management, 15,* 89-100.

Raghunathan, S. (1999). Interorganizational collaborative forecasting and replenishment systems and supply chain implications. *Decision Sciences, 30*(4), 1053-1071.

Sahin, F., & Robinson, E. P. (2002). Flow coordination and information sharing in supply chains: Review, implications, and directions for future research. *Decision Sciences, 33*(4), 505-536.

Shim, J. K., & Siegel, J. G. (1999). *Operations management.* Hauppauge, NY: Barron's Educational Series, Inc.

Silver, E. A., Pyke, D. F., & Peterson, R. (1998). *Inventory management and production planning and scheduling.* New York: John Wiley.

Simchi-Levi, D., Kaminsky, P., & Simchi-Levi, E. (2000). *Designing and managing the supply chain: Concepts, strategies, and case studies.* Boston: Irwin/McGraw-Hill.

Song, J.-S., & Yao, D. (2003). *Supply chain structures, coordination, information and optimization.* Boston: Kluwer Academic Publishers.

Sterman, J. D. (1989, March). Modeling managerial behavior: Misperceptions of feedback in a dynamic decision making experiment. *Management Science, 35*(3), 321-339.

Stevenson, W. J. (1982). *Production / operations management.* Homewood, IL: Richard D. Erwin.

Swaminathan, J. M., Smith, S. F., & Sadeh, N. M. (1998). Modeling supply chain dynamics: A multiagent approach. *Decision Sciences, 29*(3), 607-632.

Taylor, D. H. (1999). Measurement and analysis of demand amplification across the supply chain. *The International Journal of Logistics Management, 10*(2), 55-70.

Westland, J. C., & Clark, T. H. K. (1999). Supply chain management and information alliances. In *Global electronic commerce: Theory and case studies* (chapter 4). Cambridge, MA: The MIT Press.

Whang, S. (1993). Analysis of inter-organizational information sharing. *Journal of Organization Computing, 3*(3), 257-277.

Chapter IV

The Impact of IT Personnel Skills on IS Infrastructure and Competitive IS

Terry Anthony Byrd
Auburn University, USA

Bruce R. Lewis
Wake Forest University, USA

Douglas E. Turner
State University of West Georgia, USA

ABSTRACT

The knowledge and skills of information technology (IT) personnel have become of critical importance as the strategic value of IT in modern organizations has become apparent. In addition to technical skills traditionally expected of IT personnel, organizational, functional, and managerial skills have been increasingly cited as mandatory for these employees. This paper used a well-accepted typology of IT personnel knowledge and skills, and investigated its relationship to desirable technological traits in organizations and to technological variables that have been closely aligned to competitive advantage in organizations. This exploratory examination used the statistical technique of canonical correlation analysis to investigate the relationship between IT personnel knowledge and skills and the flexibility of information systems (IS) infrastructure. Additionally, the same technique was used to test the relationship between the knowledge and skills of these personnel and measures of IT contribution to competitive advantage. In both cases, the relationships were significant and positive. Implications of these findings and a call for further research into the strategic value of IT personnel knowledge and skills are discussed.

INTRODUCTION

Assessing the requisite knowledge and skills of information technology (IT) personnel has become of strategic importance as the value of IT has increased in modern organizations. In addition to technical skills traditionally expected of IT personnel, organizational, functional, and managerial skills are increasingly cited as mandatory for these technical employees (Chang & King, 2000; Cougar et al., 1995; Darais et al., 2001; Dhillion & Lee, 2000, Lee et al., 1995; McMurtrey et al., 2002). Indeed, numerous research studies indicate that organizational and behavioral knowledge and skills are crucial to programmers, systems analysts, database administrators, and other IT personnel in the organizations of today (Chang & King, 2000; Cheney et al., 1989; Darais et al., 2001; Dhillion & Lee, 2000; Lee et al., 1995; Leitheiser, 1992; McMurtrey et al., 2002; Nelson, 1991; Rockart et al., 1996; Ross et al., 1996; Tu et al., 2001; Watson et al., 1990). The IT curriculum, recommended through the collaborative efforts of professional organizations like ACM, AIS, DPMA, and ICIS, establishes organizational and managerial knowledge and skills as integral to the overall training of IT personnel (Couger et al., 1995; Darais et al., 2001; Dhillion & Lee, 2000). In the same way, the trade press promotes similar advice through articles alluding to the increased need of IT personnel to gain organizational, interpersonal, and managerial knowledge and skills (Fallon, 1997; *InfoWorld,* 1998; *Insurance & Technology,* 2003).

Recent research and practitioner literature stresses the value of a broad range of knowledge and skills for IT professionals in meeting the strategic requirements of modern organizations. To add value, IT professionals are called upon to blend technical skills with a deep understanding of the business, along with cultivating their interpersonal skills. However, empirical evidence that actually examines the relationship between IT personnel knowledge and skills with organizational success variables has not been reported in the research literature. This study attempts to fill this void by employing a well-accepted typology of IT personnel knowledge and skills to investigate relationships with desirable technological traits in organizations and technological variables that are closely aligned to competitive advantage.

Based on these relationships, this paper explores the strategic value of developing an IT organization with a broad set of skills; that is, an IT organization with technical, business, and interpersonal skills. Specifically, the study uses the multivariate statistical technique, canonical correlation analysis, to explore the relationship between: (1) IT personnel knowledge and skills and the flexibility of the information infrastructure of organizations, and (2) IT personnel knowledge and skills and IT technology variables associated with enabling competitive advantage. This exploratory analysis should serve as a foundation for further research into the strategic value of IT personnel knowledge and skills. Additionally, the study should provide guidance to practitioners regarding recruiting, training, and promoting IT professionals.

BACKGROUND

The literature related to IT personnel skills, technological infrastructure, and competitive advantage provides the conceptual basis for this study.

IT Personnel Knowledge and Skills

Most of the literature examining IT personnel knowledge and skills focuses on the types of knowledge and skills that are required for these workers. The major debate in the literature is whether IT personnel require technical skills or managerial skills or both. The debate started as far back as the 1970s. Typically during the 1970s, researchers found that technical skills were paramount for IT programmers and systems analysts, with managerial and business skills being secondary (Anderson, 1969; Roark, 1976; Strout, 1971; White, 1970). This is understandable because, during this period, IT was not viewed as a strategic or a competitive weapon. The primary task for IT during this period was as a technical support function and little more.

In the 1980s, as IT became viewed more strategically (Porter & Millar, 1985; Sethi & King, 1994), the perception of the skills needed by IT personnel appeared to change. During this time, some researchers found that although technical skills were still very important, a lack of generalist/managerial skills was seen as a hindrance to the progression of programmers and systems analysts to managerial positions (Cheney & Lyons, 1980; Harrison & Springer, 1985; Jenkins, 1986). Some researchers concluded that strong business communications were more important than technical skills for entry-level IT positions (Albin & Otto, 1987; Green, 1989). However, there were still studies during this time that put technical abilities at the top of the skills list (e.g., Watson et al. 1990).

An early study in the 1990s by Leitheiser (1992) provided evidence that interpersonal skills consistently ranked higher for systems analysts than technical skills. On the other hand, Todd, McKeen, and Gallupe (1995) used a content analysis approach on IT job advertisements from 1970 to 1990 and concluded that technical skills for both programmers and systems analysts were becoming more important, not less. They also found a decreased emphasis on business and systems knowledge for these two groups of IT staff members. Todd, McKeen, and Gallupe determined that the importance of business knowledge increased for IT managers. Other studies in the 1990s and the early 2000s have shown that today's IT professional is expected to have a combination of managerial, business, interpersonal, and technical skills (Armstrong & Sambamurthy, 1999; Couger et al., 1995; Darais et al., 2001; Dhillon & Lee, 2000; Rockart et al., 1996; Ross et al., 1996; Lee et al., 1995; MuMurtrey et al., 2002; Reich & Benbasat, 2000; Roepke, Agarwal, & Farrat, 2000; Sharma & Rai, 2003; Wixom & Watson, 2001). Looking at the results of these studies, there seems to be a consensus forming that IT professionals should possess managerial, business, and interpersonal capabilities, as well as technical skills, to be effective in today's marketplace.

This study uses a typology of IT personnel skills from Lee et al. (1995). Their typology consists of: (1) technology management skills, (2) business functional skills, (3) interpersonal skills, and (4) technical skills. Technology skills are concerned with where and how to deploy IT effectively and profitably for meeting strategic business objectives. Business skills involve the level of knowledge of the various functions within the business and the ability to understand the overall business environment. Interpersonal skill includes the ability to communicate effectively with personnel in functional areas and to work in a collaborative environment, along with the ability to lead project teams. The technical skills' measure covers the depth and breadth of the IT technical specialties (operating systems, programming languages, database management systems, networks, telecommunications, etc.) within the organization.

IS Infrastructure

An information systems (IS) infrastructure is the set of shared, tangible, technological resources forming the foundation for business applications. The tangible technological resources composing an IS infrastructure include platform technology (hardware and operating systems), network and telecommunications technologies, data, and core software applications (Byrd & Turner, 2000; Duncan, 1995). McKay and Brockway (1989) described the IS infrastructure as the enabling foundation of shared IT capabilities upon which the entire business depends. Davenport and Linder (1994) referred to IS infrastructure as that part of the organization's information capacity intended to be shared. They concluded that an infrastructure is a firm's institutionalized IT practice-the consistent foundation on which the specific business activities and computer applications are built. Rockart, Earl, and Ross (1996) stated that an IS infrastructure consisting of integrated and interconnected telecommunications, computers, software, and data is a prerequisite for doing business globally, where the sharing of information and knowledge throughout the organization is increasingly vital.

Researchers and practitioners alike have taken note of the potential value of an organization's IS infrastructure. In fact, its growing value is almost undeniable. The expenditures to develop an IS infrastructure account for 58% of an organization's IT budget and are growing at 11% a year (Broadbent & Weill, 1997). Some even see the IS infrastructure as the new competitive weapon and maintain that it is crucial in developing sustained competitive advantage (Boar, 1997; Davenport & Linder, 1994; Keyworth et al., 2001).

The IS infrastructure is a shared business resource and services-delivery base whose business functionality has been defined in terms of three dimensions: connectivity (reach), compatibility (range), and modularity (Duncan 1995; Keen, 1991, 1993). These three dimensions determine the overall flexibility of an IS infrastructure. Connectivity is the ability of a component of the IS infrastructure to attach to any other components inside and outside the organizational environment (Duncan, 1995). According to Keen (1991), connectivity (which he calls "reach") "determines the locations the platform can link, from local workstations and computers within the same department to customers and suppliers domestically, to international locations, or…to anyone, anywhere" (p. 39). Compatibility is the ability of the IS infrastructure to share any type of information across any technology components (Duncan, 1995). At one extreme of range, only simple text messages can be shared- while at the other extreme, any document, process, service, video, image, text, audio, or a combination of these can be used by any other system, regardless of manufacturer, make, or type (Keen, 1991, 1993). Modularity is the ability within the IS infrastructure to add, modify, and remove any software or hardware components with ease and with no major overall effect (Duncan, 1995). A modular infrastructure allows a wide variety of hardware, software, and other technologies to be diffused into its overall structure. It also readily supports the design, development, and implementation of a heterogeneity of business applications.

Collectively, the properties of connectivity, compatibility, and modularity determine the flexibility of the IS infrastructure. That is, an organization with high connectivity, high compatibility, and high modularity is viewed as having a very flexible IS infrastructure. A company with a flexible IS infrastructure has the potential to quickly move its technology to match many different changes in the directions of its strategy and structure. In the competitive environment of today, such agility and versatility is almost a necessity to defend against rival firms (Boar, 1997).

Competitive Advantage

Practitioners of strategic management in organizations are constantly on the lookout for resources that can bring their firms competitive advantage. The concept of competitive advantage was popularized by Porter (1980, 1985), who said that competitive advantage derives from the value a firm is able to create that exceeds the firm's cost of creating the product or service. Day and Wensley (1988) emphasized that a complete definition of competitive advantage must describe not only the state of the advantage, but also how that advantage is gained. They noted that competitive advantage consists of positional and performance superiority (outcomes or competitive advantage) as a result of relative (to the competition) superiority in the skills and resources a business deploys.

Sustained competitive advantage flows from organizational capabilities and resources that are rare, valuable, non-substitutable, and imperfectly imitable (Barney, 1986, 1991). Sustained competitive advantage is obtained by firms implementing strategies that exploit their internal strengths, through responding to environmental opportunities, while neutralizing threats and avoiding internal weaknesses (Barney, 1991; Peteraf 1993; Prahalad & Hamel, 1990).

THE VALUE OF IT PERSONNEL SKILLS

There seems to be a lack of research empirically investigating the value of IT personnel knowledge and skills, and their relationships with other strategic variables. Much of the research tends to assume that the desirability of one type of skill over another by end-users, IT personnel, educators, and managers also gives an indication of the value of those IT skills. For example, Lee, Trauth, and Farwell (1995) used a survey of IT managers, IT consultants, and user managers to ascertain the knowledge and skills needed of IT professionals. This study, like essentially all the others reviewed, assumed that the "expert" opinions of these stakeholders signify the value of the IT knowledge and skills identified in the survey. There was no objective analysis of the value of these skills in terms of other strategic variables.

The closest research that examines relationships between IT personnel knowledge and skills and other organizational variables are a few studies where the IT capabilities were part of a larger model. Boynton, Zmud, and Jacobs (1994) investigated the effect of managerial IT knowledge on IT use. Managerial IT knowledge in this study was defined as the conjunction of IT-related and business-related knowledge possessed by and exchanged among IT managers and business unit or line managers. IT use, as defined in the study, involved "the extent to which IT takes the form of cost reduction, management support, strategic planning, and competitive thrust applications: cost-reduction applications reduce the cost of business activities; management support applications support applications to assist managers' efforts to monitor, control, and design business activities; and competitive thrust applications establish competitive advantage in the marketplace" (Boynton et al., 1994, p. 300). Boynton, Zmud, and Jacobs (1994) found that higher levels of IT managerial knowledge were directly and positively related to the extent of IT use within an organization.

Sabherwal and King (1995) considered the maturity of IT within a firm as a part of a larger overall model. IT maturity was measured by: (1) the extent to which IT impacted the firm, (2) the extent to which computer technology was installed throughout the premises of the firm, (3) IT managers' knowledge of the firm's business plans and top management's knowledge about IT, and (4) the extent IT planning was formalized, took the firm's business plans into consideration, and involved top management. IT maturity and the IS department were included as two of eight variables in the development of an empirical taxonomy of the processes used to make strategic IT decisions. The other variables measured aspects of the external environment and structural characteristics of the organization. Their empirical taxonomy was developed using cluster analysis. From this analysis, five decision processes (planned decision-making process, provincial decision-making process, incremental decision-making process, fluid decision-making process, and political decision-making process) comprised the taxonomy. The success of strategic IT applications for these five decision-making processes was evaluated using a number of success variables such as: (1) contribution to market share, (2) contribution to ROI, (3) degree of innovativeness, (4) proactiveness, and (5) duration of advantage over competitors. Generally, the clusters with higher IT maturity scored better on these success variables.

In another study using the multiple-case methodology, Reich and Benbasat (1990) found that organizations considered first movers in the development of customer-oriented strategic systems were characterized by a very proactive IT function. The IT functions in these organizations were continually seeking innovative ways to utilize IT. The IT people developed high levels of competence in their skills that enabled them to design and deliver customer-oriented strategic systems. The sample for this study consisted of 11 organizations.

The results of these three studies are encouraging indicators of the strategic value of IT personnel knowledge and skills. However, they did not directly address this phenomenon. The current study was designed to open the discussion on what some practitioners and researchers think will be a core competency of the new age organization, the knowledge and skills of the IT department (Rockart et al., 1996; Ross et al., 1996). The current study examined the relationship between IT personnel knowledge and skills, and a flexible IS infrastructure. It also took a first step toward exploring the relationship between the IT personnel knowledge and skills, and measures of competitive advantage resulting from a firm's IT resources.

RESEARCH HYPOTHESES

The research questions in this study involve the relationships of IT personnel knowledge and skills with two constructs that are viewed as advantages in modern organizations.

Flexible IS Infrastructure

The first is the relationship between IT personnel knowledge and skills, and a flexible IS infrastructure. In an article in *Informationweek* (1999), a premier practitioner IT industry magazine, the development of a flexible IS infrastructure was named as the most important issue among 150 IT managers. According to these managers, a flexible IS infrastructure was seen as crucial in making existing, new, and packaged software applications come together successfully.

The importance of having flexible IS infrastructures has not escaped the notice of IT researchers. Huber (1984) argued that flexible IS infrastructures are the catalyst for the development of post-industrial organizations. Huber (1984) noted that new, more flexible technology would lead to a new type of organization with advanced communication structures, improved decision making, and decision process management. Later, Huber (1990) hypothesized that more advanced and flexible technologies could lead to attractive practices such as larger and greater variety of people participating in making organizational decisions, more uniformed communication across organizations, reductions in the number of organizational levels authorizing proposed actions, and better maintenance and access to organizational memory.

Tapscott and Caston (1993) also argued that a technology paradigm shift has enabled organizations to begin reinventing themselves around the characteristics of the post-industrial firm that featured a flexible IS infrastructure as a primary component. They stated that IT compatibility helps to break down organizational walls, empower employees, and make data, information, and knowledge in the organization readily available. Next, Tapscott and Caston affirmed that IT connectivity enables seamless and transparent organizations, organizations based on commitment instead of control, and time and space independent organizations. IT modularity allows the seemingly contradictory achievement of integration, yet independence of organizational components, businesses, and modules (Tapscott & Caston, 1993).

Weill (1992) stated that two firms investing the same amount in IT and with the same management directions would most likely have different organizational results from the IT investment. He further noted that one key factor in converting IT into productive outputs was IT knowledge and skills. McKenney, Copeland, and Mason (1995) discovered that IT success depends on the presence of a champion and a skilled technical team. From case studies they did over the years, McKenney, Copeland, and Mason found that companies depending on vendors offering the latest technological solutions alone are almost always disappointed with the results. They observed that only when an effective champion and a skilled and motivated team were present was IT implementation likely to be successful. Hwang, Windsor, and Pryor (2000) found a positive correlation between IS operations and systems success.

Additionally, researchers have found that for IT staffs to make effective use of robust technologies to build flexible IS infrastructures, a great amount of experimentation is often needed (Dumering et al., 1993; Earl, 1996). This is necessary due to the very strength of this technology — its flexible, adaptive nature. Since flexible technology can be molded in so many different ways, the IT organization needs to be able to do some experimentation to find the best fit with other organizational norms. This is one reason why uniquely advantageous IS infrastructures often emerge in these types of environments (Duncan, 1995). However, the IT personnel must have the knowledge and skills necessary to do such experimentation and build the flexible IS infrastructures that are so important to business managers. A logical conclusion from these studies is that IT personnel must possess a sufficient breadth and depth of knowledge and skills to develop flexible IS infrastructures. This leads to the first hypothesis for this study:

H1: A high level in the breadth and depth of IT personnel knowledge and skills is positively related to the presence of highly flexible IS infrastructures.

IT and Competitive Advantage

The concept of using IT as a source of competitive advantage has enjoyed extensive attention in the research literature (Benjamin et al., 1984; Clemons, 1986; 1991; Feeny, 1988; King et al., 1989; Neo, 1988; Parsons, 1983; Porter & Millar, 1985). Companies such as Wal-Mart (intra- and inter-organizational system), American Airlines (SABRE), and Baxter International (EDI System) have been cited as corporations that have gained competitive advantage from IT. In fact, a special name is given to IT applications that are utilized to provide competitive advantage to their developing companies. These applications are called strategic information systems (SISs) (Reich & Benbasat, 1990; Sabherwal & King, 1995; Sabherwal & Tsoumpas, 1993; Wiseman, 1988). SISs change the goals, operations, products, or environmental relationships of organizations to help them gain an advantage, at least temporarily, over other companies in their industries.

Despite all the attention SISs have received over the past decade or so, some researchers have cast doubt on their ability to sustain competitive advantage without other organizational resources being present (Clemons & Row, 1991; Kettinger et al., 1994; Mata et al., 1995; Neumann, 1994). In particular, Mata, Fuerst, and Barney (1995) noted the importance of technical and managerial IT skills in maintaining a sustained competitive advantage from IT. They argued that these IT skills, especially the management skills, are developed over a long period of time by trial and error learning. They wrote that "… the development and use of many of these IT managerial skills depends on close interpersonal relationships between IT managers and those working in the IT function, between IT managers and those working in other business functions, and between IT managers and customers" (p. 499).

Mata, Fuerst, and Barney (1995) cited two examples where SISs would either not have been developed at all or would not have been able to sustain their advantages for long if not for the knowledge and skills of the IT personnel. One is the SABRE system of American Airlines (Copeland & McKenney, 1988) and the other is the purchase/inventory/distribution system of Wal-Mart. In both cases, the authors argued persuasively that it was the IT personnel knowledge and skills that were really the source of sustained competitive advantage for these two systems and their firms. Kettinger et al. (1994) also found that organizations with technological and organizational "slack resources" were able to sustain competitive advantage from their SISs. This finding implies that organizations may need IT staffs with an "excess" of knowledge and skills to maintain competitive advantage from their IT resources.

The results of these studies indicate that IT personnel knowledge and skills should be considered in the development and maintenance of IT applications intended to yield a competitive advantage for their organizations. In fact, IT personnel knowledge and skills seem to be crucial in the development and maintenance of these IT applications. Therefore, the second hypothesis for this study is:

H2: A high level in the breadth and depth of IT personnel knowledge and skills is positively related to the presence of IT that gives competitive advantage to its organization.

MEASUREMENT OF THE CONSTRUCTS

The measurement items for the IT personnel skills construct were taken from a study by Lee et al. (1995) as noted earlier. The four dimensions-technology management skills, business functional skills, interpersonal skills, and technical skills-had high content validity and conceptual simplicity (Lee et al., 1995). The items measuring the four categories were taken virtually verbatim from Lee et al.'s study for use in the current study. Confirmatory factor analysis was used to check the validity, and Cronbach's alpha was used to determine the reliability of each dimension of the IT personnel skills construct.

The items to measure the flexible IS infrastructure construct were based on the typology from Duncan (1995) and Keen (1991, 1993). As noted earlier, the dimensions for this construct are connectivity, compatibility, and modularity. Three other models (Broadbent et al., 1996; Davenport & Linder, 1994; Gibson, 1993) were found to support these dimensions and were utilized to develop items for the current study. After the data were collected, confirmatory factor analysis was used as a validity check of the items for each dimension, and Cronbach's alpha was used to assess the reliability of each dimension for this construct.

The items to measure "the contribution of IT to competitive advantage" were modified from an instrument by Sethi and King (1994), called CAPITA (Competitive Advantage Provided by an Information System Application). As the terms suggest, CAPITA was developed to measure the contribution of a single information system to the competitive advantage of a firm. The items used from CAPITA were adjusted to measure the contribution of overall IT resources to the competitive advantage of a firm. The dimensions taken from CAPITA are functionality, cost efficiency, and innovativeness. Functionality represents the support of IT in completing work tasks that may focus on internal or external entities (Sethi & King, 1994). Cost efficiency refers to the extent to which IT enables a firm to produce products at a lower price relative to competing products. Innovativeness is the contribution of IT to innovative behavior in an organization. Again, confirmatory factor analysis was used to check validity and Cronbach's alpha for reliability of the dimensions in this measure.

Using these dimensions, a content analysis of the literature was employed, resulting in an initial pool of items that were used in the development of the initial instrument. The items were presented on a five-point Likert scale. The original questionnaire was pre-tested with eight IT managers, four in higher education and four in the private sector. Each manager was briefed on the purpose of the study and asked to critique the items for completeness, understandability, terminology, and ambiguity. A few items were dropped from the questionnaire as a result of this analysis. The resulting questionnaire was then pilot tested by IT personnel in three different types of firms: a textile manufacturer, a mass retailer, and a financial institution. At each location, a senior manager was asked to distribute a copy of the questionnaire to other high-level IT executives. Each participant was asked to complete the questionnaire and to offer any suggestions for improvement. Again, from this process, a few items were dropped from the questionnaire. The resulting questionnaire from these processes had 107 questions on IT personnel skills, IS infrastructure flexibility, and CAPIS. This questionnaire was then mailed to the senior IT executives in the sample organizations.

DATA COLLECTION

A questionnaire containing the items for all constructs was mailed to senior IT managers in Fortune 1,000 companies in the United States. Their titles included Chief Information Officer, Vice President of Information Services, Director of MIS, and Database Administration Directors. One-thousand executives in eight private sector industries were selected for the survey, based on a stratified random sample. A total of 207 questionnaires were returned, for a respectable 20.7% response rate. The demographic characteristics of the respondents and their companies are reported in Tables 1, 2, 3, and 4.

Non-response bias was investigated by comparing the industry distribution of the returned questionnaires to the population industry distribution using a chi-square one-sample test. The computed chi-square statistic, testing the sample industry distribution against the population distribution, was 14.04 with 7 degrees of freedom and therefore was not significant at the .05 level. This suggested that the industry distribution of firms in the sample did not significantly differ from the distribution of firms in the population, thus indicating little or no response bias.

Table 1. Industry distribution of returned questionnaires

Industry Type	Mailed	Returned	Percent
Manufacturing	493	119	24.1%
Insurance	120	10	8.3%
Health Services	91	16	17.6%
Retail	76	18	23.7%
Utilities	67	11	16.4%
Diversified Financial	60	15	25.0%
Banks	57	10	17.5%
Transportation	25	6	24.0%
Others (not specified)	11	2	18.2%

Table 2. Management level of respondents

Classification	Frequency	Percent
Executive	56	27.0%
Upper Middle Management	110	53.1%
Professional	41	19.8%

Table 3. Organization size of companies in sample

Employees in Company	Frequency	Percent
50 - 250	17	8.2%
251 –1000	38	18.4%
1001 – 5000	104	50.2%
Over 5000	48	23.2%

Table 4. Revenue distribution of companies in sample

Revenues of Company (in millions)	Frequency	Percent
$50 - $250	18	8.7%
$251 - $1000	87	42.0%
$1001 - $5000	89	43.0%
Over $5000	13	6.3%

RESULTS

The analysis of the data proceeded through two phases. First, the measurement properties of the constructs were verified. This was followed by tests of the two hypotheses.

Validity and Reliability of the Constructs

The validity of the personnel skills construct was investigated with a confirmatory factor analysis utilizing the EQS (Version 5.7a) program. The EQS for Windows program is an analytical tool that can be used for confirmatory factor analysis. The results of this analysis, shown in Table 5, indicated a reasonable fit for the factors of this construct. Each index approached or was greater than .8 with an adjusted chi-square of less than 5, which is good for an exploratory study. The reliability for each dimension of the IT personnel skills construct was determined using Cronbach's alpha. Reliability is a measure of internal consistency, and Nunnally (1978) recommended an alpha of at least .5 for exploratory studies. The reliabilities for the IT personnel skills dimensions were .74 for technical knowledge and skills, .74 for business knowledge and skills, .84 for interpersonal knowledge and skills, and .51 for technology management (Table 5). Since these reliability statistics were .5 or greater, all of the dimensions were considered reliable for the IT personnel skills construct.

The results of the confirmatory factor analysis on the flexible IS infrastructure construct are reported in Table 6. A good fit of the overall confirmatory model indicated acceptable validity for this construct. Each index approached or was greater than .9 with an adjusted chi-square of less than 2. The reliabilities for all the dimensions, as measured by Cronbach's alpha, were greater than .5, verifying that the dimensions of the flexible IS infrastructure construct were reliable.

The results of the confirmatory factor analysis of the construct representing IT contribution to competitive advantage depicted a good overall fit (Table 7). Each index approached or was greater than .9 with an adjusted chi-square of less than 2. The reliabilities for the dimensions of this construct were all greater than .5.

Examination of the Relationships Between Constructs

Canonical correlation analysis was used to examine the relationships between IT personnel skills and (1) flexible IS infrastructure and (2) the contribution of IT to competitive advantage (Hair et al., 1995) Canonical correlation analysis is a multivariate statistical procedure that facilitates the study of interrelationships among sets of multiple criterion (dependent) variables and multiple predictor (independent) variables. Whereas multiple regression investigates the relationship between a single dependent variable and a set of multiple

Table 5. Structural model fit indicators and items for IT personnel skills

Chi-Square:	868 based on 246 degrees of freedom
Adjusted Chi-Square:	< 4
Probability Value for the Chi-Square Statistic:	0.000
Bentler-Bonett Normed Fit Index:	0.790
Bentler-Bonett Nonnormed Fit Index:	0.843
Comparative Fit Index:	0.800

Technical Knowledge and Skills	**Cronbach's alpha =.74**
Our IT personnel are skilled in multiple programming languages	
Our IT personnel are skilled in multiple types of data bases.	
Our IT personnel are skilled in multiple structured programming, CASE methods.	
Our IT personnel are skilled in multiple microcomputer operating systems.	
Our IT personnel are skilled in expert systems or artificial intelligence.	
Our IT personnel are skilled in decision support systems.	
Our IT personnel are competent in managing the development life cycle of projects.	
Our IT personnel are skilled in distributed processing or distributed computing.	
Our IT personnel are skilled in network management and maintenance.	
Our IT personnel are skilled in developing web based applications.	
Our IT personnel are skilled in hardware diagnosis and maintenance.	
Our IT personnel are skilled in data warehousing, mining, or marts.	
Our IT personnel are skilled in multiple mainframe computer operating systems.	
Business Knowledge and Skills	**Cronbach's alpha = .74**
Our IT personnel understand the business environments they support.	
Our IT personnel are encouraged to learn about business functions.	
Our IT personnel are able to interpret business problems and develop appropriate technical solutions.	
Our IT personnel Our IT personnel are knowledgeable about business functions.	
Interpersonal Knowledge and Skills	**Cronbach's alpha = .84**
Our IT personnel are self-directed and proactive.	
Our IT personnel are very capable in teaching others.	
Our IT personnel have the ability to plan, organize, and lead projects.	
Our IT personnel have the ability to plan and execute work in a collective environment.	
Our IT personnel have the ability to accomplish multiple assignments.	
Our IT personnel work well in cross-functional teams addressing business problems.	
Our IT personnel have the ability to work cooperatively in a project team environment.	
Our IT personnel have the ability to work closely with clients and customers.	
Our IT personnel have the ability to write clear, concise and effective memos, reports.	
Our IT personnel have the ability to develop and deliver persuasive presentations.	
Technology Management Knowledge and Skills	**Cronbach's alpha = .51**
Our IT personnel are encouraged to learn new technologies.	
Our IT personnel closely follow the trends in current technologies.	

Table 6. Structural model fit indicators and items for flexible IS infrastructure

Chi-Square:	56.139 based on 36 degrees of freedom
Adjusted Chi-Square:	< 2
Probability Value for the Chi-Square Statistic:	0.01738
Bentler-Bonett Normed Fit Index:	0.851
Bentler-Bonett Nonnormed Fit Index:	0.904
Comparative Fit Index:	0.937

Connectivity	Cronbach's alpha = .64
Our organization utilizes open systems network mechanisms to boost connectivity.	
There are very few identifiable communication bottlenecks within our organization.	
Our organization utilizes a virtual network or VLAN to connect end users.	
Our organization utilizes online analytical processing (OLAP).	
Compatibility	**Cronbach's alpha = .60**
Software applications can be easily transported and used across multiple platforms.	
Our organization offers a wide variety of types of information to end-users (e.g., multimedia).	
Our user interfaces provide transparent access to all platforms and applications.	
Modularity	**Cronbach's alpha = .65**
Reusable software modules are widely used in new systems development.	
IT personnel utilize object-oriented technologies to minimize the development time for new applications.	
All remote, branch, and mobile offices are connected to the central office.	
Mobile users have ready access to the same data used at desktops.	

Table 7. Structural model fit indicators and items for IT contribution to competitive advantage

Chi-Square:	50.33 based on 28 begrees of freedom
Adjusted Chi-Square:	< 2
Probability Value for the Chi-Square Statistic:	0.0059
Bentler-Bonett Normed Fit Index:	0.827
Bentler-Bonett Nonnormed Fit Index:	0.854
Comparative Fit Index:	0.909

Functionality	Cronbach's alpha = .63
In our organization, IT assists the activity of upgrading a resource (e.g., adding an additional features to products).	
In our organization, IT applications assist in the order or request process for a resource.	
IT assists in our organization's ability to evaluate and select the most appropriate supplier.	
In our organization, IT reduces the cost of transferring material inputs into customer deliverable output (e.g., manufacturing technologies).	
Cost Efficiency	**Cronbach's alpha = .60**
In our organization, IT applications assists in reducing the cost of recruiting, hiring, and training organizational personnel.	
In our organization, IT reduces the cost of general management activities (e.g., planning, accounting, finance).	
In our organization, IT reduces the cost of coordinating activities (e.g., purchasing, marketing, sales).	
Innovativeness	**Cronbach's alpha = .56**
Our organization often uses IT as a component for an information based innovation.	
Our organization utilizes IT to widen the array of products without increasing costs.	

independent variables, canonical correlation simultaneously assesses the association between multiple dependent variables and multiple independent variables.
The goal of canonical correlation is to quantify the strength of the relationship
between two sets of variables, one a set of independent variables and the other
one a set of dependent variables. It has the ability to determine independent
dimensions for each set that produces the maximum correlation between
dimensions. Thus, canonical correlation identifies the optimum structure of
dimensionality of each variable set that maximizes the relationship between
independent and dependent variable sets. In situations with multiple dependent
and independent variables, canonical correlation is the most appropriate and
powerful multivariate technique (Hair et al., 1995).

In interpreting canonical correlation, three criteria should be used: (1) level
of statistical significance of the function, (2) magnitude of the canonical
correlation, and (3) redundancy measure for the percentage of variance accounted for from the two data sets. The level of significance of a canonical
correlation generally considered to be the minimum acceptable is the .05 level,
which (along with the .01 level) has become the generally acceptable level for
considering a correlation coefficient statistically significant. The rule of thumb
for the magnitude of canonical correlation is similar to the rule for factor loadings
in factor analysis, which is about .4 in many references (e.g., Hair et al., 1995).
The redundancy measure is similar to the R^2 statistic in regression and is
interpreted similarly.

In the first canonical correlation analysis, the dimensions of IT personnel
skills were used as the set of independent variables (technology management,
business knowledge and skills, interpersonal and management knowledge and
skills, and technical knowledge and skills) with the dimensions of a flexible IS
infrastructure as the set of dependent variables (connectivity, compatibility, and
modularity). The statistical problem here involves identifying any latent relationships between a respondent's perceptions about IT personnel skills and IS
infrastructure. The analysis of the data showed a definite relationship between

*Table 8. Measures of overall model fit for canonical correlation analysis
for IS infrastructure*

Likelihood Ratio	Approx. F	Num DF	Den DF	Pr > F
.5458	11.3469	12	529.44	0.0001
.8833	4.2879	6	402	0.0003
.9755	2.5377	2	202	0.0816
Statistic	**F**	**Num DF**	**Den DF**	**Pr. > F**
Wilks' Lamda	11.3469	12	529	0.0001
Pillai's Trace	10.1272	12	606	0.0001
Hotelling	12.3823	12	596	0.0001
Roy's GR	31.2320	4	202	0.0001

these two sets of dimensions. Based on the results of the canonical correlation, Hypothesis 1 was supported.

To have confidence in the results of a canonical correlation analysis, the results must be probed in a systematic fashion. The first step is to determine the overall fit of the canonical function. Table 8 shows the overall fit indices for this analysis. Two canonical functions were statistically significant with p-values of less than .01 on their F tests. Other test statistics (Wilks' Lambda, Pillai's Trace, Hotelling-Lawley Trace, and Roy's Greatest Root) also indicated that the canonical functions, taken collectively, were statistically significantly at the .01 level or less.

The next step in investigating canonical correlation results is to examine the redundancy analysis. Table 9 shows that the redundancy index for the predictor variate was .1835 for the first canonical function, while the index for the criterion variate was .1229. These numbers indicate the amount of variance of one explained by the other. Since the redundancy number is analogous to the multiple regression's R^2 statistic, we explain the results here from that viewpoint. Explaining slightly less than 20% of the variance in an organization-level study can be fairly significant considering all the other factors that can contribute to variables at this level. Because of the statistical significance of the overall canonical function and reasonable redundancy coefficients, the first function was accepted.

With the canonical relationship deemed statistically significant and the magnitude of the canonical root and the redundancy index acceptable, the analysis now turned to the substantive interpretations of the results. The three methods for interpretation are: (1) canonical weights (standardized coefficients), (2) canonical loading (structure correlations), and canonical cross-loadings. Table 9 reports all three of these indices.

The first method features the canonical weights. The magnitude of the weights represents their relative contribution to the variate. Based on these weights, the order of contribution of independent variables to the IT personnel variate was "technical skills," "interpersonal and management skills," "technology management skills," and "business skills." The sign for the interpersonal and management skills dimension was negative. The order in magnitude of the dependent variables of the flexible IS variate was "connectivity," "compatibility," and "modularity."

The canonical loadings for the independent variate, IT personnel skills, ranged from .4455 (business knowledge/skills) to .9769 (technical knowledge/skills), showing fairly high shared variance in the sample. The loadings of the dependent variate of IS infrastructure were excellent, also ranging from .5521 (modularity) to .7815 (connectivity). With the loadings of the two variates showing fairly strong consistency, the conclusion was that the variates were good representations of IT personnel skills and flexible IS infrastructure, respectively.

Table 9. Calculation of the redundancy indices for the first canonical function for IS infrastructure

Variables	Canonical Weights			Canonic Loadings	Canonical Cross-Loadings
	1st Split Sample (n=103)	2nd Split Sample (n=104)	Total Sample (n=207)		
Predictor Set – IT Personnel					
1. Technical Knowledge/Skills	1.0391	1.0373	.9951	.9769	.6039
2. Business Knowledge/Skills	. 0356	.0454	.0443	.4455	.2754
3. Interpersonal Knowledge/Skills	-.2344	-.2234	-.2565	.4579	.2830
4. Technology Mgt Knowledge/Skills	.2028	.2026	.2437	.5155	.3187
	Redundancy coefficient = .1835				
Criterion Set – Flexible IS Infrastructure					
1. Connectivity	.5640	.5504	.5124	.7815	.4841
2. Compatibility	.4992	.4775	.5035	.7247	.4480
3. Modularity	.4398	.4468	.4250	.5521	.3413
	Redundancy coefficient = .1229				
Canonical Correlation	.5963	.5968	.6182		
Canonical Root (Eigenvalue)	.5519	.5533	.6185		

Table 10. Measures of overall model fit for canonical correlation analysis for IT contribution to competitive advantage

Likelihood Ratio	Approx. F	Num DF	Den DF	Pr > F
.3847	19.1846	12	529.44	0.0001
.8485	5.7351	6	402	0.0001
.9507	5.2348	2	202	0.0061
Statistic	**F**	**Num DF**	**Den DF**	**Pr. > F**
Wilks' Lamda	19.1846	12	529	0.0001
Pillai's Trace	15.4663	12	606	0.0001
Hotelling	22.8106	12	596	0.0001
Roy's GR	60.8797	4	202	0.0001

The order of importance among the dimensions is similar to the canonical weights. There were also no negative loadings, thus facilitating the interpretation of the results.

The canonical cross-loadings for IT personnel skills ranged from .2754 (business knowledge/skills) to .6039 (technical knowledge/skills). The cross-loadings for IS infrastructure ranged from .3413 (modularity) to .4831 (connectivity). Both of these ranges are acceptable for interpretation in studies at the organizational level where any variable is likely to explain only a small amount of variance in some other variable. All cross-loadings were positive, thus giving one more indication of a valid relationship between the two variates.

The last check is a sensitive analysis of the canonical correlation results. One method is to split the sample into two equal sets and then run a canonical correlation on each set. The coefficients should roughly be the same if the overall canonical correlations are stable. As can be seen in Table 9, the canonical coefficients in this data were fairly stable and consistent. This reinforced the procedure of using the canonical loadings and cross-loadings for interpretation purposes.

The canonical relationship between the IT personnel skills and IT contribution to competitive advantage was analyzed in the same way as the first relationship. From the analysis, Hypothesis 2 was also supported. In fact, the relationship between the variables that made up these two variates was even stronger. Three canonical functions were significant at the .01 level (or better) with all additional statistical indicators significant at the .01 level or better. Table 10 shows these results. The canonical redundancy analysis was outstanding, with the redundancy index at .3617 for the amount of variance of the competitive advantage measure that was explained by IT personnel skills. The criterion's redundancy index was .2344. Table 11 reports these results.

The order of importance for the predictor variate, IT personnel skills, was the same as in the previous analysis. The cross-loadings for the predictor variate were consistent at ranges from .4095 (interpersonal knowledge/skills) to .7034 (technical skills). From the canonical coefficients, the order of importance for the criterion variate, IT contribution to competitive advantage, was "customer service," "innovativeness," and "cost efficiency." The canonical loadings for the predictor variate ranged from .5712 (technology management) to .9514 (technical skills). The canonical loadings for the criterion variate ranged from .2052 (cost efficiency) to .8645 (innovativeness). The cross-loadings for the criterion ranged from .1517 (cost efficiency) to .6391 (innovativeness). The sensitivity analysis also showed that the canonical correlation analysis for the data was stable. Table 11 reports these results.

Table 11. Calculation of the redundancy indices for the first canonical function for IT contribution to competitive advantage

Variables	Sample	Canonical Weights 1st Split Sample (n=103)	2nd Split Sample (n=104)	Total (n=207)	Canonical Loadings	Canonical Cross-Loadings
Predictor Set – IT Personnel						
1. Technical Knowledge/Skills		.8785	.8809	.8743	.9514	.7034
2. Business Knowledge/Skills		.2757	.2579	.3471	.6381	.4713
3. Interpersonal Knowledge/Skills		-.1053	-.0909	-.2734	.5539	.4095
4. Technology Mgt Knowledge/Skills		.0914	.0880	.1718	.5712	.4225
		Redundancy coefficient = .3617				
Criterion Set – IT Contribution						
1. Functionality		.5453	.5458	.5282	.7732	.5717
2. Cost Efficiency		.0151	.0198	.0561	.2052	.1517
3. Innovativeness		.6963	.6954	.6710	.8645	.6391
		Redundancy coefficient = .2344				
Canonical Correlation		.6811	.6831	.7393		
Canonical Root (Eigenvalue)		.8654	.8752	1.205		

DISCUSSION

The results of this study provide clear evidence that a high level of IT personnel knowledge and skills is positively related to both flexible IS infrastructure and to the contribution of IT to competitive advantage. As noted previously, organizational resources and capabilities that are rare, valuable, non-substitutable, and imperfectly imitable form the basis for a firm's sustained competitive advantage (Barney, 1986, 1991). The stream of research, designated as the "resource-based view," has produced substantial theoretical and empirical efforts (e.g., Amit & Schoemaker, 1993; Barney, 1991; Lado et al., 1992). The resource-based view suggests that human resources can contribute to sustained competitive advantage through facilitating the development of competencies that are firm specific, produce complex social relationships, are embedded in a firm's history and culture, and generate tacit organizational knowledge (Barney, 1991; Wright & McMahan, 1992).

The positive relationship between IT personnel knowledge and skills and the two sets of measures that have been linked to competitive advantage may give a glimpse into the possibility of these human resources being a source of sustained competitive advantage for a firm. First, the magnitude of the level of knowledge and skills of the IT personnel may determine, or perhaps enhance, the flexibility of the IS infrastructure. The use of flexible technology in developing an infrastructure does not necessarily result in the construction of a *flexible* IS infrastructure that creates positive results.

For example, General Motors spent over $650 million upgrading to more flexible technology for its infrastructure in one of its plants with absolutely no improvements in productivity or quality (Osterman, 1991). Suarez, Cusumano, and Fine (1995) reported that plants producing circuit boards and using flexible manufacturing systems (FMS) had better performance when their human operating systems were changed to match the flexible technology. In fact without such a change, they found that plants with more programmable automation actually end up with less flexibility. In comparing U.S. and Japanese companies that utilize flexible technology, Jaikumar (1986) found that the Japanese companies often performed better because the U.S. companies generally did not change their human IT organization to match their changes in technology. The difference in each one of these cases seems to be a lack of a change in the human organization. These cases might indicate that to produce a flexible IS infrastructure requires flexible technologies and IT personnel with a strong set of skills. The findings in this study would support this notion, as a high level of IT personnel knowledge and skills is positively related to the presence of a highly flexible IS infrastructure.

Second, a solid foundation of IT personnel knowledge and skills may be a prerequisite to developing IT applications that can lead to competitive advantage. The findings in this study offer some credence to the contention of Mata, Fuest, and Barney (1995) that the SISs of American Airlines, the SABRE system, and of Wal-Mart, the purchase/inventory/distribution system, would not have been possible without a strong IT organization. In fact, Wal-Mart sued Amazon.com Inc. and Drugstore.com Inc. for raiding its IT personnel department (Cole-Gomolski, 1998), alleging that Amazon and Drugstore violated the Arkansas Trade Secret Act in hiring away about a dozen Wal-Mart employees and consultants who had intimate knowledge of the retailer's proprietary purchase/inventory/distribution system. The suit asked for an injunction forbidding them from using any Wal-Mart systems knowledge.

Despite these encouraging signs that IT personnel knowledge and skills may have links to competitive advantage, further research must be done. The relationship between IT personnel knowledge and skills, flexible IS infrastructure, and IT support for competitive advantage should be investigated closer.

All three of these constructs might be examined for a relationship with other competencies that have been shown to give a sustained competitive advantage, such as mass customization (ability to customize products individually for a large number of customers) (Boynton et al., 1993; Pine, 1993), speed to market (Stalk, 1988), and organizational learning (Huber, 1991). Very little, if any, empirical evidence was found in the research literature concerning how IT personnel knowledge and skills, flexible IS infrastructure, and the contribution of IT to competitive advantage relate to other such competencies that have been linked to competitive advantage in organizations.

A somewhat surprising finding in this study is the importance of technical skills in the relationship between IT personnel and flexible IS infrastructure, and the relationship between IT personnel and the contribution of IT to competitive advantage. The literature has recently espoused the necessity of IT personnel having business skills, interpersonal skills, and technology management skills, and these skills do seem to be important (e.g., Lee et al., 1995). However, the coefficients and the cross-loadings from the canonical correlation analysis in this study indicated that technical skills are still the most important in developing a flexible IS infrastructure and developing IT support for competitive advantage. This finding was in line with the results of Todd, McKeen, and Gallupe (1995) that showed technical skills were the most sought after skill set in the IS job advertisements from 1970 to 1990.

One other interesting finding was the negative correlations of the interpersonal skills. One possibility for these negative correlations might be the uncertainty in the minds of the CIOs about how these softer skills actually fit into the success of designing, developing, and implementing IT applications. These CIOs could still believe that the softer skills are valuable. These CIOs simply did not associate these skills with the other IT variables used in this study. There are possibly other IT variables that they might associate these softer skills to, for example, end-user computing applications.

Another possibility is that interpersonal skills might be more difficult to measure than the questions used in this study. Even perceptual measures of interpersonal skills may not be as simple to measure as, for example, the relatively straightforward technical skill set. A range of social, structural, and psychological issues may need to be addressed when considering interpersonal relations.

The results for interpersonal skills might have been different if the respondents had been end users, business managers, or IT consultants. CIOs might be too concentrated on technical skills and forget that in today's world, softer skills might also be important. Further studies might look into the differences in perceptions of these various stakeholders and compare their responses.

The questions surrounding the skill mix are many and varied. What is the optimal skill mix for building a flexible IS infrastructure? Does the skill mix vary across industries? What skill mix is best for building SISs? Is it the same as the skill mix for building a flexible IS infrastructure? How does this skill mix relate to other measures that have been linked to competitive advantage such as mass customization or organizational learning? These and similar questions need to be investigated and answered.

This study also provides further evidence that the dimensions of connectivity (reach), compatibility (range), and modularity are viable measures of a flexible IS infrastructure. Duncan (1995) proposed a typology based on these dimensions, and other studies have reinforced this typology (Broadbent & Weill, 1997; Gibson, 1993).   However, the current study was the first to use statistical techniques, like confirmatory factor analysis and canonical correlation, to substantiate this typology with empirical findings. Again, other researchers should confirm and refine this typology and the set of items used to measure the dimensions in future studies.

CONCLUSION

This exploratory study provides evidence of the strategic value of IT personnel knowledge and skills. These knowledge and skills are positively related to both a flexible IS infrastructure and the contribution of IT to competitive advantage. The findings here are encouraging for those practitioners and researchers that have taken a resource-based view of the IT organization. This view sees the resource of the IT organization as a facilitator of sustained competitive advantage in today's organization. The results of this study clearly support this view and demand further research to substantiate or to refute this proposition.

REFERENCES

Albin, M., & Otto, R.W. (1987). The CIS curriculum: What employers want from CIS and general business majors. *Journal of Computer Information Systems, 27*(1), 15-19.

Amit, R., & Schoemaker, P.J.H. (1993). Strategic assets and organization rent. *Strategic Management Journal*, 14, 33-46.

Anderson, J. J. (1969). Developing an in-house systems training program. *Data Management, 7*(6), 26-31.

Armstrong, C. P., & Sambamurthy, V. (1999). Information technology assimilation in firms: The influence of senior leadership and IT infrastructures. *Information Systems Research, 10*(4), 304-327.

Barney, J. B. (1986). Organizational culture: Can it be a source of sustained competitive advantage? *Academy of Management Review, 11*, 656-665.

Barney, J. B (1991). Firm resources and sustained competitive advantage. *Journal of Management, 17*, 99-120.

Benjamin, R. I, Rockart, J. F., & Scott Morton, M. S. (1984). Information technology: A strategic opportunity. *Sloan Management Review, 25*(3), 3-10.

Boar, B. (1997). *Strategic thinking for information technology: How to build the IT organization for the information age.* New York: John Wiley & Sons.

Boynton, A. C., Victor, B., & Pine, B. J. (1993). New competitive strategies: Challenges to organizations and information technology. *IBM Systems Journal, 32*(1), 40-64.

Boynton, A. C., Zmud, R. W., & Jacobs, G. C. (1994). The influence of IT management practice on IT use in large organizations. *MIS Quarterly, 18*(3), 299-324.

Broadbent, M., & Weill, P. (1997). Management by maxim: How business and IT managers can create IT infrastructures. *Sloan Management Review, 38*(3), 77-92.

Broadbent, M., Weill, P., O'Brien, T., & Neo, B.S. (1996). Firm context and patterns of IT infrastructure capability. *Proceedings of the Seventeenth International Conference on Information Systems* (pp. 174-194).

Byrd, T. A., & Turner, D. E. (2000). Measuring the flexibility of information technology infrastructure: Exploratory analysis of a construct. *Journal of Management Information Systems, 17*(1), 167-208.

Chang, J. C., & King, W. R. (2000). The development of measures to assess the performance of the information systems function: A multiple constituency approach. *Proceedings of the 21st Annual International Conference on Information Systems* (pp. 640-646). Brisbane, Australia: Association for Information Systems.

Cheney, P. H., Hale, D. P., & Kasper, G. M. (1989). Information systems professionals: Skills for the 1990s. *Proceedings of the 22nd Annual Hawaii International Conference on Systems Science* (pp. 331-336). Honolulu, HA: IEEE Computer Society Press.

Cheney, P. H., & Lyons, N. R. (1980). Information systems skill requirements: A survey. *MIS Quarterly, 4*(1), 35-43.

Clemons, E. K. (1986). Information systems for sustainable competitive advantage. *Information and Management, 11*(3), 131-136.

Clemons, E. K. (1991). Competition and strategic value of information technology. *Journal of Management Information Systems, 7*(2), 5-8.

Clemons, E. K., & Row, M. (1991). Sustaining IT advantage: The role of structural differences. *MIS Quarterly,* 15(3), 275-292.

Cole-Gomoski, B. (1998). Employee raiding cases hard to prosecute. *Computerworld, 32*(43), 6.

Copeland, D. G., & Mckenny, J. L. (1988). Airline reservation systems: Lessons from history. *MIS Quarterly, 12*(3), 353-370.

Couger, J. D., Davis, G. B., Dologite, D. G., Feinstein, D. L., Gorgone, J. T., Jenkins, A. M., et al. (1995). IS95: Guideline for undergraduate IS curriculum. *MIS Quarterly, 19*(3), 341-359.

Darais, K., Rice, S. C., Nelson, K. M., & Buche, M. W. (2001). Identifying the enablers and barriers of information technology personnel transition. *Proceeding of the 22nd Annual International Conference on Information Systems* (pp. 289-298). New Orleans, LA: Association for Information Systems.

Davenport, T. H., & Linder, J. (1994). Information management infrastructure: The new competitive weapon. *Proceedings of the 27th Annual Hawaii International Conference on Systems Sciences* (pp. 885-899).

Day, G. S., & Wensley, R. (1988). Assessing advantage: A framework for diagnosing competitive advantage. *Journal of Marketing, 52*(2), 1-20.

Dhillon, G., & Lee, J. (2000). Value assessment of IS/IT service provision within organizations. *Proceedings of the 21st Annual International Conference on Information Systems* (pp. 647-651). Association for Information Systems, Brisbane, Australia.

Duimering, P. R., Safayeni, F., & Purdy, L. (1993). Integrated manufacturing: Redesign the organization before implementing flexible technology. *Sloan Management Review, 34*(4), 47-56.

Duncan, N. B. (1995). Capturing flexibility of information technology infrastructure: A study of resource characteristics and their measure. *Journal of Management Information Systems, 12*(2), 37-57.

Earl, M. J. (1996). The risks of outsourcing IT. *Sloan Management Review, 37*(3), 26-32.

Feeny, D. (1988). Creating and sustaining competitive advantage with IT. In M. Earl (Ed.), *Information management: The strategic dimension.* Oxford, UK: Oxford University Press.

Fallon, M. (1997). Strategic fun and games. *Informationweek*, 654, 122-123.

Gibson, R. (1993). Global information technology architectures. *Journal of Global Information Management*, 4, 28-38.

Green, G. I. (1989). Perceived importance of systems analysts' job skills, roles, and non-salary incentives. *MIS Quarterly, 13*(2), 115-133.

Hair, J. F., Anderson, R. E., Tatham, R. L., & Black, W. C. (1995). *Multivariate data analysis* (4th ed.). Englewood Cliffs, NJ: Prentice-Hall.

Harrison, W., & Springer, D. (1985). A software systems management MBA option. *Data Base, 16*(2), 19-23.

Huber, G. P. (1984). The nature and design of post-industrial organizations. *Management Science, 30,* 928-951.

Huber, G. P. (1990). A theory of the effects of advanced information technologies on organizational design, intelligence, and decision making. *Academy of Management Review, 15*(1), 47-71.

Huber, G. P. (1991). Organizational learning: The contributing processes and the literatures. *Organization Science, 2*(1), 88-115.

Hwang, M. I., Windsor, J. C., & Pryor, A. (2000). Building a knowledge base for MIS research: A meta-analysis of a systems success model. *Information Resources Management Journal, 13*(2), 26-32.

Informationweek (1999). Behind the numbers: Bond the new and the old, *716*, 108-109.

InfoWorld. (1998). Running a great IS department. *20*(16), S3-S6+.

Insurance & Technology. (2003). New NW Mutual CIO drives IT to be creative. *28*(1), 48.

Jaikumar, R. (1986). Postindustrial manufacturing. *Harvard Business Review*, (November-December), 69-76.

Jenkins, G. H. (1986). Education requirements for the entry level business systems analyst. *Journal of Systems Management, 36*(3), 30-33.

Kayworth, T. R., Chatterjee, D., & Sambamurthy, V. (2001). Theoretical justification for IT infrastrastructure investments. *Information Resources Management Journal, 14*(3), 5-14.

Keen, P. (1991). *Shaping the future: Business design through information technology.* Boston: Harvard Business School Press.

Keen, P. (1993). Information technology and the management difference: a fusion map. *IBM Systems Journal, 32*(1), 17-39.

Kettinger, W. J., Grover, V., Subashish, G., & Segars, A. H. (1994). Strategic information systems revisited: A study in sustainability and performance. *MIS Quarterly, 18*(1), 31-58.

King, W. R., Grover, V., & Hufnagel, E. H. (1989). Using information and information technology for sustainable competitive advantage: Some empirical evidence. *Information and Management, 17,* 87-93.

Lado, A. A., Boyd, N. G., & Wright, P. (1992). A competency-based model of sustainable competitive advantage: Toward a conceptual integration. *Journal of Management, 18,* 77-91.

Lee, D. M. S., Trauth, E. M., & Farwell, D. (1995). Critical skills and knowledge requirements of IS professionals: A joint academic/industry investigation. *MIS Quarterly, 19*(3), 313-340.

Leitheiser, R. L. (1992). MIS skills for the 1990s: A survey of MIS managers' perceptions. *Journal of Management Information Systems, 9*(1), 69-91.

Mata, F. J., Fuerst, W. L., & Barney, J. B. (1995). Information technology and sustained competitive advantage: A resource-based analysis. *MIS Quarterly, 19*(4), 487-505.

McKay, D. T., & Brockway, D. W. (1989). Building IT infrastructure for the 1990s. *Stage by Stage, 9*(3), 1-11.

McKenney, J. L., Copeland, D. C., & Mason, R. O. (1995). *Waves of change: Business evolution through information technology.* Boston: Harvard Business School Press.

McMurtrey, M., Grover, V., Teng, J. T. C., & Lightner, N. J. (2002). Job satisfaction of information technology workers: The impact of career orientation and task automation in a CASE environment. *Journal of Management Information Systems, 19*(2), 273-302.

Nelson, R. R. (1991). Educational needs as perceived by IS and end user personnel: A survey of knowledge and skill requirements. *MIS Quarterly, 15*(4), 503-525.

Neo, B. S. (1988). Factors facilitating the use of information technology for competitive advantage: An exploratory study. *Information and Management, 15*, 191-201.

Neumann, S. (1994). *Strategic information systems: Competition through information technologies.* New York: Macmillan College Publishing Company.

Nunnally, J. (1978). *Psychometric theory.* Englewood Cliffs, NJ: Prentice Hall.

Osterman, P. (1991). The impact of IT on jobs and skills. In M.S. Scott Morton (Ed.), *The corporation of the 1990s: Information technology and organizational transformation* (pp. 220-243). New York: Oxford University Press.

Parsons, G. L. (1983). Information technology: A new competitive weapon. *Sloan Management Review, 25*, 3-14.

Peteraf, M. (1993). The cornerstone of competitive advantage: A resource-based view. *Strategic Management Journal, 14*, 179-191.

Pine, B. J. (1993). *Mass customization: The new frontier in business competition.* Boston: Harvard Business School Press.

Porter, M. E. (1980). *Competitive strategy: Techniques for analyzing industries and competitors.* New York: The Free Press.

Porter, M. E. (1985). *Competitive advantage: Creating and sustaining superior performance.* New York: The Free Press.

Porter, M. E., & Millar, V. E. (1985). How information gives you competitive advantage. *Harvard Business Review*, (July-August), 149-160.

Prahalad, C. K., & Hamel, G. (1990). The core competence of the corporation. *Harvard Business Review*, (May-June), 79-91.

Reich, B. H., & Benbasat, I. (1990). An empirical investigation of factors influencing the success of customer-oriented strategic systems. *Information Systems Research, 1*(3), 325-347.

Reich, B. H., & Benbasat, I. (2000). Factors that influence the social dimension of alignment between business and information technology objectives. *MIS Quarterly, 24*(1), 81-113.

Roark, M. L. (1976). Information systems education: What industry thinks. *Data Management, 14*(6), 24-28.

Rockart, J. F., Earl, M. J., & Ross, J. W. (1996). Eight imperatives for the new IT organization. *Sloan Management Review, 38*(1), 43-56.

Roepke, R., Agarwal, R., & Ferratt, T. W. (2000). Aligning the IT human resource with business vision: The leadership initiative at 3M. *MIS Quarterly, 24*(2), 327-353.

Ross, J. W., Beath, C. M., & Goodhue, D. L. (1996). Developing long-term competitiveness through IT assets. *Sloan Management Review, 38*(1), 31-42.

Sabherwal, R., & King, W.R. (1995). An empirical taxonomy of the decision-making processes concerning strategic applications of information systems. *Journal of Management Information Systems, 11*(4), 177-214.

Sabherwal, R., & Tsoumpas, P. (1993). The development of strategic information systems: Some case studies and research proposals. *European Journal of Information Systems, 2*(4), 240-259.

Sethi, V., & King, W. R. (1994). Information technology application provides competitive advantage. *Management Science, 40*(12), 1601-1627.

Sharma, S., & Rai, A. (2003). An assessment of the relationship between ISD leadership characteristics and IS innovation adoption in organization. *Information & Management, 40,* 391-401.

Stalk, G. (1988). Time-the next source of competitive advantage. *Harvard Business Review, 66*(4), 41-52.

Strout, D. (1971). The activities and education of systems analyst. *Journal of Systems Management, 22*(1), 37-40.

Suarez, F. F., Cusumano, M. A., & Fine, C. H. (1995). An empirical study of flexibility in manufacturing. *Sloan Management Review, 37*(1), 25-32.

Tapscott, D., & Caston, A. (1993). *Paradigm shift: The new promise of information technology.* New York: McGraw-Hill.

Todd, P. A., Mckeen, J. D., & Gallupe, R. B. (1995) The evolution of IS job skills: a content analysis of IS job advertisements from 1970 to 1990. *MIS Quarterly, 19*(1), 1-27.

Tu, Q., Ragunathan, B., & Ragunathan, T. S. (2001). A path analytic study of the antecedents of organizational commitment of IS managers. *Information Resources Management Journal, 14*(3), 27-36.

Watson, H. J., Young, D., Miranda, S., Robichaux, B., & Seeley, R. (1990). Requisite skills for new MIS hires. *Data Base, 21*(1), 20-29.

Weill, P. (1992). The relationship between investment in information technology and firm performance: A study of the valve manufacturing sector. *Information Systems Research, 3*(4), 307-333.

White, T.C. (1970). The 70s: People. *Datamation, 16*(2), 40-46.

Wiseman, C. (1988). *Strategic information systems.* Homewood, IL: Irwin.

Wixom, B. H., & Watson, H. J. (2001). An empirical investigation of the factors affecting data warehousing success. *MIS Quarterly, 25*(1), 17-41.

Wright, P. M., & Mcmahan, G. C. (1992). Theoretical perspectives for strategic human resource management. *Journal of Management, 18,* 295-320.

This chapter was previously published in the *Information Resources Management Journal*, 17(2), 38-62, April-June, Copyright © 2004.

Chapter V

A Socio-Technical Heuristic for Analysis of IT Investments:
Results from Two Case Studies

Grover S. Kearns
University of South Florida St. Petersburg, USA

ABSTRACT

A majority of CEOs have experienced failed information technology (IT) investments. While such investments have the potential for providing competitive advantage, actual returns have varied widely. Numerous methods exist for investment evaluation, but traditional methods do not adequately account for the intangible benefits that characterize strategic investments and lack other features of portfolio selection. This chapter presents a framework based upon the analytic hierarchy process, combined with integer programming, to overcome the deficiencies associated with traditional approaches to economic evaluation of IT investments. Based on socio-technical theory and observations from two case studies in which the framework was applied successfully, a heuristic is developed for the investment process. Findings and implications are discussed.

INTRODUCTION

American Airlines' apocryphal success with the Sabre System heralded the potential of IT as a source of strategic benefits (Hammer, 1991). While the competitive advantages from superior IT investments are widely recognized, actual returns received on IT investments vary widely, and the IT productivity paradox has international recognition (Brynjolfsson & Hitt, 1998; Dewan & Kraemer, 1998; Santos & Sussman, 2000). A majority of CEOs admit to past failed IT investments but express confidence in the ability of IT to provide strategic advantages in the future (COMPASS, 1999). While most companies submit IT-based applications to some form of economic analysis, the numerous objective measures used in practice provide little relationship to the strategic direction of the firm (Liberatore, Monahan, & Stout, 1992). Moreover, despite recognition of the importance of qualitative benefits, economic analysis of IT returns relies primarily on quantitative measures. At least one author concludes that the productivity paradox may result from a bias toward quantitative measures in MIS research (Chan, 2000).

Traditional approaches to capital budgeting have not proven useful in the economic evaluation of IT-based investments. Single criteria techniques, such as discounted cash flow (DCF) and cost/benefit analysis, are biased toward the tangible benefits that can be more easily identified and quantified. Calculations of IRR or net present value may ignore the "soft," qualitative benefits of IT applications or build them into the model so creatively as to devalue the results. Traditional approaches can penalize investments with valuable soft benefits so often present in strategic applications. Hence, proper evaluation of IT-based investments requires a framework that reliably measures all benefits in a consistent manner that is understood and supported by management. Maximizing returns from IT investments also requires a total portfolio planning approach which cannot be accomplished by valuing each investment individually. In reality, some investments are mutually exclusive, other investments have mutual dependencies, and some investments should not be combined due to the total risk.

Combined with integer programming, the Analytic Hierarchy Process (AHP) supports a multi-objective, multi-criteria (MOMC) approach that addresses several issues hindering the success of IT investments. An MOMC approach, for example, can improve the alignment of the information systems plan with organizational goals. AHP has a wide variety of applications in industry and government (Vargas, 1990; Zahedi, 1986). Its use combined with integer programming for ranking IT investments has not been tested in practice.

The purpose of this chapter is to demonstrate the MOMC approach to IT investment analysis using a framework which, heretofore, has not been demonstrated in practice. This chapter first addresses the socio-technical aspects of IT investment evaluation. Next, the applicability of the proposed framework is demonstrated using an illustrative example. Two case studies, in which the framework was successfully applied, are then examined with emphasis on facilitators and inhibitors and generalizable findings. Finally, a discussion is presented with implications of the socio-technical aspects and the overall heuristic.

THE RESOURCE-BASED VIEW AND COMPETITIVE ADVANTAGE

Strategic management literature emphasizes the ability of organizations to gain a competitive advantage from the superior skills and resources the organization possesses relative to its competitors (Porter, 1980; Porter & Millar, 1985). The resource-based view (RBV) stream of research states that the advantage can be sustained only if these capabilities are rare, valuable, non-substitutable, and inimitable (Peteraf, 1993). According to the RBV, complex social relationships can yield a sustained competitive advantage by creating tacit organizational knowledge that is unique, context dependent, and non-transferable (Barney, 1991). Past research suggests that a superior process of IT investment evaluation based in a collaborative, team-based management environment could be expected to provide a competitive advantage. For example, Jones and Price (2004) found organizational knowledge sharing to be a critical element in ERP implementation, and Bharadwaj (2000) found knowledge sharing between IT and business managers led to improved IT strategies.

Lucas, Ginzberg, and Schultz (1990) found that successful implementation of IT projects was a socio-technical process. Meeting organizational strategic requirements requires that IT professionals develop an increased understanding of business needs and cultivate their interpersonal skills (Byrd, Lewis, & Turner, 2004). A key to IBM's past success with technical projects has been the fostering of collaborative teams to support the pooling and exchange of knowledge (McQueeney, 2003). A competitive environment, however, can create tensions that prevent teams from achieving a common purpose. A socio-technical dilemma is that team members often lack sufficient knowledge about IT investments because they are unwilling to share what they know with others. If the corporate culture does not support collaboration then members will hoard knowledge and place individual goals ahead of selecting the best investments (Jones & Price, 2004).

Managers are committed to achieving high returns but often make IT investment decisions without good knowledge of the true costs and benefits. This paradox can be explained by the socio-technical dimensions surrounding the selection process (Sarmad, Irani, & Baldwin, 2003). This chapter argues that the successful selection of IT investments has socio-technical dimensions. A technical framework is necessary for consistency and evaluative purposes, but it is the social aspect that promotes the knowledge sharing that leads to informed decision making.

THE IT INVESTMENT DECISION

IT investments comprise a large portion of the firm's total capital expenditure yet managers frequently commit to projects using informal methods that are based on perceptions about the strategic value of the underlying investment (Remenyi & Sherwood-Smith, 1998). This results from (1) a lack of knowledge and a reluctance to acquire the requisite knowledge and (2) the lack of an adequate framework for evaluating the investments (Irani & Love, 2001). Failure to develop and apply a precise framework, however, can have far-reaching consequences for the company in terms of lower returns and lost opportunities.

In the past, many companies have adopted traditional accounting approaches to evaluation including payback, net present value, and internal rate of return. Because these approaches do not fully reflect strategic benefits, however, management has been confused about what direction to take (Ballantine & Stray, 1999). A framework is needed that adequately measures the real costs and benefits of IT investments and achieves a common purpose. This presupposes a collaborative heuristic and a framework that values all costs and benefits including the intangible and non-financial dimensions of the IT investments, has sufficient visibility to support the human implications, and aligns with the strategies of the firm.

Although it is axiomatic that the framework for evaluation and prioritization of IT investments can heavily influence the actual return realized on the overall investment portfolio, there has been a paucity of research directed toward improving the efficacy of such a framework. Regardless of whether research can establish a direct relationship between IT investment and financial performance, those companies who are able to select the best IT investments will have a greater chance of positively influencing the financial performance of the company (Kayworth, Chatterjee, & Sambamurthy, 2001).

Past evaluation of major IT investments has relied heavily on traditional financial accounting measures. These methods suffer from (1) isolation—they do not consider alternative investments simultaneously, (2) difficulty in valuation of benefits, particularly intangibles, and (3) low explanatory power. Managers may promote their projects by overstating benefits and understating costs. They may also ignore intangible benefits critically denying the chance for many strategic investments to survive the analysis. Each investment stands on its own merits without regard to other investments and disregards mutually exclusive investments and the risk diversity of the overall portfolio.

IT-related investments represent in excess of half the annual capital expenditures for many firms. Despite this resource intensity, an agreed upon approach to measuring IT-investments does not exist (Weill & Olson, 1989) and returns on IT investments have been unsatisfactory (Compass, 1999, 2001). Researchers and practitioners have called for a more comprehensive approach to the selection and prioritization of IT investments (Kauffman & Kriebel, 1988).

Various methodologies for economic evaluation have been reviewed (Sylla & Wen, 2002). In practice, over 50 approaches to evaluation of IT investments have been identified (Irani, 1998) indicating the overwhelming lack of consensus for a preferred approach. An effective process should consistently produce the desired results and, in the case of IT, the desired result is the selection of IT-based investments that produce the highest value for the firm. That value must reflect a combination of both quantitative and qualitative criteria (Chan & Lynn, 1993).

THE ANALYTIC HIERARCHY PROCESS

Examples of real-world AHP applications are numerous and include strategic planning, microcomputer selection, software productivity measures, oil pipeline route selection, budget allocations under constrained resources, flexible manufacturing systems, manpower selection, energy policy planning, healthcare resource planning, model selection, plus numerous applications in accounting, auditing, and marketing (Finnie, Wittig, & Petkov, 1993; Hamalainen & Seppalainen, 1986; Lee, 1993; Ramanathan & Ganesh, 1995; Saaty, 1994). AHP models have been proposed for the evaluation of enterprise information technologies and project management (Kamal, 2001; Sarkis & Sundarraj, 2001).

The capabilities of AHP have been extended through combination with other techniques such as multi-dimensional scaling, and integer and linear programming in the areas of business, government, medicine, social science, and mathematics (Arbel, 1993). Thurston and Tian (1993) combined integer programming with AHP for long-range product planning. Using AHP and integer programming, Sylla and Wen (2002) proposed a conceptual framework using goal targets against which proposed IT investments would be evaluated. There have been no prior illustrations, however, of this use in practice.

The successful prioritization and selection of IT investments is made problematic by the number of issues that must be addressed. The multi-objective, multi-criteria process presented in this chapter is an effective measurement process that:

1. ranks alternative investments according to criteria that support corporate strategies;
2. is amenable to the strict time constraints of the planning process;
3. supports consensus among a diverse group of individuals;
4. can reflect investment precedence or exclusivity constraints;
5. can incorporate both quantitative and qualitative criteria; and
6. can be understood by management.

THE IT INVESTMENT MODEL

Corporate Strategies Used as Project Ranking Criteria

The selection of IT investments can be highly political, requiring a considerable amount of negotiation. Two factors which appear to influence the selection mechanism's credibility and acceptability is the degree of management involvement and alignment with corporate strategy (McKeen & Guimaraes, 1985). IT often does not support management involvement, embracing a technical focus and being "unaware of the human and organizational factors" that account for IT investment failures (McDonagh & Coghlan, 1999, p. 43). Alignment is critical. Strategic linkage and competitive response are highly important evaluative criteria in allocating resources to competing projects (Bacon, 1992). Companies which support alignment between their IT plan and corporate strategies outperform those that do not (Das, Zahra, & Warkentin, 1991). AHP facilitates specification of criteria based upon corporate strategies. In fact, the criteria can be the specific strategies that the investment alternatives support.

Level of Difficulty

The issue of process implementation depends upon the level of difficulty. This includes technical expertise required to perform the prioritization, requisite understanding of the related theory, the effort and time required collecting and entering data, and the time required to perform the analysis and analyze results. Closely associated is the flexibility of the measurement process in reflecting changes, performing sensitivity analysis, producing viable alternative solutions, and providing an explanatory trail. AHP methodology uses a paired-comparisons approach with semantic anchors. These criteria indicators represent typical investment alternatives. Each investment can then be assigned an indicator value for each criterion. The sum of these values becomes the investment's global score that is used for final ranking. The ranking of a large number of investments can thus be accomplished with a limited number of semantic anchors (Wedley, 1990).

Explanatory Power

For IT professionals to create an effective dialogue with senior management, it must be clear how potential projects fit into the overall corporate context. Perhaps the most valuable feature of AHP is its explanatory power. The hierarchy is simple to communicate and the weighting process is highly intuitive. Moreover, it offers a convenient framework for concise representation of the most critical elements that affect the funding decision (Lauro & Vepsalainen, 1986). The relative weight of each decision alternative and criterion can readily be compared to the weights of other elements and discussion centered upon a single element or a level of elements. Managers are able to see into the process as opposed to accepting results from a "black box." This supports participation and future commitment to the investment decisions.

Creating Consensus

Using the method of paired (also known as pairwise) comparisons, AHP is highly effective in distilling information from groups and fostering consensus—an important foundation for acceptance when IT projects are later transferred back to users. In the absence of an absolute scale, all people have the ability to perform relative comparisons between alternatives. As the number of such comparisons increases, however, the consistency tends to decrease simply due to the limits of human cognition. Using this notion, AHP organizes this thought process and creates quantitative rankings using a systematic approach to capture priorities and measures the consistency of the overall process. AHP allows for the simultaneous consideration and evaluation of both quantitative and qualitative criteria, the inclusion of managerial judgments in a direct manner, and managerial focus on those parts of the decision that pose the most uncertainty.

Cost, Precedence, and Exclusivity Constraints

Portfolio selection for stocks using AHP has been described by Saaty (1980). A difficulty arises, in ranking investments with significantly different costs. Resource constraints limit the number of investments that can be selected. Rankings may be deceptive as in the case where a top ranked investment costs as much as two other projects that were precluded due to limited resources, but the sum of the benefits of the two precluded investments exceed the benefits of the more highly ranked investment. Problems can arise. One investment, for example, may preclude selection of another. Selection may be predicated upon another investment's selection.

Structuring the AHP Hierarchy

Because it is a hierarchical process, decisions in AHP are made at various levels descending from the overall goal at the top level, to decision criteria at the second level and proceeding on down to the decision alternatives at the lowest level. A general schematic of such a hierarchy is presented in Figure 1. Note that there are n alternatives and k levels possible. Each criteria may or may not affect each alternative. In practice the total number of levels rarely exceeds nine and is frequently limited to three: *goal*, *criteria*, and *alternatives*.

AN INFORMATION SYSTEMS EXAMPLE

To illustrate the multi-objective, multi-criteria model, five investment proposals that include both financial and non-financial criteria are assumed:

1.   design and install a new *customer relationship management system* ($210,000);
2.   purchase and install software for **material acquisitions system** ($107,000);
3.   purchase and install software to perform **manufacturing control system** ($185,000);
4.   expand and enhance an existing **logistics control system** ($75,000); and
5.   purchase and install software for a **data warehouse** ($160,000).

These investments will be compared on the basis of five criteria representing the following corporate strategies: investment risk, revenue enhancement, operating efficiency, customer satisfaction, and market growth.

The first step in AHP is to define the decision hierarchy. The goal is to rank the decision alternatives (i.e., IT investments) in order of preference as

Figure 1. AHP decision schema

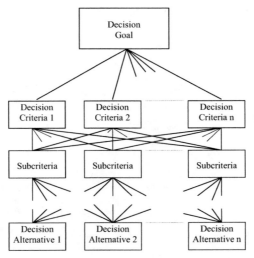

determined by the priority weights of the criteria. The second step is to input the data. This step may take one of several forms depending upon how the decision maker has formulated the problem criterion. *Expert Choice™*, an AHP applications software package, provides simple step-by-step instructions for data entry. After entry, the input data are manipulated using matrix algebra to produce the relative weights or priorities for each level of the hierarchy. *Expert Choiceä* provides a visual result of each step in the ranking process including presentation of both local and global priorities which indicates the relative importance of each alternative at various stages. A "consistency index" for each criterion measures the degree of consistency inherent in the decision maker's ranking of alternatives. The final step is aggregation of all weights to produce a vector of composite relative weights between the criteria and the alternatives (Zahedi, 1986). These weights, which are displayed visually, represent the contribution of the alternative and criterion to the overall goal. Each column of weights sums to the criterion's priority.

For the sample problem, the final solution, shown in Table 1, ranks the market evaluation model first with an overall weight of 0.394. Not presented in this chapter, is the visual presentation of results at each stage of the process, which increases management's understanding of the process and how the final results were achieved. By doing so, it improves the overall explanatory power and credibility of the process.

Optimizing Using Integer Programming

The final rankings do not reflect several criteria that have been purposefully omitted: investment cost, precedence, and exclusivity. An effective approach to solving multi-criteria resource allocation problems is to convert them into integer programming maximization-type problems. The investment alternatives are used as variables and priorities are used as the variable coefficients in the model's objective function (Ramanathan & Ganesh, 1995).

Table 1. Final rankings of IT investments

Proposed Investments	Rank	Overall Rating
Customer Relationship Mgmt System	1	.394
Materials Acquisition System	2	.203
Manufacturing Control System	3	.149
Logistics System	4	.142
Data Warehouse System	5	.112
total all ratings		1.000

Formulating the problem to maximize the AHP priority weights with the resource constraint completes the measurement process by including these remaining evaluative factors. Generally, the mathematical statement for an integer programming problem is:

Maximize $\sum aij\ xi$, subject to a given constraint set

where *aij* are the performance coefficients in the integer programming model that, for our purpose, become *pi* or the priority weights from the AHP rankings (Ramanathan & Ganesh, 1995). For our problem, assume the following costs for each of the five variables in Table 2.

To illustrate cases of exclusivity and dependence, assume that:

a.   a budget constraint of $500,000 exists for all investments;
b.   management has decided that it is not necessary to purchase both the CRM system and the data warehouse system immediately; thus the solution will include either the purchase of one or none of the two models, but not both;
c.   the manufacturing control system cannot be installed without the materials acquisition system; thus the latter may be purchased without the former but not vice-versa.

Using the priority coefficients of our AHP rankings in the objective function and the above three constraints, the model is:

$$
\begin{array}{llllll}
\text{Maximize} & 0.394X1 & +0.203X2 & +0.149X3 & +0.112X4 & +0.142X5 \\
\text{subject to} & 210\ X1 & +\ 107\ X2 & +\ 185\ X3\ + & 75\ X4\ + & 160\ X5\ \leq\ 500 \\
& X1 & & & + & X5\ \leq\ 1 \\
& -\ X2 & +\ X3 & & & <\ 1 \\
& & & & & Xi\ =\ 0,1
\end{array}
$$

Table 2. Costs for IT investment example

IT Investment	variable	cost ($000)
Customer Rel Mgmt System	X_1	210
Materials Acquisition System	X_2	107
Manufacturing Control System	X_3	185
Logistics System	X_4	75
Data Warehouse System	X_5	160
total cost all investments		737

The last constraint ensures that the result variables will be binary (e.g., we either fund an investment or do not fund an investment). The optimal solution is (1,1,0,1,0) with an objective function value equal to 0.709. Higher values for the objective function signify higher overall returns for the IT investments. Alternatives with explicit cost and associated benefit can quickly be derived.

Thus, the MOMC model has the capability to prioritize investments by a set of criteria and to select the optimum set of investments given cost, precedence, and exclusivity constraints.

EVIDENCE FROM TWO CASE STUDIES

Research Methodology

Evidence was elicited from two case studies performed using the IT-investment framework. The case approach was selected because it was believed that contextual conditions could impact the outcomes. The author acted as investigator with the goals of (1) ascertaining the efficacy of the proposed ranking mechanism, and (2) collecting and reporting the attitudes, behaviors, and perceptions of the CEO, CIO, and other managers toward the process. Results of the investigation were reviewed by the CIOs of the two companies with only minor corrections and revisions. The approach elected is in the interpretivist tradition in which the investigator enters the organizational setting without an *a priori* model but with a good understanding of the underlying literature and theory. The purpose is to further understanding of the phenomenon (Cavaye, 1996). Using multiple cases allows the investigator to replicate the results and improves generalizability.

The study will show that management involvement is necessary for the successful ranking and prioritization of IT investments. The study will also show that organizational structure affects the success of the ranking process. Because of the sensitive nature of the information gathered and discussed, both companies requested complete anonymity. For reasons that will become apparent, the companies are referred to herein as Hot and Lukewarm. The backgrounds of the companies are now presented in order to provide the reader with a contextual framework.

Case Study Background of Companies

The multi-criteria IT investment model was tested on two U.S. utility companies, one in the north-central region and the other in the southern region. The two companies, each with assets in excess of $2 billion, shared several operating similarities. They were both generators of electricity, had retail and wholesale markets, sold surplus power, and controlled their own transmission and distribution systems. Both had CIOs committed to IT planning. They also had differences. Hot was a smaller company under greater competitive pressure, had a higher cost of electricity, which caused customer complaints and pressure from regulators, and had wholesale markets that were currently threatened by competition. Hot had a highly participative management structure with younger management who had previous experience in non-regulated industries. From the beginning, Hot was highly committed to planning and the strategic use of IT.

Lukewarm, the larger company, was known as a low-cost provider of electricity, had relatively secure markets but recognized the ensuing issues of deregulation that would shortly put wholesale markets under competitive pressures. Management was hierarchical with traces of political rivalry. The engineering and financial areas were highly insular. Marketing had played a lesser role in the past but was slowly developing. With the exception of the CEO and CIO, top management was without experience outside their field and had limited experience outside of the utility industry. Both the CEO and CIO had previous experience in non-regulated industries and were committed to planning and increasing returns on IT investments.

IT Planning and Evaluation

Hot initially developed the set of decision criteria and subcriteria that was subsequently adapted by Lukewarm. Hot's management took an interest in IT planning, was interested in using IT strategically, and wanted a system that would satisfy all areas of management as to the final selection of projects. Several members of management had recently participated in an MBA program where they took classes together. It was during this period that they recognized the need for improved selection techniques for IT investments. In developing business strategies, Hot often asked IT management for assistance in identifying technologies that might allow revision of business processes to improve efficiencies and customer service.

Lukewarm's management delegated all IT planning to the CIO, and complained about the time and cost of implementing systems. An IT steering committee composed of several senior managers reviewed major projects prior to funding but relied heavily on the opinion of the CIO. IT investments were identified after completion of the business plan. The IT plan contained a "wish list of applications that continually changes with the political climate."

Hot had used a combination of project evaluation tools including ROI, payback, and a corporate model. Management admitted that they did not understand how the project rankings were arrived at and considered the methods "useful but probably unreliable." Lukewarm used a cost/benefit and payback approach wherein total costs were simply divided by total benefits. Selection of projects were often based on how well managers could creatively assign dollars to benefits to get projects approved. A payback period of over three years required a meeting with the board for final approval. Lukewarm also used a financial planning model to evaluate certain investments but the model did not lend itself to a broad range of IT-based investments.

Hot had approached the author about implementing a comprehensive methodology that would support management participation, have high explanatory power, and would be easy to manipulate. The proposed investment model used decision criteria initially developed by Hot and later refined during the study.

Lukewarm's management was convinced by Hot's management of the superiority of the multi-criteria IT investment model and asked to be included in the study. They agreed to use the same decision criteria if they could stipulate their own sub-criteria and assign their own weights. Both Hot and Lukewarm asked that the decision criteria, weights for the decision criteria, the sub-criteria, or their weights not be disclosed.

The Hot Results

The decision criteria and sub-criteria were originally developed by a team of IT managers and later modified by other members of management. (The decision criteria included two business and two technical dimensions supported by greater detail in the sub-criteria.) The concept was introduced in a two day joint application development (JAD) session held off-premises. An outside consultant, familiar with AHP, facilitated the process. Many members of management, particularly the engineers and financiers, had attended a four-hour workshop and developed familiarity with AHP prior to the JAD session. Most managers were enthusiastic and several later stated that they could apply the AHP methodology to other decision-making problems.

The first day was spent discussing the importance of IT investments and attendant problems, introducing the AHP multi-criteria investment concept, and reviewing the major IT investments currently under investigation. Much of the day was spent in answering questions about the IT investments, and it was decided to separate the investments by category and apply the new process to only ten investments that were strategic in nature, cost in excess of $300,000 each, and had higher than average risk. The second day was spent in explaining the weights for the decision criteria. Discussion centered on understanding how the weights were derived which was clarified by a handout (from IT management). Using a modified Delphi technique in which groups made adjustments to the weights, compared results, and made further modifications, a final set of weights was derived. Finally, preliminary paired-comparisons were made. During the process, IT management played an impartial advisory role. Strong leadership was provided by managers that were either project leaders or closely associated with the projects.

Over a period of two weeks, the paired-comparisons and other parameters—primarily costs, benefits, and risks—were refined. It was agreed upfront
that the initial analysis would not be binding and that, with support, changes could
be made to the parameters after reviewing the initial model results.

Working with managers from finance, engineering, and marketing, it took
approximately a week for IT to complete the initial analysis that used both the
AHP and integer programming models. Results were provided to the management steering committee for review. Within two weeks, comments were
gathered, adjustments made, and a final analysis completed.

Post interviews with managers revealed a general consensus on perceived
benefits derived from the process. All agreed that the process was effective, fair,
understandable, and could easily be replicated and modified. Several managers
had collected articles on AHP and had become intricately acquainted with the
theory. This was expected to positively influence future use of the model.

One disadvantage was the total time involved in making the paired-
comparisons and estimating other parameters. However, most agreed that their
understanding of the process would help to make future estimates easier and cut
the time requirement. The results were used to select five IT investments with
a capital requirement in excess of $18.5 million.

The Lukewarm Results

The Lukewarm study was expected to benefit from the results of the Hot
experience. The JAD approach, which had proved highly successful in the
previous case, was only partly implemented and with less success. One day, on-
site, was devoted to the session. The session was facilitated by the CIO.
Managers were previously briefed about the purpose of the meeting in a memo
from the CEO. The meeting agenda paralleled the first day of the Hot session.
However, other members of management generated little discussion, and the
focus kept returning to who would create and who would approve the paired-
comparisons. Managers initially objected to the process stating that they could
not compare their projects to projects for which they were not responsible. They
also questioned the amount of time the process would require, where administrative responsibility would reside, and approval of parameters.

During the session, several managers were called away to phone calls,
which disrupted the continuity of the meeting. At the end of the meeting, it was
agreed that all managers would attempt to provide an initial set of paired-
comparisons for those projects of which they had some responsibility. A cross-
functional management team would review and refine the comparisons after
individual discussions with managers. It was further decided that the management team would have final authority and that appeals would be made to the team
first and the CEO second. After three weeks, the management team circulated
the final results. Several appeals were made to the team that resulted in minor

adjustments, but no appeals were made to the CEO. The CEO later admitted that complaints had been voiced, but no manager had requested altering the final decision of the management team. The CEO supported the process but did not participate directly other than to proclaim, "Information technology is our strategic weapon of the future."

After two more weeks, the management team circulated the initial results of the analysis. On the advice of the team, a categorization of IT projects was made, and only those investments identified as strategic, high cost, and high risk were evaluated. In total, 26 investments were analyzed (many were overlapping and mutually exclusive). A total of eight investments were selected with a capital cost in excess of $34 million.

Post interviews with management revealed several positive findings. IT management was pleased that the process shielded them from complaints that they controlled the process and allocated much of the decision making to a cross-functional team. In fact, IT had made it clear at the beginning that they did not want responsibility for the final selection of investments. Several managers made positive comments. One stated, "I think we trust the process more than in the past." Another said, "IT is going to be more important to us in the future and the process will be appreciated then."

There were also problems. It was clear that most of the work was pushed upon the management team. Many managers continually requested revisions of the management team. The revisions were quickly made using a spreadsheet program, and the team viewed this as minor harassment that would disappear in the future. A few managers continued to complain about the outcomes and questioned the parameters. However, the management team quickly countered by issuing a memo reminding management that they could make any adjustments to the parameters that could be supported. They also performed a modified ROI analysis on the selected projects to mollify any outstanding complaints. The analysis showed returns in excess of the company's cost of capital for all of the selected investments.

At the request of the management team, the CEO issued a memorandum of support, reminding management that they owned the process and that results reflected their own decisions. Although the process did not initially run smoothly, and all managers did not participate fully, IT managers felt that the direction was an improvement over past experiences and would improve over time. They also decided that a two-day, off-site JAD session should be held annually to start the process of reviewing IT investments.

RESULTS OF INVESTMENT DECISIONS

A review of progress was undertaken eleven months after the initial analysis. Information was collected from the CIO, the CEO, and other members of management at both companies with the objective of determining (1) how the project selection method had been accepted by all managers, (2) the status of the IT investments selected, (3) the status of the selection process, and (4) if there were findings that could be generalized.

Acceptance

Managers of both companies voiced enthusiasm for the methodology with some qualifications. Several managers from both companies commented that the documentation for the methodology improved their understanding and made it easier for new managers to grasp. An engineering manager at Hot voiced this opinion:

We have strict limits on spending. As a result, there has been some frustration about which projects would be funded. I'm sure every manager has had projects delayed or cancelled. This can be a morale breaker. Particularly if you think some other guy is getting funded for the wrong reasons. This approach gives me more faith in the system. Now, if I can defend my assumptions I have a fair chance of getting the project funded. I think the playing field is more level now than in the past.

The CIO at Hot believed that the new methodology had "proven itself" as evidenced by the status of the IT investments selected. An executive from marketing provided one of the reasons for the acceptance of the approach:

I've been here for nearly ten years and came from a company where there were plenty of turf issues. Managers here have so much turf that they don't feel threatened. The CIO has more business sense than most techies and our managers seem to be technically aware. They were early adopters of PDAs, in fact there were arguments over which one was best. And you see everyone carrying around notebooks. They opt for those so they can take them on trips and home for the weekend. They trade them in every two years and go cutting edge. I don't know if we became this way consciously or not but it seems that all of the hires over the past five years or so have certainly had technical orientations.

Hot is rather unique in the limited political rivalries and the congruence of a CIO with business acumen and managers with technical acumen. The internal environment and organizational structure are more conducive to acceptance of new processes, even those with technical orientations. This supports prior research that found hierarchical decentralization and lateral communications important to strategic investment decision processes (Papadakis, 1995).

The CIO at Lukewarm stated that acceptance of the methodology had removed a major burden from IT planning and that he no longer incurred the wrath of managers who had not been funded. Lukewarm's CEO commented:

This hasn't solved all our problems but I believe we're on the right track. This used to be a political football and you knew that there would be resistance against these systems every time we put them in place. I could count on one hand the successful ones [i.e., IT investments] over the past ten years. Now, I believe every project underway is going to be successful. I call that progress.

This supports recent findings of Sylla and Wen (2002) that one of the benefits of the MOMC approach is the balancing of conflicting objectives of different users and stakeholders. It also supports the previous findings of Koksalan and Sagala (1995) that MOMC methods, while still evolving, have generally been successful where preferences and personal judgments can be reflected in the selection process.

Status of the IT Investments Selected

Despite the economic downturn, only two of the projects initially funded had been delayed. Utility earnings are partly protected, and both companies had continued to earn a satisfactory accounting return. Thus, there was no immediate pressure to cut capital investments. Of the two companies, however, Hot had lower earnings-per-share, and management had delayed one project to conserve cash and deploy resources to the other projects in order to realize the benefits more quickly. Also, Hot wanted to see a return on two projects, targeted at cutting costs, before further IT investments were undertaken. These two projects were scheduled to be completed within the next three months. The projects were on schedule, and both were running slightly under budget. In fact, all of the projects at Hot were on or under schedule and, in total, under budget.

Lukewarm's CEO stated that the process may have benefited from reduced political tensions but admitted that remnants of politics remained. Although implementation of the selection methodology was highly centralized, project management and implementation for many systems took place at the operating companies. Most of the projects were on schedule and within budget. One project, involving an intranet that would ultimately be installed at all of the operating companies, had experienced a major delay. The CIO who had technical responsibility for the project stated that the delayed project had suffered from a political tug-of-war about infrastructure issues. Rather than risk later opposition, the CIO had asked the steering committee to shelve the project until the underlying problems were resolved.

Overall, stated the CIO of Lukewarm, the IT projects were an outstanding success. Management seemed to be "more in synch" and ready to work with project members. One particular area of improvement, identified by the CIO, was in the creation of service-level agreements (SLA). The SLA process, which had evolved over a period of several years, had been the basis for several battles that had created ill-will among some of the company managers toward IT and the CIO. In discussing several SLAs for the new systems, the CIO found managers more literate and understanding about the functionality and limitations of the new system. The CIO stated:

They [the managers] appear to have more rational expectations about what to expect from these systems. In the past, I don't really think they had been involved or knew what to expect. Now they're forced to be involved. As a result, they have an appreciation for the complexities and the tradeoffs.

Status of Selection Process

Managers of Hot were continuing to modify and enhance the model. They wanted to be able to analyze individual investments on a stand-alone basis. The approach would include four "surrogate" investments, with favorable parameters, to establish a threshold against which proposed investments could be ranked. A continuing effort was the use of a program to quickly generate an initial set of paired-comparisons based upon a set of questions that the manager could answer by checking boxes on a one-page questionnaire. This initial solution made deriving a final solution much faster.

In addition, Hot had decided to categorize IT investments into five categories: strategic over $1 million; strategic under $1 million; non-strategic over $1 million; non-strategic under $1 million; and mandatory. The mandatory class usually consisted of smaller projects that were demanded by regulatory bodies. By their nature, these were not subjected to the analysis. Four separate sets of criteria and sub-criteria were developed for the four remaining classes. The two strategic categories had greater emphasis on valuation of intangible benefits. The two over $1 million categories had greater emphasis on risk analysis, an area that had been largely ignored in past analysis.

The major area of difficulty was in establishing the paired-comparisons. With the revised criteria, the CIO of Hot realized that managers would lose some of the familiarity gained earlier. Also, it was not feasible to create the paired-comparisons by comparing to all other projects within the category, and it was impractical to prescribe a single point in time for all managers to make the comparisons. To address these two problems, the CIO asked a team comprised of financial, marketing, and engineering managers to develop a surrogate investment for each category. The surrogate would possess benefits that would make it an attractive investment for each of the criteria. Criteria for proposed investments could then be pairwise compared with the surrogate. These comparisons would then serve to develop the paired comparison matrices between the actual IT investments. Thus, given actual investments A and B and surrogate C, knowledge of matrices AC and BC provides the matrix for AB. This eliminated the temporal dependency of the paired-comparisons and allowed for a less complex analysis. Furthermore, changes in the criteria for a single investment could quickly and easily be reflected.

Hot had also begun assimilating IT investment proposals for the next round of evaluations. Although a temporary freeze had been placed on funding of new projects, it was expected to be lifted with the successful completion of two IT projects within three months. More standardization was being added to the investment proposals. IT investments were submitted using a set of forms for outlining costs, benefits, human resource requirements, risks, and alternatives. The steering committee would screen out any unsound proposals or ones that lacked proper support. For those investments that were tentatively accepted, paired-comparisons would be made. The objective of the screening process is to force sponsors to provide sufficient and precise information to support the investment proposal.

In about the same period of time, Lukewarm had accomplished much less. Although the CEO supported the process, he did not participate with the exception of attending quarterly steering committee meetings. At these meetings, he did champion several IT issues and tended to support the CIO, as when he decided to shelve one project until questions had been resolved between managers whose disputes were hindering the project. The CEO had to contend with several presidents of the operating companies and had less time to focus on IT. Some of the company presidents had greater knowledge of IT and were supportive of the new process. The CEO had increased the operating budget of the centralized IT function, but the time-period was not sufficient to show productivity gains by the hiring and training of new IT personnel. For that reason, little had been accomplished toward improving the process, primarily documentation of the process and the training of new managers. The CIO, however, was confident that the next round of investment proposals would be handled more expeditiously than in the past. Queried as to why this would be, he replied:

There is a new attitude. I see more managers today. They ask more questions. I have managers asking me if their new systems can be used with our intranet or if the intranet server will be centralized, things like that. They seem to be taking charge. Some are actually enjoying it. Even the ones who still grumble are not grumbling about how we approach ranking the investments, its just about things like doing these [paired] comparisons.

Generalizable Findings

Research has shown CEO involvement to be a predictor of SISP success (Basu et al., 2002). In this study, the new process was supported by the CEOs of both firms. In one firm, the CEO had greater knowledge of information systems opportunities and how they had been used strategically by other firms. This CEO worked closely with the CIO, and other managers followed the lead. In the other firm, the CEO had superficial knowledge but was convinced that IT investments were an important strategic tool, particularly for the future. This conviction appeared to be based on discussions with CEOs at other companies and articles from journals, periodicals, and industry reports. The CEO's support was encouraging for the CIO, particularly in creating an improved environment in which to implement systems. However, while voicing strong support, this CEO did not work closely with the CIO, concluding that the IT area was capable of managing the process.

In a relatively short period of time, Hot had capitalized on the new process by extending the model and adding administrative controls to further insure success and reduce the time requirement on management. In an almost equal time-period, Lukewarm had accomplished much less.

Managers in both firms had an improved attitude. This was perhaps even more noticeable at Lukewarm where the relationship had evolved from one that could be described as approaching adversarial. The new process improved the quality of information available to measure investment proposals, increased the involvement of managers who were most knowledgeable about the proposed investments, and added credibility to the final results.

A key problem is that an investment's potential return may be reduced because of implementation problems. For example, a software application project may fail because of the inability to control quality during system development. Westland (2002) showed that unresolved software errors became exponentially more costly with each new phase in the project. While it is uncertain what influence the selection and prioritization mechanism has upon this problem, it is possible that, when the process lacks credibility, management will be less motivated to actively participate and help insure the success of the projects. The current cases could not adequately address this possibility but, in both cases, an increase in management participation was matched with overall success of implementation.

Summary

These findings represent only two case studies from an industry that is not truly competitive. One company, however, was under-increasing competitive pressures, and both companies were interested in strategic level systems that would improve the quality of their customer relationships and prepare them for deregulation. Despite these limitations, researchers and practitioners alike would probably agree that the findings are noteworthy and could be generalized to other firms.

First, the role of the CEO in supporting the new prioritization and measurement process is essential. Other managers are unlikely to participate, and may resist, unless they are convinced that the CEO is fully behind the process. Second, the AHP and integer programming framework has several attributes, as discussed earlier that make it superior to other measurement tools. The framework will only succeed if managers are made aware of these attributes and understand how they work. Third, the framework is not the process, it is a part of the process. Other parts include management participation, especially in creating paired-comparisons and reviewing results. Without participation by managers who are closest to the initiatives for the IT investments, there will not be an improvement in the information made available to the process. A collaborative environment is essential for overall success of the framework. Less hierarchical organizational structures may be more conducive to its acceptance and participation.

Fourth, the process is flexible and scalable. It can be extended to use various sets of criteria and sub-criteria, and it can accommodate a reasonably large number of proposals. Fifth, the process can be improved administratively. The use of a steering committee for screening can filter out unsound proposals. The use of questionnaires can assist in deriving paired-comparisons. Sixth, if successful, the process may provide serendipitous results. The attitude of managers toward IT planning and service-level agreements may improve. These findings are summarized in Table 3.

Table 3. Generalizable findings

1	CEO support of the IT investment process is essential
2	Managers outside of IT must be trained and made aware of how the process works.
3	Managers must realize that participation is as important to success as the measurement tool. Managers closest to the IT initiatives must participate fully in the process.
4	The multi-objective, multi-criteria approach is flexible, scalable, and able to accommodate various sets of criteria.
5	Administrative steps can improve upon the IT investment ranking process and reduce the burden for managers.
6	Implemented correctly, the process may provide serendipitous results. For example, the process may lower political tensions.

DISCUSSION

Two case studies supported the overall effectiveness of AHP and linear programming in prioritizing and selecting IT investments. Occasionally, investments must be approved on a stand-alone basis and cannot await the next IT planning cycle. These investments can be evaluated independently using an economic evaluation model or be ranked against a surrogate project that possesses criteria that would make it a desirable investment.

Neither company used the model for risk balancing, preferring to add this functionality at a future date. Although both had mutually exclusive investments, neither identified dependencies. Both companies made adjustments to sub-criteria weights during the studies. After the analysis, both companies experimented with small revisions to weights to test their sensitivity. At the conclusion, the majority of managers appeared to be reasonably satisfied with the prioritization and selection of investments.

Benefits and Limitations

Both companies identified the following benefits:

- the ability of the model to handle a large number of criteria,
- the ability to represent both tangible and intangible items,
- the ability to model exclusivity and dependency of investments,
- the ability to quickly reflect revisions,
- the explanatory power of the model, and
- the support for group decision-making.

The following limitations were also noted:

- the lack of a financial measure of profitability,
- the overall time requirements for management, and
- the problem of valuing intangibles, although ameliorated, remained.

Both companies agreed that the model, while not simple, was understood and accepted by the majority of managers. Hot identified the process as one of continuous improvement. Over time, as managers gained experience with using the model and results of investments were evaluated, adjustments could be made to reflect the new knowledge. Both companies stated that the model would be useful for supporting expenditures with regulators who frequently asked for such justification.

Facilitators and Inhibitors

Process facilitators and inhibitors are summarized in Table 4 for Hot (Case 1) and Lukewarm (Case 2). While both companies used JAD, only Hot used an outside facilitator and maintained focus by allowing sufficient time and holding it at a remote location. Both companies benefited from the support of the CEO although the CEO of Hot led a more participative role. Without the support of Lukewarm's CEO, however, success would have been in doubt. Both companies stated that the process was time-consuming, requiring the attention of many managers over a span of several weeks. Hot had the advantage of a smaller and younger management team that had previous experience in a non-regulated, more competitive environment. Lukewarm's management, less familiar with SISP and IT opportunities, were less enthusiastic but participated at a higher rate than in the past. Both companies benefited from a cross-functional management team that provided the requisite expertise for making the paired-comparisons. The team may also have been responsible for reducing political tensions. Displeasure with past approaches and CEO support had motivated both sets of management to adopt a new approach, but Hot appeared to better understand the use of strategic criteria for aligning the investments with business strategies. Use of JAD, the process facilitator, the CIOs, and the written documentation fostered an overall understanding of the new approach. This understanding made the step-by-step procedures and numerous adjustments that were necessary in the initial implementation much easier to communicate.

Several process inhibitors were apparent. Lukewarm's top-down style of management was more rigid and created a less harmonious environment that had undermined the JAD session and resulted in more adjustments to the paired-comparisons. The absence of competition may also have made Lukewarm's

Table 4. Process facilitators and inhibitors

Facilitators	Case 1	Case 2
Focused JAD Session	X	
CEO Support	X	X
Other Management Support & Participation	X	?
Cross-Functional Management Team	X	X
Strategic Use of IT	X	?
Desire for Improved Rankings of Investments	X	X
Process Understanding	X	X
Inhibitors		
Bureaucratic Management Structure		X
Low Level of Competition		X
Time Requirement of Management	X	X

management more complacent and less concerned about the strategic value of IT investments and the alignment with business objectives. Both companies identified the time requirement for producing acceptable paired-comparisons as being the most imposing challenge. Hot was taking steps to address this problem.

An important process facilitator was the adeptness of certain managers in both firms with the more quantitative aspects. Managers had little difficulty in using the application software, and some had read several articles on AHP to gather a more complete understanding of the process and develop methods for handling the paired-comparisons. Both companies had existing computer models for integer programming, with which several of the engineering managers were highly skilled. The cross-functional team approach was very useful in adding a broader perspective to the identification of items to be included in the constraints for the integer programming model.

IT Investment Heuristic

Results of the two case studies supported the value of the framework for ranking and evaluation of the IT investments. Based on the cultures of the two firms, it was also apparent that this was a socio-technical process that rewarded knowledge sharing and a collaborative corporate culture. The IT investment heuristic in Figure 2 combines socio-technical theory with the observations from the case studies. While the heuristic appears to be oversimplified, achieving a collaborative environment is a daunting task.

Figure 2. IT Investments evaluation heuristic

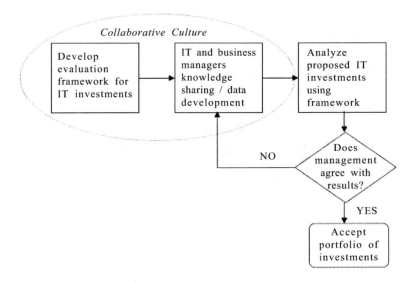

STUDY CONTRIBUTIONS

According to the RBV, competitive advantage cannot be derived from IT alone because it is readily transferable. However, socially complex processes such as the framework and heuristic provided in this study are not easily imitated. Thus, they can yield a competitive advantage if they lead to the superior selection of IT investments. While the framework supports the process heuristic, it cannot provide a competitive advantage without the collaborative environment that supports knowledge sharing. That environment is fostered by senior management. In a recent survey for London Business School, over 50% of the CEOs claimed a major involvement with IT strategic planning. When appraising IT investments, they cited strategic criteria equally important to traditional financial measures (Compass, 2001). These CEOs would be more likely to establish a corporate culture of knowledge sharing and seek to derive the greatest value from IT investments.

The study has presented a heuristic and framework for IT investment evaluation that addresses the problems identified with current methodologies. The framework was tested in two case studies and found to be a useful tool. Case results supported the importance of knowledge sharing for IT and business managers and interpersonal relationships for IT managers in particular.

This study makes several useful contributions. First, it provides a tested framework for prioritization and selection of IT investments that can improve future returns. Researchers can further test and modify the framework in a manner that parallels this study and note its effectiveness. Practitioners can implement the process as part of their own IT planning practices.

Second, the study identifies benefits and limitations inherent within the process.

Third, the study identifies facilitators and inhibitors and generalizable findings to the approach. Researchers would be interested in how these are related to the contextual environments of other industries. Practitioners can benefit by knowing the social implications of the heuristic which requires a collaborative environment.

Suggestions for Future Research

The measurement process for prioritization of information technology investments proposed herein has profound implications for practice. To test applicability of the methodology, further case studies are suggested wherein a portfolio of IT investments from different industries is evaluated. It would be interesting to see what criteria and sub-criteria are developed by different companies. Further case studies would provide more insights into the completeness of the approach, the time requirements, and the level of consensus and management support achieved.

Researchers could also examine the impact of contextual variables on the success of the IT investment model. How do organization structure, size, and IT maturity impact the usefulness of the process? Are bureaucratic organizations more or less likely to benefit from the process? The balancing of investment risk was not tested in this study. The process lends itself to identifying the types of risk associated with each investment. Using an integer program constraint, each risk type could be limited so as to achieve a balance of risk for the overall investment portfolio. At minimum, each risk type could be measured for the portfolio.

Finally, a paramount question for researchers is the extent to which corporate culture impacts investment evaluation. Can firms that pit managers against one another really exploit IT? Change management could be prescribed for implementation of large and pervasive IT systems. The process leads to greater employee participation and final acceptance. It is possible that elements of this process could also lead to higher levels of knowledge sharing (Sherer, Kohli, & Baron, 2003).

CONCLUSION

The framework utilizing AHP and integer programming merits attention as an investment selection and ranking tool. The positive features, evidenced by two successful applications, include (1) incorporation of tangible and intangible benefits, (2) ease of use and flexibility, (3) intuitive appeal, (4) a forum for participatory decision making which can help depoliticize the process, (5) a measure of consistency, and (6) availability of user friendly software.

Basing selection criteria on business strategies ensures the alignment of IT investments with these strategies and increases the communicative power of the process to top management. While assessing the value of intangible benefits cannot be done with absolute accuracy, the process offers multiple advantages and overcomes the deficiencies of a strictly objective approach. The success of two companies using the framework provides evidentiary support for its future usefulness and provides insights into how corporate culture impacts the IT investment selection process.

REFERENCES

Arbel, A. (1993). A weighted-gradient approach to multiobjective linear programming problems using the analytic hierarchy process. *Mathematical and Computer Modeling, 17*(4-5), 27-40.

Bacon, J. C. (1992). The use of decision criteria in selecting information systems/technology investments. *MIS Quarterly, 16*(3), 335-354.

Ballantine, J., & Stray, S. (1999). Information systems and other capital investments: Evaluation practice compared. *Logistics and Information Management, 12*(1-2), 78-93.

Barney, J. B. (1991). Firm resources and sustained competitive advantage. *Journal of Management, 17*(1), 99-120.

Basu, V., Hartono, E., Lederer, A., & Sethi, V. (2002). The impact of organizational commitment, senior management involvement, and team involvement on strategic information systems planning. *Information & Management, 39*, 513-524.

Bharadwaj, A. S. (2000). A resource-based perspective on information technology capability and firm performance: An empirical investigation. *MIS Quarterly, 24*(1), 169-196.

Brynjolfsson, E., & Hitt, L. (1998). Beyond the productivity paradox. *Communications of the ACM, 41*(8), 49-55.

Byrd, A., Lewis, B. R., & Turner, D. E. (2004). The impact of IT personnel skills on IS infrastructure and competitive IS. *Information Resources Management Journal, 17*(2), 38-62.

Cavaye, A. (1996). Case study research: A multi-faceted research approach for IS. *Information Systems Journal, 6*, 227-242.

Chan, Y. E. (2000). IT value: The great divide between qualitative and quantitative and individual and organizational measures. *Journal of Management Information Systems, 16*(4), 225-261.

Chan, Y. L., & Lynn, B. E. (1993). Hierarchical analysis as a means of evaluating tangibles and intangibles of capital investments. *MidAtlantic Journal of Business, 29*(1), 59-74.

Compass Group. (1999). *The COMPASS international IT strategy census 1999.* Rotterdam: Compass Publishing.

Compass Group. (2001). *The COMPASS world IT strategy census 2001.* Rotterdam: Compass Publishing.

Das, S. R., Zahra, S., & Warkentin, M. (1991). Integrating the content and process of strategic MIS planning with competitive strategy. *Decision Sciences, 22*, 953-984.

Dewan, S., & Kraemer, K. L. (1998). International dimensions of the productivity paradox. *Communications of the ACM, 41*(8), 56-62.

Expert Choiceä Version 8, *Expert Choice, Inc.: The Decision Support Software Company*, Pittsburgh, PA.

Finnie, G. R., Wittig, G. E., & Petkov, D. I. (1993). Prioritizing software development productivity factors using the analytic hierarchy process. *Journal of Systems & Software, 22*(2), 129-139.

Hamalainen, R. P., & Seppalainen, T. O. (1986). The analytic network process in energy policy planning. *Socio-Economic Planning Sciences, 20*(6), 399-405.

Hammer, M. (1991, September-October). Reengineering work: Don't automate, obliterate. *Harvard Business Review*, 104-112.

Irani, Z. (1998). *Investment justification of information systems: A focus on the evaluation of MRPII.* PhD dissertation, Brunel University, Department of Engineering Systems, UK.

Irani, Z., & Love, P. E. D. (2001). The propagation of technology management taxonomies for evaluating investments in manufacturing resource planning. *Journal of Management Information Systems, 17*(3), 161-177.

Jones, M. C., & Price, R. L. (2004). Organizational knowledge sharing in ERP implementation: Lessons from industry. *Journal of Organizational and End User Computing, 16*(1), 21-40.

Kamal, M. (2001). Application of the AHP in project management. *International Journal of Project Management, 19*, 19-27.

Kauffman, R. J., & Kriebel, C. H. (1998). Modeling and measuring the business value of information technologies. In P. Strassmann, P. Berger, B. Swanson, C. Kriebel, & R. Kauffman (Eds.), *Measuring the business value of IT* (pp. 93-119). Washington, DC: ICIT Press.

Kayworth, T., Chatterjee, D., & Sambamurthy, V. (2001). Theoretical justification for IT infrastructure investments. *Information Resources Management Journal, 14*(3), 5-14.

Koksalan, M. M., & Sagala, P. N. (1995). Interactive approaches for discrete alternative multiple criteria decision making with monotone utility functions. *Management Science, 41*(7), 1158-1176.

Lauro, G. L., & Vepsalainen, A. (1986). Assessing technology portfolios for contract competition: An analytic hierarchy process approach. *Socio-Economic Planning Sciences, 20*(6), 407-415.

Lee, H. (1993). A structured methodology for software development effort prediction using the analytic hierarchy process. *Journal of Systems & Software, 21*(2), 179-186.

Liberatore, M. J., Monahan, T. F., & Stout, D. E. (1992). A framework for integrating capital budgeting analysis with strategy. *Engineering Economist, 38*(1), 31-43.

Lucas, H., Ginzberg, M., & Schultz, R. (1990). *Information systems implementation.* Norwood, NJ: Ablex Publishing Corp.

McDonagh, J., & Coghlan, D. (1999). Can O.D. solve the IT dilemma? O.D. in IT-related change. *Organization Development Journal, 17*(4), 41-47.

McKeen, J. D., & Guimaraes, T. (1985). Selecting MIS projects by steering committee. *Communications of the ACM, 28*(12), 1344-1352.

McQueeney, D. F. (2003) IBM's evolving research strategy. *Research Technology Management, 46*(4), 20-25.

Papadakis, V. M. (1995). The contribution of formal planning systems to strategic investment decisions. *British Journal of Management, 16*, 15-28.

Peteraf, M. A. (1993). The cornerstones of competitive advantage: a resource-based view. *Strategic Management Journal, 14*(3), 179-191.

Porter, M. E. (1980). *Competitive strategy: Techniques for analyzing industries and competitors.* New York: The Free Press.

Porter, M. E., & Millar, V. E. (1985). How information gives you competitive advantage. *Harvard Business Review,* 149-160.

Ramanathan, R., & Ganesh, L. S. (1995). Using AHP for resource allocation problems. *European Journal of Operational Research, 80,* 410-417.

Remenyi, D., & Sherwood-Smith, M. (1998). *Another look at evaluation to achieve maximum value from information systems.* Working Paper HWP 9609. Henley Management College, UK.

Saaty, T. L. (1980). Portfolio selection through hierarchies. *Journal of Portfolio Management, 6*(3), 16-21.

Saaty, T. L. (1994). Highlights and critical points in the theory and application of the analytic hierarchy process. *European Journal of Operational Research, 74,* 426-447.

Santos, B. D., & Sussman, L. (2000). Improving the return on IT investment: The productivity paradox. *International Journal of Information Management, 20,* 429-440.

Sarkis, J., & Sundarraj, R. P. (2001). A decision model for strategic evaluation of enterprise information technologies. *Information Systems Management, 18*(3), 62-72.

Sarmad, A., Irani, Z., & Baldwin, L. (2003) Benchmarking information technology investment and benefits extraction. *Benchmarking, 10*(4), 414-423.

Sherer, S., Kohli, R., & Baron, A. (2003) Complementary investment in change management and IT investment payoff. *Information Systems Frontiers, 5*(3), 321-333.

Sylla, C., & Wen, H. J. (2002). A conceptual framework for evaluation of information technology investments. *International Journal of Technology Management, 24*(2/3), 236-261.

Thurston, D. L., & Tian, Y. Q. (1993). Integration of the analytic hierarchy process and integer programming with linear constraints for long range product planning. *Mathematical and Computer Modeling, 17*(4/5), 41-54.

Vargas, L. G. (1990). An overview of the analytic hierarchy process and its applications. *European Journal of Operational Research, 48,* 2-8.

Wedley, W. C. (1990). Combining qualitative and quantitative factor—An analytic hierarchy approach. *Socio-Economic Planning Sciences, 24*(1), 57-64.

Weill, P., & Olson, M. H. (1989). Managing investment in information technology: Mini-case examples and implications. *MIS Quarterly, 13*(1), 3-16.

Westland, J. C. (2002). The cost of errors in software development: Evidence from industry. *The Journal of Systems and Software, 62*, 1-9.

Zahedi, F. (1986). The analytic hierarchy process—A survey of the method and its applications. *Interfaces, 16*(4), 96-108.

Chapter VI

Global Service Provider Strategies and Networking Alternatives

Ron Landi
WorldCom, USA

Mahesh S. Raisinghani
University of Dallas, USA

ABSTRACT

Deregulation and liberalization of the telecommunications markets has led to tough international competition. This chapter presents well-established approaches used by large telecom service providers in assessing the technical and market forces impacting their network planning and strategies. This paper, in the form of a tutorial, takes the reader through the assessment and analysis processes dealing with the requirements, design and implementation issues facing global communications carriers today. Four generic telecommunication network models (varying based on the degree of capital intensity required) are presented to demonstrate that a strategy of employing these generic models to appropriate settings generates cost savings and network efficiencies. A specific case analysis conducted by the global communications carrier for a regional network in Italy is included that discusses strategic planning for the provision of new data and Internet services, and assesses alternative network designs and technologies to provide optimized solutions and service delivery.

INTRODUCTION

The deregulation in the European telecommunication markets since the beginning of the 1990s and the liberalization of telecommunication deals across state boundaries has brought about significant changes in the communications industry. On February 15, 1997, in a resolution of the 68 countries of the World Trade Organisation (WTO), it was decided to prepare the ground for global competition gradually. (Kollmann, 2000). This is similar to the competitive situation in other countries where deregulation and other telecom-focused government actions are rapidly changing the industry landscapes and extending key aspects of telecommunications beyond regional and national boundaries into the global arena.   The boundaries that have previously defined the telecom competitive landscape in the recent past, such as long-distance or toll-service provider vs. incumbent local (PTT) service provider vs. competitive service provider (see Appendix A for list of acronyms), are blurring in a market being defined by mergers, acquisitions and joint ventures (Martin, Deskey, and Pihl, 1999).   In addition, distinctions between local and long-distance services, LATAs, and voice and data services are gradually breaking down.   At the same time, there is a growing trend away from traditional voice services to data-centric IP-based services.   The communications customer is also becoming more sophisticated with new technical and service requirements, while the traditional markets and segments are fast changing.   Telecommunications end users are increasingly savvy, gaining insight into provider capabilities and raising their expectations of provider performance as a result (Martin et al., 1999). Customer satisfaction and loyalty depend more than ever on the carrier's ability to understand and meet these changing requirements. This tutorial describes some industry-established processes and presents a structure used by global service providers to assess and analyze their telecommunications networking requirements and alternatives. Large telecom carriers, due to the inherent technical and market forces they work in, often use the approaches outlined and presented in this article. The processes and structures are very important because they help the carrier identify and understand regional characteristics of a given locality (i.e., country or state).   It also helps in assessing city types, which may vary by functionality and market potential.   The carrier needs to consider other key attributes such as: demand for voice and data services; volume of traffic staying and leaving varied parts of the country network; geometry of network elements and facilities; and competition.   As the global carrier considers entry into new markets, its strategic planning should include: analysis of target countries; assessment of regional transport networks connecting targeted cities; and assessments of the metropolitan (metro) transport and local loop network requirements within targeted cities.   These requirements will be driven by the local market conditions, and the carrier's requirements for network build and deployment.

The main objectives of this paper include:

- Presentation of a tutorial discussion on network modeling and analysis to support international business development with strategies for metropolitan and local access networks;
- Determination of the network cost drivers for providing voice and IP services to various market segments, including the small and medium sized enterprise (SME) and multi-dwelling unit (MDU) markets;
- Identification of the market and cost synergies for combining voice and IP services on common carrier facilities; and
- Comparison of leasing verses building alternatives for metropolitan transport and last mile access networks.

The discussion opens with a description of the general problem and then talks to a specific business case analysis. It continues by identifying and discussing key drivers and factors, trade-offs and alternatives that are faced by the global communications carrier. The discussion closes with some general recommendations, insightful thoughts regarding the changes over the next few years and a summary of conclusions.

DISCUSSION OF BUSINESS STRATEGIES FOR SERVING LOCAL/METRO MARKETS

Business Opportunities

The strategic planning for a global communications carrier involves the interplay of business, marketing, technology and regulatory factors. While some of these factors are independent of one another, most are inter-dependent on each other. One example of an inter-dependent factor is a country's policy regarding wireless spectrum–this may influence the technology choices, network costs and services offered. Figure 1 (and all illustrations in this article are based on the authors' original research and work) identifies some of the dynamic factors of network planning that the global communications carrier may consider. Carriers entering new markets must deal with these dynamics. They must determine how to take advantage of technology, the changing regulatory environment, existing competitive service providers and new customer demands–to build optimal networks and successful businesses (Wrede, 2000).

The choice of network technology is more important than ever due to today's rapidly changing market and new services. Business opportunities influence the service provider's strategic decisions and impact the network architectures and how technology is deployed to deliver services. A service

Figure 1. Dynamics of network planning

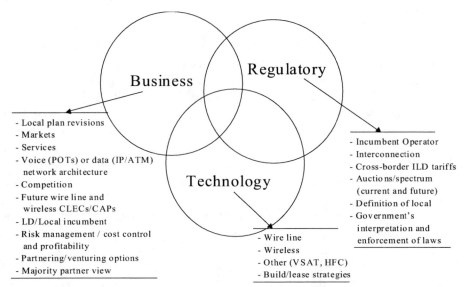

- Local plan revisions
- Markets
- Services
- Voice (POTs) or data (IP/ATM)
  network architecture
- Competition
- Future wire line and
  wireless CLECs/CAPs
- LD/Local incumbent
- Risk management / cost control
  and profitability
- Partnering/venturing options
- Majority partner view

- Incumbent Operator
- Interconnection
- Cross-border ILD tariffs
- Auctions/spectrum
  (current and future)
- Definition of local
- Government's
  interpretation and
  enforcement of laws

- Wire line
- Wireless
- Other (VSAT, HFC)
- Build/lease strategies

provider may choose to offer IP-only wholesale services, PTT by-pass services, or a full suite of voice and data telecom services. A second service provider consideration centers on target market segment decisions–will the service provider focus on the residential customer base, SME customers or large/corporate enterprises. A third decision is network infrastructure ownership, such as end-to-end ownership of the network, leasing capacity or facilities, or partnering with other entities. And a fourth issue regards positioning decisions to specific market segments — such as IP-only services to SMEs and large enterprises, or wholesale IP dial-up access to residential focused Internet service providers (ISPs). Wymbs (2002) found that complex interactions among country market size, government role, technology, industry dynamics, firm strategy, and project sequencing strategy affect a company's decision of entry into the European telecommunications markets during the 1990s and that an eclectic evolutionary theory of telecommunications investment appears most appropriate. This suggests that an evolutionary theory based on project learning, competitive adaptiveness and institutional dynamics is the only theory that is sufficiently broad to adequately explain the diverse behaviors of firms in the emerging, rapidly innovating telecommunications industry. The service provider business objectives, coupled with their short and long-term strategic initiatives and plans, will serve as important elements in setting these important business opportunity decisions.

Target Market Segment and Positioning Decisions

The global communications carrier must clearly define its strategy with respect to market segments, customers served, and services and applications delivered. This must include a view of today's market demand, including competition, and a view of the near-term future. The market requirements will be an integral component to meeting carrier objectives, and will drive its decisions relating to technologies and network architectures. The carrier must consider various aspects in its marketing decisions. Among these include: the market segment(s) served; the positioning decisions (i.e., wholesale, retail, full service) to specific market segments; the market demand — both current and future; the customer requirements; the competitive factors and environment; and the specific set of telecom services, features and applications provided to their customers.

Many of these factors have a current "today" element and a future element (i.e., a few years out). These marketing decisions and overall plans drive technology choices that best deliver the services and applications demanded. They also drive network architecture choices regarding scalability (to grow), flexibility (to meet changing needs) and how best to leverage available access technologies. Large service providers need to focus on market opportunities that leverage their core strengths, including technology and networks, while at the same time recognizing that there are smaller carriers pursuing niche markets with differentiated capabilities (Strouse, 2001). Different market segments will require different services and varying amounts of access bandwidth or capacity. These different market segments will be served by alternative technologies that minimize overall costs, and meet customer requirements of security, reliability, scalability and flexibility. The perception that if broadband services — provided by DSL, satellite, wireless, or cable — were made available, a user would automatically sign up, is a myth. There are plenty of big threats looming to Internet service providers (ISPs) as they fight to provide their users with faster speeds. As countries deregulate their telecom industries, government bodies establish new rules that may impact incumbent providers and new competitors in different ways. In some cases, incumbent carriers may be forced to open up their networks, or some portion, to new competitors. In other cases, these new rules and requirements may be unclear and take longer to implement, affording incumbent carriers more time to determine the competitive aspect of their network strategies. Another black cloud hanging over ISPs is the business practice of cable operators and incumbent carriers, which are already offering broadband service. Content itself will remain a big hurdle for the Internet industry and the sell to broadband (McGinity, 2002). Broadband technology has evolved at a faster pace than the marketplace — while the technical capabilities exist today to offer broadband access, the vast majority of services that could be provided by the carriers, via broadband, have not yet been developed. This is due to a number of events, including: the economic downturn starting in 2000; the Internet bust and a rationalization of its growth and impact on the global economy; over-zealous expectations by service providers to build-out networks and capacity, without clearly defining the services to be provided; irrational pricing models (i.e., bandwidth is free) and incomplete/unrealistic business cases relating to market penetration and take-up of new services; over-estimating the true demand and timing of broadband services; and failing to recognize that reliable voice services, with a select small set of basic class features, is still a dominant requirement by a majority of residential and business customers. Most customers, even today, mainly want reliable voice and basic data services — such as Internet access and secured networking (i.e., virtual private networks) between their sites. In addition, these customers have limited, and in many cases, shrinking telecommunications budgets. Service providers will need to develop content — services, products and access to information and valuable data — at a reasonable cost and that meets specific customer needs. As the global economy rebounds and excess network capacity is used up, customer demands will grow. Once these new services and products are in place to meet existing market demands, then the justification for broadband access pipes to intercon-nect the users will exist. Even today, some service providers are providing broadband capabilities, with limited services — examples include commercial high-speed storage services; residential high-speed Internet access via cable modems and DSL; and picture messaging via mobile phones on 3G (third/next generation) wireless networks.

Figure 2 illustrates example market segments and their respective band-width, services and technologies. Most large enterprises will require a high

Figure 2. Market segmentations

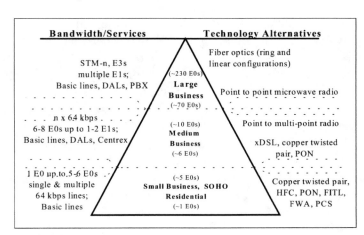

amount of bandwidth (i.e. multiple E-3s or STM-1s) that support voice and data private lines, and virtual enterprise networking. Fiber optic connections built directly into a physical serving location (i.e., customer building) may be an optimal solution. SMEs that require less bandwidth may be better served with other alternative access technologies, including fixed wireless access (FWA), digital subscriber line (DSL) and existing copper facilities.

The key for the service provider is to accurately match bandwidth and service needs to the optimal telecommunications technologies that deliver the maximum value to the customer. This balance of bandwidth/services and technology alternatives needs to be monitored on an on-going basis to ensure that as the customer needs change (i.e., growth of business, expansion into new markets), the optimal technology is deployed by the service provider. It is important to note that customer requirements of network security, availability, reliability, restoration and scalability will vary greatly based upon their core businesses and applications. The network planning, architectural choices and technology deployed will be fundamental in successfully meeting these customer needs.

Network Infrastructure Ownership Decisions

Network infrastructure decisions relate to the different aspects of the global carrier's network. The network can be divided into four segments. The first segment is the core or backbone network, which includes plant and facilities that span across a country or countries. This part of the network typically uses high-speed optical transport technologies to carry bits of information across national boundaries. The second segment of the network is the regional network. This is a sub-network of the core network interconnecting cities within a geographic region or area of a country. This network also uses high-speed optical transport technologies to carry traffic between cities. The third segment covers the network within a city — connecting various switching, routing and traffic aggregation facilities across a metropolitan or city area. The final network segment comprises the access network or last mile. This is the portion of the network that connects the customer sites to the carrier's network facilities. Figure 3 shows a conceptual city network — focusing on the metropolitan (city) and access (last mile) networks. This network may be made up of various metropolitan and collector fiber optic rings, in addition to: point-to-point fiber connections, radio or wireless access and leased facilities. The global carrier must consider various network infrastructure ownership decisions. One important decision is leasing verses building or buying plant and facilities — this decision impacts costs, control of infrastructure, and time to market. It is more likely that a carrier will build core and regional infrastructure, and lease the metro/access plant and facilities. The carrier may choose to lease last mile facilities (i.e., leased lines) from incumbent carriers in lieu of deploying alterna-

Figure 3. Conceptual city network

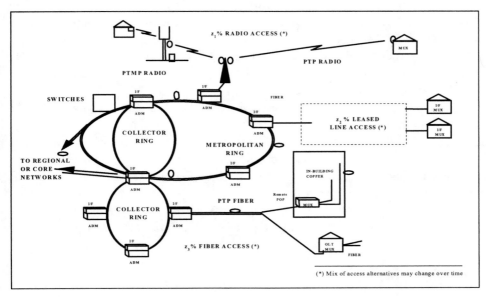

(*) Mix of access alternatives may change over time

tive technologies such as FWA or DSL to connect to the customers. These alternatives may require building infrastructure and additional capital outlays for required customer and networking equipment. Again, the costs, regulations regarding the unbundling of incumbent carrier networks and the competitive environment will influence this decision.

As the global carrier weighs these decisions, the business, market positioning, regulatory and technology dynamics come into play. Albright (2001) talks about the impact of disruptive technologies to the carrier. Global carriers are going through a significant transition in their networks and associated technologies. They must identify disruptive technologies at the right time during this transition — taking advantage of innovations by turning them into strategic opportunities. Albright describes these new technologies as having the following characteristics: revolutionize cost structures, increase network capacity, enhance quality of service, improve performance; but notes that they are difficult to incorporate into legacy carrier networks and systems. Examples of disruptive technologies include: gigabit ethernet, packetized voice and dense WDM technologies. Gigabit ethernet has the potential to deliver high-speed data across local and wide area networks at lower cost, due in part to less complex networks and cheaper/mature Ethernet switches. Packetized voice is a real alternative to PSTN circuit-switched voice. Digitizing voice and transporting as IP packets allows for more efficient utilization of network capacity and lower operating costs. A key issue surrounding packetized voice presently being addressed by industry experts and the vendor communities is "quality of the voice service".

Dense wave division multiplexing and advancements in optio-electronics have resulted in transporting more than 160 separate wavelengths on a single fiber. This dense DWDM technology exist today, has been trailed by major telecom carriers and is deployed, on a limited basis, in core network routes warranting this significantly increased transport capacity. While disruptive technologies are coming online, the ability for service providers to take advantage of them has been limited. Many of these technologies have been trialed by the carriers, and in some cases deployed in their networks on a limited basis. As the general global economy starts to rebound and the telecom services industry recovers, the opportunity to deploy these new disruptive technologies will increase. In addition, commercial services and applications that could be supported by these technologies have been slow to develop — broadband data and third generation mobile wireless are vivid examples. Wrede (2000) further explains that successful service providers will need to understand the economics of delivering advanced services to their customers and how technology will impact those economics.

CONSIDERATIONS OF GENERIC MODELS

Services, Market Segments, Network Architectures and Cost Drivers

This section continues to develop the general problem and challenges faced by the global communications carrier. Tobin (2002) found that optimal capacity placement under a given budget can be reduced to a two-dimensional implicit search over 2 multipliers: one that governs technology selection and one that governs project sizing. There are different network architectures that provide varied levels of service to the customer. Each of the architectures vary in complexity, network functionality, services supported and overall network costs. As the carrier defines its business objectives, it can then determine an appropriate market strategy. The carrier objectives and market strategies drive the selection of the architectures and technologies that best meet these plans. The network architectures and technologies will vary by cost, risk, flexibility, scalability, complexity and time to market considerations. Four generic network models are presented in the following section.   he model that best meets the carrier objectives and customer requirements should be deployed.

Low Capital Intensity: IP Services Only

The first model, "low capital intensity — IP services only" network model, provides the carrier with an option to sell public Internet access and IP virtual private networking services with minimal infrastructure build-out. The IP-only network requires the lowest outlay of capital investment — a minimal set of services would require only network router/server facilities in the metropolitan and regional networks, and associated back-office systems. Refer to Figure 4 and note the required network infrastructure, denoted in gray — the rest of the infrastructure being leased. The carrier could increase the amount of capital investment by varying how much of the network is leased, owned or partnered with other entities. This network could serve large enterprise, SME and residential markets — in addition to wholesaling capacity to residential focused ISPs.

Medium Capital Intensity: IP + International Voice

The second model, "medium capital intensity — IP + international voice" network model, expands on the first model. This network adds voice over Internet (VoIP) and competitive PTT services, such as: local by-pass, toll and international switched voice, private line and data services. As the IP services grow, the carrier needs to introduce private line and digital cross connect (DXC) capabilities into the network to more efficiently groom the access traffic. This network also includes long-distance (LD) voice switches. Frame relay and ATM may also be needed to serve as data link layer technologies for the transport of IP services. This network infrastructure will support frame relay and ATM data services, private line services, and connectivity to international PSTN dial services. Refer to Figure 5 and note additional infrastructure, which is denoted in gray — again the remainder being leased. As infrastructure is added, the capital investment, ownership and control of the network increases for the carrier.

Figure 4. Low capital intensity network

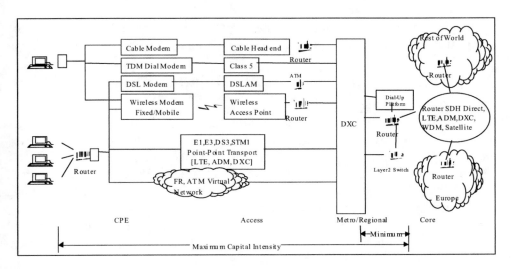

Figure 5. Medium capital intensity network

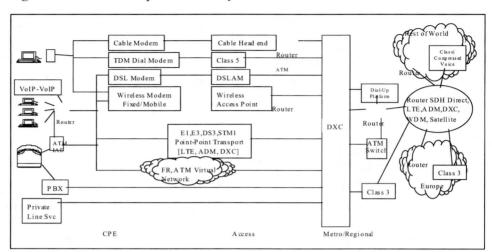

High Capital Intensity: IP + International Voice + Select Local PSTN Voice

The third model, "high capital intensity — IP + international voice + select local PSTN voice" network model, expands on the first and second models. This network adds IP-only services such as: VoIP to PSTN, web hosting, security, mirroring of sites, and alternative service provider (ASP) services. It also provides switched local voice to selected market segments (i.e., SME, large enterprise) and international voice to residential customers. The network requires VoIP to PSTN gateways, intelligent customer equipment and local/LD voice switches. Refer to Figure 6 and note the additional infrastructure, denoted in gray — the remainder being leased. This network targets local services to support Pan-European and international customers.

Very High Capital Intensity: Full Suite of Local to Global Services

The final model, "very high capital intensity — full suite of local to global services" network model, expands on the previous three models. This network adds VoIP, switched local voice, international voice, and private line and data services to the residential market segment. This network requires local voice switches deployed in the metro/local networks. Refer to Figure 7, noting additional infrastructure, denoted in gray the remainder being leased.

This network has the highest outlay of capital investment, but supports a full suite of local to global services. This network architecture focuses on the entire local market, including the residential market segment.

Figure 6. High capital intensity network

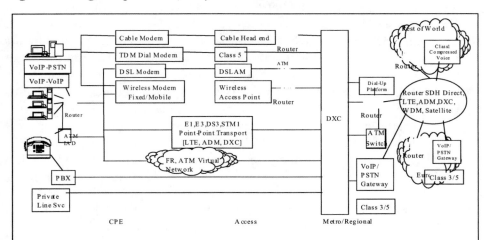

Figure 7. Very high capital intensity network

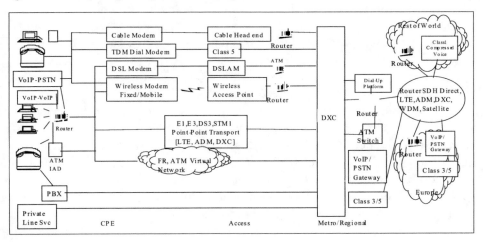

NETWORK DESIGN CONSIDERATIONS

Network Design

The service provider network planning team would use a network design process to facilitate their planning decisions. There are a number of general steps in such a network design process. The first step is to establish unconstrained design goals — lowest capital outlay, scalability, flexibility to offer array of services, performance. The second step is to perform network modeling and analysis of backbone, regional, metro and access networks — this step requires various inputs such as equipment architecture options, network topology, traffic demand data, design parameters, equipment cost parameters, and network selection criteria. The next step includes the development of "internal" designs of the network using internal software tools, including simulation software tools. The team will also coordinate "external" vendor network designs, including equipment costs and counts. A critical step for the team includes a comparison of "internal" and "external" network designs–and based upon selection criteria, they select the best architectures and technologies to meet the design goals. The team proceeds to identify prioritized requirements based upon carriers' resource constraints. They next assess selected architectures and technologies based upon cost and performance trade-offs. If the selected architectures and tech-nologies do not meet cost and performance criteria, the team repeats their network modeling and analysis steps with revised assumptions and information/ cost inputs. Selected architectures and technologies meeting cost and perfor-mance trade-offs would yield viable alternatives.These network design alterna-tives would provide the team with estimates over a multi-year period of: the network evolution plan; the network capital outlays (costs); the power and space requirements for network facilities (i.e., switch/router sites); the costs of back-hauling traffic verses switching traffic locally within a city or metro area; and the network operational costs, including systems and information technology (IT) costs.

Other Future Network Considerations

The global communications carrier might consider additional aspects of network design and planning. One aspect is distributed switching and moving network intelligence closer to the customer to reduce costs and provide network flexibility. A second aspect is packet technologies and packet-based network architectures to reduce costs, and improve access and transport efficiencies. And a final aspect is optical capabilities to reduce costs, increase efficiencies, and improve service delivery in the regional and metro networks. These future network design and technology considerations are discussed in the following sections.

Distributed Switching and Pushing Intelligence to Network Edge

Many vendors and service providers are working together to develop next generation switch architectures. These new switches will distribute processing functions and intelligence out into the network closer to the customer. The distributed switch architecture promises to: lower carrier costs; support domi-nant data and IP network traffic; provide deployment flexibility; extend control and capabilities to the customer to manage their services; and provide intelligence to allow the network to manage services. A big driver of the next generation switch is the ability for carriers to provide new services — faster and easier. The next generation switch provides: a distributed network architecture; logical connection of gateways, controllers, broadband core and services; best-of-breed components based on industry standard protocols; and supports IP and ATM core technologies. The "soft switch" is an example of the next generation switch.

In contrast, the traditional switch uses a centralized architecture that provides ports, switch matrix, call control and feature processing in a common physical platform. The soft or distributed switch architecture separates these components. It distributes the ports and switch matrix throughout the network, to the edge where the customer resides. It also separates the control and feature server functions for added flexibility. It takes advantage of various gateway devices that connect and provide intelligence across the network. It is these network gateway functions that enable new, innovative services and potentially simplify the network architecture and lower the costs of delivering services. Some examples of these potentially new services include high-quality IP voice; IP virtual private networks (VPNs); and SIP (session initiation protocol)-enabled voice features, such as advanced directory and "follow-me services. The network intelligence and gateway capabilities could reduce service provider costs in the following ways: improve bandwidth utilization and efficiencies by processing IP packets instead of translating various voice and data protocols; the ability to statistically multiplex data from various customers and sources; the ability to over-subscribe bandwidth by setting traffic priorities and establishing service classes; and leveraging cheaper and faster network gear (i.e. intelligent routers) and customer equipment. According to Katz (2000), the carrier move from PSTN to the next generation packet network is in its third stage of development. The first stage was the build out of optical networks for efficient transport. The second stage was the development and deployment of soft-switch (next generation switch) technologies necessary to direct call traffic on the new networks. This stage also included the development of new protocols and standards, to which basic features could be supported across the network. The third stage focuses on the development of enhanced services and feature sets. With the recent global economic downturn and the adverse impacts on the telecommunications industry, the deployment of next generation switching capabilities and the promise of new IP services has been stalled significantly. Many of the telecom industry leaders — including the service providers, vendors, and standards bodies — are continuing their work, but at a more cautious and pragmatic pace.

Packet Technologies and Packet-Based Architectures

Another area of recent interest by carriers has been in packet aggregation and switching capabilities, leveraging LAN-based technologies. Carriers are interested in packet-based technologies for the following reasons. There is a new LAN paradigm—today's LAN technology has evolved to support high-speed full duplex gigabit Ethernet (GbE) packet networks. The overly aggressive global forecasts and projections of data and IP traffic growth of the last few years — Ethernet being a significant share of this projected data growth — fueled much industry optimism and activity, with packet technologies promising to be efficient for means of handling this future data traffic. There are key enablers of native data technologies — such as the availability of high bandwidth resources (i.e., fiber) and wavelength division multiplexing (WDM) technologies. New service and cost models are driving carriers to look at packet-based technologies. And finally, there are major potential benefits, including: lower costs to customers and carriers; enabler of new services and revenue sources; ability to support existing carrier services; easier provisioning and service delivery; and lower operational costs (i.e., network maintenance labor).

Packet aggregation and switching technologies become important as customer profiles change to more data-centric services and applications. Services can be provided over a single access facility and switch/router interface resulting in cost savings. In addition, the carrier may aggregate multiple customers onto shared over-provisioned access transport facilities. Packet technologies are also better adapted to real-time service provisioning. The carrier can realize savings from packet aggregation technologies by: more efficiently filling access pipes, interfaces and network devices; more efficiently utilizing switch interfaces and matrix capacity; and grooming smaller interfaces into larger, more cost effective interfaces. These technologies will be used in areas where high data throughput is required, and metro/wide area network integration and strict quality of service (QoS) are not main concerns. Packet-based technologies are optimized to support the following: network traffic that is primarily data, packetized video or voice; where delay sensitive applications can operate with less stringent QoS; where network migration and simplicity is needed; where bandwidth and installation costs are a concern; and where it is important for the carrier to leverage an installed base of Ethernet knowledge for network management, monitoring and trouble-shooting. Henderson (2001) notes that service providers can improve cost structures by aggregating presentation, delivery and support for IP-based communications services via communications portals. Communications portal providers are an emerging breed of IP-enabled carriers who are providing Net (Internet) telephony, unified messaging, and collaboration (i.e., application sharing, Web-casting, voice chat) services. Rosenbush and Einhorn (2000) describe voice-on-the-Net as a growing international business. Companies around the globe are beginning to use new systems based on Internet technology in place of their old phone networks–not only because they are cheaper but also because they can do so much more. Internet technology allows many calls to share the same phone line. Voice-on-the-Net is expected to account for more than 30% of total global telecom traffic by the year 2005. As call quality via IP approaches or exceeds traditional circuit-switched calls, carriers will increasingly recognize the economic advantage to routing calls via the Internet (Dukart, 2001). The British-based global carrier, Cable & Wireless, recently announced a major initiative to build a national state-of-the-art optical fiber network in Japan. This advanced network will enable the carrier to deliver a new standard in IP and data services to business customers throughout Japan (Stober, 2000).

Optical Capabilities in the Access/Metro and Regional Networks

Global communications carriers are also keenly interested in and pursuing optical networking capabilities such as high-speed transmission, dense wavelength division multiplexing (DWDM), optical layer management and optical packet switching. In addition, they are working with vendors to develop next generation fiber, ultra broadband and optical cross connect systems, and more efficient wavelength amplifier systems. Much of this work is being driven by some of the following carrier challenges and objectives. These include: a forecasted significant increase in capacity demand in the near future (driven by data growth); a need for automated service provisioning capabilities; requirements for higher spectral density to increase capacity on a per fiber basis; an on-going need to reduce cost, power consumption and physical size of future generations of transmission, transport and access equipment; and carrier requirements for scalability, reliability and flexibility in the transport network.

Optical capabilities and WDM have traditionally been used in the regional and core or backbone networks. As capacity requirements increase and economics improve, these technologies are moving into the metropolitan transport network, and in some special cases, into the access network. Some of the larger ISPs, incumbent (PTT) end offices and carrier hotel transport customers in major metropolitan cities may warrant WDM directly to their buildings to transport data at higher optical rates. A few of the main drivers for metro and access network optical capabilities include: relief of fiber exhaust in metro areas via WDM; improved utilization of fiber facilities through packet technologies and statistical multiplexing; a need to deploy next generation fiber that maximizes wavelength counts, improves performance, and minimizes signal dispersion and loss; the use of wavelength switching and optical cross connects for wavelength management; the need to deploy more efficient amplifiers to extend optical signals and lower costs; and the requirement to offer convergent services over efficient optical transport systems and networks.

According to Walter (2000a), a new class of products called optical access or WAN platforms, is bringing multi-service capabilities to metropolitan optical networks. These products aggregate a variety of inputs to an optical network — IP, ATM, Ethernet, TDM — onto SDH/SONET rings or DWDM wavelengths. They can extend access to optical networks as far out as an office building, or can groom metro rings into large multi-protocol streams ready for backbone networks (Walter, 2000b, & 2000c). Li (2000) talks about Carrier1, a European-based global supplier of long distance communications services. Carrier1 is deploying a new fiber that increases the distance an optical signal can travel without dispersion compensation. Underground ducts are being constructed with this new fiber technology in Amsterdam; Carrier1 plans to build in 20 other major European cities, including Paris, Berlin and Zurich. The customer is demanding service flexibility, speed of provisioning, low cost per bit, and low cost per connection. Although previous results about the obstructive influence of distance on technical communication are valid, empirical evidence has shown that factors such as the recognition of highly interdependent team members, the existence of strong organizational bonds and the use of electronic communication media can influence technical communication in the telecommunications industry (Sosa et al., 2002). WDM and other optical technologies are proving to be essential tools in the metropolitan market to meet these evolving needs.

OTHER CARRIER CONSIDERATIONS AND FUTURE TRENDS

Vendors, equipment manufacturers and systems/software companies have developed, and continue to develop, new technologies for the telecom industry. Much of the research & development and introduction of these technologies have slowed due to the uncertain global economic conditions. In addition, there has been significant industry consolidation and contraction, which has further slowed the pace of deploying new technologies. The anticipated worldwide demands for new services and increased capacities have not come to fruition. As the economic conditions improve, network over-capacity absorbed and the telecom industry returns to growth, service providers will look to the vendors and manufacturers for these new technologies and networking capabilities. The service providers, in conjunction with their vendor partners, will most likely bear most of the risk and costs of developing and deploying these new technologies. Telecommunications remains a high capital investment business — it will be critical for the service providers and vendors to work together to develop and deploy optimal technologies with optimal cost structures. They will need to optimize and minimize upfront capital investments by designing more modular and scalable equipment and platforms. In addition, the service provider will need to carefully assess the market opportunities to sell new services and develop "success-based business models" that ensure economic viability. Their success will be based, in part, on achieving a minimum level of market penetration to reduce their unit costs to deliver profitable services. The service providers will also require intelligent platforms that can reduce operational costs and simplify the network — remote provisioning of services, dynamic control of bandwidth, and prioritization of packets and data flows — are some examples. These new technologies will allow the service provider to lower overall cost of delivering services, increase network efficiencies, more effectively manage operational costs and achieve the necessary economies of scale to develop viable businesses. Components of the service provider's success-based business models may include the following: vendor financing that equitably balances the risks and returns for the manufacturers; service contracts and pricing strategies where the customer purchases, or leases over a period of time, a greater portion of their premise and access equipment; and the deployment of new last mile technologies — such as wireless and packet-centric solutions — that allow the service provider to deliver capacity and services at a lower overall cost. These new investments and introduction of advanced technologies will yield many tangible benefits to the public. Some of these benefits include the following: lower cost reliable services that are available to a wider range and geographic scope of customers; new capabilities that support services — such as tele-conferencing, distance learning, telemedicine, electronic commerce and wireless messaging/ voice. These services will allow the public to gain wider access to information; provide services across geographic boundaries; bring educational benefits and heathcare opportunities closer to people; increase convenience, flexibility (i.e., mobility) and timeliness of leisure, business and emergency communications; provide a higher degree of reliability and quality of service; and drive costs down to make these services more affordable to more members of society. These new technologies will be critical for under-developed and developing countries as their governments/private entities move forward with deploying network infrastructure to deliver services to their under-served populations — this in turn will improve basic standards of living and begin to stimulate economic growth.

While it is difficult, and sometimes dangerous, to make predictions regarding the future, it is important to look ahead and try to understand the impact of new technologies on the telecom industry. Some of the trends we believe will occur over the next five years include the following:

- Continued advancement, growth and industry dominance in wireless technologies. Reliable voice will continue to be a dominant service, followed by non-voice services such as picture imaging, downloadable gaming and

Internet access. People will continue to demand rich services, at low costs, with the freedom (via mobility) that wireless allows. Wireless, both mobile and fixed technologies, will be critical to service providers in meeting the demands for under-developed and developing countries and markets.

• Packet technologies — such as voice over IP and Ethernet-based services — will become dominant. These new data technologies will provide higher bandwidth — but with allow for more efficient utilization of bandwidth and delivery of services by the service providers/operators. This will allow service providers to provide broadband capabilities at lower costs, and leverage these capabilities across the access and transport networks.

• As the economy rebounds, we will see renewed investment in new technologies and network capabilities. This will provide more bandwidth to the customer, broadband capabilities to more people, and richer services at lower costs. It will also further expand telecom and it's benefits (i.e., safety, learning, easily and reliably connecting people) into the daily lives and workplaces, allowing people to be more efficient, productive and connected.

SUMMARY AND CONCLUSION

There are many factors influencing the global communications carrier's network planning decisions and strategy. There are marketplace factors such as Internet growth, new IP services, voice and data convergence, non-traditional competitors, and global expansion. There are technology factors such as high-speed switching, the proliferation of new access technologies, and developments in optical technologies, declining costs, and new routing/control protocols. There are regulatory factors such as global de-regulation and price arbitrating in traditional telecom services (i.e., VoIP by-pass and circuit-switched voice using incumbent carrier switching). And there are business factors such as declining profit margins, the need for new services and revenue growth — and the need to reduce access costs, operations costs and service intervals. All or some of these factors will be part of the global carrier's strategic decision-making process. The ability to reasonably, objectively and comprehensively identify and assess critical factors, and consider alternative scenarios, becomes vital to the carrier. The carrier can learn valuable lessons from analyzing and studying specific business cases. This tutorial described the experiences of a major global carrier's network planning efforts, in addition to a detailed case study they used to evaluate their European network activities. The combination of past experiences from seasoned industry personnel, lessons learned from studies and analyses based on real experiences, sound business sense, clear corporate vision, and flexible objectives — will ensure the global communications carrier's success as it moves forward in planning and implementing new networks.

REFERENCES

Albright, P. (2001). An innovator's dream es another's disruptive technology. *Wireless Week, 1,* 18-19.

Dobrushin, A. (2000). Convergence revisited: Will intersection of optics, IP finally realize promise of a single network. *X-CHANGE, 1,* 32-36.

Dukart, J. (2001). IP, Latin America emerge as major growth markets. *Phone+, 1,* 58-59.

Henderson, K. (2001). Service on a portal: Web-user interface enables enhanced communications. *Phone+, 1,* 36-42.

Kollman, T. (2000). The price/acceptance function: Perspectives of a pricing policy in European telecommunication markets. *European Journal of Innovation Management, 3,* 1.

Li., J. (2000). DWDM moves into the metro. *Outside Plant, 1,* 46-51.

Martin, S., Deskey, B., & Pihl, A. (1999). 5th annual telecommunications customer expectations survey report. *Deloitte Consulting LLC, 1,* 1-16.

McGinity, M. (2002). Broadband to go. *Communications of the ACM, 45*(6), 21.

Rosenbush, S., & Einhorn, B. (2000). The Talking Internet: Special Report Telecommunications. *Business Week, 1,* 174-196.

Seals, T. (2001). Bundled services: No sign of dwindling in 2001. *Phone+, 1,* 52.

Sosa, M., Eppinger, S., Pich, M., Mckendrick, D., & Stout, S. (2002). Factors that influence technical communication in distributed product development: An empirical study in the telecommunications industry. *IEEE Transactions on Engineering Management, 49*(1), 45.

Stober, S. (Ed). (2000). News: Cable & wireless creates optical fiber network in Japan. *Outside Plant, 1,* 16.

Strouse, K. (2001). Planning, measuring, managing market share. *Phone+, 1,* 94-96.

Summerill, S. (2000). Next-gen networks: Got features? *Sounding Board, 1,* 38-45.

Tobin, R. (2002). Relief period optimization under budget constraints. *European Journal of Operational Research, 139*(1), 42.

Wede, D. (2000). A business case for fiber-to-the-home. *Optical Solutions, Inc., 1,* 1-16.

Walter, C. (2000a). Optical access rides the waves. *X-CHANGE, 1,* 8-14.

Walter, C. (2000b). Mighty mice: Fledging companies make waves at optical fest. *X-CHANGE, 1,* 26-32.

Walter, C. (2000c). Making next-gen friends: VoDSL vendors, softswitch makers partner up for the new networks. *Sounding Board, 1,* 46-50.

Wymbs, C. (2002). U.S. firms' entry into the European telecommunications market: A question of modality choice. *Journal of High Technology Management Research, 13*(1), 87.

APPENDIX A: GLOSSARY OF TECHNICAL ACRONYMS

ADM: add drop multiplexer
ASP: alternative service provider
ATM: asynchronous transfer mode
CAP: competitive access provider
CLEC: competitive local exchange provider
CPE: customer premise equipment
DAL: direct access line
DSL: digital subscriber line
DSLAM: digital subscriber line access module
DWDM: dense wave division multiplexing
DXC: digital cross-connect
FR: frame relay
FWA: fixed wireless access
GbE: gigabit Ethernet
GDP: gross domestic product

IAD: intelligent access device
ILEC: independent local exchange carrier
IP: Internet protocol
ISDN: integrated services digital network
ISP: Internet service provider
IT: information technology
LAN: local area network
LATA: local access and transport areas
LD: long distance
MDU: multi-dwelling unit
MUX: multiplexer
OLT: optical line termination
PBX: private branch exchange
PCS: personal communications services
PL: private line
PON: passive optical network
POP: point of presence

POTS: plain old telephone services
PSTN: public switched telephone network
PTMP: point to multi-point
PTP: point to point
PTT: postal telephone & telegraph
QoS: quality of service
SDH: synchronous digital hierarchy
SME: small and medium enterprise
SOHO: small office/home office
SONET: synchronous optical network
STM-n: ETSI standard optical carrier
TDM: time division multiplexing
VoIP: voice over the Internet
VSAT: very small aperture terminal
WAN: wide area network
WDM: wave division multiplexing

This chapter was previously published in the *Information Resources Management Journal, 17*(1), 19-36, January-March, Copyright © 2004.

Chapter VII

Toward a Greater Understanding of End-Users' Acceptance of ERP Systems

Fiona Fui-Hoon Nah
University of Nebraska - Lincoln, USA

Xin Tan
University of Nebraska - Lincoln, USA

Soon Hing Teh
Singapore Power, Singapore

ABSTRACT

Despite huge investments made by organizations in ERP implementation, maintenance, and user training, ERP implementation failures and less than expected productivity improvements are not uncommon. End users' reluctance to use newly implemented ERP systems is often cited as one of the main reasons for ERP failures. To understand the lack of end-user acceptance of ERP systems, we examined end users' attitude toward system use and symbolic adoption; the latter refers to users' voluntary mental acceptance of a system. Four instrumental beliefs—perceived usefulness, perceived ease of use, perceived compatibility, and perceived fit—were modeled as the antecedents. The research model was tested using a survey on end users' perceptions in adopting and using a newly implemented ERP system. The findings show that perceived compatibility and perceived ease of use have both direct and indirect effects (mediated by attitude) on symbolic adoption, while perceived fit and perceived usefulness influence symbolic adoption via attitude. The study provides managerial implications for organizations in engendering positive user acceptance of enterprise systems and applications.

INTRODUCTION

Enterprise resource planning (ERP) systems provide an integrated enterprise-wide business solution to organizations to help achieve their competitive goals. An ERP system can be viewed as an enterprise-wide information system that integrates all aspects of a business. At the core of an ERP system is a single comprehensive database, which collects data from and feeds data into modular applications supporting virtually all of a company's business activities—across functions, across business units, across the world (Davenport, 1998).

To reap the benefits of ERP systems, organizations across the globe have invested heavily in ERP implementation, maintenance, and user training. Despite the huge investments, there are many cases of implementation failures and less-than-satisfactory productivity improvements (Davenport, 1998). One of the commonly cited reasons for ERP failures is end users' reluctance to use the newly implemented ERP system (Barker & Frolick, 2003; Scott & Vessey, 2002; Umble & Umble, 2002; Wah, 2000). The lack of user acceptance can lead to rote rather than sophisticated use of the system and cause disgruntled morale problems in the organization. Therefore, a good understanding of end users' acceptance of ERP systems is vital to ERP implementation success.

A literature review of past ERP studies indicates that only a few studies have empirically investigated end users' acceptance of ERP systems. The majority of them drew heavily on the technology acceptance model (TAM) (Davis, 1989; Davis, Bagozzi, & Warshaw, 1989). An analysis of the findings of these studies, together with a review of literature on end users' acceptance of information technology (IT) in mandatory settings, led us to contend that TAM needs to be revised and extended in the ERP context.

By drawing on established theories and empirical findings in IT adoption, we developed a model of end users' acceptance of ERP systems. Specifically, our model depicts the effect of users' instrumental beliefs regarding an information system on their attitude and voluntary mental acceptance of the system. This proposed model was tested using a survey of ERP end users in a large institution.

Our chapter is organized as follows. First, we review TAM (Davis, 1989; Davis et al., 1989) and other studies that have examined users' acceptance in the ERP context. Then, we discuss the problems of directly applying TAM in understanding end users' acceptance of ERP systems. Second, based on the relevant literature and theoretical foundations, we develop our research model and related hypotheses. Third, a survey of end users' perceptions concerning adopting and using a newly implemented ERP system is used to test the research hypotheses. Fourth, we discuss the implications of the results. Finally, the chapter concludes with a discussion of future research directions.

BACKGROUND

As several studies (Barker & Frolick, 2003; Scott & Vessey, 2002; Umble & Umble, 2002; Wah, 2000) have revealed, a common reason for ERP failures can be attributed to end users' reluctance to use newly implemented ERP systems. Hence, a better understanding of factors leading to users' acceptance (or lack of acceptance) of ERP systems is necessary to facilitate successful ERP implementation and usage. One widely used theory that examines user adoption is the technology acceptance model (TAM) (Davis, 1989; Davis et al., 1989). The few existing studies on end users' perceptions and attitudes on adopting and using ERP were primarily based on TAM. We briefly introduce TAM before reviewing other empirical studies.

Technology Acceptance Model (TAM)

As an adaptation of the Theory of Reasoned Action (TRA) (Ajzen & Fishbein, 1980), TAM (Davis, 1989; Davis et al., 1989) has emerged as a powerful and parsimonious way to represent the antecedents of system usage . TAM theorizes that an individual's behavioral intention to use a system is determined by two beliefs: perceived usefulness, defined as the extent to which a person believes that using the system will enhance his or her job performance, and perceived ease of use, defined as the extent to which a person believes that using the system will be free of effort (Davis, 1989).

According to TAM, perceived usefulness is also influenced by perceived ease of use because, other things being equal, the easier the system is to use, the more useful it will be (Davis et al., 1989). Many empirical tests of TAM indicate that perceived usefulness is a strong determinant of behavioral intention, while perceived ease of use is a relatively weak determinant of intention (Venkatesh & Davis, 2000). The original TAM (see Figure 1) depicts that attitude is a mediating variable between the two determinants and behavioral intention. Studies demonstrated that without the mediating attitude construct, the explanatory power of the model is equally good, and the model is more parsimonious

(Davis et al., 1989). As a result, it has become a norm to exclude the attitude construct from TAM. Figure 1 and Figure 2 show the original formulation of TAM and the parsimonious formulation of TAM.

Specifically tailored for modeling user acceptance of information systems, TAM has very good explanatory power (explaining about 40% of the variance in usage intentions and behavior, according to Venkatesh & Davis, 2000). However, TAM by itself may not be suitable for explaining end users' acceptance in the ERP context. We will articulate this point by referring to some existing studies on end users' acceptance in ERP and similar contexts.

Studies in End Users' Acceptance of ERP Systems

Among the limited number of empirical studies that investigated end users' acceptance of ERP systems, many drew heavily upon TAM.

Some researchers directly applied TAM to test the model in the ERP context (Brown et al., 2002; Rawstorne, Jayasuriya, & Caputi, 2000). The findings are mixed. While TAM may successfully predict ERP adoption behavior in some cases, some strong links in TAM are absent (or not statistically significant) in some other cases.

Amoako-Gyampah and Salam (2004) chose to extend TAM by examining the influence of antecedent variables on TAM constructs of perceived useful-

Figure 1. Original formulation of TAM

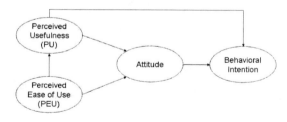

Figure 2. Parsimonious formulation of TAM

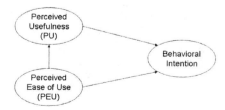

ness (PU) and perceived ease of use (PEU). The findings of their study indicate that project communication, training, and shared beliefs in the benefits of an ERP system affect both PU and PEU, directly or indirectly. Another interesting finding is that the link between PU and behavioral intention is not statistically significant.

Finally, one study (Bagchi, Kanungo, & Dasgupta, 2003) drew extensively on the research model proposed by Hartwick and Barki (1994), which itself is an adaptation of the TRA (Ajzen & Fishbein, 1980). The study evaluated the effects of end users' participation and involvement on their acceptance of ERP systems. Their findings also indicate that traditional models have to be modified to be relevant for ERP context. Table 1 summarizes existing studies in end users' acceptance of ERP systems.

Problems of Directly Applying TAM in the ERP Context

By analyzing the findings of existing studies on users' acceptance of ERP systems, we are able to identify some problems of directly applying TAM in the ERP context.

The Settings of ERP Implementation

TAM has been tested primarily in the environments where the technologies are relatively simple to use, such as in e-mail and word processors. ERP systems, however, are implemented in the organizational settings and are very complex to use. Several researchers (Adamson & Shine, 2003; Amoako-Gyampah & Salam, 2004; Brown et al., 2002; Legris, Ingham, & Collerette, 2003; Rawstorne et al., 1998) have pointed out that TAM needs to be extended or revised in order to be suitable for explaining end users' acceptance of complex and advanced IT in organizational settings.

Table 1. Prior studies in user acceptance of ERP systems

Study	Method	Theoretical foundations	Major findings related to TAM
Brown et al., 2002	Survey	TAM (both original and parsimonious formulation) and Theory of Planned Behavior (TPB)	1. PEU has a much higher total influence on intention than PU. 2. The link between attitude and intention is insignificant
Rawstorne et al., 1998, 2000	Survey	TAM and TPB	1. Neither TAM nor TPB could explain all ERP adoption behaviors
Amoako-Gyampah and Salam, 2004	Survey	TAM with extended determinants	1. The link between PU and intention is insignificant 2. Low reliability score and factor loading of questionnaires capturing intention
Bagchi et al., 2003	Survey and qualitative case studies	Hartwick and Barki (1994), which is an adaptation of the Theory of Reasoned Action (TRA) (Ajzen & Fishbein, 1980)	1. Low factor loading of questionnaires capturing intention 2. The link between attitude and intention is positive in one model, but negative in the other two

Voluntary or Mandatory Use

An implicit assumption of TAM is that users of IT have a choice about the extent to which they use the technology. As a matter of fact, the majority of studies based on TAM have been conducted in environments in which adoption was voluntary, as noted by Brown et al. (2002) and Melone (1990). Such environments are very different from the ERP settings. ERP usage is characterized as mandatory for its users. Brown et al. (2002) and Pozzebon (2000) pointed out that ERP is a mandatory context where one user's tasks on the ERP system are tightly coupled and integrated with other users' tasks. In other words, one generally does not have the choice not to use the system, regardless of their attitude and mental acceptance of the system.

Appropriateness of the Construct "Behavioral Intention"

Due to ERP's mandatory adoption context, many scholars argue that "behavioral intention," which has been typically used as a gauge of usage behavior, is inappropriate in a pure mandatory adoption environment because the variable would be extremely skewed and thus unsuitable in model testing (Rawstorne et al., 1998, 2000).

In view of the aforementioned problems of directly applying TAM in the ERP context, we concur with other researchers (Bagchi et al., 2003; Brown et al., 2002; Legris et al., 2003; Rawstorne et al., 1998) and contend that TAM needs to be revised and extended in order to be useful in explaining end users' acceptance of ERP systems. By drawing on established theories and empirical findings in information technology (IT) adoption, we developed a research model to further our understanding of end users' acceptance of ERP systems.

THEORETICAL FOUNDATIONS AND RESEARCH MODEL

Robey, Ross, and Boudreau (2002) organized the academic research on ERP into two categories: variance research and process research. Variance research on ERP seeks to explain variation in outcome variables by associating those outcomes with antecedent conditions and predictor variables. Such studies include those on critical success factors of ERP implementation, and studies on effects of ERP implementation. Process research on ERP seeks to explain outcomes by examining sequences of events over time.

Accordingly, our study can be classified as variance research because we want to identify factors that lead to variation in users' acceptance of ERP systems. In this section, we discuss the theoretical foundations for our research model.

Symbolic Adoption

The adoption and usage of ERP systems take place in a mandatory environment: in other words, the decision to adopt and implement an ERP system is often made by the management; end users are mandated to use the ERP system to carry out their tasks; and the level of interdependence across departmental and functional boundaries is very high due to the integration. As discussed in the literature review, behavioral intention is not appropriate for understanding and predicting users' acceptance in mandatory adoption and usage contexts. The intention-behavior relation only applies when the behavior is under a person's volitional control (Ajzen & Fishbein, 1980). In addition, typical items used in questionnaires to probe users' behavioral intention, such as "Assuming I have access to the system, I intend to use it" or "I intend to use the system frequently in the next 6 months," seem to be irrelevant in the mandatory contexts (Rawstorne et al., 1998).

To address this issue, Rawstorne et al. (1998) and Karahanna (1999) suggested an alternative variable to substitute for behavioral intention—Symbolic Adoption (or SA for short)—in the mandatory context. Coined by Klonglan and Coward (1970), symbolic adoption refers to one's mental acceptance of an innovation, distinct from actual adoption which refers to actual use of technology. Karahanna (1999) asserted that symbolic adoption precedes actual adoption and is a necessary but not sufficient condition for actual adoption in voluntary contexts. In the case of mandatory adoption, symbolic adoption is not necessary for actual adoption, but it is necessary for infusion. Rawstorne et al. (1998) contended that in a mandatory environment, people are likely to display differences in symbolic adoption of the new system. Identifying and analyzing such differences is likely to help predict initial resistance or lack of acceptance of technology in a mandatory adoption environment.

Therefore, we will use *symbolic adoption* as the primary variable for assessing end users' acceptance of ERP systems in this study.

Users' Attitude Toward System Use

Users may form attitudes toward using a system, which in turn influence their productivity through quality or amount of system usage and other important traits, such as job satisfaction, and loyalty toward the organization. Attitude refers to the affect that one feels for or against some object or behavior (Ajzen & Fishbein, 1980). In IS research, a user attitude can be defined as "a predisposition to respond favorably or unfavorably to a computer system, application, system staff member, or a process related to the use of that system or application" (Melone, 1990, p. 81). As a strong relationship can be expected between attitude and performance of a particular behavior, attitude concerning system use has been extensively studied.

Attitudes have been found to correlate with behavioral intention in voluntary contexts. However, it may not be the case in mandatory contexts, such as in the case of ERP. Brown et al. (2002) show that attitudes are not related to behavioral intention in a mandatory adoption environment. Other studies (Bagchi et al., 2003; Hartwick & Barki, 1994) reported contradictory results, which support the positive relationship between attitude and intention in mandatory contexts. We attribute the mixed findings to the inappropriate inclusion of the behavioral intention construct, which may be either highly skewed or irrelevant to research subjects and thus make the link unstable in the research model. As indicated by Rawstorne et al. (2000), the seemingly positive relationship may also have arisen due to "cognitive dissonance" in cross-sectional studies, causing respondents to psychologically associate intention with actual use.

The role of users' attitude in a mandated environment is important and should not be overlooked. Brown et al. (2002) specifically noted that excluding the attitude construct would not provide an accurate representation of users' acceptance of IT in the mandated adoption contexts. Therefore, attitude is included in our research model.

Consistent with earlier research, it is reasonable to assume that users' mental acceptance of an ERP system is highly influenced by their attitude toward using the system. That is, there is a positive relationship between attitude and symbolic adoption. Karahanna (1999) provides empirical evidence that users' attitude toward system use is a significant predictor of symbolic adoption. Hence, we hypothesize that:

- **Hypothesis 1:** Attitude toward system use will have a positive direct effect on symbolic adoption in the ERP context.

Antecedents: Instrumental Beliefs

While users' attitude toward system use constitutes an affective dimension of symbolic adoption, other instrumental beliefs are also important in determining one's symbolic adoption of an ERP system. Two important constructs in TAM—perceived usefulness (PU) and perceived ease of use (PEU)—may have direct effects on symbolic adoption. Karahanna (1999) provides empirical support for the direct effects (PU-SA and PEU-SA). Rawstorne et al. (1998) proposed that the effects of PU and PEU constructs on symbolic adoption are mediated by attitude, though these indirect effects have not been empirically tested. In this study, we hypothesize that:

Direct effects:

- **Hypothesis 2:** Perceived usefulness will have a positive direct effect on symbolic adoption in the ERP context.

- **Hypothesis 3:** Perceived ease of use will have a positive direct effect on symbolic adoption in the ERP context.

Indirect effects mediated by attitude:

- **Hypothesis 4:** Perceived usefulness will have a positive direct effect on attitude toward system use in the ERP context.

- **Hypothesis 5:** Perceived ease of use will have a positive direct effect on attitude toward system use in the ERP context.

Perceived usefulness and perceived ease of use as instrumental beliefs have been widely studied in general IT adoption settings (Agarwal & Karahanna, 2000). In the case of ERP implementations, which occur in organizational settings, other instrumental beliefs may become significantly relevant by influencing one's attitude and symbolic adoption.

One attraction or major benefit of ERP is that it boasts the ability to offer companies best business practices. The true meaning of best practices is elusive, but Miranda (1999) cited several implications associated with the adoption of best practices (as defined by software companies), including promotion of standardized processes, organizational discipline, and cross-functionality. ERP implementations "force" organizations to streamline and standardize their processes across the organization and within individual business units. This characteristic of ERP systems is more than likely to create concerns among end users about the compatibility and fit of the system.

According to Rogers' (1995) theory of Diffusion of Innovations, compatibility is defined as "the degree to which an innovation is perceived as consistent with the existing values, past experiences, and needs for potential adopters" (p. 224). Several studies (Agarwal & Prasad, 1997; Karahanna & Straub, 1999; Moore & Benbasat, 1991) have demonstrated that compatibility is an important factor in influencing end users' attitudes in adopting or using a new IT. In the ERP context, we refer to perceived compatibility as the degree to which the ERP system is perceived to be consistent with past business processes that users have been accustomed to. As ERP implementations usually involve business process reengineering, end users of ERP systems are likely to display strong variance in perceived compatibility, which in turn affects their attitude and symbolic adoption. Therefore, we hypothesize that:

- **Hypothesis 6:** Perceived compatibility will have a positive direct effect on attitude toward system use in the ERP context.

- **Hypothesis 7:** Perceived compatibility will have a positive direct effect on symbolic adoption in the ERP context.

The extent to which an ERP package encompasses the desired business processes for an organization is referred to as fit (Hong & Kim, 2002; Sieber et al., 2000). We define perceived fit from an end user's perspective as the degree to which the ERP software is perceived by a user to meet his/her organization's needs. While fit-gap analysis is often conducted at the organization level (i.e., as part of the implementation process), individual end users would cognitively process and perceive the fit at both the organizational and divisional (e.g., departmental) levels.

Soh and her colleagues (Soh et al., 2003; Soh, Kien, & Tay-Yap, 2000) used the terms "misfit" and "misalignment" interchangeably to refer to the situation where the company-specific, public sector-specific, or country-specific requirements did not match the capabilities of the ERP package. In their study (Soh et al., 2000), the observed misfits were clustered into three broad categories: data misfits, functional misfits, and output misfits. These misfits reflect a complex combination of compatibility and fit issues, which are often inevitable in ERP implementations because organizations often change their internal processes to fit the "industry best practices" available in ERP software (Nah, 2003; Siau, 2004). Due to the nature of ERP software, organizations will try to customize the software as little as possible. Hence, the issue of perceived fit is likely to take on heightened importance and relevance in influencing end users' attitude and symbolic adoption. Therefore, we hypothesize that:

- **Hypothesis 8:** Perceived fit will have a positive direct effect on attitude toward system use in the ERP context.

- **Hypothesis 9:** Perceived fit will have a positive direct effect on symbolic adoption in the ERP context.

Based on the above discussions on the theoretical foundations and research hypotheses, we develop the research model as shown in Figure 3.

Our research model is an extension of the original formulation of TAM. However, In view of the deficiency and inappropriateness of using the behavioral intention construct in the ERP context, we replaced it with a more meaningful construct—symbolic adoption. In addition to the two primary determinants of TAM (perceived usefulness and perceived ease of use), we added perceived compatibility and perceived fit because they are highly relevant and influential in the ERP context.

In this research, we are interested in examining to what extent the salient instrumental beliefs regarding using ERP systems impact end users' accep-

Figure 3. The research model

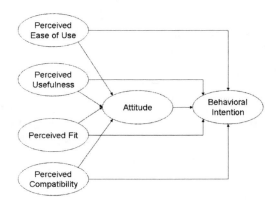

tance. The effects of the characteristics of other factors (e.g., characteristics of users and contextual environment) are outside the scope of this chapter. To focus on the key aspects of this research (i.e., assessing the impact of the four determinants on users' acceptance in terms of attitude and symbolic adoption) and to maintain parsimonious to our model, the interrelationships among the four antecedents (exogenous variables) are not examined in this study.

RESEARCH METHOD

The survey approach is used to test the research model. The survey was conducted in a midwestern public institution in the U.S. that implemented SAP R/3, a popular ERP package. The SAP R/3 system went live in July 1999 to support the administration functions of the institution. At the time of initial implementation, five SAP modules were utilized: Financial Accounting (FI), Controlling (CO), Human Resources (HR), Materials Management (MM), and Project Systems (PS). Subsequently, the Asset Management (AM) and Treasury (TR) modules were implemented. Survey questionnaires for this study were sent out to the users around the end of 2000.

Instrument Development

We developed a survey questionnaire to capture each of the constructs in the research model (as shown in Figure 3). Most of the theoretical constructs were operationalized using validated items from prior research. The items measuring perceived usefulness, perceived ease of use, and perceived compatibility were derived from Taylor and Todd (1995). The items measuring attitude toward system use were adopted from Hartwick and Barki (1994). The items measuring symbolic adoption were adopted from Karahanna (1999). The two items for perceived fit were developed specifically for this study. The constructs were measured on a 7-point Likert scale (see appendix).

Data Collection

Out of the surveys sent to all 525 SAP end users, 229 usable responses were received, resulting in an overall response rate of 44%. Majority of the SAP end users were department secretaries, purchasing clerks, general clerks, and other clerical staff. Female users comprise 84% of the sample, which is consistent with the user population. In terms of education level, 75% of the respondents hold diplomas or bachelor's degrees. Most respondents (about 70% of them) have attended 2 to 6 (SAP end user) training classes provided by the institution.

DATA ANALYSIS

Table 2 shows the descriptive statistics of the data collected. As shown in Table 3, Cronbach's Alpha coefficients range from 0.90 to 0.95, indicating very high reliability. The results of confirmatory factor analysis (CFA) are also included in Table 3, which demonstrate satisfactory convergent and discriminant validity of the constructs.

We conducted multiple linear regressions to test the research model. In order to obtain more precise estimates of the significant effects among constructs, regressions omitting non-significant variables were run, and the results are shown in Figure 4. The result of hypothesis tests is summarized in Table 4.

DISCUSSION OF RESULTS

In this study, we developed our research model based on the review of literature on users' acceptance of IT in mandatory contexts. We conducted a survey of end users' perceptions about using a newly implemented ERP system to test the hypotheses related to our model. By contrasting the results of our study with prior research, we draw conclusions concerning enterprise system adoption in the mandatory context and discuss the implications of our findings.

Table 2. Descriptive statistics

	No. of Items	Mean	Std. Deviation	Minimum	Maximum
perceived usefulness	3	3.11	1.40	1	7
perceived ease of use	3	3.51	1.62	1	7
perceived fit	2	3.64	1.49	1	7
perceived compatibility	3	3.79	1.42	1	7
attitude toward system use	2	3.02	1.49	1	7
symbolic adoption	3	3.16	1.41	1	7

Table 3. Results of confirmatory factor analysis and reliability analysis

	Perceived usefulness	Perceived ease of use	Perceived Compatibility	Perceived Fit	Attitude toward system use	Symbolic adoption
Cronbach's Alpha	.95	.94	.90	.91	.91	.91
perceived usefulness1	**0.778**	0.336	0.238	0.232	0.178	0.217
perceived usefulness2	**0.845**	0.234	0.186	0.184	0.103	0.271
perceived usefulness3	**0.799**	0.251	0.253	0.179	0.257	0.183
perceived ease of use1	0.273	**0.778**	0.236	0.212	0.195	0.262
perceived ease of use2	0.272	**0.832**	0.186	0.138	0.117	0.263
perceived ease of use3	0.285	**0.760**	0.274	0.205	0.242	0.277
perceived compatibility1	0.233	0.220	**0.819**	0.248	0.034	0.172
perceived compatibility2	0.316	0.257	**0.673**	0.223	0.323	0.327
perceived compatibility3	0.252	0.343	**0.638**	0.152	0.395	0.333
perceived fit1	0.246	0.221	0.251	**0.741**	0.283	0.328
perceived fit2	0.339	0.273	0.319	**0.721**	0.175	0.225
attitude1	0.239	0.211	0.181	0.303	**0.785**	0.320
attitude2	0.299	0.362	0.243	0.161	**0.626**	0.460
symbolic adoption1	0.222	0.311	0.181	0.166	0.240	**0.793**
symbolic adoption2	0.303	0.338	0.178	0.208	0.215	**0.764**
symbolic adoption3	0.169	0.165	0.251	0.200	0.177	**0.770**

Extraction Method: Principal Component Analysis.
Rotation Method: Varimax with Kaiser Normalization.
The factor loadings for each item on its construct are in bold

Figure 4. Final model with only significant relationships

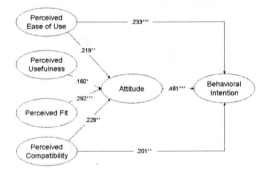

Table 4. Summary of hypothesis tests

Hypothesis	Support
H1: Attitude > Symbolic Adoption	Yes
H2: Perceived Usefulness > Symbolic Adoption	No
H3: Perceived Ease of Use > Symbolic Adoption	Yes
H4: Perceived Usefulness > Attitude	Yes
H5: Perceived Ease of Use > Attitude	Yes
H6: Perceived Compatibility > Symbolic Adoption	Yes
H7: Perceived Compatibility > Attitude	Yes
H8: Perceived Fit > Attitude	Yes
H9: Perceived Fit > Symbolic Adoption	No

Attitude Toward System Use

As shown in the final model (Figure 4), the basic relationships (PU-Attitude, PEU-Attitude) of the original TAM are found to be significant, which are in line with prior empirical studies (Davis et al., 1989; Mathieson, 1991; Taylor & Todd, 1995). In addition, our results also show that two additional determinants—perceived fit and perceived compatibility—account for a significant amount of variance in attitude. These two determinants have higher standardized coefficients than PU and PEU, suggesting that they have higher explanatory power than PU and PEU in the ERP context. A plausible explanation is that most of the prior studies were conducted in voluntary end-user computing contexts where users' perceived usefulness and ease of use are the primary factors in forming their attitude toward using the system. In the case of ERP, usefulness and ease of use cannot sufficiently explain end users' attitudes toward using the new system. Instead, the issue of compatibility and fit is of heightened relevance and importance because organizations implementing ERP systems often change their business processes to fit the software in order to take full advantage of the "best practices" offered by the ERP system (Nah, 2003; Siau, 2004). It is a difficult balancing act for the management of organizations to optimize their investment in ERP software through business process reengineering. End users may bear different feelings toward the heightened responsibility and accountability through the reengineering process. For some end users, the added responsibility and accountability through business process reengineering are regarded as an element of empowerment (Shang & Seddon, 2000); for others, they may be regarded as significant job burden. Therefore, users' beliefs concerning compatibility and fit are highly relevant in forming their affective feelings toward using the new system.

Symbolic Adoption

The final model (Figure 4) also indicates that perceived ease of use, attitude, and compatibility are significant determinants of symbolic adoption, with attitude as the primary determinant. This result, as well as the discriminant validity shown earlier (Table 3), provides support for the assertion by Rawstorne et al. (1998) and Karahanna (1999) that attitude and symbolic adoption are two distinct constructs. While attitude toward system use is the key driver of symbolic adoption, both compatibility and perceived ease of use also have direct positive effects on symbolic adoption. On the other hand, perceived usefulness and fit affect symbolic adoption only through attitude. This finding casts some light on our understanding of end users' acceptance of enterprise systems in mandatory usage contexts. Prior studies often use behavioral intention as the criterion variable, which may not be appropriate when system use is mandated. Symbolic adoption, the degree of voluntary mental acceptance of the idea component of an IT innovation, may well be a more appropriate construct to explain IT adoption when usage is mandated (Karahanna, 1999). Together with the findings from Brown et al. (2002), which demonstrate the lack of relationship between attitude and behavioral intention in mandatory contexts, our results provide another support for using symbolic adoption to assess end users' acceptance.

Perceived Usefulness and Perceived Ease of Use

As per TAM, PU and PEU are regarded as the dominant instrumental beliefs as drivers of individual usage intention. In addition, many empirical tests of TAM indicate that perceived usefulness is a strong determinant of behavioral intention, while perceived ease of use is a relatively weak determinant of intention (Venkatesh & Davis, 2000). Our study, however, shows a different pattern about the explanatory power of PU and PEU. First, PU and PEU have lower explanatory power than perceived compatibility and perceived fit in the ERP context. Second, compared with PU, PEU is a relatively strong determinant of attitude and symbolic adoption. As shown in a follow-up test (see Table 5), which examines the total influence of PU and PEU on symbolic adoption, PEU has a significantly higher coefficient than that of PU.

We attribute the weaker influence of PU on user's acceptance to the specific setting of mandatory ERP use. When the usage is mandated, the instrumental beliefs regarding the ERP system lean heavily toward how to use the system to perform the routine work, rather than how to improve productivity. Therefore, users may regard compatibility and fit as more important consider-ations. Compared with PU, PEU's influence is relatively elevated in the ERP context. We argue that in mandatory usage context, ease of use will have a higher instrumental value than usefulness.

Implications

In summary, our findings show a different pattern of relationships between important instrumental beliefs and users' acceptance constructs (attitude and symbolic adoption), as compared with prior studies that were conducted mainly in voluntary contexts. Our findings have significant implications for organizations striving to engender positive attitudes toward newly adopted enterprise-wide software packages and mandatory applications. In order to create positive mental acceptance among end users, organizational interventions should also focus on the issue of compatibility, which has both direct and indirect effects on

Table 5. The standardized regression coefficients

	Beta	t	Sig.
perceived usefulness	.298	4.70	.000
perceived ease of use	.485	7.66	.000

Dependent Variable: symbolic adoption
Adjusted R square: .520
Regression Sig.: .000

symbolic adoption, as well as the issue of technology fit with organizational context, which influences symbolic adoption through attitude.

In order for an ERP system to be accepted by its end users, the system must not only be perceived as useful and easy to use, it is also important that the end users perceive the system to be compatible with their values and past experiences, and to be a good fit with the organizational context. Organizational fit with ERP is critical and has been found to be a critical success factor of ERP implementation (Hong & Kim, 2002).

User acceptance is necessary for effective use and appropriation of an ERP system, so organizations can gain maximum benefits from the system (Boudreau, 2003). For an ERP system to be perceived as useful and easy to use, training must be provided to the end users. In order for end users to understand the system and perceive it to be compatible with their values and past experiences, ample training and hands-on experiences are needed. Such training should not only focus on the keystrokes and procedures to complete the transactions, but should also provide users with a high-level view and understanding of the business process and their corresponding mappings to the system procedures. If the mappings between the business process and the current and previous procedures are apparent to users, they are more likely to perceive the ERP system to be compatible with their previous experiences. Hence, end-user training should be designed in such a way that it covers the different levels of abstractions and mappings between the business processes and the ways they are represented in the ERP system.

Users also need to perceive a fit between the ERP software and the business and organizational needs for them to accept the system. One way to achieve fit is to involve functional experts in the selection and evaluation of the ERP software package. Another complementary approach is to carry out a fit-gap analysis (Nadkarni & Nah, 2003; Sieber et al., 2000) to thoroughly understand the fits and gaps between the available ERP software packages and the needs of the organizations before selecting the package that fits the best. Appropriate customization should also be carried out to achieve optimal fit.

CONCLUSION

To address the key issues in end users' acceptance of complex, integrated, enterprise-wide information systems such as ERP, researchers are thriving in two fronts. Some researchers attempt to effectively conceptualize and operationalize the variable of system use. For instance, Straub, Limayem, and Karahanna (1995) claimed that the wide variation of system usage measures hinders the efforts of MIS researchers to compare findings across studies. Their study reveals the difference between self-reported and computer-reported system use. Saga and Zmud (1994) classified system use based on three levels of infusion: extended use, integrative use, and emergent use. They stressed the infusion of technology as a key variable, that is, the extent to which an innovation's features are used in a complete and sophisticated way. More recently, Boudreau (2003) emphasized on the quality of use, which refers to one's ability to correctly exploit the appropriate capabilities of a software system in the most relevant circumstances. In another front, some researchers focus on users' acceptance of an IT innovation, which is a key factor influencing effective system use. Symbolic adoption (Karahanna, 1999) is conceptualized as one measure of users' mental acceptance and is proposed to replace adoption intention in contexts where use is mandated. Its determinants may include attitude, the characteristics of the technology, the characteristics of the users, such as self-efficacy (Agarwal & Prasad, 1997), and the characteristics of the contextual environment, such as subjective norms and facilitating conditions.

Accordingly, the present study can be classified in the latter group. The results of this study provide some empirical support for the construct of symbolic adoption. In addition, we investigated the impact of the characteristics of technology on users' attitude and symbolic adoption. The findings also have significant managerial implications on successful implementation of ERP systems, which is more complex and integrated than many other types of systems.

In conclusion, users' acceptance of ERP systems remains a complex and important phenomenon. Future research is needed to investigate other factors that contribute to ERP user acceptance and to study the importance and consequences of end-user acceptance in the ERP context.

REFERENCES

Adamson, I., & Shine, J. (2003). Extending the new technology acceptance model to measure the end user information systems satisfaction in a mandatory environment: A bank's treasury. *Technology Analysis & Strategic Management, 15*(4), 441-455.

Agarwal, R., & Karahanna, E. (2000). Time flies when you're having fun: Cognitive absorption and beliefs about information technology usage. *MIS Quarterly, 24*(4), 665-694.

Agarwal, R., & Prasad, J. (1997). The role of innovation characteristics and perceived voluntariness in the acceptance of information technologies. *Decision Sciences, 28*(3), 557-582.

Ajzen, I., & Fishbein, M. (1980). *Understanding attitudes and predicting behavior*. Englewood Cliffs, NJ: Prentice Hall.

Amoako-Gyampah, K., & Salam, A. F. (2004). An extension of the technology acceptance model in an ERP implementation environment. *Information & Management, 41*(6), 731-745.

Bagchi, S., Kanungo, S., & Dasgupta, S. (2003). Modeling use of enterprise resource planning systems: A path analytic study. *European Journal of Information Systems, 12*(2), 142-158.

Barker, T., & Frolick, M. N. (2003). ERP implementation failure: A case study. *Information Systems Management, 20*(4), 43-49.

Boudreau, M.-C. (2003, January 6-9). Learning to use ERP technology: A causal model. *Proceedings of the 36th Hawaii International Conference on System Sciences,* Big Island, Hawaii (p. 235).

Brown, S. A., Massey, A. P., Montoya-Weiss, M. M., & Burkman, J. R. (2002). Do I really have to? User acceptance of mandated technology. *European Journal of Information Systems, 11*(4), 283-295.

Davenport, T. H. (1998). Putting the enterprise into the enterprise system. *Harvard Business Review, 76*(4), 121-131.

Davis, F. D. (1989). Perceived usefulness, perceived ease of use, and user acceptance of information technology. *MIS Quarterly, 13*(3), 318-340.

Davis, F. D., Bagozzi, R. P., & Warshaw, P. R. (1989). User acceptance of computer technology: A comparison of two theoretical models. *Management Science, 35*(8), 982-1003.

Hartwick, J., & Barki, H. (1994). Explaining the role of user participation in information system use. *Management Science, 40*(4), 440-464.

Hong, K. K., & Kim, Y. G. (2002). The critical success factors for ERP implementation: An organizational fit perspective. *Information and Management, 40*(1), 25-40.

Karahanna, E. (1999, July). Symbolic adoption of information technology. *Proceedings of the International Decision Sciences Institute,* Athens, Greece.

Karahanna, E., & Straub, D. W. (1999). Information technology adoption across time: A cross-sectional comparison of pre-adoption and post-adoption beliefs. *MIS Quarterly, 23*(2), 183-213.

Klonglan, G. E., & Coward, E. W. J. (1970). The concept of symbolic adoption: A suggested interpretation. *Rural Sociology, 35*(1), 77-83.

Legris, P., Ingham, J., & Collerette, P. (2003). Why do people use information technology? A critical review of the technology acceptance model. *Information & Management, 40*(3), 191-204.

Mathieson, K. (1991). Predicting user intentions: Comparing the technology acceptance model with the theory of planned behavior. *Information Systems Research, 2*(3), 173-191.

Melone, N. P. (1990). A theoretical assessment of the user-satisfaction construct in information systems research. *Management Science, 36*(1), 76-91.

Miranda, R. (1999). The rise of ERP technology in the public sector. *Government Finance Review, 15*(4), 9-17.

Moore, G. C., & Benbasat, I. (1991). Development of an instrument to measure the perceptions of adopting an information technology innovation. *Information Systems Research, 2*(3), 192-222.

Nadkarni, S., & Nah, F. (2003). Aggregated causal maps: An approach to elicit and aggregate the knowledge of multiple experts. *Communications of the Association for Information Systems, 12*, 406-436.

Nah, F. (2003). Introduction: Special issue on enterprise resource planning. *International Journal of Human-Computer Interaction, 16*(1), 1-3.

Pozzebon, M. (2000, August 10-13). *Combining a structuration approach with a behavioral-based model to investigate ERP usage.* Paper presented at the Americas Conference on Information Systems, Long Beach, CA.

Rawstorne, P., Jayasuriya, R., & Caputi, P. (1998, December 13-16). An integrative model of information systems use in mandatory environments. *Proceedings of the International Conference on Information Systems,* Helsinki, Finland (pp. 325-330).

Rawstorne, P., Jayasuriya, R., & Caputi, P. (2000, December 10-13). Issues in predicting and explaining usage behaviors with the technology acceptance model and the theory of planned behavior when usage is mandatory. *Proceedings of the International Conference on Information Systems,* Brisbane, Australia (pp. 35-44).

Robey, D., Ross, J. W., & Boudreau, M.-C. (2002). Learning to implement enterprise systems: An exploratory study of the dialectics of change. *Journal of Management Information Systems, 19*(1), 17-46.

Rogers, E. M. (1995). *Diffusion of innovations* (4th ed.). New York: Free Press.

Saga, V., & Zmud, R. W. (1994). The nature and determinants of it acceptance, routinization, and infusion. In L. Levine (Ed.), *Diffusion, transfer, and implementation of information technology* (pp. 67-86). New York: North-Holland.

Scott, J. E., & Vessey, I. (2002). Managing risks in enterprise systems implementations. *Communications of the ACM, 45*(4), 74-81.

Shang, S., & Seddon, P. B. (2000, August 10-13). A comprehensive framework for classifying the benefits of ERP systems. *Proceedings of the Americas Conference on Information Systems,* Long Beach, CA (pp. 1005-1014).

Siau, K. (2004). Enterprise resource planning (ERP) implementation methodologies. *Journal of Database Management, 15*(1), 1-6.

Sieber, T., Siau, K., Nah, F., & Sieber, M. (2000). Sap implementation at the University of Nebraska. *Journal of Information Technology Cases and Applications, 2*(1), 41-72.

Soh, C., Kien, S. S., Boh, W. F., & Tang, M. (2003). Misalignments in ERP implementation: A dialectic perspective. *International Journal of Human-Computer Interaction, 16*(1), 81-100.

Soh, C., Kien, S. S., & Tay-Yap, J. (2000). Cultural fits and misfits: Is ERP a universal solution? *Communications of the ACM, 43*(4), 47-51.

Straub, D. W., Limayen, M., & Karahanna, E. (1995). Measuring system usage: Implications for IS theory testing. *Management Science, 41*(8), 1328-1132.

Taylor, S., & Todd, P. A. (1995). Understanding information technology usage: A test of competing models. *Information Systems Research, 6*(2), 144-176.

Umble, E. J., & Umble, M. M. (2002). Avoid ERP implementation failure. *Industrial Management, 44*(1), 25-33.

Venkatesh, V., & Davis, F. D. (2000). A theoretical extension of the technology acceptance model: Four longitudinal field studies. *Management Science, 46*(2), 186-204.

Wah, L. (2000). Give ERP a chance. *Management Review, 89*(3), 20-24.

APPENDIX: SURVEY QUESTIONNAIRE

Strongly Agree	Agree	Somewhat Agree	Neutral	Somewhat Disagree	Disagree	Strongly Disagree
1	2	3	4	5	6	7

Perceived Usefulness

1. Using the SAP system will make my work more efficient.
   1   2   3   4   5   6   7

2. Using the SAP system will increase my job performance.
   1   2   3   4   5   6   7

3. Using the SAP system will increase the productivity of my work.
   1   2   3   4   5   6   7

Perceived Ease of Use

1. My interaction with the SAP system is clear and understandable.
   1   2   3   4   5   6   7

2. It is easy for me to remember how to perform my regular job assignments using the SAP system.
   1   2   3   4   5   6   7

3. Overall, I find the SAP system easy to use.
   1   2   3   4   5   6   7

Strongly Agree	Agree	Somewhat Agree	Neutral	Somewhat Disagree	Disagree	Strongly Disagree
1	2	3	4	5	6	7

Perceived Compatibility

1. The setup of the SAP system is compatible with the way I worked before.

1	2	3	4	5	6	7

2. Using the SAP system is compatible with the way I like to work.

1	2	3	4	5	6	7

3. The setup of the SAP system is compatible with my style of work.

1	2	3	4	5	6	7

Perceived Fit

1. The SAP system fits well with the business needs of my campus.

1	2	3	4	5	6	7

2. The SAP system fits well with the business needs of my department.

1	2	3	4	5	6	7

Attitude concerning System Use

1. Using the SAP system is a good idea.

1	2	3	4	5	6	7

2. I like the idea of using the SAP system to perform my job.

1	2	3	4	5	6	7

Symbolic Adoption

1. I am enthusiastic about using the SAP system.

1	2	3	4	5	6	7

2. I am excited about using the SAP system in my workplace.

1	2	3	4	5	6	7

3. It is my desire to see the full utilization and deployment of the SAP system.

1	2	3	4	5	6	7

Chapter VIII

Inclusion of Social Subsystem Issues in IT Investment Decisions:
An Empirical Assessment

Sherry D. Ryan
University of North Texas, USA

Michael S. Gates
University of North Texas, USA

ABSTRACT

Researchers have attempted to augment the traditional cost/benefit analysis model used in the IT decision process. However, frequently social subsystem issues are inadequately considered. Survey data, collected from a U.S. sample of 200 executives, provides an empirical assessment of how these issues compare with other IT decision criteria given differing decision types. The social subsystem issues considered most important by decision makers are also identified and the manner by which they consider these issues is investigated.

INTRODUCTION

In the last several decades, organizations around the world have made enormous investments in information technology (IT) (Siegel, 1998). However, some claim that nearly one third of the outlays for IT are wasted (Alter, 1997). The Standish Group research (The Chaos Report White Paper) shows that 31% of IT projects are canceled before they are completed. Further, results indicate that 53% of IT projects will cost nearly double the original estimates (Webb, 1997). While there are many factors that lead to high failure rates and cost overruns, a contributor is the lack of foresight in IT acquisition or investment processes (Holme, 1997; GAO, 1993).

IT investment decisions have traditionally focused on financial or technological issues, using cost versus benefit analysis. Responding to what appears to be underperformance in anticipated IT investment payoffs, both researchers and practitioners have suggested that traditional valuation analyses are inadequate, and have called for additional research to identify seldom-considered costs and benefits (Hitt & Brynjolfsson, 1996).

Researchers have augmented the traditional cost/benefit approach by adding a strategic perspective to IT investment decisions (e.g., Clemons & Weber, 1990; Post et al., 1995). However, while strategic criteria are increasingly being recognized in IT decisions (Bacon, 1992), some have suggested the dimension that is inadequately considered concerns the organizational issues associated with *employees* in the IT implementation and adoption process (Slater, 1995; Ryan & Harrison 2000). Consistent with the terminology and principles of socio-technical systems (STS) theory (Trist, 1982), we define these issues originating from employees' assessments, capabilities, decisions, and task interdependencies as *social subsystem issues* (Emery, 1962). Social subsystem benefits and costs do accrue when an IT is acquired (Markus & Benjamin, 1996). However, without awareness or formal consideration of social subsystem issues, organizations have no way of understanding their impact on the success and potential payoff of the chosen IT.

Some prior research focusing on IT valuation has examined social subsystem issues. For example, Hochstrasser (1990) and Keen (1991) addressed techniques to evaluate "soft" organizational costs, some of which were in the social subsystem domain. Belcher and Watson (1993) included certain social subsystem benefits when assessing the returns of an Executive Information System (EIS). Holden and Wilhelmij (1995) used a knowledge value-added technique to evaluate people, culture and knowledge. Ryan and Harrison (2000) investigated the types of social subsystem costs and benefits decision makers incorporate into their decision process.

Our investigation continues this stream of research, taking a descriptive approach to understanding the incorporation of these issues. It was motivated by two primary research questions:

- **(RQ1):** What weight does the decision maker place on social subsystem issues as compared with technological or financial factors?
- **(RQ2):** To what extent are social subsystem issues considered in an explicit manner, an implicit manner, or not at all?

In examining these questions, we first present the theoretical foundation for our work and detail our research hypotheses. We then describe the methodology used to conduct our study. Finally, we present our research findings and discuss their implications. We believe our findings extend prior research by: (a) providing an empirical assessment of how social subsystem issues compare with other IT decision criteria given differing decision types, (b) identifying which social subsystem issues are considered most important by decision makers, and (c) distinguishing the manner by which these social subsystem issues are considered.

THEORETICAL BACKGROUND AND RESEARCH HYPOTHESES

Sociotechnical systems (STS) theory provides a strong theoretical basis for investigating issues in the technological and human resource domains. The social subsystem consists of employees and the skills, knowledge, abilities, interrelationships, ideas, attitudes, and needs they bring to work. The technological system incorporates the tools, devices, and techniques used within the social subsystem to accomplish organizational tasks (Pasmore, 1995). Relying on the key concept of joint optimization, which states that an organization will perform optimally only if the interdependency between social and technological subsystems is explicitly recognized, the STS approach views the social subsystem and the technological subsystem as interrelated components of the organizational whole. Each subsystem must be designed to fit the requirements of the other, so that superior results can be achieved (Pasmore et al., 1982). In this interdependent relationship, incorrect specifications in one subsystem may greatly impact the performance of the overall organizational system (DeGreene, 1973; Pasmore et al., 1982).

The STS approach can also be applied to the IT investment process, and it provides a conceptual framework with which to consider the close interrelationship between the technological and social subsystems. When new IT is introduced, it must be implemented in both the technological subsystem (for example, the IT must be installed and integrated into the existing systems architecture) and in the social subsystem (for example, by training end-users how to use the technology). However, many social subsystem issues, which are prescribed as crucial considerations in literature evaluating IT implementations, are never included in the evaluation process. Ryan and Harrision (2000) found that executives seldom considered such important concepts as increased role conflict or greater employee empowerment. In fact, better communication, which is defined as enhanced interaction enabling greater lateral coordination (Migliarese & Paolucci, 1995), was incorporated into only 3% of the investment decisions, while only 3% of executives sampled ever mentioned considering such important employee-related concerns as morale or job dissatisfaction.

But all IT decisions do not have the same interdependency or "spill-over" effect in the social subsystem. Using STS theory as a theoretical basis also, Daft (1978) proposed a dual-core model to explain varying attributes of administrative and technical innovations. Swanson (1994) extended this work to account for the unique nature of IS innovation by proposing a tri-core model. Type I, or what Swanson termed Information Core innovations, focus on the management and administrative support of IS work or the technical IS task itself. Large-scale relational DBMS or CASE tools are typical examples. Other examples might include language compilers, developer's toolkits, or communication network monitors. Type II, or Administrative Core innovations, support functions of the business such as payroll systems or e-mail. Type III, Technical Core innovations, are those embedded in the elemental technology for producing the organization's goods and services, and examples in this category include CAD/CAM or MRP systems.

Building upon Swanson's tri-core model, Ryan and Harrison (2000) created a two-dimensional framework consisting of Swanson's innovation types on one dimension and the degree of change induced by an IT decision (Orlikowski, 1993) on the other dimension.

Based on interviews with IT decision makers, their data suggested that when taken together, these two dimensions implied a single continuum they termed "social subsystem disruption." This social subsystem disruption continuum suggests that not all decisions engender the same degree of social subsystem cost and benefit consideration. At the low end of the continuum, Type I (Information Core) investments induce little process change, and therefore typically create little social subsystem disruption. However, IT investment decisions at the high end of the disruption continuum, associated with radical change or major

Figure 1. Social subsystem disruption continuum

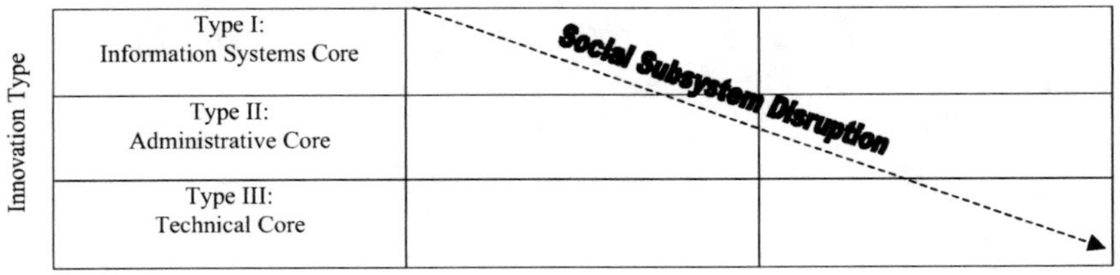

reengineering of core business processes, cause significant social subsystem disruption. This overall framework provides a rich lens through which actual IT investment decisions and their incorporation of social subsystem issues can be evaluated.

At the low end of the social subsystem disruption continuum, because Type I (Information Core) decisions induce little social subsystem change, one might suppose that these issues will not be the predominant IT decision criteria. However, because these Information Core decisions frequently involve IT infrastructure, one would expect that technical issues be carefully considered for these decision types.

We propose that financial issues will also be predominant decision criteria. IT investment decisions often rely heavily on traditional financial models. A recent study showed that the number of U.S. firms requiring IS executives to demonstrate the potential payback, revenue, or budget impact of their IT projects is sharply on the rise (Violino, 1998). Therefore, we propose:

- **H1:** Social subsystem issues will be considered less than (a) technical or (b) financial issues in decisions that will induce little disruption.

A continuum of social subsystem disruption incorporates the idea that not all decisions about IT engender the same degree of social subsystem consideration. The organizational context matters fundamentally, and this implies that the amount of change in the technological subsystem is not linked one-to-one with consequences for the social subsystem. Executives are likely to consider more social subsystem issues when the potential for social subsystem disruption is high (Ryan & Harrison, 2000). For example, high disruption often leads to strong employee resistance, requiring significant change management to overcome. Grover et al. (1995) found that this increased attention to managing change in the social subsystem is critical for the success of IT implementations that alter core business processes. Therefore, we propose:

- **H2:** Social subsystem issues will be considered more than technical issues in decisions that will induce great disruption.

Despite the increased importance of social subsystem issues at the high end of the disruption continuum, we propose that financial issues continue to be the predominant decision criteria in the investment decision process. IT executives are under increasing pressure to justify the contribution of IT expenditures (Myers et al., 1997). Often IT decision makers are required to present financial analyses of the impact their proposed IT changes will have on the corporate "bottom line" (Violino, 1998). We therefore propose:

- **H3:** Social subsystem issues will be considered less than financial issues in decisions that will induce great disruption.

Many of the social subsystem issues do not have well-established metrics or algorithms by which they can be evaluated (e.g., an employee's learning curve). As a result, formal or explicit evaluation of these issues may not be part of the decision process. Yet, evidence exists that decision makers think about these issues, at least on some occasions (Ryan & Harrison, 2000). While social subsystem issues may not be formally included in the decision process, they may be informally or implicitly considered to some degree. Therefore, we propose:

- **H4:** Implicit consideration of social subsystem issues will be considered to a greater extent for both (a) decisions that induce little disruption and (b) decisions that induce great disruption.

METHODOLOGY

Conduct of the Study

Our investigation consisted of three phases: exploratory interviews used as basis for survey development, an extensive pilot study to modify the survey instrument, and the administration of the final survey. Each phase is described below.

Interviews

Thirty semi-structured interviews were performed to obtain insight on issues decision makers consider when making an IT investment decision. The target population for this phase consisted of individuals who have decision-making authority at the organizational or divisional level regarding whether an IT innovation should be acquired. A key objective was to obtain broad variance in the set of responses; therefore these IT executives were selected from organizations in diverse industries with varying organizational sizes. Sixteen executives were from small firms (less than 1,000 employees) and 14 executives from large firms (greater than 1,000 employees). Firms from both service and manufacturing industries were represented.

The interviews began with background and broad domain questions, and were subsequently funneled into three specific areas: social subsystem, financial, and technical. For example, a broad domain question that was asked was: "What are the steps in your organization's IT decision process?" A more specific question in the financial area was: "Do all projects go through a budgetary process?" The interviews, which ranged from 40 to 60 minutes in length, were tape recorded and transcribed. Based upon these interviews, survey questions were developed.

Pilot Study

The survey was refined through four stages. First, several academic experts in the IS field reviewed the survey, and modifications were made based on expert comments. Next, seven IT executives from the Society of Information Management (SIM) organization completed a pilot survey and provided comments as to the appropriateness and clarity of the questions and the scenarios. After further modifications, 12 additional content experts reviewed a third iteration of changes to the questionnaire, and based on their recommendations, the survey was finalized.

Survey

Firms in diverse industries and regions with varying organizational sizes were selected for the mail survey. This deliberately maximized the breadth and potential generalizability of results from the sample, while mitigating against the findings being specific to a particular type of firm. Firms from major industry categories such as aerospace, agriculture, construction, government, health care, real estate, and many others were represented. In each firm, decision makers with overall or division-level authority regarding IT investments were surveyed.

Three sources were used for firm contacts. The first source was a list of 539 IT manager names, organizations and addresses provided by the executive education branch of a large, international hardware and software manufacturing company. The second source was provided by a computer research company, Applied Computer Research, from their database of over 15,000 IT professionals. The 575 names and addresses used in this research were randomly selected from individuals classified as a " top computer executive." A third source of contacts was obtained from the 1997 Edition of the CORPTECH database, produced by Corporate Technology Information Services. A list of 401 companies was selected from this database with contacts for the top executive responsible for MIS.

Measures

Social Subsystem Issues

The social subsystem issues decision makers most frequently incorporate into their decisions are: productivity, quality, improved decision-making ability, labor savings, training, change management, communication with the employees about the new IT, and on-the-job learning curve (Ryan & Harrison, 2000, Ryan, Harrison & Schkade, 2002). Ryan and Harrison (2000) note that some of these categories approach the boundary between the social and technical subsystems (e.g., productivity and labor savings). They state, "while these costs and benefits are clearly 'human-related' and result from employee effort, judgments, or presence, they are also highly dependent upon the technical tools used by these social subsystem members, demonstrating the high degree of interdependency between the social and technical subsystems" (Ryan & Harrison, 2000, pp. 19-20). Two items were created for each of these categories. One item represented implicit consideration of a specific social subsystem issue, and the other item represented explicit consideration of the same social subsystem issue. For example, for Productivity, these items were created:

- **Implicit:** In my organization, we would spend effort or resources thinking about the impact this project will have on end-user productivity.
- **Explicit:** In my organization, we would spend effort or resources forecasting, with input from the line managers, how much the choices will affect the amount of work employees can handle.

A seven-point Likert scale was used for responses to the items with anchors ranging from No to An Extraordinary Amount. The anchors were considered by subject respondents to be equally spaced (Bass, Cascio & O'Conner, 1974).

Explicit versus implicit consideration of social subsystem issues can be viewed from several perspectives. One perspective is that explicit consideration means that each item is quantified. However, Bacon (1992) indicated that even large companies do not always make their decisions strictly on the basis of quantification techniques. Therefore, this perspective of equating quantification with explicit may be too narrow.

A broader definition in which explicit refers to "clearly developed or formulated," and implicit refers to "implied, tacitly understood, rather than expressly stated" was used to develop a more inclusive perspective with which to evaluate when decision makers explicitly or implicitly consider social subsystem issues. When an IT decision maker engages in specific, observable or manifest actions to determine the issues associated with an IT investment decision, he or she is acting explicitly; on the other hand, if the considerations are solely cognitive in nature, then the executive is viewed as acting implicitly only.

Financial and Technical Issues

Based upon the exploratory interviews, five questions were developed to measure technical decision issues and three questions were developed to measure financial issues. These questions were refined through the pilot process previously discussed.

The social subsystem, financial and technical issues scales used in this study were found to be internally consistent. The most common method of assessing the reliability of an instrument is through the use of Cronbach's alpha (Zmud &

Boynton, 1989). The reliability estimate of each measure is reported in Table 1, demonstrating the internal consistency of these measures.

Another important criterion for a well-developed survey includes validity, which is often discussed in terms of two distinguishable types: content and construct (Zmud & Boynton, 1989). A content valid scale is one that has drawn representative questions from a "universal pool" (Kerlinger, 1986). Cronbach (1971) indicated that content validity could be established by having the instrument reviewed by experts in the field. The content validity of this survey was established in two ways. First, the items were derived from the exploratory interviews with IT executives. Second, the field experts who participated in the pilot study gave written and oral feedback concerning the survey.

The second type of validity, construct validity, determines whether the scale measures what it purports to measure. As suggested by Zmud and Boynton (1989), this was assessed through factor analysis. An iterated principal axes analysis was conducted using an orthogonal rotation (Loehlin, 1992). Three factors were apparent when inspecting a scree plot of successive eigenvalues against their ordinal position (Cattell 1966). As shown in Table 2, one pertained to social subsystem issues only, a second to technical issues only, and the third to financial issues only, supporting the validity of these three distinct constructs.

Manipulated Variable: Decision Type

Two scenarios were written to represent IT decisions along opposite ends of the social subsystem disruption continuum: (1) a Type I, Information Systems Core, decision inducing little process change, represented a *low social subsystem disruption* decision, and (2) a Type III, Technical Core, decision inducing great process change, represented a *high social subsystem disruption* decision. The respondents were asked to read each scenario, then answer the questions regarding how much effort or resources they would spend considering each of the social, financial, and technical issues mentioned above.

The scenarios were counter-balanced so that half of the surveys had the "high disruption" scenario placed first in the survey (Form 1) and the other half had the "low disruption" scenario placed first (Form 2). T-tests showed that the sequence of the survey form had insignificant effects, ($p < 0.05$). To make sure that executives' clearly differentiated the "low" and "high" social subsystem disruption decisions, after each scenario each executive was asked: "How much do you think this project will affect the way the users do their business from day

Table 1. Instrument reliabilities (Cronbach's α)

Measure	Alpha
Social Subsystem Issues	0.97
Technological Decision Issues	0.84
Financial Decision Issues	0.89

Table 2. Factor analysis

Category	Disruption Scenario	Item	Factor 1	Factor 2	Factor 3
SS	High	Calculating the extra time managers will need to spend managing this change.	0.87		
SS	High	Forecasting , with input from the line managers, how much the choices will affect the amount of work employees can handle.	0.81		
SS	Low	Calculating the extra time managers will need to spend managing this change.	0.81		
SS	Low	Evaluating the costs of telling and "selling" the decision to the users.	0.81		
SS	Low	Thinking about the costs of communicating information about the change to users.	0.80		
SS	High	Projecting the decrease in performance due to the employees' learning curve.	0.80		
SS	High	Evaluating the costs of telling and "selling" the decision to the users.	0.76		
SS	High	Thinking about the costs of communicating information about the change to users.	0.76		
SS	Low	Forecasting, with input from the line managers, how much the choices will affect the amount of work employees can handle.	0.76		
SS	High	Considering the time managers will need to spend overseeing the change.	0.76		
SS	High	Projecting the effect this project will have on the quality of employee work.	0.76		
SS	Low	Considering the time managers will need to spend overseeing the change.	0.74		
SS	Low	Projecting the decrease in performance due to the employees' learning curve.	0.74		
SS	High	Considering the impact that the users' learning curve will have on productivity.	0.74		
SS	Low	Thinking about the amount and the cost of training that end users will need.	0.66		
SS	Low	Considering the impact that the users' learning curve will have on productivity.	0.73		
SS	Low	Projecting the effect this project will have on the quality of employee work.	0.69		
SS	Low	Projecting the benefits of more timely decisions that result because of this project.	0.68		
SS	High	Thinking about the amount and the cost of training that end users will need.	0.67		
SS	High	Estimating the expense of training the users.	0.64		
SS	High	Mulling over how much these options will help end users make quicker decisions.	0.60		
SS	High	Thinking about the effect this will have on the quality of the employees' work.	0.60		
SS	High	Projecting the benefits of more timely decisions that result because of this project.	0.60		
SS	Low	Mulling over how much these options will help end users make quicker decisions.	0.58		
SS	Low	Estimating the expense of training the users.	0.58		
SS	Low	Thinking about the effect this will have on the quality of the employees' work.	0.57		
SS	Low	Quantifying the possible savings from head count reductions.	0.55		
SS	High	Thinking about the impact this project will have on end user productivity.	0.54		
SS	Low	Considering whether this decision will consolidate or eliminate jobs.	0.48		
SS	High	Considering whether this decision will consolidate or eliminate jobs.	0.48		
SS	Low	Thinking about the impact this project will have on end user productivity.	0.45		
SS	High	Quantifying the possible savings from head count reductions.	0.42		
TECH	Low	Evaluating system performance and capacity characteristics		0.83	
TECH	Low	Investigating the ability to expand or modify our option to meet changing requirements.		0.72	
TECH	Low	Assessing the need for additional co-requisite hardware or software.		0.72	
TECH	Low	Evaluating how easily the options can be integrated with our existing systems		0.64	
TECH	High	Investigating the ability to expand or modify our option to meet changing requirements.		0.61	
TECH	High	Evaluating how easily the options can be integrated with our existing systems.		0.58	
TECH	High	Evaluating the performance and capacity characteristics		0.53	
TECH	High	Assessing the need for additional co-requisite hardware or software.		0.50	
TECH	High	Evaluating if we have the technical skills to implement and support the options.		0.48	
TECH	Low	Evaluating if we have the technical skills to implement and support the options.		0.43	
FIN	Low	Considering whether the budget allows for this project.			0.82
FIN	High	Considering whether the budget allows for this project.			0.82
FIN	High	Gathering information about the total financial outlay of each option.			0.75
FIN	Low	Gathering information about the total financial outlay of each option.			0.72
FIN	High	Weighing the monetary costs and benefits of the various options.			0.69
FIN	Low	Weighing the monetary costs and benefits of the various options.			0.67

to day?" A matched-pair t-test ($t194 = 7.52, p < 0.01$), supported the validity and soundness of the manipulation.

Demographic Profile

Surveys were mailed to 1,515 firms. Of those, 1,242 were deliverable to the addressee; 200 firms replied to the written survey, yielding a 16% response rate. Other national surveys of top executives have had comparable response rates (e.g., Chan et al., 1997; Rai & Patnayakuni, 1996). Non-response bias was evaluated by the frequently used method of treating responses received after the deadline given (three weeks after the survey was mailed to the respondents) as being representative of non-respondents' bias (Karahanna, Straub, & Chervany, 1999). T-tests on important demographic variables and constructs showed no significant differences between respondents and non-respondents. Although the possibility of lack of representativeness to the population of IT executives is not completely removed, it should be noted that the survey responses were from a diverse range of firms and persons, ensuring multiple sources of variance and supporting the generalizability of its conclusions.

The firms responding to the survey represented a wide-ranging and varied sample in terms of organizational size, geographical distribution, and types of technologies used. Responses were received from firms in 37 states. Median annual revenue of the firms was reported as $150 million, with a median annual IT budget of $1.7 million. The median number of employees in these firms was 650, with a median of 17 IT workers. Twenty-eight percent of the responding firms were non-profit organizations. When asked to categorize their firm as either manufacturing or service, 125 responded service, 68 manufacturing, and seven gave no response.

The target respondent from this study was the senior IT executive responsible for making IT investment decisions, consistent with previous IT investment and planning research (Bacon, 1992; Premkumar & King, 1994). The use of the senior IT executive as a "key informant" is a common approach used in empirical IS studies (Segars & Grover, 1998). In survey research, these IT executives take on the role of a key informant, and provide information on collective organizational properties rather than personal attitudes and behaviors (Venkatraman, 1989). With this approach, such informants are chosen because of their particular qualifications such as rank, experience, or expert knowledge. To ensure the suitability of the responses, we selected the top computer executive in each organization as described above. Two percent of those who responded were presidents, 50% were vice presidents or directors of IS/IT, 34% held the title of chief information officer or IS/IT manager, 4% were chief financial officers or controllers, and 10% held some other title. These titles show the appropriateness of the sample.

Seventy-eight percent of the respondents were male. The executives' average tenure in their current position was 7.2 years (median = 5 years) and their average age was 47. The average number of years the executives had made IT decisions was 13.2 years and 72% had spent at least half their career in Information Systems.

RESULTS

Hypotheses 1-3 relate to our first research question concerning the weight decision makers place on social subsystem issues compared with technical or financial issues. The mean responses to the technical, financial and social subsystem issues are depicted by decision type in Figure 2. For both decisions, financial issues had the highest mean response, followed by technical issues, with social subsystem issues lowest in both cases. In the low process disruption

Figure 5. Implicit vs. explicit consideration—High process disruption decision.

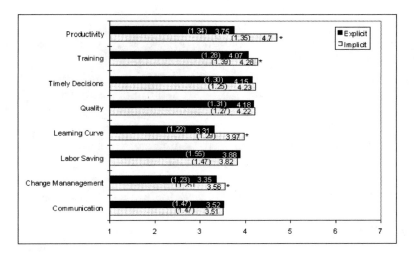

Table 4. Differences in the means of implicit vs. explicit social subsystem issues—High disruption decision

Social Subsystem Issue	t-test statistic	p-value
Productivity	10.37	0.01*
Training	2.67	0.01*
Timely Decisions	1.04	0.30
Quality	0.36	0.71
Learning Curve	8.92	0.01*
Labor Saving	-0.90	0.37
Change Management	3.21	0.01*
Communication	-0.11	0.92

decision, the difference between the financial mean and the social subsystem mean was significant, $t189 = 16.47$, $p < 0.01$, as was the difference between the technical and social subsystem mean, $t189 = 14.13$, $p < 0.01$, thus supporting Hypotheses 1a and 1b.

For the high process disruption decision, the difference between the technical and social subsystem mean was significant, $t189 = 11.36$, $p < 0.01$. However, while we had hypothesized that the social subsystem issues mean would be higher than that of the technical issues, our data show it to be lower. Thus, Hypothesis 2 is not supported. Hypothesis 3, however, which posits a significant difference between the financial mean and the social subsystem mean, was strongly supported, $t189 = 13.07$, $p < 0.01$.

Our second research question investigated whether social subsystem issues are considered explicitly or implicitly. As illustrated in Figure 3, using repeated measures analysis of variance, a significant difference between implicit and explicit consideration of social subsystem issues for both the low disruption ($F 1,187 = 58.52$, $p < 0.01$) and high disruption ($F 1,187 = 74.99$, $p < 0.01$) scenarios was found.

To further investigate implicit versus explicit consideration of social sub-system issues, a paired *t-test* was used to compare the responses an individual provides for implicit and explicit consideration of each social subsystem issue. Table 3 shows the results of the Paired *t-tests* for the low disruption decision. Figure 4 depicts the differences in means graphically.

Implicit consideration of Productivity, Learning Curve, and Change Management are significantly greater, $p < .01$ from the explicit consideration of these social subsystem issues when decision makers consider a low disruption decision. Similarly, Productivity, Learning Curve, Change Management, and additionally Training were considered implicitly to a greater extent for the high process disruption decision. Table 4 shows the results of tests for the high disruption decision. Figure 5 depicts the differences in means graphically. Note, that the pattern of responses was almost identical for both low and high disruption decisions, with implicit consideration of social subsystem issues outweighing explicit consideration. Note also that implicit consideration of Productivity changes had the highest overall mean in both decision types. While many decision makers are attempting to assess the impact a proposed IT investment will have on productivity, it appears that they are grappling with how to formally evaluate and incorporate this impact into their decision processes. Explicit consideration is also significantly less for assessing the learning curve that users will have to overcome when a new technology is introduced and the management of change required to successfully implement that technology. These issues might be considered by some executives, but formal incorporation of these issues is done less frequently.

DISCUSSION

Our first research question compared the weights decision makers place on social issues as compared with technical and financial issues. Figure 2 shows that for both decisions, financial issues had the highest average score followed by technical issues, and lastly social subsystem issues. While not surprising, this reaffirms our initial argument that organizations place the most importance on financial and technical considerations and substantially less importance on social subsystem issues.

The predominance of financial consideration is congruent with prior research that indicates that organizations often require IT investments to be evaluated using traditional financial measures such as net present value and return on investment (Violino, 1998). Financial quantification is considered desirable because alternatives are easy to compare and choices easy to justify.

Technical issues were also weighed more heavily than social subsystem issues. One explanation could be that these issues also tend to be more tangible, and therefore, easier to quantify and include in the investment decision (Ryan & Harrison, 2000). From an STS perspective, this indicates a lack of systemic thinking in terms of failing to jointly optimize both the technological and the social subsystems.

An interesting observation is that financial and technical issues were weighed almost identically in both the low and high disruption decisions. In addition, the technical issues were secondary to financial issues in both decision types. This is somewhat surprising because, at least some interviewees in the exploratory phase expressed the opinion that technical issues were the primary consideration in low disruption decisions that dealt mainly with IT infrastructure.

Some may argue that in low disruption decisions dealing with fundamental information technologies that affect the daily work flow of employees only minimally, it may be reasonable to consider social subsystem issues substantially less than other decision factors. However, even in a high disruption environment, where core business processes change significantly, note that social subsystem issues were also considered substantially less. This is contrary to the business process reengineering literature, which emphasizes the importance of social subsystem issues (Grover et al., 1995) and warns that inattention to these issues often leads to failure (Alavi & Yoo, 1995).

This study also found that decision makers may think about social subsystem benefits and costs when making an IT investment decision, but far less often do they formally or explicitly include them in the decision process. This suggests that better techniques are needed for formally evaluating the impact an IT will have on social subsystem benefits and costs. Particularly, there appears to be a need for procedures that consider the effect an IT will have on productivity, the end-users learning curve, and change management.

A principal concern is that if these social subsystem issues are not formally considered in the acquisition decision process, yet are realized during implementation, the anticipated outcomes of the project may vary from the original projection. Organizations may argue that the management of an IT implementation is merely a part of the functional managers' and the IT group's responsibility, therefore considering the additional time or effort it takes to manage the social side of the technical implementation is unwarranted. Yet, without formal consideration of these issues, organizations have no way of capturing the magnitude of the impact.

Several of the social subsystem issues that showed no significant differences in explicit and implicit consideration have quantifiable metrics available. In terms of labor saving, the number of jobs eliminated as a result of an IT implementation can be easily measured. Next, much work has been done in the quality area recently, including the development of metrics such as the Cost of Quality Index (Strassman, 1995). Third, methodologies are available for calculating training costs (e.g., Fitz-enz, 1988). It is interesting to note that while implicit and explicit considerations of training were not significantly different in the low disruption decision, they were in the high process disruption decision. When core business process changes are proposed, it may be difficult to ascertain exactly what training will be required because employees may need to learn new work skills above and beyond those required for new IT. If the training requirements are not well understood, any type of quantification is more difficult. Therefore, while decision makers may think about training issues in a process redesign setting, they may not be formally assessed in the decision process.

LIMITATIONS AND FUTURE RESEARCH

As with all research, this investigation has several limitations. First, this study is cross-sectional. Therefore, no long-term trends or causal inferences can be established. In the future, it might be possible to track IT decisions in a longitudinal study to obtain this type of data.

Common method variance is another possible limitation of this study (Podsakoff & Organ, 1986). Because all the data were obtained from one executive per organization, concerns might arise regarding potential respondent biases which might constitute systematic error. In the future, obtaining responses from multiple executives in different functional areas within the same organization might yield additional insights into the IT decision making process.

No commonly accepted framework or methodology for determining social subsystem issues is available. Work has been done, however, in attempting to quantify intangible strategic benefits. Parker, Benson, and Trainor (1988) proposed a "value-linking framework" that measures, based on the organization's value-added chain, intermediate level process variables in the transformation of inputs to outputs. Based upon this framework, the value of an IT investment is equated to the summation of the investment's economic impact, business (strategic) domain assessment, and technology domain assessment. Noticeably missing is the social subsystem domain assessment. Parker et al.'s framework could potentially be extended to include a social subsystem domain assessment in the evaluation of IT value.

Cross-cultural research investigating how and when social subsystems issues are incorporated into IT decisions in various national cultures is also warranted. As the world continues to become a global economy, an interesting question is, "What national cultures do a more thorough job of including social subsystem considerations in their IT decisions?" A critical issue, both within and across cultures, is whether firms that do take these issues into consideration perform better as a result.

CONCLUSION

This study investigated an important, but under considered, aspect of IT investment decisions: the social subsystem dimension. This study empirically shows that IT decision makers do consider some social subsystem issues in their IT investment decisions. However, the consideration of these issues is not weighed heavily, as compared with financial or technical issues, nor is it frequently done formally or explicitly. Bacon (1992, p. 338) warns that formal consideration is important because, "otherwise there may be an absence of disciplined analysis, no real basis of objective measurement, and limited awareness of the true costs and benefits of IT investments."

Findings from this study imply that greater consideration should be given to social subsystem issues when the IT under consideration will substantially alter employees' daily work processes. Yet, even when a proposed IT will cause considerable disruption, IT decision makers view social subsystem issues as significantly less important than financial or technical factors.

While the focus of this research was descriptive in nature, it also has normative implications. Namely, when making an IT decision, organizations should consider the type of IT under consideration and the degree to which an IT under consideration will disrupt employees' daily work processes. The greater the disruption, the more effort and resources should be expended in evaluating the social subsystem implications.

REFERENCES

Alavi, M., & Yoo, Y. (1995). Productivity gains of BPR: Achieving success where others have failed. *Information Systems Management, 12*(4), 43-47.

Alter, A. (1997). Top firms spend more on IT. *Computerworld, 31*(22), 74.

Bacon, C. J. (1992). The use of decision criteria in selecting information systems/technology investments. *MIS Quarterly, 16*(3), 335-349.

Bass, B. M., Cascio, W. F., & O'Connor, E. J. (1974). Magnitude estimations of expressions of frequency and amount. *Journal of Applied Psychology, 59*(3), 313-320.

Belcher, L. W., & Watson, H. J. (1993). Assessing the value of Conoco's EIS. *MIS Quarterly, 17*(3), 239-253.

Brynjolfsson, E. (1993). The productivity paradox of information technology. *Communications of the ACM, 35*(12), 66-77.

Cattell, R. B. (1966). The scree test for the number of factors. *Multivariate Behavior Research, 1,* 245-276.

Chan, Y. E., Huff, S. L., Barclay, D. W., & Copeland, D. C. (1997). Business strategic orientation, information systems strategic orientation, and strategic alignment. *Information Systems Research, 8*(2), 125-150.

Clemons, E. K., & Weber, B. W. (1990). Strategic information technology investments: Guidelines for decision making. *Journal of Management Information Systems, 7*(2), 9-28.

Cronbach, L. J. (1971). Test validation. In R. L. Thorndike (Ed.), *Educational measurement* (2nd ed., pp. 443-507). Washington, DC: American Council on Education.

Daft, R. L. (1978). A dual-core model of organizational innovation. *Academy of Management Journal, 21*(2), 193-210.

DeGreene, K. B. (1973). *Sociotechnical systems: Factors in analysis, design, and management.* Englewood Cliffs, NJ: Prentice-Hall.

Emery, F. (1962). *Characteristics of sociotechnical systems.* Tavistock Institute of Human Relations, London, Doc. T-42.

Fitz-enz, J. (1988). Proving the value of training. *Personnel, 65*(3), 17-23.

GAO, Information Management and Technology Issues, United States General Accounting Office, Office of the Comptroller General, Report No. GAO/OCG93-STR, 5-6.

Grover, V., Fiedler, K., & Teng, J. (1997). Empirical evidence on Swanson's tri-core model of information systems innovation. *Information Systems Research, 8*(3), 273-287.

Grover, V., Jeong, S. R., Kettinger, W.J., & Teng, J.T.C. (1995). The implementation of business process reengineering. *Journal of Management Information Systems, 12*(1), 109-144.

Hitt, L. M., & Brynjolfsson, E. (1996). Productivity, business profitability, and consumer surplus: Three different measures of information technology value. *MIS Quarterly, 20*(2), 121-141.

Hochstrasser, B. (1990). Evaluation of IT investments—Matching techniques to projects. *Journal of Information Technology, 5*(4), 215-221.

Holden, T., & Wilhelmij, P. (1995-1996). Improved decision making through better integration of human resource and business process factors in a hospital situation. *Journal of Management Information Systems, 12*(3), 21-41.

Holme, M. R. (1997). Procurement reform and MIS project success. *International Journal of Purchasing and Materials Management, 33*(1), 2-7.

Karahanna, E., Straub, D. W., & Chervany, N. L. (1999). Information technology adoption across time: A cross-sectional comparison of pre-adoption and post-adoption beliefs. *MIS Quarterly, 23*(2), 183-213.

Keen, P. G. W. (1991). *Shaping the future.* Cambridge, MA: Harvard Business School Press.

Kerlinger, F. N. (1986). *Foundations for behavioral research* (3rd ed.). New York: Harcourt Brace Jovanovich.

Loehlin, J. C. (1992). *Latent variable models* (2nd ed.). Hillsdale, NJ: Lawrence Erlbaum Associates.

Markus, M. L., & Benjamin, R. I. (1996). Change agentry—The next IS frontier. *MIS Quarterly, 20*(4), 385-407.

Migliarese, P., & Paolucci, E. (1995). Improved communications and collaborations among tasks induced by groupware. *Decision Support Systems, 14*(3), 237-250.

Myers, B. L., Kappelman, L. E., & Prybutok, V. R. (1997). A comprehensive model for assessing the quality and productivity of the information systems function: toward a theory for information systems assessment. *Information Resources Management Journal, 10*(1), 6-25.

Norburn, D., & Birley, S. (1988). The top management team and corporate performance. *Strategic Management Journal, 9,* 225-237.

Orlikowski, W. J. (1993). CASE tools as organizational change: Investigation of incremental and radical changes in systems development. *MIS Quarterly, 17*(3), 309-341.

Parker, M. M., Benson, R. J., & Trainor, H. E. (1988). *Information economics: Linking business performance to information technology.* Englewood Cliffs, NJ: Prentice Hall.

Pasmore, W. A. (1995). Social science transformed: The sociotechnical perspective. *Human Relations, 48*(1), 1-21.

Pasmore, W., Francis, C., & Haldeman, A. (1982). Sociotechnical systems: A North American reflection on empirical studies of the seventies. *Human Relations, 35*(12), 1179-1204.

Podsakoff, P. M., & Organ, D. W. (1986). Self-reports in organization research: problems and prospects. *Journal of Management, 12,* 531-544.

Post, G. V., Kagan, A., & Lau, K. N. (1995). A modeling approach to evaluating strategic uses of information technology. *Journal of Management Information Systems, 12*(2), 161-187.

Premkumar, G., & King, W. R. (1994). Organizational characteristics and information systems planning: An empirical study. *Information Systems Research, 5*(2), 75-109.

Rai, A., & Patnayakuni, R. (1996). Structural model for case adoption behavior. *Journal of Management Information Systems, 13*(2), 205-234.

Ryan, S. D., & Harrison, D. A. (2000). Considering social subsystem costs and benefits in it investment decisions: a view from the field on anticipated payoffs. *Journal of Management Information Systems, 17*(4), 11-38.

Ryan, S. D., Harrison, D. A., & Schkade, L. L. (2002) .Information technology investment decisions: When do costs and benefits in the social subsystem matter? *Journal of Management Information Systems, 19*(2), 11-38.

Segars, A. H., & Grover, V. (1998). Strategic information systems planning success: an investigation of the construct and its measurement. *MIS Quarterly, 22*(2), 139-163.

Siegel, M. (1998). Do computers slow us down? *Fortune, 137*(6), 34-38.

Slater, S. F. (1995). Learning to change. *Business Horizons, 38*(6), 13-20.

Straub, D. W. (1989). Validating instruments in MIS research. *MIS Quarterly, 13*(2), 147-169.

Strassman, P. (1985). *Information payoff: The transformation of work in the electronic age.* New York: Free Press.

Swanson, E. B. (1994) Information systems innovation among organizations. *Management Science, 40*(9), 1069-1092.

Trist, E. L. (1982). The sociotechnical perspective. In A. H. Van de Ven & W. F. Joyce (Eds.), *Perspectives on organization design and behavior.* New York: Wiley.

Venkatraman, N. (1989). Strategic orientation of business enterprises: The construct, dimensionality, and measurement. *Management Science, 35*(8), 942-962.

Violino, B. (1998). ROI in the real world. *Information Week, 679,* 60-72.

Webb, G. (1997). Make IT work. *Airfinance Journal, 197,* 52-53.

Zmud, R. W., & Boynton, A. C. (1991). Survey measures and instruments in MIS: inventory and appraisal. *HBS Research Colloquium, 3,* 149-180.

APPENDIX A

Scenario 1:
Network Servers (Low Process Disruption)

You have heard complaints that access to information on the network is slow. Your technical people say that the applications are written and tuned properly; however, the server(s) do not have enough processing capability. You are thinking about several options:

1. Upgrade the server(s)
2. Partition the workload by getting another server(s), so that some users can access one server, while the others access another
3. Set up a multi-tiered environment, so the database or file access is on one system and the application access is on another
4. Move the application to a midrange or mainframe system

Scenario 2: Integrating Business Functions (High Process Disruption)

The managers in your organization have expressed concern that the information systems supporting your core business functions are not well integrated. You recognize the need for streamlining business processes to become more efficient. The suggestion has been made to reengineer these business processes using IT capabilities to better support the business areas. You are considering these options:

1. Modify the existing software, to the extent possible, so that the business functions can become more integrated
2. Purchase an integrated package that contains modules for your core business functions
3. Have either in-house programmers or a consultant custom design a solution

You know options 2 and 3 will affect organizational structure, the work sequence, and the sources of data.

This chapter was previously published in the *Information Resources Management Journal*, 17(1), 1-18, January-March, Coyright © 2004.

Chapter IX

Effect of Tasks, Salaries, and Shocks on Job Satisfaction Among MIS Professionals

Fred Niederman
Saint Louis University, USA

Mary Sumner
Southern Illinois University, Edwardsville, USA

ABSTRACT

This chapter contrasts attitudes and attributes of current and former positions of IT professionals who have changed jobs within the IT field. It also examines relationships among key variables of tasks performed, salary, job satisfaction, and external influences or "shocks" that may have precipitated turnover. Survey data were collected from 169 MIS professionals. Results showed significant changes in task, salary, and job satisfaction between former and current jobs. Detailed examinations show significant increases in project management and business analysis and decrease in 3GL and maintenance programming as well as differences in the amount of change for different elements of job satisfaction. A number of significant relationships among variables between some tasks and salary, some tasks and job satisfaction, and low former job satisfaction and response to particular "shocks" relative to turnover emerged from the data.

INTRODUCTION

Over the past two decades, investigators have studied IT professionals and job satisfaction largely in relation to workforce shortages as well as to employee turnover. Much evidence has been collected in recent years regarding the existence of an IT worker shortage (West & Bogumil, 2001), although not without some dissenting views also being voiced (Matloff, 1997). Much of the discussion regarding IT workforce shortages focuses on the ability of universities to produce enough computer science and MIS graduates; but another stream of discussion focuses on issues such as attrition from the field and job stress (Moore, 2000), difficulties for older workers (e.g., Cowley, 2001) and unequal gender presence in the field, particularly in the most technical and highest wage areas (ITAA, 2000). Goman (2000), in her discussion of high tech personnel based on wide ranging interviews with leading HR staff at high tech firms, repeatedly mentions the goal of recruiting younger employees. Fraser (2001) is even more explicit in describing incidents of alleged age discrimination among white-collar workers particularly in high-tech firms.

Information technology (IT) employee turnover has been a problem since the 1970s (Bartol, 1983) and has been studied regularly ever since. More recently, Jiang and Klein (1999-2000) report a 25%-35% turnover rate for IS employees in Fortune 500 firms and Shellenbarger (1996) provides a conservative estimate of 15%-20% turnover for IT workers. However, research on employee turnover has largely focused on individual attitudes that lead to organizational commitment and job satisfaction which in turn are viewed as leading to intention to remain on the job. In light of the many issues pertaining to the nature of IT work and the composition of the IT workforce overall, it may be time to broaden the discussion of employee turnover.

Employee turnover is an important issue both to high tech firms and to traditional firms that also need IT personnel for development of new systems and maintenance of their information infrastructure. Turnover is generally expensive and disruptive to employers. As noted by Reichheld (1996), even changes in 1% or 2% of turnover can make a significant difference in firm profitability. This is due to the accumulation of direct costs of hiring new personnel with the indirect costs of lost productivity if there is a gap between an employee leaving and finding a replacement as well as time for the new employee to descend the learning curve for technical and organizational knowledge. In spite of the common view that turnover is expensive and to be avoided, some information technology firms are comfortable with and even encourage high levels of turnover (Agarwal & Ferratt, 2001; Fraser, 2001).

Studies of IT personnel typically take a snap shot of employees of a number of firms or of members of an MIS/computer science society at a point in time (e.g., Baroudi & Igbaria, 1994-1995; Guimaraes & Igbaria, 1992). These types of studies generally test a set of attitudinal variables aimed at showing the relationships among job satisfaction and its precursors, organizational commitment and intent to leave. Alternatively, they show differences between demographic groups by gender, age, or race for these different attitudinal positions. From the perspective of the IT personnel employer, these traditional studies do not resolve the issue of how to influence the "intent to leave" or even more simply how to know the current state of intention to leave for a given employee at a given time.

In the management literature, Lee et al. (1999) have suggested the importance of taking a different approach. They argue that the traditional approach to turnover studies, while providing some predictive power, are not adequate to explain "why and how people leave". They suggest adding variables from the external environment to the psychological attitudes commonly studied in the turnover literature for a fuller picture of the precursors and steps leading to turnover. Given the extraordinary external environment that MIS professionals have faced in recent years with the enormous growth of demand for IT professionals, followed by the the waning of the high-tech workforce crisis, IT professionals have increasingly been affected by external environmental factors.

The current study focuses on concrete variables, salary, tasks, and shocks in addition to the job satisfaction attitudes considered at two points in time contrasting former job position with current job position. It is acknowledged that more recent experiences may color judgments regarding preceding ones (e.g., a poor job may look even worse after seeing what a good one looks like), and it may be more difficult to accurately recall attitudes about prior circumstances. However, such an approach has some offsetting advantages in that it does provide some ability to assess the relative strength of different contrasting factors between former and current positions, and also it focuses on IT employees who in fact turned over rather than rely upon the intention to turnover.

In the remainder of this chapter, we will review recent literature regarding employee turnover with an emphasis on information technology employees and present research questions, describe the methodology used in the study, present results, and discuss the implications of our findings.

LITERATURE REVIEW

Understanding Turnover

Employee turnover is one of the most studied issues in organizational behavior and human resource management literatures. Such studies have focused on employee attitudes toward work and the employer testing relationships among these attitudes. Studies in these areas have generally shown some positive relationship between intention to turnover (leave an employer) and actual turnover. However, the strength of this relationship has varied greatly from study to study and "suggest[s] some limits in intent to quit as a surrogate of turnover" (Tett & Meyer, 1993). Studies in this area have also generally shown some influence of job satisfaction and organizational commitment on the intention to turnover. An additional set of variables has been examined as possible influences of job satisfaction and organizational commitment. These variables include boundary spanning, role ambiguity and conflict, perceived workload as well as demographic variables such as age, years in position, and gender.

Although studies in employee turnover often use subjects from a particular field, such as attorneys or accountants, theories of turnover appear to be based on the premise that all employees regardless of field should follow a similar pattern of influences. Prior research in motivation has shown that information systems professionals may react differently from other employees (Couger; 1986, 1988, 1992; Couger & Zawacki, 1978), particularly those in more technical positions (Myers, 1992). Some research, notably Baroudi and Igbaria (1994-1995) and Guimaraes and Igbaria (1992), have targeted information systems personnel in terms of intention to turnover. Where Guimaraes and Igbaria (1992) found positive influence on intention to turnover from five variables (boundary spanning, role ambiguity, role conflict, overall job satisfaction, and organizational commitment), Baroudi and Igbaria (1994-1995) found no influence from gender (the only variable examined in the study) on intention to turnover. Additional studies have shown the influence of boundary spanning, role ambiguity, and role conflict on job satisfaction and organizational commitment (Guimaraes & Igbaria, 1992; Igbaria & Guimaraes, 1999).

Igbaria, Greenhaus, and Parasuraman (1991) compared results of Schein's career orientation instrument with actual work in technical vs. managerial IT roles. Based on this comparison, four categories of employee were defined: matched managerial orientation and role; matched technical orientation and role; mismatched managerial orientation and technical role; and mismatched technical orientation and managerial role. For the matched subgroups, job satisfaction, career satisfaction, organizational commitment, and intention to stay were all reported significantly higher than for mismatched subgroups. For those with a managerial orientation, those in managerial positions showed significantly higher values for all four dependent variables. For those with a technical orientation, those in technical positions showed significantly higher job satisfaction and career satisfaction, but not significantly different organizational commitment or intention to stay.

Another strand of research has focused more on racial and gender equity in information technology. For example, Igbaria and Wormley (1992) focused on racial differences among IT workers based on both employee surveys and matched and supervisor assessments. Among the key findings were positive associations between job performance and job discretion, career support, and participation in training activities, but no such association with feelings of acceptance and met expectations. Additionally, their data showed that advancement prospects were positively related to job performance and to higher levels of satisfaction with their careers. Finally, they reported that career satisfaction was related to organizational commitment. Baroudi and Igbaria (1994-1995) focused primarily on gender and found influences on salary and boundary spanning but not on overall job satisfaction, organizational commitment, or intention to turnover.

Alternate Views

Among MIS employee turnover researchers, there has been some movement to alternative research approaches. Moore (2000) used the concept of work-exhaustion (burnout), a tendency to which MIS professionals are particularly susceptible, as a mediator of several attitudinal antecedents to higher turnover intention. Indeed, work-exhaustion was the strongest significant predictor of intention to turnover. Individual attitudinal measures of fairness of rewards and individual workload seemed to play a significant role in both work exhaustion and in intention to turnover. Interviews with respondents suggested that leading causes of work exhaustion were insufficient staff and resources, changes in technology and/or business environment, unrealistic deadlines and target dates, organizational restructuring, expectations and needs of users, and unclear objectives. Although these causes may apply to a variety of jobs, several particular changes in technology and unrealistic deadlines are found rather frequently among IT workers. In the study, the number of individuals classified as "exhausted" was 48 out of a sample of 283, or 17%. Even if 100% of all those reporting exhaustion left the firm, it would still not account for the many organizations experiencing even higher levels, sometimes estimated as high as 20% or 30% per year.

Shock Theories

In the unfolding model of voluntary turnover, Lee and Mitchell (1994) argue that leaving is more complex than originally thought. In this analysis, turnover is influenced sequentially by a variety of variables, including shocks (unexpected job-related or unrelated major life events), the following of scripts, searching for alternatives, experiencing of image violation, and experience of job satisfaction. According to Lee and Mitchell (1994), a "shock" is a particular, jarring event (e.g., unsolicited job offers, transfers, acquisitions, and mergers) that initiates the psychological analysis involved in quitting a job. An engaged script ties to a shock and is a preexisting plan of action, which can be upon pre-experience, observation of others, or social expectations. An image violation occurs when an individual's values, goals, and strategies for goal attainment do not fit with those implied by the shock. Searching for job alternatives involves looking for and evaluating alternatives to a current job. Finally, lower levels of job satisfaction occur when people come to feel, over time, that their jobs no longer provide the intellectual, emotional, and financial benefits they desire.

An individual can pursue a number of paths in making a decision to leave an organization. In the case of MIS professionals, approximately 50% of respondents (e.g., 50 of the 109 respondents) reported receiving a "shock" (e.g., such as an unsolicited job offer), following an engaged script (e.g., pursuing the opportunity), and following a path of searching for alternatives. This finding may reflect the IT labor market at the time of the data collection (2000). In this labor market, IT professionals who were relatively well-satisfied with their current positions were still in a position to maximize their opportunities by responding to an unsolicited job offer.

Career Anchors

The career anchors of IT professionals have been examined in several research studies. Crepeau et al. (1992) reported a variety of career anchors, including managerial and technical competence, identity, service, organizational stability, and variety. Their data suggested a clustering of respondents around three dimensions, including the leadership dimension (consisting of the anchors managerial competence, service, identity, and variety), the organizational stability dimension (characterized by the organizational stability anchor), and the technical competence dimension (characterized by the technical competence anchor).

Jiang and Klein (1999-2000) examined the relationship between career anchors and career satisfaction for entry level IS employees. They found correlations with career satisfaction only for variety and service and not with managerial competence, identity, technical competence, geographic security, autonomy, or organizational stability. In the same study, Jiang and Klein did find relationships between supervisor support and both perceived external career opportunity and career satisfaction as well as between external career opportunity and career satisfaction.

Igbaria, Greenhaus, and Parasuraman (1991) compared results of Schein's career orientation instrument with actual work in technical vs. managerial IT roles. Their research showed that systems programmers, application programmers, and software engineers tended to be technically oriented, whereas systems analysts, project leaders, and computer managers tended to be managerially oriented. In their study, employees whose career orientations matched their job settings were more satisfied with their job and career, more committed to their organization, and less inclined to leave their organization than those employees who did not display a match. For example, the managerial-oriented employees holding managerial positions reported higher satisfaction with job and career, greater organizational commitment, and lower intention to leave the organization. The findings provided considerable support for the importance of matching career orientation and job setting.

In a recent study designed to identify the career anchors possessed by IT personnel, Sumner, Yager, and Franke (2005) found four predominant career anchors among IT personnel: creativity, autonomy, identity, and variety. They also sought to identify the career anchors that were the strongest determinants of organizational commitment. Further analysis that included a weighted variation of time in job, variety, autonomy, and identity explained 38% of the variation in organizational commitment expressed by the respondents. These new career anchors may be related to the change in labor market demands for IT personnel due to outsourcing and increasing reliance on contract personnel. This labor market situation makes it important for IT professionals to maintain state-of-the-art skill sets to maximize their market value and to manage their own careers more effectively.

In summary, this review of literature on turnover of MIS professionals shows a base of understanding regarding relationships between attitudinal variables and intention to turnover. However, recent work has shown that external factors play a significant role in illuminating turnover behaviors among MIS professionals. The purpose of this chapter is to continue the effort to enrich our understanding of the turnover phenomenon by examining in detail several external factors potentially affecting MIS professionals. Additionally, this chapter takes a slightly different approach from previous work on turnover in that we are not investigating the difference between those who turnover and those who do not but rather are looking in depth only at those who have chosen to turnover. This study also illustrates emerging labor market trends affecting the IT professional and points to changing priorities and expectations.

RESEARCH QUESTIONS

- **Research Question 1:** Does the amount of performance of common IT tasks change between former and current jobs?

It would seem that little would be more fundamental to attitudes regarding work than the nature of the work itself. Little attention has been given in the turnover literature to differentiate IT workers based on what they do. The one exception was Guimaraes and Igbaria (1992) contrasting attitudes of information systems and information center (largely help desk) workers. Individuals differ in their preference for and skills to perform various tasks. Being in a position that does not match one's skill set or preferences should lead to significant levels of change in IT task. Presumably individuals shift from poorly matched to well-matched tasks when changing positions.

Some tasks lend themselves to entry-level positions—maintenance programming is often viewed this way—while others, such as project management or working with the infrastructure requiring architecture, may require a broader array of experiences and skills. Performance of traditional entry level tasks should tend to diminish between former and current job where performance of the more previous job experience should tend to improve between former and current job.

Additional changes should be created simply by the evolution of technology within the IT field. For example, many firms have been shifting from third generation language programming to relational database and object-oriented approaches. This should be reflected in a movement from former to current positions in the amount of work done particularly with 3GL in contrast to 4GL programming.

- **Research Question 2:** Do starting and ending salaries change significantly between former and current jobs?

The literature regarding information technology personnel says very little about the role of changing salary in influencing turnover. Baroudi and Igbaria (1994-1995) do show that there are significant differences between male and female IT workers in terms of salary, but do not extend this to consideration of the role of salary in job change. It is possible to envision scenarios where employees shift to lower paying jobs, for example, if those jobs are more congruent with skills and preferences or if threatened with layoff. However, for the most part, we expect IT workers to progress in salary between starting and ending of each job as well as when shifting from one employer to another.

- **Research Question 3:** Do overall job satisfaction and its various components change significantly between former and current jobs?

We can see from Igbaria, Parasuraman, and Badawy (1994) as well as Guimaraes and Igbaria (1992) that a number of factors including boundary spanning, role ambiguity, and role conflict can influence the level of job satisfaction. It is not as clear, however, whether job satisfaction changes between the former and current job. Moreover, job satisfaction may be comprised of satisfaction with various aspects of the job. The desire to change jobs signals some kind of dissatisfaction and potential improvement that results in an actual job change. It is expected that on average job satisfaction will rise with the new job, but it is not clear that all factors contributing to job satisfaction will contribute equally to this change.

- **Research Question 4:** Are there higher levels of salary for some IT tasks in either former or current jobs?

It is not unreasonable that some people change employers in order to shift from performing one set of tasks to another. In some cases, the tasks themselves may be associated with higher levels of pay either because they are more managerial in nature, they require more technical acumen, or simply have fewer people willing to perform them. When someone works for a company that does not want to change them to a more profitable task (for any number of reasons including local value for the current job, managerial politics, or seniority), they may seek that change outside. With the changing IT job market, it is likely that IT professionals will want to move to positions which will enable them to develop and to maintain state-of-the-art skill sets because these skill sets will enable them to maximize their market value. By maximizing their market value, they can shield themselves from economic factors and work effectively as free agents, particularly in an environment in which contracting for IT skills is more and more prevalent.

- **Research Question 5:** Are there higher levels of job satisfaction for some IT tasks in either former or current jobs?

Some tasks may inherently be more or less appealing to a majority of practitioners. In all likelihood, there is some matching between interests/skills and job. Although several organizational attitudes such as boundary spanning have been found to correlate with job satisfaction and intention to turnover, studies have not considered that some frequently performed MIS tasks may correlate with different attitudes. Therefore, this study considers whether there is a relationship between tasks and level of job satisfaction.

- **Research Question 6:** Are there higher levels of job satisfaction based on differences in demographics, salary, or shocks?

It is not clear from prior studies whether demographic differences among IT workers lead to differences in job satisfaction. Igbaria and Wormley (1992) did find positive correlations between job satisfaction and both gender and race. In contrast, neither Guimaeras and Igbaria (1992) nor Baroudi and Igbaria (1994-1995) found differences in job satisfaction based on gender (neither tested for racial differences). Salary was found to correlate with higher job satisfaction in Igbaria et al. (1994), but was not measured in the other studies.

A major ingredient in the extensions to the range of variables beyond attitudes is the concept of a "shock" (Lee et al., 1999). In our data, all respondents have shifted jobs. It will be interesting to determine whether they leave as a result of an external shock (e.g., such as an unsolicited job offer) or if they leave because of low job satisfaction. With the change in labor market demand for IT professionals, more IT professionals may choose to remain in their current positions even if they are not satisfied with these positions because the likelihood of finding a suitable alternative is not as great as it was in the 2000-2001 timeframe.

METHOD

This study is based on data gathered through distribution of a survey and analysis of responses. Such a method allows for detailed quantification of the variables of interest. This offers the ability to present quantitative analysis regarding the relationships among the variables of interest and offer provisional inference regarding IT professionals in general.

Survey Creation and Distribution

Survey questionnaires were mailed in June 2000 to 280 alumni who had graduated from Saint Louis University with undergraduate business degrees with concentrations in MIS between 1990 and 1999. Thirty of these were returned due to unknown current address. A second round of mailings was sent to the alumni in August 2000. This time 25 were returned for unknown current address. Usable responses were received on the first round from 21 respondents with 11 additional responses on the second round for a total of 32 responses (12.5% response rate). A possible factor influencing the response rate of the survey was its length. To completely cover all aspects of this research, the full survey spanned seven full pages of questions.

The same survey questions were mailed to 1500 alumni of Southern Illinois University at Edwardsville in August 2000. Surveys from 137 of these alumni (9.1%) have been returned. At each school, we extracted from alumni databases student name and address information from among those who graduated in MIS undergraduate and graduate programs. Any differences in demographics or content among respondents from the two schools will be reported in a later section. Note that these respondents, though formerly students, have been out of school and into the workforce for up to 20 years. Some were in the workforce before and during their school years. It must be noted though, that IT workers without BA degrees were not represented in the sample.

Questionnaires were mailed with response envelopes. No information on the questionnaire or on the envelope can be linked to the identity of the respondent as known from the content of the original mailing list. A separate post card was included so that respondents could request a summary of the study findings. These summaries were sent in January 2000. Additionally, respondents received a cover letter explaining the purpose of the survey, that participation was voluntary, how they might contact the investigators with questions, and how anonymity has been maintained.

Measures

Demographics

Respondents were asked their gender, age, and the year that they graduated with a bachelor's degree. These were all single response items. Additionally, they were asked to state the industry in which they are employed, however, the relatively small number of respondents did not allow for statistical utilization of this measure.

Salary Levels

Respondents were asked the starting and ending salary of their former job as well as the starting and ending salary of their current job. These were all single response items.

Employment Shocks, Offers, and Alternatives

Respondents were asked if there was a single particular event that caused them to think about leaving, how many alternative positions they considered before taking a new position, and how many offers they received before taking the new position. These were each single item responses.

MIS Job Tasks

The authors listed 12 frequently reported MIS tasks. Most of these conformed to particular courses that are frequently found in academic MIS programs. These tasks map fairly closely to the list of MIS skills developed and studied in Lee, Trauth, and Farwell (1995). Where the list used in this study differentiated between 3rd and 4th generation language programming, Lee et al. differentiated a number of stages in the SDLC which our listing would have considered part of project management. Room on the survey was also available for other or "write-in" responses. These "other" answers were generated by six Saint Louis University and 41 Southern Illinois at Edwardsville students and ranged from 5% other (not specified) to 100% management or training. Management activities were mentioned by 10 of the respondents. Those job tasks mentioned by two participants were: testing, knowledge management; software installation, helpdesk; ERP, web development, and training. On average, the tasks noted by respondents from among those listed represented 88.6% of all former employment tasks and 93.1% of all current employment tasks. The questionnaire is attached as Appendix A.

Job Satisfaction

Respondents were asked 10 questions about their level of satisfaction pertaining to their former job and again pertaining to the current job. Eight of these questions were derived from Lee et al. (1999, p. 461). Two additional questions were posed concerning whether personal goals and career were progressing as expected. All questions were presented on 5-point Likert type scales anchored by 1 = very dissatisfied and 5 = very satisfied. Questions were analyzed separately from the perspective that individuals could differ in their weighting of these elements of satisfaction. They were also analyzed combined into two constructs, former satisfaction (Cronbach alpha = .86) and current satisfaction (Cronbach alpha = .90) based on the sum of the assessments for the individual items (10 for current employment and 10 for former employment).

Data Analysis

Responses were entered into an Excel spreadsheet and read into SPSS for standard statistical processing. Two kinds of data analysis were used to analyze the five research questions proposed in this study. Comparisons between former and current task activity levels and job satisfaction were analyzed using matched sample t-tests. Analyses of the correlations between other constructs were tested using Pearson correlations. All analysis was conducted using SPSS. Additional analysis of the structure of former and current job tasks as well as changes between these were examined using exploratory factor analysis with verimax rotation and a 1.0 eigenvalue cut off.

Composition of the Sample

The average age of the respondents was 27.6 years old with a range from 23 to 35 years old (see Table 1). ITAA statistics (2000) show that 35% of computer systems analysts and scientists and 33.6% of operations and systems researchers and analysts fall in this age range (about 4% are younger than this age range and about 60% are older than this age range). Additionally, 42.7% of programmers are in this age range with 7% younger and about 50% older. In the sample, 62.5% of respondents were male (see Table 2). This contrasts with 72% of computer systems analysts and scientists, 57% of operations and systems researchers and analysts, and 69% of computer programmers (ITAA, 2000).

For this sample, it took an average time of 2.5 months to decide to leave an employment situation and almost a month to actually leave once the decision has been made (see Table 1). Consideration of the averages for these measures, however, should be tempered by knowledge of the wide range of responses (1-300 and 2-75 days respectively). More than half of respondents indicated it took either 1 or 2 months to decide to leave an employment situation and 11 of 24 respondents took 2 weeks to leave once the decision was made.

Table 1.   Characteristics of the sample

	Mean	Std. Deviation	Range
Age (n=164)	37.9	9.5	23-70 years
Time to decide to leave firm (days) (n-124)	104.5	149.4	0-980 days
Time to leave firm after decision (days) (n=124)	51.2	98.7	1-730 days
Amount of job search (n=126) (scale 1 -- no search; -5 extensive search)	2.67	1.36	1-5
Number of alternatives located during job search (n=123)	2.50	3.81	0-25
Number of offers received during job search (n=126)	1.78	1.67	0-10

Table 2.   Event precipitating job change of the sample

	Yes	No
Job change precipitated by an event (n=133)	89	44

Table 3.   Gender of the sample

	Male	Female
Gender (n = 168)	77	91

Not surprisingly, salaries on average increased from former job starting to former job ending and from current job starting to current job ending (see Table 1). The current job ending salary was on average 67% higher than the former job starting salary. Again, it should be understood that there were a wide diversity of responses on this question. The amount of job search leaned slightly to the extensive search side (3.23 on a scale of 1-5). On average respondents considered nearly four alternative employment opportunities and had more than two job offers. Just under half of those leaving for alternative employment were triggered by a sudden event (see Table 2).

The sample was comprised of a slightly higher number of female than male respondents (see Table 3). Based on figures from ITAA (2000), the number of female and male IT employees is relatively similar when summed across all IT job categories, with males highly disproportionately represented in electrical engineering and females in data entry. As the preponderance of graduates from business MIS programs should fall between these job categories—in systems analysis and programming, a sample more evenly divided by gender is not overly unusual, although ITAA figures show 57% of systems analysts and 69% of programmers to be male.

On the whole, while some differences between the Saint Louis University and Southern Illinois University at Edwardsville groups were noted, it is argued that regarding major variables of task, salary, and job satisfaction, there are few differences between the two groups. Where some differences exist, it actually broadens the overall representation of the combined sample relative to the population of IT employees.

RESULTS

- **Research Question 1:** Does the amount of performance of common IT tasks change between former and current jobs?

There is a wide variance in percentage of time spent across the 12 tasks (see Table 4). The top five tasks (project management, interacting directly with users, analysis of business processes, coding 3GL, and maintenance coding) remain the same and account for 62% of work activity for both former and current jobs. However, there is contrast when considering the top three tasks with only

Table 4. Former vs. current job percentage of tasks sorted by amount at current firm

	Former Job		Current Job			
	Mean	STD	Mean	STD	Gap	P-value
Project management (n=114)	.108	.17	.168	.22	.060	.00
Interacting directly with users (n=115)	.164	.21	.166	.19	.002	.90
Analysis of business processes (n=115)	.108	.13	.134	.16	.026	.06
Coding 3GL (COBOL, Fortran) (n=115)	.111	.20	.081	.19	-.030	.09
Maintenance coding (n=115)	.125	.21	.075	.14	-.050	.01
Design application architecture (n=115)	.065	.11	.065	.08	.000	.98
Coding retrieval language (SQL, Oracle) (n=115)	.067	.14	.061	.12	-.006	.68
Database administration (n=114)	.053	.14	.048	.13	-.005	.62
Design infrastructure architecture (n=115)	.026	.07	.037	.08	.011	.02
Network administration (n=114)	.028	.08	.023	.09	-.005	.52
Hardware installation (n=115)	.031	.07	.019	.05	-.012	.07
Hardware selection (n=115)	.011	.03	.009	.02	-.002	.58
Average	0.069		0.068			

interacting directly with users remaining a top activity along with coding 3GL and maintenance coding among the top three in the former jobs, however, project management and analysis of business processes becoming a larger focus in current jobs. This finding is not inconsistent with some shifting of the IT environment away from 3GL, nor is it inconsistent with a maturation of IT professionals from coding to project management and new application design. Designing infrastructure architecture, network administration, hardware installation, and hardware selection remain the bottom four alternatives for both former and current jobs.

It is also clear from the data that a number of tasks that change significantly from former to current jobs. At the high end, project management jumps by 64% (10.8% to 16.8%). A significant increase of 41% (from 2.6% to 3.7%) in performing the design infrastructure architecture was also observed. It is reasonable that those with increasing levels of experience to be in a better position to see the breadth of the architecture and be able to perform this task effectively. At the same time, maintenance coding declined by 40% (12.5% to 7.5%), which is consistent with the view of maintenance coding as an entry-level position. While not significant at the 0.05 p-value threshold, the data showed a 24% increase in analysis of business process task performance (from 10.8% to 13.4%) and a drop of 39% in hardware installation (from 3.1% to 1.9%). The data indicate change across the whole sample and may not reflect the numbers of individuals experiencing changes in these directions.

Three trends in job tasks observed in our data have continued. These trends include: the increasing emphasis on project management, user support, analysis of business processes, and the design of information architecture. The emphasis on these skill sets has continued to occur because of the global outsourcing of routine, mechanized IT jobs (e.g., programming, maintenance programming), the move toward implementing commercial off-the-shelf ERP packages instead of in-house development, and the increasing complexity of managing the information infrastructure.

• **Research Question 2:** Do starting and ending salaries change significantly between former and current jobs?

At each measured point, from start to end of former job, end of former to start of current job, and from start of current to end of current job, salaries significantly increase (see Table 5). Although the size of increase from end of the former job to the start of the current job is a tiny bit smaller than the increases from start to end of the former job and start to end of the current job, it should be kept in mind that this increase will typically occur across a much shorter time period. Although this data cannot show whether or to what degree salary increase is part of the motivation for turnover, in this sample, the indication clearly shows increased compensation as an element in changing jobs.

Table 5. Former vs. current job salary   (N = 101, first job respondents excluded)

		Mean	St.D.	Gap	P-value
Former job	Start	$37,053	$15,722		
				$ 9,494	.000
	End	$46,547	$17,629		
				$ 9,117	.000
Current job	Start	$55,665	$23,214		
				$16,474	.000
	End	$72,140	$29,038		

The issue of salary change is complicated by emerging IT workforce trends. In 2000, during the high-tech worker shortage, IT salaries were driven upward by market demand for IT skills. By 2004, the IT bubble had burst, and salaries for IT professionals stabilized and, in some cases, decreased. In addition, an increasing percentage of IT professionals are contract professionals. An interesting question is "What is the impact of the transition from using internal IT personnel to contract IT personnel on the salaries of IT professionals?" Although contract IT personnel may command a higher wage rate than internal IT personnel, they may not be able to command these wage rates on a consistent, recurring basis.

- **Research Question 3:** Do overall job satisfaction and its various components change significantly between former and current jobs?

It stands to reason that job satisfaction levels would be higher with current than with former employment (see Table 6). Those who are highly satisfied are less likely to change jobs. In addition, most job changers in this sample had at least one offer prior to leaving and were in a position to be somewhat selective in locating a new job that more directly addressed their needs. Alpha levels for combining the 10 different elemental job satisfaction questions into one overall measure were high for former (alpha = .86) and current (alpha = .90) job satisfaction levels.

Considering the high alpha scores and the fact that all individual questions comprising the job satisfaction scale were significantly different between former and current employment, this sample provides strong evidence that all aspects of job satisfaction tend to move together and in an upward direction with job change. However, unlike scales that essentially ask the same question with slight variation in wording, the content of these questions targets somewhat different aspects of job satisfaction, and it is worthwhile to look at the individual questions in a little more detail.

Table 6. Former vs. current job satisfaction sorted by size of gap (n=87, first job respondents excluded, listwise exclusion for missing data)

	Former Firm		Current Firm			
	Mean	STD	Mean	STD	Gap	P-value
Overall job satisfaction (sum of 10 questions)	28.68	7.60	37.06	7.60	8.38	.000
Satisfied with my coworkers	3.47	1.13	4.05	.81	.57	.000
Satisfied with the nature of the work	3.17	1.23	3.86	.95	.69	.000
Satisfied with the fringe benefits	2.98	1.19	3.56	1.20	.59	.002
Satisfied with the firm as an employer	2.97	1.25	3.95	.94	**99**	.000
Satisfied with the recreational activities	2.91	1.32	3.32	1.15	.41	.025
Satisfied with the supervision I received	2.84	1.27	3.70	1.16	.86	.000
Career progressing as I expected	2.70	1.15	3.60	1.03	.90	.000
Personal goals progressing as I expected	2.70	1.15	3.64	.99	.94	.000
Satisfied with the career opportunities	2.38	1.14	3.64	1.08	1.26	.000
Satisfied with the financial rewards	2.38	1.14	3.72	1.08	1.16	.000
Average (excluding overall)	2.85		3.70		.84	

For both former and current employment, respondents were most satisfied with coworkers with the nature of the work ranking second highest for former and third highest for current employment. Satisfaction with the firm as an employer was ranked fourth highest for the former and second highest for the current employer. It would be of interest to further test whether these are consistent judgments of IT employees regarding IT work across jobs and firms.

In contrast, satisfaction with career opportunities and financial reward were tied for the lowest ranking in the former job but rose to near the average of the current job rankings. Personal and career goal expectations being met were also low both for former and current employment. It is suggestive that these aspects of job satisfaction were influential in the decision to leave and may represent areas where specific firms and the IT field overall need improvement for retaining experienced IT personnel.

While much is made in the trade literature about recreational activities and luxury perks at high tech firms, this was a question frequently left blank by respondents and one that may be viewed by many as not relevant either because it is not offered by the employer or not of interest to the respondent. Fringe benefits, while one of the higher ranked elements in the former job was ranked below average in the current job, which may reflect on the tendency of many firms to be cutting back on the extent of health benefits, even as costs rise. It could also be that the respondents are not receiving the kinds of stock options so prevalent in high tech start-ups and that the actual fringe benefits may be nearer to static or even slowly increasing, but at a slower rate than expected.

The issue of job satisfaction is also complicated by emerging IT workforce trends. From our data, job satisfaction was higher in current positions, as compared with former positions. Yet, in today's market, IT professionals have an increasing tendency to stick with their current positions, even if they are not satisfied with their current positions. This is because external market demand for IT professionals is less, and they may not be able to locate an alternative position. If they choose to pursue contract IT work, the whole picture is changed, and new issues are raised. An interesting question becomes "what is the overall impact of the shift to IT contract work on the job satisfaction of the contractors?"

- **Research Question 4:** Are there higher levels of salary for some IT tasks in either former or current jobs?

A relatively strong number of comparisons (17 out of 96—18%) were significant with a 0.05 or less p-value (see Table 7). By normal distribution, it would be expected that 4 or 5 of the combinations would be significant at that level. This suggests that the significance among task-salary relationships do stand out as more than random chance findings.

Considering the correlations between tasks and the starting and ending salaries for both former and current positions, 17 of 48 (35%) combinations were statistically significantly correlated at p-value = 0.05. The tasks most strongly positively correlated with salary were project management (4 of 8 combinations correlated) and business analysis (4 of 8 combinations correlated). Both former and current amount of project management correlate with current end salary. Former position project management also correlated with former position start salary and current position start salary. Both former and current amount of business analysis correlated with current end salary. Current business analysis also correlates with former end salary and current start salary. This would provide strong, though not unequivocal, support for a positive influence on salary of both project management and business analysis. Additionally, former position 4GL programming correlated with current start salary.

On the other hand some tasks were negatively correlated with salary. The strongest negative relationships with salary were 3GL coding (3 of 8 combinations negatively correlated) and maintenance programming (2 of 8 combinations negatively correlated). Former job amount of 3GL coding negatively correlated with current start salary and current amount of 3GL coding negatively correlated

Table 7.   Correlation of salary measures and specific tasks

Variable	Former start salary	Former end salary	Current start salary	Current end salary
Former job task				
Project management	.20*	.10	.31**	.24*
Hardware selection	.13	-11	-.01	-.05
Infrastructure architecture	.12	.07	.11	.10
Business analysis	-.06	.00	.14	.21*
Application architecture	.06	.02	.07	.08
4GL	.11	-.01	.28**	.13
Network administration	-.06	-.07	-.04	-.09
Working directly with users	-.10	-.07	-.04	.05
Database administration	-.08	-.05	.12	-.03
Hardware installation	-.12	-.12	-.14	-.23*
3GL coding	-.08	-.10	-.20*	-.13
Maintenance programming	-.14	-.12	-.23*	-.10
Current job task				
Project management	-.01	.07	.02	.32**
Business analysis	-.08	.26**	.22*	.25*
Hardware selection	.16	-.16	-.06	.10
Infrastructure architecture	.14	.11	.02	.11
Application architecture	.01	-.01	.05	.05
Database administration	.04	.03	.15	.06
Network administration	-.07	-.15	.02	- **.12**
Working directly with users	-.09	-.06	-.02	-.19*
Hardware installation	.01	-.23*	-.07	-.17
4GL	-.13	.01	-.02	-.13
Maintenance programming	-.02	.00	-.08	-.20*
3GL coding	.08	-.05	-.17*	-,26**

* p-value < .05, ** p-value < .01

with both current start and end salaries. Former job maintenance programming was negatively correlated with current start salary, and current job maintenance programming was negatively correlated with current end salary. Additionally, former job hardware installation negatively correlated with current end salary, and current job working with end users negatively correlated with current end salary.

Overall, based on salary data, we see that employers have been generally rewarding project management. They also seem to have been shifting to higher rewards for 4GL programming and lower rewards for 3GL programming. Having done more maintenance programming has tended to lower salaries at the time of job change; doing more maintenance programming at present seems to go along with a slower rate of increasing salary. The negative correlation of working with end users and current end salary is a surprise because the authors would have expected higher levels of working with end users to go along with project management and business analysis, both of which positively correlated with current end salary.

The increasing need for experienced IT project managers and their ability to command higher salary rates is a recurring trend which persists in a marketplace in which there is increasing reliance on purchasing commercial off-the-shelf ERP packages and contracting for external IT personnel. This trend is expected to continue.

- **Research Question 5:** Are there higher levels of job satisfaction for some IT tasks in either former or current jobs?

A modest number of comparisons (4 out of 48—8%) were significant with a 0.05 or less p-value (see Table 8). By normal distribution, it would be expected that 2 or 3 of the combinations would be significant at that level. This suggests that the significant among the job satisfaction-salary relationships may stand out as more than random chance findings.

The only item that was positively correlated with job satisfaction was former job project management and former job satisfaction. Since project management did not show significant correlation with current job satisfaction measures, it is difficult to conclude that this is a robust relationship. Both former and current levels of hardware installation were significantly negatively correlated with former job satisfaction. However, both former and current levels of hardware installation were positively correlated, though not significant at the 0.05 p-value level, suggesting that this also is difficult to conclude as being robust. Finally, former amount of 3GL coding was negatively correlated with current job satisfaction. However, since current amounts of 3GL programming are correlated with neither former nor current job satisfaction, this again is difficult to view as being a robust relationship.

Considering the overall pattern of correlations between current and former tasks with current and former job satisfaction, it is difficult to conclude that the specific jobs have much impact on job satisfaction. Specific tasks such as project management, hardware installation, and 3GL programming would seem the most likely targets for further investigation.

The issue of job satisfaction and various IT skill sets (e.g., managerial vs. technical) seems to be reminiscent of Igbaria et al.'s (1991) findings that IT professionals with a managerial orientation are most satisfied with managerial jobs (e.g., project management, business analysis), and IT professionals with a technical orientation are more satisfied with technical responsibilities (e.g., network infrastructure).

Table 8. Pearson correlations of job satisfaction with specific tasks

Variable	Former Job Satisfaction	Current Job Satisfaction
Current Job Satisfaction		1.0
Former Job Satisfaction	1.0	.45**
Current job tasks		
3GL coding	.07	.04
4GL	-.09	-.11
Application architecture	.02	.07
Business analysis	-.13	-.06
Database administration	-.11	.05
Hardware installation	-.25*	.16
Hardware selection	-.12	-.02
Infrastructure architecture	.07	.11
Maintenance programming	-.02	-.07
Network administration	.01	.13
Project management	.06	.01
Working directly with users	.04	.01
Former job tasks		
3GL coding	-.10	-.20*
4GL	-.02	-.16
Application architecture	.13	-.03
Business analysis	.09	.14
Database administration	-.17	.14
Hardware installation	-.27**	.14
Hardware selection	-.04	.04
Infrastructure architecture	.19	.10
Maintenance programming	-.12	-.04
Network administration	-.15	.13
Project management	.25*	.09
Working directly with users	-.04	-.06

*p-value < .05, ** p-value < .01*

- **Research Question 6:** Are there higher levels of job satisfaction based on differences in demographics, salary, or shocks?

A relatively strong number of comparisons (4 out of 24—17%) were significant with a -0.05 or less p-value (see Table 9). By normal distribution, it would be expected that 0 or 1 of the combinations would be significant at that level. This suggests that the significant among the job satisfaction-demographic relationships do stand out as more than random chance findings.

The only item that was positively correlated with job satisfaction (former or current) was former job ending salary. Time to leave after the decision was negatively correlated with former job satisfaction meaning that the lower time to leave matched higher job satisfaction. Further examination of this item showed

Table 9. Pearson correlation of satisfaction with former and current employment and various demographic and job-related factors

Variable	Former Job Satisfaction	Current Job Satisfaction
Demographics		
Gender	.07	-.05
Age	.07	-.09
Year BA awarded	-.04	.02
Salary		
Former starting salary	.13	-.28**
Former ending salary	.28**	-.12
Current starting salary	.14	.02
Current ending salary	.17	.02
Shocks		
Time to decide to leave (days)	-.02	.01
Time to leaving after decision to leave (days)	-.23*	-.20
Event as trigger to job change (yes/no)	-.23*	-.02
Number of offers before new job	-.06	.03
Number of alternatives considered before new job	.05	.09

* significant at p-value .05 (two-tailed), ** significant at p-value .01 (two-tailed)

two respondents with times in the 700-800 day range and low prior job satisfaction scores. Though technically not outliers, as the data from these two respondents appears in all ways to be accurate relative to their entire set of answers, removal of these two data points showed no relationship between time to leave after the decision and former job satisfaction. Therefore, it appears coincidental that two individuals taking a very long time between deciding to leave and leaving correlated with low job satisfaction. It would stand to reason, though, that people desiring to leave a firm but staying for whatever reason might have that experience affect their perceived satisfaction with the job.

Quite unexpectedly, the data show a negative relationship between former job starting salary and current job satisfaction. The authors would expect a consistently positive relationship between more salary at instances and more satisfaction with both former and current.

Finally, the nature and impact of "shocks" on the IT workforce seems to be a significant issue. In the 2000-2001 timeframe, the IT workforce shortage created a high labor market demand for IT professionals, and the occurrence of unsolicited shocks (e.g., external job offers) which led many of them to test their market value and to make job changes, even though they were satisfied with their current positions. In contrast, in the 2004-2005 timeframe, the IT workforce shortage has waned, and the "shocks" can be slightly different in nature. This time, the "shocks" can be negative (e.g., having your IT job outsourced). IT professionals must continuously assess their labor market potential and be aware of the job alternatives which exist—many of which are on a contract basis. To maintain their market value, IT professionals must increasingly manage their own careers and seek to acquire state-of-the-art skill sets which enable them to compete successfully for jobs, both technical and managerial.

DISCUSSION

Changes Between Former and Current Jobs

Project management and infrastructure architecture both significantly increased while both maintenance programming and 3GL programming both decreased. This finding is consistent with the increasing implementation of commercial off-the-shelf ERP systems and other software packages, and the decrease in in-house development.

There was no big surprise that salaries for respondents moved up when they changed jobs. The data collected do not rule out change in salary as a motivation for turnover. In the current environment, it is more difficult to measure the impact of job transitions on salary progression. An interesting question becomes "What is the impact of the shift from internal IT jobs to contract IT jobs on salary progression?"

Responses regarding each element of job satisfaction rise significantly between prior and current job (see Table 6). The simplest explanation would be that changing jobs has the desired effect of raising job satisfaction levels for the individual. Gaps between satisfaction with current and former jobs were largest for financial reward, progress on personal goals, supervision, and career opportunities. These issues represent areas where individuals are seeking improvement in shifting jobs.

The current decline in labor market demand for IT professionals makes it less likely that IT professionals will switch jobs, even when they may not be satisfied with their current positions. It is more difficult to make job transitions in the current labor market environment, particularly when many IT jobs are contract jobs. An interesting question is "What is the impact of the shift from internal IT jobs to contract IT jobs on job satisfaction?"

Satisfaction with coworkers was ranked most highly for both former and current jobs, though the difference between them was significant (largely due to lower variance among respondents). This is a provocative finding that suggests a potential point of leverage for managers desiring to build higher levels of job satisfaction (e.g., stimulate greater strength of coworker relationships) and calls into question the finding of IT professionals being only very weakly motivated by social relations (Couger, 1986, 1988, 1992; Couger & Zawacki, 1978).

An Additional Observation

Although not targeted in this study for hypothesis testing, the authors observed that this sample of respondents reported a higher level of performance of "soft" information technology activities such as project management, working with end users, and business process design (see Table 4). This contrasts with moderate amounts of "hard" IT activities such as programming in third and fourth generation languages and low amounts of activities such as hardware selection.

These data may be pointing to three new challenges for IT professionals in the years ahead: First, IT professionals must maintain state-of-the-art skill sets to maximize their market value; second, IT professionals may gain these skill sets by providing contract IT services; and third, IT professionals may have to switch jobs to assure their ability to operate in environments where they have an opportunity to continuously update their skills.

In terms of managerial trends, there will be an increasing emphasis on project management skills, business analysis, and an understanding of the business context for making investments in information technology applications and infrastructure.

CONCLUSION

Overall, the findings of this study lend weight to the position that external market conditions, particularly events precipitating job change, should be accounted for along with attitudes, such as low job satisfaction. Findings also show that tasks tend to evolve from former to current positions; that salaries do indeed rise during the changeover from a former to current job; and that employees are inclined to view a new position as more satisfying in almost all ways (at least in retrospect) compared to the former job.

Limitations

The approach to this study differed from prior IT employee turnover studies in asking respondents to consider both their former and current job. While this has some strengths in terms of allowing for comparisons, it also has some limitations. Responses regarding former employment occurred further in the past and are subject to retrospective interpretation. Genuine longitudinal panel studies are needed to more completely address the full range of issues in this domain.

This study also differed from prior IT employee turnover studies in focusing on the alumni of two particular IT programs. While the respondents are fully enfranchised IT workers and no longer students, they may not represent a cross section of the entire IT workforce as they do not include those without a college degree and those coming to the IT workforce from computer science, general business (not MIS), and other areas.

FUTURE RESEARCH

First, it would also be interesting to consider different time periods. The shortage of IT personnel created many unsolicited job offers, but more recent changes in labor market demand have caused many IT professionals to stay in their current position. It would be interesting to compare the current sample with a sample of current IT professionals to determine tasks, salaries, and satisfaction. The increasing number of contract IT personnel presents further interesting research opportunities. What is the difference in tasks, salaries, and job satisfaction between internal IT professionals and contract IT professionals? Are contract IT professionals able to develop state-of-the-art skill sets more readily? Does their ability to maintain these state-of-the-art skill sets enable them to enhance their market value and to enjoy more significant salary progression as compared to IT professionals who choose to maintain their roles as internal IT professionals? Does job mobility enhance the salary progression of IT professionals? Does job mobility enable IT professionals to operate in environments in which they can continuously update their skill and knowledge sets? These issues will provide ample topics for further research.

Final Word

No one study is likely to provide the definitive understanding of a topic as broad and complex as IT employee turnover. However, we believe that this chapter makes a significant contribution in extending the discussion of turnover among MIS personnel by providing insight into the effects of turnover, in terms of tasks, salary, and job satisfaction. As IT professionals become increasingly mobile, understanding these changes will help many of them manage their careers more effectively.

REFERENCES

Agarwal, R., & Ferratt, T. W. (2001). Crafting an HR strategy to meet the need for IT workers. *Communications of the ACM, 44*(7), 58-64.

Baroudi, J. J., & Igbaria, M. (1994-1995). An examination of gender effects on career success of information system employees. *Journal of Management Information Systems, 11*(3), 81-201.

Bartol, K. M. (1983, October). Turnover among DP personnel: A causal analysis. *Communications of the ACM, 26*(10), 807-811.

Couger, J. D. (1986). Effect of cultural differences on motivation of analysts and programmers. *MIS Quarterly, 10*(2), 189-196.

Couger, J. D. (1988, June). Motivators versus demotivators in the IS environment. *Journal of Systems Management, 39*(6), 36-41.

Couger, J. D. (1992). Comparison of motivation norms for Pacific Rim programmer/analysts vs. those in the United States. *International Information Systems, 1*(3).

Couger, J. D., & Zawacki, R. A. (1978). What motivates DP professionals? *Datamation,* pp. 19-20.

Cowley, S. (2001). Survey: Age bias seen by over-45 techies. Network World Fusion. Retrieved July 29, 2005, from http://www.nwfusion.com/news/2001/0423agebias.html

Crepeau, R. G., Crook, C. W., Goslar, M. D., McMurtrey, M. E. (1992). Career anchors of information systems personnel. *Journal of Management Information Systems, 9*(2), 145-160.

Fraser, J. A. (2001). *White-collar sweatshop: The deterioration of work and its rewards in corporate America.* New York: W. W. Norton and Company.

Goman, C. K. (2000). *The human side of high-tech.* New York: John Wiley & Sons.

Guimaraes, T., & Igbaria, M. (1992, September). Determinants of turnover intentions: Comparing IC and IS personnel. *Information Systems Research, 3*(3), 273-303.

Igbaria, M., & Baroudi, J. J. (1995, March). The impact of job performance evaluations on career advancement prospects: An examination of gender differences in the IS workplace. *MIS Quarterly, 19*(1), 107-123.

Igbaria, M., Greenhaus, J. H., & Parasuraman, S. (1991, June). Career orientations of MIS employees: An empirical analysis. *MIS Quarterly, 15*(2), 151-169.

Igbaria, M., & Guimaraes, T. (1999). Exploring differences in employee turnover intentions among telecommuters and non-telecommuters. *Journal of Management Information Systems, 16*(1), 147-164.

Igbaria, M., Parasuraman, S., & Badawy, M. K. (1994, June). Work experiences, job involvement, and quality of work life among information systems personnel. *MIS Quarterly, 18*(2), 175-201.

Igbaria, M., & Wormley, W. M. (1992, December). Organizational experiences and career success of MIS professionals and managers: An examination of race differences. *MIS Quarterly, 16*(4), 507-529.

ITAA (2000). Bridging the gap: Information technology skills for a new millennium, executive summary. Retrieved July 29, 2005, from http://www.itaa.org/workforce/studies/hw00execsumm.htm

Jiang, J. J., & Klein, G. (1999-2000). Supervisor support and career anchor impact on career satisfaction. *Journal of Management Information Systems, 16*(3), 219-240.

Lee, D. M. S., Trauth, E. M., & Farwell, D. (1995, September). Critical skills and knowledge requirements of IS professionals: A joint academic/industry investigation. *MIS Quarterly, 19*(3), 313-340.

Lee, T. W., Mitchell, T. R., Holtom, B. C., McDaniel, L. S., & Hill, J. W. (1999). The unfolding model of voluntary turnover: A replication and extension. *Academy of Management Journal, 42*(4), 450-462.

Matloff, N. (1997). Critique of the Department of Commerce report entitled "America's New Deficit, The Shortage of Information Technology Workers." American Engineering Association, Inc. Retrieved July 29, 2005, from http://www.aea.org/news/doc_critique.htm

Moore, J. E. (2000, March). One road to turnover: An examination of work exhaustion in technology professionals. *MIS Quarterly, 24*(1), 141-168.

Myers, M. (1992). The information systems profession and the information systems professional- fit or misfit? In A. Lederer (Ed.), *Proceedings of the 1992 ACM SIGCPR Conference on Computer Personnel Research* (pp. 350-351). Cincinnati, OH.

Reichheld, F. F. (1996). *The loyalty effect.* Boston: Harvard Business School Press.

Shellenbarger, S. (1996, November 13). Flexible hours allow company to crack tight labor market. *The Wall Street Journal*, p. B1.

Sumner, M., Yager, S., & Franke, D. (2005). Career orientation of IT personnel. *Proceedings of the 2005 ACM SIGMIS and SIGCPR Conference*, Atlanta, Georgia.

Tett, R. P., & Meyer, J. P. (1993). Job satisfaction, organizational commitment, turnover intention, and turnover: Path analysis based on meta-analytical findings. *Personnel Psychology, 46*(2), 259-293.

West, L. A., & Bogumil, W. A. (2001, July). Immigration and the global IT work force. *Communications of the ACM, 44*(7), 34-39.

Chapter X

Empirical Evaluation of an Integrated Supply Chain Model for Small and Medium Sized Firms

Toru Sakaguchi
Northern Kentucky University, USA

Stefan G. Nicovich
University of New Hampshire, USA

C. Clay Dibrell
Oregon State University, USA

ABSTRACT

With increased global competitive pressures, companies operating in these competitive environments are not only looking to their distribution division to save money, but also to generate competitive advantages. One technique is the integrated supply chain. However, this process has not met with success for all companies, leading some managers to consider the appropriateness of an integrated supply chain. This dearth of success could be attributed to the lack of scholarship to guide managers in their efforts to formulate and then implement their integrated supply chain strategies. In an effort to fill this gap, our paper draws on resource dependency theory and the realities of ever-increasing information technology sophistication as enablers of successful supply chain integration, resulting in the creation of our model to guide managers throughout this process. Through a Web-based survey, 329 responses were collected and analyzed through a structural equation modeling technique using LISREL to confirm the relationships in the model.

INTRODUCTION

Five days before the release of the fourth Harry Potter book, *Harry Potter and the Goblet of Fire,* Amazon.com found its supply chain strained. Over 275,000 copies of the book had to be delivered on time within the next few weeks (King, 2000). By working closely with members in their supply chain such as FedEx, Amazon was able to handle the orders and avert a potentially damaging situation. While not every company is as dependent upon its partners as Amazon is, global pressures are forcing more and more companies to reassess the importance of working with others. Indeed much of the blame for K-mart's bankruptcy and subsequent restructuring lay in its inability to compete with the likes of Target and Wal-Mart (Sliwa, 2002). Both Target and Wal-Mart had been able to streamline their supply chains, whereas K-Mart had struggled to keep up. Both of these incidents show that successfully managing the supply chain has become not just a means of distribution, but a means of competitive advantage as well.

The rapid advancement of information technologies, such as the explosive growth of enterprise resource planning (ERP) and the continuing development of e-commerce applications and the Internet, has forced many companies to reevaluate their roles and positions within their competitive environments. This new business paradigm is forcing business processes to be reconsidered and redesigned (Hackney, Burn, & Dhillon, 2000). As such, many companies like K-mart are modifying their logistics functions by forging strategic alliances with suppliers and buyers to more thoroughly integrate their supply chains.

An integrated supply chain is simply "taking those functions that originate at point of origin and ultimately end up at a point of consumption" and integrating them together through alliances (Bowman, 1997, p. 30). As stated by Hertz (2001), for example, an integrated supply chain involves greater coordination and collaboration among all members of a company's supply chain. It is sharing information across organizational boundaries within a network of alliances, including suppliers and end-users. The potential benefits of employing an integrated supply system include overall cost and time reduction in the design through product stages (Davenport & Short, 1990). However, within both academic and practitioner journals, there has been inconclusive evidence that an integrated supply chain is an essential strategic tool for companies to succeed (Bowman, 1997). While most (but not all) voices state that an integrated supply chain is a benefit, several voices have argued that an integrated supply chain is not necessarily beneficial in all situations (Cox, 2001; Cox & Thompson, 1998). Indeed many attempts at integrating the supply chain have not been successful (Handfield, Krause, Scanwell, & Monezka, 2000). To date there has been limited discussion as to the conditions under which a company should integrate its supply chain. Our primary purpose of this paper is to conceptualize and test a model drawing from resource dependency theory and the realities of information technologies as enablers of a successfully integrated supply chain. By doing so, it is our hope to aid managers of such firms facing the decision of joining or forming an integrated supply chain.

LITERATURE REVIEW

Resource dependency is applicable to an integrated supply chain perspective, as an integrated supply chain is based upon inter-enterprise relations or alliances and the building of supply networks (Trienkekens & Beulens, 2001). Likewise, resource dependency posits a firm is a collection of strategic coalitions created to secure critical resources for the firms including suppliers and buyers (Olavarrieta & Ellinger, 1997). Resource dependency provides an additional perspective to other supply chain management theories. We argue that resource dependency theory complements the extant integrated supply chain management literature (Trienkekens & Beulens, 2001).

Resource dependency theory suggests that a company will attempt to generate alliances with other organizations in order to maintain a consistent supply of critical resources (Pels, Coviello, & Brodie, 2000; Pfeffer & Salancik, 1978; Scott, 1987). In essence, the initiating company will create an alliance with another company that possesses a needed resource, and in doing so, will attempt to create a mutual interdependence between the two alliance members through buyer-seller exchanges and through access to other members of the initiating company's strategic alliance network. Strategic alliances allow the company to create a web that is dedicated to the survival of both the company and to the other companies in the network (Arthur, 1996; Mitchell & Singh, 1996).

Unfortunately, not all companies possess the trust and openness necessary to create and to sustain an integrated supply chain (Ratnasnigam & Phan, 2003). The success of an integrated supply chain directly depends on the performance of all the members in the alliance or network and the ability to coordinate among the different network members effectively (Swaminathan, Smith, & Sadeh, 1998). Some companies are unwilling to allow internal, sensitive data to flow to suppliers, whereas others may not be resource-dependent on external companies, and choose to compete and operate on their own. One reason for considering an alliance is the need to maximize supply chain power (Kanter, 1979; Pfeffer, 1981). Resource dependency theory posits that companies increase power by forming alliances that will reduce dependencies on external sources and will gain influence over supply chain partners (Pels, Coviello, & Brodie, 2000; Pfeffer & Salancik, 1978). In addition, strategic alliances are often borne out of environmental uncertainty caused by a multitude of factors including increased competitive forces (Barringer & Harrison, 2000).

Strategic alliances provide the company with the ability to cope with environmental uncertainty without vast increased investments in internal new-venture processes and the associated exposure to risk, while providing essential external resources and flexibility to the company (Burns, 1990; Mitchell & Singh, 1996). These alliances or networks do not have fixed boundaries but continue to contract and expand over time (Thorton & Tuma, 1995). For instance, Song's (1995) analysis of the effects of resource dependency on the hospital industry indicates that hospitals create alliances in order to better manage the process of external dependence upon other companies while protecting their core competencies.

Resource dependency has three theoretical assumptions that must be considered:

1. Companies consist of both internal and external networks or coalitions (Pfeffer & Salancik, 1978).
2. The environment plays a critical role, as it contains vital resources that are necessary for the survival of the company (Pfeffer, 1981).
3. All companies attempt to attain two objectives:
    a. To minimize the demand of essential resources by acquiring control of these resources, thus limiting external dependency.
    b. To maximize the resource dependency of other organizations to the company (Pfeffer, 1981).

In summary, "organizations attempt to alter their dependence relationships by minimizing their own dependence or by increasing the dependence of other organizations on themselves" (Ulrich & Barney, 1984, p. 472). However, resource dependency cannot always be reduced. One method of reducing the uncertainty around resource dependency is through information exchange. Information is shared among the members, and is not constrained by time and boundaries. As members of the alliance become more familiar with each other, inter-firm trust is formed and becomes embedded within the alliance group over time (Gulati, 1995; Gulati & Singh, 1998). The resulting increased information flows among channel members reduces the propensity for opportunistic behavior (Contractor & Lorange, 1988; Ratnasnigam & Phan, 2003). Mutual dependence on network partners reduces opportunistic behavior as long as the resource is critical to all members. Alliances based on non-critical resources are more likely to result in opportunistic behaviors by supply chain members.

Resource dependency theory aids in explaining the necessity for alliances and the potential value of an integrated supply chain to a company in search of critical resources. Furthermore, resource dependency suggests why companies that are able to stand-alone should not attempt to engage in an integrated supply chain. Likewise, resource dependency provides a foundation for understanding why it is necessary for a company to invest in information technologies that enable a company to integrate its supply chain by practicing greater control and coordination of the alliance.

The electronic data interchange (EDI) system is one of the means to coordinate and communicate among organizations. The capability of interorganizational systems, like EDI, to connect supply chains has been predicted and demonstrated extensively (e.g., Cash & Konsynski, 1985; Gupta, Peters, Miller, & Blyden, 2002; Narasimhan & Kim, 2001; O'Callaghan, Kaufmann, & Konsynski, 1992). More recently, Clark and Stoddard (1996) describe that technical innovations such as EDI are enablers of process innovations such as BPR (business process redesign). Narasimhan and Kim (2001) in their study examined the effects of integrating the functional level components to the entire supply chain through information technology, while Gupta, Peters, Miller, and Blyden (2002) studied the integration of strategic planning to the integrated supply chain through information technology. Additionally, supply chain electronic commerce, coupled with the commercial availability of the Internet and development of sophisticated software including ERP tools, make the integrated supply chain attainable for more organizations (e.g., Jenson & Johnson, 1999; Zheng, Yen, & Tarn, 2000). IT sophistication (Chwelos, Benbasat, & Dexter, 2001) captures the level of such technological expertise within the organization. IT sophistication, therefore, should be regarded as one of the necessary conditions that contributes to the ability to integrate supply chains. However, none of the aforementioned studies have investigated the effects of a company's external task environment, extent of resource dependency, and IT sophistication on its supply chain integration and the resulting impact on company financial performance.

RESEARCH MODEL

As stated previously, our purpose is to create and test a model of supply chain integration empirically with a theoretical foundation grounded in resource dependency theory and the IT sophistication. Chwelos, Benbasat, and Dexter (2001) have summarized various EDI-adoption studies in terms of their usage of dependent and independent variables. According to their model, Perceived Benefits of EDI, External Pressure, such as Dependency on Trading Partner, and Organizational Readiness, such as IT Sophistication, have positive impacts on a construct: "Intent to Adopt EDI." In this paper, the authors simplified this model and incorporated it so that the argument of this paper stands out. Our model is illustrated in Figure 1.

Figure 1. Proposed research model

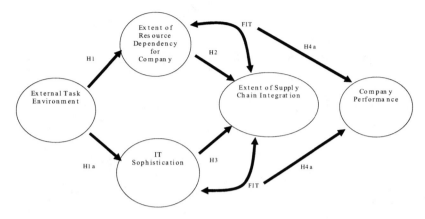

Hypotheses

The level of resource dependency will aid in predicting the company's potential benefit gained through either joining or forming an integrated supply chain. Several articles imply that the company's task environment plays a role in the level of exhibited resource dependency (e.g., Pfeffer & Salancik, 1978). The external task environment can be defined as parties that the firm interacts or conducts transactions with such as suppliers, buyers, and competitors (Dess & Beard, 1984; Dill, 1958; Brown & Eisenhardt, 1998). If a company resides in a benevolent task environment, then external resources will be non-critical. For example, a concrete manufacturer needs a constant supply of rocks, sand, and water to make concrete. These resources are in abundant supply and most likely can be controlled by the company. However, a company that is in a highly volatile environment, such as in the biotechnology industry sector, must rely on external suppliers to satisfy their demands for critical resources (Lukas, Tan, & Hult, 2001).

- **H1:** Companies in highly volatile task environments will exhibit a higher degree of Resource Dependency than companies in benevolent task environments.
- **H1a:** Companies in highly volatile task environments will exhibit a higher extent of IT Sophistication than companies in benevolent task environments.

Companies considering whether or not to initiate or to join an integrated supply chain should consider their level of resource dependency and level of information technology. Opportunistic behaviors could be more self-evident for alliances based on non-critical resources. Even if just joining an established integrated supply chain, expertise in IT is necessary to participate in such an alliance. Only companies that are high on both resource dependency and information technology will be able to fully integrate their systems and realize the full potential of an integrated supply chain, while simultaneously reducing opportunistic behavior of its members.

- **H2:** Companies with a higher degree of Resource Dependency are more likely to integrate their supply chains than companies with a lower Resource Dependency.
- **H3:** Companies with a higher extent of IT Sophistication are more likely to integrate their supply chains than companies with a lower IT Sophistication.

Companies that integrated their supply chains to manage their logistics and development costs will be more likely to show some evidence of their success in financial performance. The study also attempts to show that the match between the level of integration and the level of resource dependency and IT sophistication affects the company's performance.

- **H4:** Companies with a higher degree of integration in their supply chain management will perform better than companies with a lower degree of integration.
- **H4a:** Companies whose level of supply chain integration matches their resource dependency and information systems sophistication will perform better than companies with a mismatch between them.

RESEARCH METHODOLOGY

Instrument Development

The first phase of the study developed an instrument to measure the constructs listed in the model. The survey instrument was developed and its validity tested according to the general guidelines as set by Churchill (1979). The list of measures used is reported in Table 1.

Table 1. Scales

Construct	Source	# of items
External Task Environment (EX)	Lukas, Tan, and Hult (2001)	12
Resource Dependency (RD)	Chwelos, Benbasat, and Dexter (2001)	3
IT Sophistication (IT)	Chwelos, Benbasat, and Dexter (2001), developed from Paré and Raymond (1991)	8
Extent of Supply Chain Integration (SCI)	Developed for this study (adopted from Chwelos, Benbasat, and Dexter, 2001)	3
Company Performance (CP)	Dess and Robinson (1984)	4

Data Collection

The instrument was disseminated in the form of an html Web page driven by a FileMaker Pro database. E-mails inviting participation in this study were sent over a period of eight days from January 29 to February 7, 2003 (no e-mailing was done over the weekend). Recipients selected were all members of the U.S. Small Business Administration's procurement marketing and access network. This network has more than 195,000 members, and services small, disadvantaged, and women-owned businesses. Using this database we compiled a list of 8,000 small and medium businesses with employees of 50 or more headquartered in the U.S. All respondents contacted were considered to be top management team members, including reporting assistants and middle managers (Woolridge & Floyd, 1990). We received 820 bounced e-mails back, including 117 distinct users-not-found undeliverable error messages and 109 warnings. We also received 67 automated replies, such as "out-of-office" notifications. There were 12 positive responses for participation, as well as 52 e-mails declining participation. Sixty-seven other communications received included errors in accessing the website, clarification of questions, and notices of e-mail forwarding because of wrong addressing divisions or the addressee had moved. The Web survey yielded 329 usable responses, delivering a response rate of 4.2%. This response rate is somewhat lower than traditional mailed surveys, yet comparable with other Web-based surveys targeting top management team members (e.g., Davis, Dibrell, & Janz, 2002).

To test for non-response bias effects in our sample, we sent an additional e-mail survey invitation to non-respondents asking for information on their demographic variables of job title, total company size, and industry profiles after the questionnaire data collection period had closed (Ramaswami, 2002). Using Pearson's chi-square test of data differences between groups on each variable, we found no statistical differences between respondents and non-respondents, indicating no evidence of non-response bias associated with our sample.

The industry profiles for the responses are summarized in Table 2. The survey asked very detailed classification questions of industries, but as they yielded scattered variability (each group contained only a few data points), we aggregated them into larger classifications. The respondents, however, are representative of many types of businesses.

The distribution of questionnaires through e-mail and Web pages may have been one of the weaknesses of this data collected. It is very hard to make sure that the respondents reached were not only willing and able to participate, but were also qualified to fill in the survey instrument. A total of 329 respondents representing their company at the rank of CEO, CFO, VP, general manager, and other line management areas were recorded. Thirty-three of the respondents did not identify their job titles. Table 3 summarizes the distribution of job titles of survey respondents.

Table 2. Industry type of responding companies

	Frequency	Percent
Manufacturing (subtotal)	**157**	**47.7**
Aerospace	14	4.3
Agriculture/Forestry/Fisheries	4	1.2
Computer/Network (Software)	2	.6
Construction/Architecture/Engineering	35	10.6
Manufacturing and Processing (Other)	100	30.4
Mining/Oil/Gas	2	.6
Services (subtotal)	**110**	**33.2**
Business-Services	34	10.3
Computer/Network Consultant	7	2.1
Consultant	12	3.6
Data Processing Services	9	2.7
Education	4	1.2
Environmental	7	2.1
Marketing/Advertising	3	.9
Medical/Dental/Healthcare/Pharmaceutical	3	.9
Research/Development Lab	5	1.5
Telecom	4	1.2
Transportation	5	1.5
Utilities	2	.6
Wholesale/Trade/Retail/Distribution	15	4.6
Non-Profit/Government (Subtotal)	**10**	**3.0**
Government: Federal (including military)	5	1.5
Government: State/Local	1	.3
Nonprofit/Trade Association	4	1.2
Other	**2**	**.6**
Missing[*]	**50**	**15.2**
Total	**329**	**100.0**

* Non-Profit/Government (10) and Missing (50) data were disregarded from further analyses because of possibly different measurements of company performance.

Table 3. Job titles of respondents

	Frequency	Percent
CEO/President/Chair	96	29.2
General Manager	20	6.1
VP/Head Sales/Marketing	63	19.1
CFO/VP/Head Finance	18	5.5
CIO/VP/Head of Information Technology	4	1.2
Mgr/Dir Product/Operation/Materials	17	5.2
Mgr/Dir Proposals/Contracts/Estimates	7	2.1
Mgr/Dir Purchasing/Supply Chain	5	1.5
VP/Head Logistics	3	.9
VP/Head Procurement/Purchasing	5	1.5
Treasurer/Account Mgr	5	1.5
Other	33	10.0
Missing[*]	53	16.1
Total	329	100.0

DATA ANALYSIS AND RESULTS

Analysis of the Instrument

Following the procedures suggested by Churchill (1979), the scales were analyzed for their reliability and validity. According to Churchill, the sample of items generated from the literature search and other sources should be tested for reliability and purified by eliminating the items with low-item-to-total correlations. Table 4 summarizes the internal consistency measures (Cronbach's coefficient alpha) before and after this process.

The low scores in coefficient alphas for external environment and resource dependency (Nunnally & Bernstein, 1994, suggest .70 or higher) may hamper further investigation of this research. However, since the resource dependency construct is a significant component in this study; we decided to proceed with caution.

Churchill (1979) suggests that after the iterative process of calculating coefficient alpha, the elimination of items, and the subsequent calculation of alpha until a satisfactory coefficient is achieved, factor analysis can then be used to confirm whether the number of dimensions conceptualized can be verified empirically.

The data was factor analyzed using principal component analysis with a varimax rotation (Kim & Mueller, 1978). After refining the scales, most of the constructs factor loaded as expected except for one item (EX6), which loaded on two factors. To purify the instruments, item EX6 was eliminated from further analysis. The rotated component matrix is reproduced in Table 5.

The above analysis supports a claim of reliability and validity for four of the constructs (Resource Dependency, IT Sophistication, Extent of Supply Chain Integration, and Company Performance). The remaining construct was somewhat problematic and deserves further discussion. "External Task Environment" appears to be multidimensional. The analysis identified four sub-dimensions of this construct:

Table 4. Reliability of measures

Construct	Source	Initial		After Purification	
		# of Items	Coefficient Alpha	# of Items	Coefficient Alpha
External Task Environment (EX)	Lukas, Tan, and Hult, 2001	12	.60	9	.60
Resource Dependency (RD)	Adopted from Chwelos, Benbasat, and Dexter, 2001	3	.24	2	.52
IT Sophistication (IT)	Chwelos, Benbasat, and Dexter, 2001	8	.90	6	.91
Extent of Supply Chain Integration (SCI)	Adopted from Chwelos, Benbasat, and Dexter, 2001	3	.83	3	.83
Company Performance (CP)	Dess and Robinson, 1984	4	.81	3	.89

- predictability of technology and regulations;
- international changes;
- rapid change in customers and regulations; and
- suppliers, economic, and socio/cultural impact.

This is suggesting more complexity in this factor than was identified in the model. The measurement model for this construct was modified to reflect this complexity first using a two-tier model. A confirmatory Factor Analysis using LISREL 8.51 was conducted to assess the fit of this model. Figure 2 depicts the results of this analysis.

Structural Equation Modeling

The results of our measure development process yielded the following main research model. The main model assumes external task environment (EX) affects both resource dependency (RE) and IT sophistication (IT), and in turn RE and IT affect the extent of supply chain integration (SCI). Finally, a high level of SCI leads to better performance, and thus SCI affects corporate performance (CP). All the variables were entered in our structural equation model (LISREL

Table 5. Factor loadings of the variable on each of the eight constructs

	EX Predict	EX Int'l	EX Change	EX Supplier	Resource Dependency	IT Sofistication	SC Integration	Company Performance
EX2	.792							
EX3	.807							
EX4		.796						
EX12		.766						
EX5			.648					
EX7			-.756					
EX8				.570				
EX10				.628				
EX11				.704				
RD1					.719			
RD3					.857			
IT3						.726		
IT4						.845		
IT5						.798		
IT6						.819		
IT7						.816		
IT8						.827		
SCI1							.764	
SCI2							.755	
SCI3							.660	
CPA1								.866
CPA2								.881
CPA3								.889

Extraction Method: Principal Component Analysis. Rotation Method: Varimax with Kaiser Normalization. Rotation converged in 10 iterations

Figure 2. Second-order factor model for external task environment

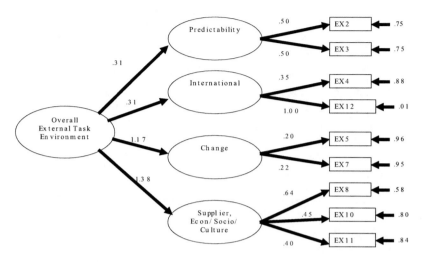

Table 6. Fit indices for external task environment measurement model

	χ^2	df	$\Delta\chi^2$	χ^2/df	GFI	AGFI	NNFI	CFI	RMSEA
One second order-factor (two-tier)	60.18*	23	-	2.62	.95	.91	.69	.80	0.078
Four first-order factor	55.91*	21	-4.27	2.66	.96	.90	.68	.81	0.079
One first-order factor	87.41*	27	27.23*	3.24	.93	.88	.54	.65	0.096
Null model	274.06 *	27	213.88*	10.15	.81	.69	-.39	0.0	0.190

* Chi-square is significant at the 0.05 level (2-tailed)

Version 8.51) at the same time. As external task environment is a two-tier construct, only the second-level construct (overall external task environment) has a link to other constructs of resource dependency and IT sophistication. The other constructs are linked according to the hypotheses described earlier. These paths and fit indices are reported in Table 9 and are shown in Figure 3. The goodness of fit index (GFI) for the initial model is 0.89, and the adjusted goodness of fit index (AGFI) is 0.86. While higher values of these indices indicate better fit, no absolute threshold levels for acceptability have been established (Hair, Anderson, Tatham, & Black, 1995). Bollen (1989) observes that cut-offs in fit indices are often arbitrary; he instead suggests comparing the fit of one's model to the fit of other prior models of the same phenomenon. Although there are

Table 7. Error variance (Zeta) and covariance matrix of ETA

	Zeta (ζ)	Predictability	International	Change	Supplier, econ/socio/culture
Predictability	0.22	0.25			
International	0.91	0.05	1.01		
Change	-0.02	0.04	0.08	0.05	
Supplier, Econ/Socio/ Culture	-0.38	0.14	0.28	0.23	0.42

None of zetas are significant at the 0.05 level (2-tailed)

Table 8. Correlation table among scale variables

	Mean	Std. D.	1	2	3	4	5
1. External Task Environment	4.27	.68	1				
2. Resource Dependency	4.06	1.50	.086	1			
3. IT Sophistication	5.71	1.23	.255**	.115	1		
4. Supply Chain Integration	3.10	1.80	.327**	.180*	.412**	1	
5. Company Performance	5.10	1.59	-.109	.145	.030	.033	1

** Correlation is significant at the 0.01 level (2-tailed); * Correlation is significant at the 0.05 level (2-tailed). Note 1: These scales are standardized to adjust to 7-point scale. Note 2: Listwise N=154

Figure 3. Structural equation model showing path

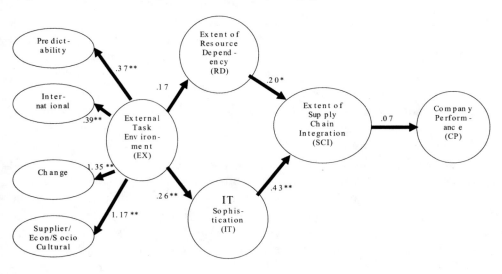

Table 9. Path and fit indices for integrated supply chain model

	Path	Standardized Solution	t-value
G11 (γ_{11})	EX → RD	0.17	1.21
G22 (γ_{22})	EX → IT	0.26	3.37**
B31 (β_{31})	RD → SCI	0.20	2.41**
B32 (β_{32})	IT → SCI	0.43	5.93**
B43 (β_{43})	SCI → CP	0.07	0.91
Z1 (ζ_1)	Error RD	0.97	1.31
Z2 (ζ_2)	Error IT	0.93	6.31**
Z3 (ζ_3)	Error SCI	0.77	6.88**
Z4 (ζ_4)	Error CP	1.00	7.07**

** indicates the p-value is less than .01

χ^2	374.53 (df= 221, p<.001)
χ^2/df	1.69
GFI	0.89
AGFI	0.86
NNFI	0.90
CFI	0.92
RMSEA	0.051

# of Observations = 266; linear trend at point missing value replacement (regression imputation; see, e.g., Olinsky, Chen, & Harlow, 2003)

alternative models of general system adoption, there are no prior models including all the factors used in our conceptualization. A focus of this research is to find relationships among resource dependency, IT sophistication, and extent of supply chain integration, not to find an exact fit of a particular model.

Hypotheses 1 and 1a

The results presented in Figure 3 shows mixed support for these hypotheses. Linking external task environment to IT sophistication was supported, but not from external task environment to resource dependency. It seems that the level of resource dependency is irrespective of the current external environment. It might be argued that even in a volatile environment, the importance of resources for buyers may not change—it is important. However, this result should be taken cautiously, as the measurement reliability for resource dependency and external task environment constructs were very low; thus the relationship between them could have been attenuated. On the other hand, the level of IT sophistication is well linked with the extent of volatility in the external environment. This result is consistent with previous studies in which a rapidly changing environment is a driver of automation and utilization of information technology.

Hypotheses 2 and 3

As indicated by the significant coefficients shown in the Figure 3, resource dependency and IT are both related to the level of supply chain integration, supporting both Hypotheses 2 and 3.

Hypothesis 4

Hypothesis 4 assumed better company performance in the organizations as a result of supply chain integration. Unfortunately this hypothesis was not supported. As in many cases of IT/IS research, it is very difficult to link IT with corporate financial data, especially with cross-sectional data like this. It may take some time to realize the full benefit of an IT investment that results in better communications and streamlined operations attained by integrating the supply chain. A longitudinal study might find better support for the relationships described here.

Hypothesis 4a

The final step of data analysis was testing for the effects of fit between RD and SCI, and IT and SCI on the company performance. Following the nested goodness-of-fit strategy test suggested by Jaccard and Wan (1996, p.25), a three-step sequence was employed for analyzing the effect of fit. First, subjects were divided into two groups based on a median split of company performance; LISREL 8.51 was then used to generate the goodness-of-fit in terms of Chi-square when each group's path coefficients were estimated freely. In the second step, one of the coefficients was restricted to impose an across-group constraint to limit the interaction effect. In the third step, the difference in model fit (Chi-square) for the restricted solution and free solution was calculated, and based on the size of this difference (with df=1), a conclusion about the interaction effect was made.

The p-values for the Chi-square differences were both not significant, indicating that the same coefficients were estimated regardless of whether they were estimated freely or the same structure was imposed on both groups. Therefore, Hypothesis 4a was not supported. However, notice that in the low performance group, the path from resource dependency to supply chain integration became non-significant. This could be the effect of a mismatch between resource dependency and the supply chain integration, which resulted in low performance. Likewise, the (insignificant) result could be caused by the weaker statistical power due to the smaller sample size (i.e., when dividing the sample into two groups); however, the linkage between resource dependency and supply chain integration was significant for the high performers.

Table 10. Results of the analysis of effects of fit on performance

Path	Low Performance Group (n=133)		High Performance Group (n=133)		Restricted Model		χ^2	$\Delta\chi^2$	p-value
	coefficient	t-value	coefficient	t-value	coefficient	t-value			
RD → SCI	0.24	1.43	0.48	2.35**	0.33	2.58**	711.65	2.70	0.1003
IT → SCI	0.41	3.59**	0.63	5.14**	0.52	5.94**	712.42	3.47	0.0625

Restricted model's χ^2 is 720.35 (df=497), and completely free model's χ^2 is 708.95 (df=473). The difference in χ^2 is 6.92 (df=24), (p=0.998).

DISCUSSION AND CONCLUSIONS

As seen in our results section, we found mixed outcomes for our hypotheses. Our findings, however, do provide a greater understanding of the roles of external task environment, degree of resource dependency, and extent of IT sophistication on a company's supply chain integration. First, our findings indicate that the external task environment does play a critical role in relation to a company's extent of IT sophistication. IT enables managers to feel more confident in their decision making by allowing better information to flow to them. Managers in more unpredictable environments seemingly have a strong affinity to use IT to make decisions and to use more sophisticated forms of IT.

Second, we found interesting results in relation to the unpredictability and impact of the external task environment on a company's degree of resource dependency on its largest supply chain partner. This is somewhat surprising, as we expected to find a greater dependency on a company's largest supplier as the external task environment became more unpredictable. A possible explanation to our finding is that most firms use a competitive bidding process to keep suppliers in line and attempt to have several suppliers supplying them in order to remove uncertainty from their supply chain. Conversely, the role of industry effects may a play greater role than we had anticipated (c.f., Powell, 1996). A compelling point of our research design is that we have strong external generalizability due to the industry cross-section of our sample. In this instance, our sample may actually be a weakness, as some industries may place a greater emphasis on having strong supplier relationships (e.g., Intel and Dell Computers) than other industries (e.g., consultants or government agencies).

Third, our potentially most influential finding can be seen in the robust relation to the extent of supply chain integration with resource dependency and IT sophistication. In essence, the degree of resource dependency on key suppliers and the extent of IT sophistication play a critical role in the extent of supply chain integration. As resource dependency theory suggests, firms in need of vital resources will attempt to remove uncertainty. As seen in our model, these firms attempt to remove uncertainty through an integrated supply chain. Likewise, firms that demonstrate a high extent of IT sophistication will be more likely to employ an integrated supply chain. The strength of this finding is that it cuts across manufacturing and service sectors.

Fourth, our findings indicate a lack of support for the direct path between an integrated supply chain and company performance. Once again, this finding could be the case of our cross-sectional industry research design masking possible industries where an integrated supply chain does have a strong impact on financial performance. Conversely, an integrated supply chain could be considered to be a support activity in a company's internal value chain (Porter, 1980), and thus the direct effects of an integrated supply chain may not be visible (similar to the research of IT on company performance). We propose that the indirect effects of an integrated supply chain do have an effect on a company's performance, as noted in the extant literature (e.g., Wisner, 2003). Furthermore, the fit between resource dependency and supply chain integration, along with the fit between IT sophistication and supply chain integration, had nothing to do with performance. The model hypothesized that the fit between the supply chain integration and resource dependency or IT sophistication would affect company performance positively. Unfortunately, this might be the result of weaker statistical power, but the data did not support this hypothesis. Also another possible explanation is that the result of the integrated supply chain has not been materialized in company performance because this study was performed at a single point in time; some companies may be realizing the effect of streamlined processes and responsive communication later on.

From our discussion, we believe that managers can take something of value from our findings with regard to the importance of IT sophistication and the degree of resource dependency when deciding upon the need or desire to more fully integrate their company's supply chain. The value of a company's degree of IT sophistication should also be evident in our findings, as IT plays a pivotal role in allowing managers to better interpret their external task environment, and to implement and manage their integrated supply chain successfully. For firms that do not possess a strong IT sophistication capability, they may wish to consider either sourcing for this capability or acquiring it in the open market if they wish to operate an integrated supply chain.

This study does not come without limitations. One of the largest limitations is that even though we used previously validated scales, they were validated in different contexts, and thus may not be completely applicable to the issues at hand. It might be necessary to further investigate the phenomena using newly developed scales for this purpose. Another limitation is the sample. A Web-based survey used in conjunction with email solicitations resulted in a very low response rate and a large variation in respondents in terms of industries and positions in the organization. The sample shows great generalizability to industries of all kinds, except for non-profit and government organizations that are excluded from our sample. However, our sample is limited to small and medium sized companies, and may not be generalizable to large corporations. Also, the sample contains variability in the positions within the supply chain from upstream manufacturing companies to downstream customers. The way companies utilize the integrated supply chains is different among these positions, and thus, the benefits they enjoy should be different. This may have resulted in the insignificant effect of supply chain integration on company's performance.

Despite these limitations, we argue that full benefits of an integrated supply chain cannot be achieved by all firms, as the literature has consistently postulated. Levels of resource dependency and information-based technology sophistication play integral parts in the potential rewards of an integrated supply chain. Without the ability to share information throughout the alliance, the integrated supply chain would be unthinkable. This paper has attempted to explain why some firms perform better in an integrated supply chain than others. The hope of the authors was not to dampen the enthusiasm regarding integrated supply chains, but to point out potential fallacies that are illuminated through theory, but have largely been ignored by both practitioner and academic writers. Thus, this paper provides a point of reference for managers who are contemplating entering into an integrated supply chain.

REFERENCES

Arthur, W. B. (1996). Increasing returns and the new world of business. *Harvard Business Review, 74*(4), 100-111.

Barringer, B. R., & Harrison, J.S. (2000). Walking a tightrope: Creating value through interorganizational relationships. *Journal of Management, 26*(3), 367-403.

Bollen, K.A. (1989). *Structural equations with latent variables.* New York: John Wiley & Sons.

Bowman, R.J. (1997). The state of the supply chain. *Distribution, 96*(1), 28-36.

Brown, S. L., & Eisenhardt, K. M. (1998). *Competing on the edge: Strategy as structured chaos.* Boston: Harvard Business School Press.

Burns, L. R. (1990). The transformation of the American hospital: From community institution toward business enterprise. *Comparative Social Research,* (12), 77-112.

Cash, J. I. Jr., & Konsynski, B. R. (1985). IS redraws competitive boundaries. *Harvard Business Review, 63*(2), 134-143.

Churchill, G.A. (1979). A paradigm for developing better measures of marketing constructs. *Journal of Marketing Research, 16,* 64-73.

Chwelos, P., Benbasat, I., & Dexter, A.S. (2001). Research report: Empirical test of an EDI adoption mode. *Information Systems Research, 12*(3), 304-321.

Clark, T. H., & Stoddard, D. B. (1996). Interorganizational business process redesign: Merging technological and process innovation. *Journal of Management Information Systems, 13*(2), 9-28.

Contractor, F. J., & Lorange, P. (1988). *Cooperative strategies in international business*. Lexington, MA: Lexington Books.

Cox, A. (2001). Understanding buyer and supplier power: A framework for procurement and supply competence. *Journal of Supply Chain Management, 37*(2), 8-15.

Cox, A., & Thompson, I. (1998). On the appropriateness of benchmarking. *Journal of General Management, 23*(3), 1-20.

Davenport, T. H., & Short, J. E. (1990). The new industrial engineering: Information technology and business process redesign. *Sloan Management Review, 31*(4), 11-27.

Davis, P. S., Dibrell, C. C., & Janz, B. (2002). The impact of time on the strategy-performance relationship: Implications for managers. *Industrial Marketing Management, 31*(4), 339-347.

Dess, G., & Beard, D. (1984). Dimensions of organizational task environments. *Administrative Science Quarterly, 29,* 52-73.

Dess, G. G., & Robinson, R. B. (1984). Measuring organizational performance in the absence of objective measures: The case of the privately held firm and conglomerate business unit. *Strategic Management Journal, 5,* 263-272.

Dill, W.R. (1958). Environment as an influence on management autonomy, *Administrative Science Quarterly, 2,* 409-443.

Gulati, R. (1995). Does familiarity breed trust? The implications of repeated ties for contractual choice in alliances. *Academy of Management Journal, 38,* 85-112.

Gulati, R., & Singh, H. (1998). The architecture of cooperation: Managing coordination costs and appropriation concerns in strategic alliances. *Administrative Science Quarterly, 43,* 781-814.

Gupta, V., Peters, E., Miller, T., & Blyden, K. (2002). Implementing a distribution-network decision-support system at Pfizer/Warner-Lambert. *Interfaces, 32*(4), 28-45.

Hackney R., Burn J., & Dhillon G. (2000). Strategic planning for e-commerce systems (SPECS): A new approach to strategic planning for e-commerce systems. *Proceedings of the Americas Conference on Information Systems* (pp. 843-847), Long Beach, California, August 10-13.

Hair, J. F., Anderson, R. E., Tatham, R. L., & Black, W. C. (1995). *Multivariate data analysis* (4th ed.). Englewood Cliffs, NJ: Prentice-Hall.

Handfield, R., Krause, D., Scanwell T., & Monezka R. (2000). Avoid the pitfalls in supplier development. *Sloan Management Review, 41*(2), 37-49.

Hertz, S. (2001). Dynamics of alliances in highly integrated supply chain networks. *International Journal of Logistics: Research & Applications, 4*(2), 237-256.

Jaccard, J., & Wan, C.K. (1996). *LISREL approaches to interaction effects in multiple regression.* Thousand Oaks, CA: Sage Publications.

Jenson, R. L., & Johnson, I. R. (1999). The enterprise resource planning system as a strategic solution. *Information Strategy: The Executive's Journal, 15*(4), 28-33.

Kanter, R.M. (1979). Power failure in management circuits. *Harvard Business Review, 57*(4), 65-75.

Kim, J. O., & Mueller, C. (1978). *Factor analysis: Statistical methods and practical issues.* Beverly Hills, CA: Sage Publications.

King, J. (2000). *Pottermania strains e-commerce supply chain.* Retrieved on July 5, 2000, from http://www.cnn.com/2000/TECH/computing/07/05/rowlings.book.idg/index.html.

Lukas, B. A., Tan, J. J., & Hult, G. T. (2001). Strategic fit in transitional economies: The case of China's electronics industry. *Journal of Management, 27*, 409-429.

Mitchell, W., & Singh, K. (1996). Survival of businesses using collaborative relationships to commercialize complex goods. *Strategic Management Journal,* (17), 169-195.

Narasimhan, R., & Kim, S.W. (2001). Information system utilization strategy for supply chain integration. *Journal of Business Logistics, 22*(2), 51-75.

Nunnally, J. C., & Bernstein, I. H. (1994). *Psychometric theory.* New York: McGraw-Hill.

O'Callaghan, R., Kaufmann, P. J., & Konsynski, B. R. (1992). Adoption correlates and share effects of electronic data interchange systems in marketing channels. *Journal of Marketing, 56*(2), 45-56.

Olavarrieta, S., & Ellinger, A. E. (1997). Resource-based theory and strategic logistics research. *International Journal of Physical Distribution & Logistics Management, 27*(9/10), 559-587.

Olinsky, A., Chen, S., & Harlow, L. (2003). The comparative efficacy of imputation methods for missing data in structural equation modeling. *European Journal of Operational Research, 151*(1), 53-79.

Paré, G., & Raymond, L. (1991). Measurement of information systems sophistication in SMEs. *Proceedings of Administration Sciences Association of Canada* (pp. 90-101).

Pels, J., Coviello, N. E., & Brodie, R. J. (2000). Integrating transactional and relational marketing exchange: A pluralistic perspective. *Journal of Marketing Theory & Practice, 8*(3), 11-20.

Pfeffer, J. (1981). *Power in organizations*. Marshfield, MA: Pitman.

Pfeffer, J., & Salancik, G. (1978). *The external control of organizations*. New York: Harper and Row.

Porter, M. E. (1980). *Competitive strategy: Techniques for analyzing industries and competitors*. New York: The Free Press.

Powell, T. C. (1996). How much does industry matter? An alternative empirical test. *Strategic Management Journal*, 17, 323-334.

Ramaswami, S. N. (2002). Influence of control systems on opportunistic behaviors of salespeople: A test of gender differences. *Journal of Personal Selling & Sales Management*, *22*(3), 173-188.

Ratnasnigam, P., & Phan, D. D. (2003). Trading partner trust in B2B e-commerce: A case study. *Information Systems Management*, *20*(3), 39-50.

Scott, J. (1987). *Organizations*. Englewood Cliffs, NJ: Simon and Schuster.

Sliwa, C. (2002). Analysis: IT troubles helped take K-Mart down. *CNN.com.Sci-Tech*. Retrieved on January 29, 2002, from http://www.cnn.com/2002/TECH/industry/01/29/kmart.bankruptcy.idg/index.html.

Song, Y. I. (1995). Strategic alliances in the hospital industry: A fusion of institutional and resource dependence views. *Academy of Management Journal, Best Paper Proceedings* (pp. 271-275).

Swaminathan, J. M., Smith, S. F., & Sadeh, N. M. (1998). Modeling supply chain dynamics: A multiagent approach. *Decision Sciences, 29*(3), 606-632.

Thorton, P. H., & Tuma, N. B. (1995). The problem of boundaries in contemporary research on organizations. *Academy of Management Journal, Best Paper Proceedings* (pp. 276-280).

Trienekens, J. H., & Beulens, A. J. M. (2001). Views on inter-enterprise relationships. *Production Planning & Control*, *12*(5), 466-477.

Ulrich, D., & Barney, J.B. (1984). Perspectives in organizations: Resources dependence, efficiency, and population. *Academy of Management Review, 9*(3), 471-481.

Wisner, J. D. (2003). A structural equation model of supply chain management strategies and firm performance. *Journal of Business Logistics*, *24*(1), 1-26.

Woolridge, B., & Floyd, S. W. (1990). The strategy process, middle manager involvement, and organizational performance. *Strategic Management Journal*, 11, 231-241.

Zheng, S., Yen, D. C., & Tarn, J. M. (2000). The new spectrum of the cross-enterprise solution: The integration of supply chain management and enterprise resources planning systems. *The Journal of Computer Information Systems, 41*(1), 84-93.

This chapter was previously published in the *Information Resources Management Journal, 17*(3), 1-19, July-September, Copyright © 2004.

Chapter XI

Identifying and Managing the Enablers of Knowledge Sharing

W. A. Taylor
University of Bradford, UK

G. H. Wright
Manchester Metropolitan University Business School, UK

ABSTRACT

Knowledge sharing in public services has not yet received much attention in the research literature. This chapter investigates knowledge sharing in one public service context, the UK National Health Service (NHS), and identifies factors that influence the readiness of an organization to share knowledge effectively. Using participant observation, document analysis, interviews, and a survey of managers, data are presented to highlight enablers of effective knowledge sharing in health care service delivery. Through factor analysis and regression modeling, we have isolated six factors that are significant predictors of effective knowledge sharing. Our research is broadly consistent with previous findings that an innovative culture, a capacity to learn from failure, and good information quality are strong predictors of successful knowledge sharing. However, we also identify factors associated with change management and a predisposition to confront performance indicators that significantly influence the knowledge sharing process. We suggest that the peculiar nature of the public sector environment poses unique challenges for health care managers who seek to develop a knowledge sharing capability.

INTRODUCTION

This chapter contributes to our understanding of an increasingly important practical problem, namely, the effectiveness of adoption of knowledge management in organizations. As with many other managerial innovations, knowledge management (KM) appears to have been adopted firstly by manufacturing firms and is only now beginning to permeate the service sector, predominantly in professional services such as consulting (Hansen, Nohria, & Tierney, 1999; Sarvary, 1999). Public services, traditionally slower to embrace innovative management practices, are only beginning to recognize the importance of knowledge management. There is, as yet, little published research of its implementation in this context (Bate & Robert, 2002; Sharifuddin & Rowland, 2004; van Beveren, 2003).

This chapter examines knowledge sharing in the context of public services partnerships between organizations mandated by government policy to jointly improve the delivery of health care services. In particular, the chapter explores the central roles of knowledge sharing, learning, and information provision in the improvement of service delivery in the UK National Health Service (NHS). Our research question focused on the issue of how to make knowledge sharing more effective. In other words, are there broader organizational factors, beyond the dynamics of individual sharer-receiver interactions, that significantly influence knowledge sharing? To that end, the chapter firstly reviews what can be learned about knowledge management from previous research, which has predominantly been grounded in the private sector. We then discuss the public sector context of health care in general and the concept of partnership working in particular. We outline possible external influences that may uniquely affect knowledge sharing therein. Results are then presented from our empirical study of UK health and social care partnerships, highlighting some significant enablers of knowledge sharing practice. The findings support the small but growing body of evidence that motivational and reward factors are not the main influencers of knowledge sharing (Bock & Kim, 2002; Stonehouse, Buehring, & Pemberton, 2002; Szulanski, 1996).

KNOWLEDGE MANAGEMENT

Studies of knowledge management practices have been predominantly of two types to date: (a) surveys, often sponsored by consulting groups, with limited reporting of the underpinning methodologies, and (b) case studies in individual firms. These studies provide some insight into KM implementation and have influenced our research design. For example, in Ernst and Young's survey of 431 private organizations (Ruggles, 1998), it was concluded that the main barriers to implementing knowledge management were all people related, that is, a culture that inhibited knowledge sharing, a lack of top management leadership, and poor understanding of what KM involved. Similar studies by KPMG (1999) of 100 UK companies, and by the Conference Board (Hackett, 2000) of 200 companies broadly confirmed these findings.

However, these three surveys highlighted some differences. For example, lack of time and lack of perceived benefits were cited in the KPMG survey as the most significant barriers to knowledge sharing, while the Conference Board survey added that there was little observed integration between firms' activities in knowledge management and the promotion of organizational learning. Leidner (2000) underlined the same point: "Although a well-established tradition of organizational learning research could be considered an adumbration if not a forerunner of organizational KM, KM as a research discipline has drawn less from organizational learning than from strategy research" (p. 100).

Nonaka (1994) also recognized the link between knowledge sharing and organizational learning in his discussion of the interactions between tacit and explicit knowledge and their subsequent spiraling through different organizational levels. Although his work is largely related to knowledge creation, all four of his tacit-explicit transformation processes could apply equally to knowledge sharing. Nonaka's SECI model has become very influential in both research and practice; however, less recognition has been given to the importance he placed upon information in this process: "Information is a necessary medium for initiating and formalizing knowledge … in short, information is a flow of messages, while knowledge is created and organized by the very flow of information, anchored on the commitment and beliefs of its holders" (p. 15).

This critical interdependence of information and knowledge was underscored by Blumentritt and Johnston (1999) who argued that information is not only a necessary antecedent to knowledge creation and use, but it is also the medium by which knowledge is transferred. McDermott (1999) echoed the same theme, commenting that while the knowledge revolution was inspired by new information systems, it is ironic that it takes people to make knowledge management happen. In McDermott's terms, this is not because people are reluctant to use IT, but rather because knowledge involves thinking with information: "To leverage knowledge we need to enhance both thinking and information" (p. 116). It is this dependence on the enabling role of information resources that makes knowledge management so challenging.

McDermott's comment also stresses the importance of people in the knowledge sharing process—people who allegedly need to be motivated to engage in an activity that requires additional time and carries a threat of loss of power or status (Porter, 1985). More recent research (Bock & Kim, 2002; Szulanski, 1996) has challenged this view. Szulanski's study of intra-firm transfer of best practices found that three factors dominated motivational barriers to knowledge sharing, namely, lack of absorptive capacity, causal ambiguity, and arduous relationships between sharer and receiver. Similarly, Bock and Kim found that motivational factors were negatively correlated with knowledge sharing in a study of four Korean organizations, while Huber (2001) questioned the strongly held view of practitioners (and some researchers) that motivation is the key to effective knowledge sharing. Huber's assertion that "what we know about the transfer of knowledge is greatly exceeded by what we do not know" (p. 73) is sustained by the comparatively small amount of substantive research published to date. There appears to be a need to look beyond incentives and rewards for knowledge sharing and to focus scarce resources and managerial attention on developing the learning capabilities of the organization (Szulanski, 1996).

This perspective on developing organizational capabilities for knowledge sharing was expanded by Gold, Malhotra, and Segars (2001) who postulated that such capabilities were necessary preconditions for effective knowledge management to flourish, and without which, launching a knowledge sharing initiative, however well-intentioned, might be "doomed before it begins" (p. 208). Assessing an organization's readiness for knowledge sharing is a compelling argument that has the potential to complement much of the existing research on the dynamics of interactions between knowledge sharer and receiver at the individual level, as propounded by Szulanski, Bock and Kim, and others. Thus, the literature suggests that implementation of knowledge sharing places a renewed focus on the importance of information and on organizational factors such as learning capability and culture.

In one of the few studies of knowledge management in the UK health care sector, Bate and Robert (2002) evaluated three collaborative partnerships, formed as part of the government's modernization agenda. While they observed that these collaborative arrangements seemed apposite for knowledge sharing among NHS organizations, because of their emphasis on network structures, they concluded that, as presently constituted, they are not effective mechanisms for knowledge sharing, primarily because of a neglect of the softer, people aspects of these partnerships. Bate and Robert's research provides a point of departure for this chapter, based on their call for more research that identifies "the organizational impediments to the transfer of good practice in the NHS and the mechanisms that will be required to allow the necessary knowledge conversions and boundary crossings to occur" (p. 660).

RESEARCH METHOD

Background

It was against this background that we selected care partnerships in the UK NHS, with the objective of identifying factors that significantly influence the knowledge sharing process at the organizational rather than the personal (sharer-receiver) level. The UK health care sector has been experiencing "relentless, almost hyperactive government intervention in the last five years" (Appleby & Coote, 2002). Increased external regulation and accountability in public services is commonplace in many developed countries, with performance measurement and performance management high on the agenda (Rashid, 1999; Smith, 1995, 1996). Such are the pressures imposed on UK health care managers that there have been recent instances of deliberate distortion of performance statistics, where patient records were altered, their names were not added to lists, or they were taken off the list even though they had not been treated (Audit Commission, 2003; National Audit Office, 2001).

Public Sector Partnerships

Another government policy intervention is the requirement for partnership working between purchasers and providers of care services (Department of Health, 1998; HMSO, 2001) to breakdown inter-organizational barriers in the service value chain, and to provide integrated health and social care to each patient as a unified service. This notion of "joined-up" or "seamless" service delivery seeks to share good practices across the value chain through better interconnection and mutual support among National Health Service departments, local authority social services departments, private sector providers of residential care, and the voluntary/charity sector. Working in partnership implies the sharing of best practices, both within each organization and among the partners. Fundamental to this partnership approach to service delivery is therefore the sharing of information and knowledge across organizational and professional boundaries (Irvine & Haman, 2001).

Research Design

We chose one UK NHS region where partnership working among care providers was being implemented.

The research design comprised:

- 30 key informant interviews
- participant observation
- an in-depth service study of four key areas of health care service provision involving services for (a) the elderly, (b) children with severe disabilities, (c) food and nutrition initiatives, and (d) community policing
- a region-wide survey of all care professionals (n = 132)
- document analysis of national, local, and project-based health care policies and plans

The 30 key informant interviews were used to complement our literature review on knowledge sharing. Given that most of the knowledge sharing literature derives from the private sector, it was important to understand the public sector context. Therefore, these 30 interviews, representing over 50 hours of discussion, were tape-recorded and examined using content analysis, and the identified themes were incorporated into the questionnaire design.

Sample and Survey Instrument

The sample population was care managers working in the partnerships. The survey instrument was a six-page questionnaire consisting of statements relating to service delivery, knowledge sharing, and organizational practices associated with performance improvement, including information provision and change management. A total of 132 responses were received from the 500 question-naires distributed, representing a response rate of 26%. As a preliminary survey, we consider this response rate to be acceptable.

Analysis Procedures

The first stage involved the selection of questions to include in the final data set for this analysis. We chose 30 variables that, from the qualitative analysis of the interviews and based on the literature, we judged to be associated with effective knowledge sharing. The initial case-to-variable ratio fell slightly short of the recommended minimum of 5:1 (Hair et al., 1998), although we note that some exploratory studies have gone as low as 2:1 (Fuller & Swanson, 1992). The critical assumptions underlying factor analysis were tested using the Bartlett test of sphericity and the Kaiser-Meyer-Olkin measure of sampling adequacy (KMO = 0.860). Reverse scoring was applied to some variables to prevent a canceling out of items with positive and negative valences. The independent variables were subjected to exploratory factor analysis using Principal Components Analysis as the extraction method and Varimax rotation with Kaiser normalization. All factors with eigenvalues greater than 1.0 were extracted.

Factor loadings were evaluated on two criteria: the significance of the loadings and the simplicity of the factor structure. Items were deleted from the analysis according to guidelines developed by Churchill (1979) and Kim and Mueller (1978), namely, loadings of less than 0.5 or cross-loadings greater than 0.35 on two or more factors. On this basis, after the first factor analysis, two items were deleted. A second iteration resulted in one more item being deleted. This iterative process is recommended as an effective way of deriving a stable factor structure (Rai, Borah, & Ramprasad, 1996; Sethi & King, 1991). After three iterations, all remaining 27 variables loaded satisfactorily onto the six latent factors. The data were tested for acceptable levels of variable communality and multicollinearity by way of the Variance Inflation Factor (VIF). Based on the generally accepted threshold (VIF = 10), no problems were found in the data. We then used multiple regression with the six composite independent factors, expressed as factor scores calculated from the item responses, regressed with the dependent variable of effective knowledge sharing.

RESULTS

Table 1 shows the construct strengths for the six latent factors extracted from the 27 variables and the loadings for the principal factor to which each variable contributes. Item statements with reversed valences are indicated "R".

Table 2 shows the multiple regression of the dependent variable, effectiveness of knowledge sharing, regressed onto all six latent factors.

The results were examined for validity and reliability. Three different types of validity were considered: content, construct, and criterion validity.

Content Validity

A factor is considered to have content validity if there is theoretical support from the literature that items included in each summated factor representatively sample the intended domain of the concept it is intended to measure. The discussion in the preceding literature review reflects the genesis of our constructs in the relevant literature, and this, alongside the findings from our 30 exploratory interviews, establishes the content validity of our instrument. More insight into the interview findings is contained in the following discussion section, through the inclusion of selected quotations.

Construct Validity

A factor possesses construct validity if it measures the theoretical construct that it was designed to represent. The construct validity of each factor was evaluated by using Principal Components Analysis, using a minimum factor loading of 0.5 to screen out variables that were weak indicators of the constructs. All 27 items loaded acceptably well onto the factors.

Table 1. Factor analysis

ITEMS	FACTOR					
	1	2	3	4	5	6
Open leadership climate **α = 0.9346**						
Accepting new ideas	.823					
Motivating staff to develop new ideas	.770					
Encouraging staff to suggest new things	.701					
There is a rigid and hierarchical structure [R]	.662					
Recognizing the importance of people	.657					
Strategic inclusion of all staff	.641					
Change seen as a positive challenge	.638					
Systematically reflecting on success	.580					
Token consultation with staff [R]	.535					
Systems exist to facilitate learning	.501					
Strong leadership	.500					
Learning from failure **α = 0.8869**						
Systematically learning from failure		.718				
Regularly reflecting on what doesn't work		.691				
Having a user focus for continuous improvement		.653				
Satisfaction with change processes **α = 0.7672**						
Constantly high levels of stress [R]			.731			
Continuous changes of target outcomes [R]			.678			
Experiencing discomfort with change [R]			.652			
Results of innovation not apparent to staff [R]			.508			
Information quality **α = 0.7974**						
User focused information				.829		
Appropriate information systems				.787		
Service quality performance data reviewed				.640		
Performance orientation **α = 0.7439**						
Defensiveness impedes improvement [R]					.820	
Ignoring performance statistics [R]					.693	
Imperative to be seen as successful [R]					.678	
A vision for change **α = 0.7471**						
Lack of urgency to change [R]						.837
Perceived need to improve user responsiveness						.759
Desiring the status quo [R]						.552
Eigenvalues	12.0	2.7	1.7	1.5	1.3	1.1
% of variance explained	43.2	9.2	5.9	5.2	4.7	3.7
Cumulative % of variance explained	43.2	52.4	58.3	63.5	68.2	71.9

Table 2. Multiple regression analysis

Factor	Beta	T	Significance
Open leadership climate	0.516	7.693	0.000
Information quality	0.235	3.508	0.001
Satisfaction with change processes	0.216	3.220	0.002
Learning from failure	0.204	3.036	0.003
A vision for change	0.130	1.932	0.009
Performance orientation	0.103	1.542	0.056

Model Summary	R	R^2	Adjusted R^2	Std error of estimate
	0.661	0.437	0.410	1.05

Analysis of Variance

	Sum of squares	Df	Mean Square	F	Significance
Regression	106.531	6	17.755	16.198	0.000
Residual	137.015	125	1.096		
Total	243.545	131			
Dependent variable: Effective knowledge sharing					

Criterion Validity

Criterion validity is concerned with the degree to which the model's independent variables explain or predict the dependent (criterion) variable. The coefficient of determination was used to assess the proportion of the variance in the dependent variable (effective knowledge sharing) about its mean that was explained by the six independent latent variables. With a coefficient of determination value >0.40, for the specified sample size and the number of independent variables, the results indicate the six factors have a reasonably high degree of criterion-related validity (Nunally, 1978).

Reliability

Reliability is an assessment of the degree of consistency between multiple measurements of a variable. Cronbach's alpha is the most widely used measure with a generally agreed lower limit of 0.70. Hair et al. (1998) caution that where a factor has a high number of items, the Cronbach's alpha value should be subject to more stringent requirements. The reliability measures for each factor in Table 1 meet these acceptability requirements, even for factor 1 ($\alpha = 0.9346$) where there are 11 items.

DISCUSSION OF RESULTS

The central research objective was to identify factors that significantly influence the knowledge sharing process at the organizational, rather than the personal (sharer-receiver), level in NHS partnerships. Our results suggest that effective knowledge sharing is indeed shaped by wider organizational issues beyond the dynamics of interactions between individual sharer-receiver dyads. They represent significant challenges for the management of an organization, without which knowledge sharing is likely to be ineffectual. The six factors in our model are all associated with the culture and information infrastructure of the organizations. Moreover, the multiple regression analysis reveals the influence of each factor on effective knowledge sharing, relative to the other factors. In so doing, the resultant regression model (Figure 1) gives managers further insight into what they must do to make their organizations ready for, and to encourage knowledge sharing, that is, to nurture an appropriate organizational context that develops knowledge sharing enablers or facilitators and eliminates obstacles (Stonehouse et al., 2002).

In Figure 1, each of the factors is significantly and positively associated with the dependent variable, with five of the factors being highly significant ($p < 0.01$). In the following sections, we consider the logic and practical implications of each of these factors, using selected quotations to illuminate the discussion.

Figure 1. Knowledge sharing model

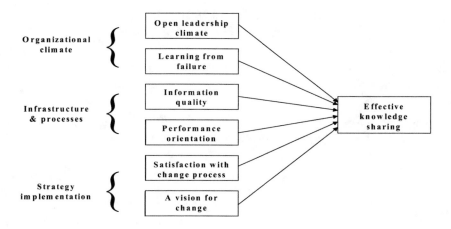

Creating an Open and Innovative Climate

An innovative climate is one where new ideas are welcomed and accepted and where people feel motivated to engage in improvement activities. Several respondents commented on the peculiar difficulties this posed for the public sector, where opportunities to incentivize staff are comparatively limited:

We're not like private sector companies who can offer share options or pay annual bonuses to staff; everybody gets the same rate of pay, even if you just sit at your desk and shuffle the paperwork, day after day.

Respondents also referred to the problems posed by the highly regulated, hierarchical, and top-down nature of the sector, where government decides on policies and procedures:

I try to get staff to think about new ways of working but they are all stuck in a mindset of procedures and going by the book.

Most of them are happiest when they simply follow the 'rules'; they'd rather think about next month's holiday or last night's sports results than come up with a good work idea.

We are rewarded for doing things the way we always have, and discouraged, at the very least, to challenge this. Our protocols mitigate against any change whatsoever.

In some of the organizations, managers talked about how they had over-come these challenges, by consulting staff about key decisions and by instituting non-monetary rewards for suggestions and by publicizing improvement ideas in in-house publications:

I find that most staff want to do the best for the public, and once you make them feel that they can make a difference, it snowballs.

While it is true that there is a reluctance to look at new ideas, there really is a lot of latitude for how we implement things at the local level—people at the customer interface know what works best and if you give them a hearing you can get a lot of leveraged improvement for very little cost.

Above all, you've got to let them see that you are listening, and willing to try out their ideas. If you give them time to reflect on what has worked well in the past, and put them into regular discussion groups, the flow of innovation can be staggering. Monetary incentives don't matter—they want to have pride in their work and the satisfaction of doing things better.

This factor emphasizes the need for health care managers to provide clear and exemplary leadership, to empower employees to challenge the rules, and to proactively search for better working methods and systems. Without the lever of extrinsic monetary rewards, managers should concentrate on the intrinsic motivation of taking pride in doing a good job and performing well. While health care policies are externally defined by government, managers need to facilitate local participation of staff in policy implementation. This should promote ownership and involvement, and foster the necessary bottom-up flow of innovative ideas (Kim & Mauborgne, 1997). Health care managers should complement this with regular review sessions with groups of staff to stimulate reflection on what has worked well previously.

Learning from Failure

Interestingly, while learning from what works well featured in the first factor, the analysis reveals a second, related but distinct, issue concerned with learning from things that do not work well. Organizations are often very comfortable examining successes, but it takes extra effort to subject mistakes and failures to wider scrutiny. This is something that recent research has identified as being of particular salience for the health care sector (Tucker & Edmondson, 2003; Weick & Sutcliffe, 2003), and it seemed to be an especially sensitive topic for the respondents:

Private sector firms can often bury their mistakes and keep them secret; in the public sector we have the threat of public enquiries, or accountability to the Government's Public Accounts Committee. The last thing we need is for mistakes to become public.

The press just love to get their hands on a mistake in public sector health care; it makes great headlines, so we just keep our heads below the parapet.

You don't progress in this sector by owning up to mistakes. Promotion goes to the safe-pair-of-hands. You've just got to stay out of trouble and not rock the boat.

Nevertheless, as Garvin (1993) observes, as much, if not more can be learned from failure as from success using the terms "unproductive successes" and "productive failures" to underline his point. In the public sector, the need for accountability for taxpayers' money cannot be removed, and the level of public and media scrutiny makes it more difficult to overcome a fail-safe mentality. Even so, these comments suggest a need for public sector managers to create an environment where staff will not be adversely affected by "owning up" when things go wrong, and where there is no stigma attached to failure. They also need to overcome perceptions that promotion prospects can be jeopardized by trying new things. Government also has a part to play by recognizing that improvement will be hindered by not addressing problems and failures. Senior health care managers should lobby civil servants and government officials to moderate the punitive nature of external control and oversight.

Information Quality

Effective knowledge sharing also depends on the quality of the information infrastructure (Hult, 2003). To enable people to engage in the organization's decision making processes and to capture knowledge and new ideas generated from reflective learning, there must be an appropriate information infrastructure to inform and empower employees (Macdonald, 1998). Interviewees commented that:

Too often, nobody knows how well we are doing because we can't get access to the information.

We can tell how much everything costs but we have no idea whether the customer is getting a good service or not. We just don't gather the right data.

Employees also need access to good quality information that supports their specific work tasks and provides information in timely and appropriate formats (Marchand, Kettinger, & Rollins, 2001). This too seemed important to respondents:

IS tell us that the information is all there, but try finding it. It takes too long and usually needs a special report written. Nobody can wait three weeks for that to happen.

Without pertinent information support, exhortations to learn and share knowledge and to generate new ideas for improving performance will only lead to even more employee frustration:

The only information I can get is what we need to send to government, but the cost per bed or the length of the waiting list does not tell me what I need to do to make things better. I feel so dissatisfied with our Information Systems I tend to ignore them most of the time.

While it is understandable that health care managers are preoccupied with the need for external performance reporting to government, they must also make certain that information provision addresses internal user needs as well. Without high quality information support, employees will struggle to execute their work effectively and will be starved of the feedback that stimulates innovation and learning. However, appropriate information alone is not sufficient; employees need also to be prepared to accept the signals and messages that it contains about current performance levels. This is the essence of the next factor.

Performance Orientation

This fourth factor is concerned with attitudes to information about performance. It relates to a climate of honesty and openness, and a willingness to face the realities of service performance levels. It is epitomized by one respondent's candid observation that:

We just collect lots of statistics to keep the Government off our backs. Most of the numbers are pretty meaningless, so we just carry on doing things the way we know works best.

This factor is also linked to the pervasive fear of punishment for poor performance alluded to earlier:

We are so busy portraying a rosy picture of our performance that we lose sight of the real issues—we delude ourselves most of the time.

If anyone thinks I'm going to admit that we're not performing as well as we should, they're crazy. I'd have the management crashing down on top of me like a pile of bricks—it's just not worth it.

Lack of customer focus is also a contributory factor. If staff have difficulty obtaining feedback on service performance levels and if customer feedback is sparse, there is a tendency to believe that current performance is acceptable.

We make it difficult for customers to complain, and even when they do, we don't want to know. Complaints are swept under the carpet as quickly as possible. You get no medals in this job for admitting that all is not well.

Managers need to instill a real desire to serve the public well and to achieve high levels of customer satisfaction. This should create a hunger for meaningful and realistic performance data and a willingness to address the issues signaled by this information. Consequently, in so doing, there should be increased involvement with IS departments to provide appropriate and meaningful user reports.

Satisfaction with Change Processes

Performance improvement through knowledge sharing will almost inevitably require changes to working practices, measurement systems, and to people's behaviors. Such changes on their own may not be too daunting or difficult to implement, but managers need to assess the overall level of change that is being demanded from their staff. If several changes are introduced in quick succession, staff may become disenchanted or over-stressed (Lawrence, 1998), perceiving a lack of constancy of purpose or direction. While our examination of policy documents showed that government has tried to inculcate more customer focus into the health care sector for over 20 years, this has been packaged in a series of different initiatives with confusing labels (Sharifuddin & Rowland, 2004), as underlined by the following interviewee comments:

We've had Customer First, Best Value, Partnership Working; there seems no end to the stream of changes we've had to wrestle with. People just get confused and give up.

Another government, another policy. It's all the same meaningless drivel. Too many gray people in gray suits writing more policy documents to gather dust on my bookshelf. I'm getting tired of all these changes and so are my staff. I'm just looking forward to an early retirement package.

Managers need to understand that there is consistency in the various change initiatives and communicate this to their staff. If people can grasp that there is constancy of purpose in the goal of achieving customer-focused performance improvement, feelings of stress and disenchantment will be attenuated:

It's quite simple, really. We just need to realize that we are here to serve the public, not for our own ends. The government message has been consistent for as long as I can remember. Most healthcare people still haven't got it.

What is more, if specific change initiatives are not followed through to a stage where the benefits are manifest before another change is introduced, this can foster cynicism among employees (Strebel, 1996) who may do one of two things. Either they will feel frustrated that the "goalposts are always changing," or they will endeavor to ignore changes because they believe that something else will soon come along to replace it:

Right now we have the Modernization Agenda, but if we wait another few years it will be something else, so why bother?

Moreover, too much unwelcome change leads to an uncomfortable and stressful working environment that may exceed peoples' mental and physical capacity to cope:

It feels so uncomfortable working in an environment where everything is changing so much. I reckon most of our absenteeism is stress-related.

It feels like drowning because of so many changes—like you can't get above the surface to catch your breath. After a while you just let go and let it all wash over you. There is too much change to get to grips with and not enough time. Too many changes of language, procedures, forms, reporting structures, performance measures and so on.

If knowledge sharing is to flourish, then managers need to consider the timing and pace of its introduction relative to the overall level of change within the organization. However, in the public sector, change usually emanates top-down from government and is perceived to be imposed for politically expedient reasons. In such circumstances, change is more likely to be resisted. Therefore health care managers need to make great efforts to involve staff in change processes and to communicate and persuade, given that the ultimate sanction for dealing with vehement resisters, that is, termination of employment, is not as easy to invoke as in the private sector.

A Vision for Change

The preceding five factors have all involved change, including changes to the working environment, to attitudes to failure, to information provision, and to a willingness to address real performance levels. To introduce knowledge sharing into public sector agencies, managers must ensure these preceding factors are addressed so that their organizations are ready to implement knowledge sharing. However, people also need a clear and compelling reason to embrace such change (Kotter, 1996) and to convince them that knowledge sharing is necessary (Huysman & de Wit, 2004). We detected considerable complacency among interviewees about the need to change, who expressed views such as:

Things are working just fine. There is no real need to change anything we are doing.

We've been in this business for decades and I can see no reason to depart from tried and trusted healthcare systems.

I just wish we could be left alone to get on with the job. You don't change a winning team, so why make all these changes? Too much unnecessary interference from people who ought to know better—but they don't.

Weick and Sutcliffe (2003) provide an especially insightful explanation of how one UK hospital's mindset became largely impervious to change, by reconstructing history, not to fool others, but to fool themselves and to rescue order from disorder, such that:

Through repeated cycles of justification, people enact a sensible world that matches their beliefs, a world that is not clearly in need of change. Increasingly shrill insistence that change is mandatory changes nothing. (p. 81)

Our data resonate with this quotation and suggest that health care managers face a formidable challenge to invoke knowledge sharing behaviors. In the inter-organizational context of this study, there were also concerns about sharing knowledge across agency boundaries:

Why should we share what we know with other agencies? We'll only make them look better at the expense of our budgets.

We're not measured on how well other agencies operate so why should we help them? Our position in the Government's league tables is all that matters.

Unless and until such resistance and inertia is removed, public sector organizations will not be ready to implement knowledge sharing initiatives, echoing Gold et al.'s (2001) prognosis, quoted earlier, that knowledge sharing will be doomed before it begins. The imperative for changing is perhaps easier to grasp in the private sector, particularly when there is falling market share, a downturn in customer demand, or dissent from dissatisfied and influential shareholders. Professionally dominated public sector agencies are relatively protected from such turbulence and so it is more difficult to instill a sense of urgency to do things differently. Health care managers need to communicate a credible argument for sharing knowledge that connects with improved service performance for the benefit of the customer. This message will act as the engine of change, to overcome prevailing attitudes that the status quo is acceptable and that health care service delivery need not strive for excellence.

CONCLUSION

This chapter has identified six organizational enablers of effective knowledge sharing, within the context of public services. Using selected quotations from our 30 key informant interviews, we have illuminated the unique challenges facing public sector health care managers who seek to implement knowledge sharing processes. Many of these distinctive challenges seem to emanate from the highly regulated nature of government intervention in the sector. The dynamics of this government-agency relationship can be characterized by the following dimensions:

1. It seems to engender a rule-based culture that seeks compliance rather than intrapreneurship, innovation, and improvement;
2. The pressure for accountability for taxpayers' money and the concomitant media scrutiny and litigation risks erode the willingness of staff to reflect upon and learn from mistakes;
3. Changes emanate predominantly from government policies that are perceived to be imposed, and consequently received as unnecessary and unwelcome external interference;
4. The focus on individual agency performance is at variance with the need for inter-agency collaboration across the entire service value chain.

Nevertheless, health care managers acknowledged that they have considerable scope to improve current attitudes and practices within these externally imposed constraints. The model of knowledge sharing in Figure 1 can be used by health care managers as a framework by which to assess their organizations' current readiness to embrace a knowledge sharing culture. The model provides pointers to what needs to be addressed in such public sector agencies.

Referring back to McDermott's earlier assertion, the two strongest factors in the model, an open and innovative climate and information quality, support the need to "think with information." In other words, innovation and change thrive on the supply of appropriate and relevant information, which in turn stimulates people to generate new ideas for improving service delivery. We have also identified a separate but related factor, learning from failure, that has some precedent in the literature. Due to the highly regulated, top-down nature of the public service environment, it is not surprising that this has emerged separately. In a public service where managers have already been found to manipulate and deliberately misreport performance statistics and where performance league tables dominate the budget process, it is essential for managers to create a climate of openness, where everyone is prepared to confront real performance levels, rather than ignore them or pretend that all is well and change is not necessary. This is not helped by declarations from government ministers that poor performers will be "named and shamed" (Carvel, 2000).

The results have highlighted two antecedents to knowledge sharing associated with change management. These two factors relating to the management of change (i.e., specifically change overload and vision) have not featured prominently in previous empirical research on knowledge sharing. Nevertheless, this is a caveat to all managers that they must recognize the impact that too much change can have on their staff. Managers must also create a sense of urgency that conveys a compelling need to embrace knowledge sharing and the contingent changes that this implies. For public service partnerships, this model of knowledge sharing can guide efforts to share good practices across the service value chain.

Moreover, organizations cannot assume that if they move toward a knowledge sharing process, staff will embrace it wholeheartedly (McKenzie, Truc, & van Winkelen, 2001). Managers must assess their organization's readiness to adopt knowledge sharing attitudes and behaviors, that is, to evaluate the extent to which there exists a knowledge friendly culture and a supportive set of enabling conditions (Davenport, DeLong, & Beers, 1998). The model presented here articulates what this might mean in practice.

These results represent a contribution to knowledge in that little of the extant research on knowledge sharing has integrated all of these organizational factors in one empirical study. Moreover, by considering the public sector context and by including selected interview quotations, we have pointed to the ways in which managers in government-agency relationships must influence each of the factors. If they do not assess their organization's current status on each of these six dimensions, the identified enablers may conversely represent serious obstacles and impediments.

REFERENCES

Appleby, J., & Coote, A. (2002). *Five-year health check: A review of health policy, 1997-2002.* London: King's Fund.

Audit Commission. (2003). *Waiting list accuracy: Assessing the accuracy of waiting list information in NHS hospitals in England.* Wetherby, UK: Audit Commission Publications.

Bate, S. P., & Robert, G. (2002). Knowledge management and communities of practice in the private sector: Lessons for modernizing the National Health Service in England and Wales. *Public Administration, 80*(4), 643-663.

Blumentritt, R., & Johnston, R. (1999). Towards a knowledge management strategy. *Technology Analysis and Strategic Management, 11*(3), 287-300.

Bock, G. W., & Kim, Y-G. (2002). Breaking the myths of rewards: An exploratory study of attitudes about knowledge sharing. *Information Resources Management Journal, 15*(2), 14-21.

Carvel, J. (2000, July 1). Failing hospitals to be named and shamed. *The Guardian*, p. 23.

Churchill, G. A. (1979). A paradigm for developing better measures of marketing constructs. *Journal of Marketing Research, 16*(1), 64-73.

Davenport, T. H., DeLong, D. W., & Beers, M. C. (1998). Successful knowledge management projects. *Sloan Management Review, 39*(2), 43-57.

Department of Health. (1998). *Partnership in action: New opportunities for joint working between Health and Social Services* (Paper No. 13684). p. 38.

Fuller, A. L., & Swanson, E. B. (1992). Information centers as organizational innovation. *Journal of Management Information Systems, 9*(1), 47-68.

Garvin, D. A. (1993). Building a learning organization. *Harvard Business Review, 71*(4), 78-91.

Gold, A. H., Malhotra, A., & Segars, A. H. (2001). Knowledge management: An organizational capabilities perspective. *Journal of Management Information Systems, 18*(1), 185-214.

Hackett, B. (2000). *Beyond knowledge management: New ways to work and learn* (p. 70). New York: The Conference Board.

Hair, J. F., Anderson, R. E., Tatham, R. L., & Black, W. C. (1998). *Multivariate data analysis.* NJ: Prentice Hall.

Hansen, M. T., Nohria, N., & Tierney, T. (1999). What's your strategy for managing knowledge? *Harvard Business Review, 77*(2), 106-116.

HMSO. (2001). *Joining up to improve public services.* London: Report by the Comptroller and Auditor General, HC383 p. 15.

Huber, G. P. (2001). Transfer of knowledge in knowledge management systems: Unexplored issues and suggested studies. *European Journal of Information Systems, 10*(2), 72-79.

Hult, G. T. M. (2003). An integration of thoughts on knowledge management. *Decision Sciences, 34*(2), 189-195.

Huysman, M., & de Wit, D. (2004). Practices of managing knowledge sharing: Towards a second wave of knowledge management. *Knowledge and Process Management, 11*(2), 81-92.

Irvine, S., & Haman, H. (2001). *Spotlight on general practice.* Abingdon, UK: Radcliffe Medical Press.

Kim, J., & Mueller, C. W. (1978). *Factor analysis: Statistical methods and practical issues.* Beverly Hills, CA: Sage Publications.

Kim, W. C., & Mauborgne, R. (1997). Fair process: Managing in the knowledge economy. *Harvard Business Review, 75*(4), 65-75.

Kotter, J. P. (1996). *Leading change.* Boston: Harvard Business School Press.

KPMG. (1999). *Knowledge management research report* (p. 20). London: KPMG Consulting.

Lawrence, D. (1998). *Leading discontinuous change: Ten lessons from the battlefront.* In D. C. Hambrick, D. A. Nadler, & M. L. Tushman (Eds.), *Navigating change* (Chapter 16). Boston: Harvard Business School Press.

Leidner, D. (2000). Editorial. *Journal of Strategic Information Systems, 9*(2/3), 100-105.

Macdonald, S. (1998). *Information for innovation: Managing change from an information perspective.* Oxford: Oxford University Press.

Marchand, D. A., Kettinger, W. J., & Rollins, J. D. (2001). *Information orientation.* Oxford: Oxford University Press.

McDermott, R. (1999). Why information technology inspired but cannot deliver knowledge management. *California Management Review, 41*(4), 103-117.

McKenzie, J., Truc, A., & van Winkelen, C. (2001). Winning commitment for knowledge management initiatives. *Journal of Change Management, 2*(2), 115-127.

National Audit Office. (2001). *Inappropriate adjustments to National Health Service waiting lists* (HC 452).

Nonaka, I. (1994). A dynamic theory of organizational knowledge creation. *Organization Science, 5*(1), 14-37.

Nunnally, J. (1978). *Psychometric theory.* New York: McGraw-Hill.

Porter, M. E. (1985). *Competitive advantage: Creating and sustaining superior performance.* New York: Free Press.

Rai, A., Borah, S., & Ramprasad, A. (1996). Critical success factors for strategic alliances in the information technology industry: An empirical study. *Decision Sciences, 27*(1), 141-155.

Rashid, N. (1999). *Managing performance in local government.* London: Kogan Page.

Ruggles, R. (1998). The state of the notion: Knowledge management in practice. *California Management Review, 40*(3), 80-89.

Sarvary, M. (1999). Knowledge management and competition in the consulting industry. *California Management Review, 41*(2), 95-107.

Sethi, V., & King, W. R. (1991). Construct measurement in information systems research: An illustration in strategic systems. *Decision Sciences, 22*(3), 455-472.

Sharifuddin, S. O., & Rowland, F. (2004). Knowledge management in a public organization: A study on the relationship between organizational elements and the performance of knowledge transfer. *Journal of Knowledge Management, 8*(2), 95-111.

Smith, P. (1995). On the unintended consequences of publishing performance data in the public sector. *International Journal of Public Administration, 18*(2/3), 277-310.

Smith , P. (Ed.). (1996). *Measuring outcomes in the public sector*. London: Taylor and Francis.

Stonehouse, G., Buehring, A., & Pemberton, J. (2002, May 19-22). Managing knowledge in UK primary healthcare: Some mixed messages (pp. 663-666). *Proceedings of 2002 Information Resources Management Association International Conference*, Seattle, Washington. Idea Group Publishing.

Strebel, P. (1996). Why do employees resist change? *Harvard Business Review, 74*(3), 139-158.

Szulanski, G. (1996). Exploring internal stickiness: Impediments to the transfer of best practices within the firm. *Strategic Management Journal, 17*(Winter special issue), 27-43.

Tucker, A. L., & Edmondson, A. C. (2003). Why hospitals don't learn from failures: Organizational and psychological dynamics that inhibit system change. *California Management Review, 45*(2), 55-72.

van Beveren, J. (2003). *Does health care for knowledge management? Journal of Knowledge Management, 7*(1), 90-95.

Weick, K. E., & Sutcliffe, K. M. (2003). Hospitals as cultures of entrapment: A re-analysis of the Bristol Royal Infirmary. *California Management Review, 45*(2), 73-84.

Chapter XII

Tranquilizing the Werewolf that Attacks Information Systems Quality

Evan W. Duggan
University of Alabama, USA

ABSTRACT

After years of research and experimentation with information systems building, delivering high-quality systems remains a largely elusive objective. Since the prophetic assertion of Fred Brooks that the essential difficulties of "software engineering" would frustrate the search for a "silver bullet" to slay the legendary werewolf that beset its quality, IS delivery has become more difficult, and organizations have magnified the struggle to overcome what has been called "the software crisis." There is unlikely to be a silver bullet. Only the disciplined, effective management and selection of appropriate approaches by knowledgeable and committed participants in the delivery process are likely to increase the odds of producing high-quality software products. This article discusses a variety of available user-centered and process-oriented systems delivery methods, philosophies, and techniques, which may be used in innovative permutations to tranquilize the dragon beyond its capacity to generate terror. The application context for these approaches, their strengths and weaknesses as indicated by the research literature, and reported practitioner experiences are also discussed.

INTRODUCTION

Despite the information technology (IT) innovations of the past several years, the persistent theme is that there is an information systems (IS) delivery crisis[1] resulting from the failure to exploit IT capability to produce high-quality systems (Brynjolfssen, 1993; Gibbs, 1994). Many organizations have established successful IS; however, several have not obtained the expected benefits from their large investments in software products, and even successfully deployed IS consume a disproportionate share of systems development resources for maintenance activities (Banker, Davis, & Slaughter, 1998; Hoffer, George & Valacich, 2002). Consequently, organizations (and eventually the national economy) seldom derive commensurate benefits from IT investments. This, presumably, has contributed to the perception of a productivity paradox, which was first insinuated by economist Robert Solow.

Brooks (1987) suggested that software engineering problems emerged from both accidental and essential difficulties. According to him, accidental difficulties derive from the incidental properties of the delivery environment; they are controllable. However, there is no solution for the essential difficulties and no silver bullet existed or was imminent to slay this "werewolf." Brooks attributed essential difficulties to four factors: (1) conformity—the need for new software to conform to organizational politics and policy and other systems, both social and technical; (2) changeability—the corrections, adaptations to business process changes, and extensions that software experiences in delivery and evolution; (3) invisibility—the inability to create visual models to make intangible design products appreciable; (4) complexity—the inherent difficulty involved in working with and communicating about this largely intangible product.

None of these problem factors has disappeared. In fact, the complexity of IS delivery has increased (Al-Mushayt, Doherty, & King, 2001). As organizations rely more on IT to enable their strategic priorities and support value chain operations, advanced IS are required to apply sophisticated information and communications technologies, to accommodate a variety of data distribution and application architecture strategies, support cross-functional business processes and global operations, and mitigate the information security risks that now attend the greater movement of data. This increased reliance on IT accentuates the challenges that face IS developers and other stakeholders to interact more effectively (Vessey & Conger, 1994).

It is generally acknowledged that there is no painless therapy for software development maladies—no single silver bullet. However, Cox (1995) asserted that the werewolf may be slain by those who will summon the tenacity to shift from the software building paradigms that we have embraced. Such a shift requires more focused preproject analysis to select the appropriate combinations of approaches that are best suited to the IS delivery context. IS developers may have to emulate the resilience of the organizations they serve. Most are forced to pursue a multilevel attack on the werewolf of profitability by simultaneously addressing technology adoption, product design, process management, and customer relationship management.

In this chapter, I describe potential IS quality-enhancing techniques and recommend a disciplined, multisource attack on the problem of poor software quality with faithful application of relevant combinations of philosophies, methods, and techniques—perhaps silver pellets—that may assist developers and users chip away at the vital areas of the monster's anatomy to tranquilize it beyond its capacity to generate terror. However, many IS delivery methods have been over-hyped by zealous originators and enthusiastic proponents who often hyperbolize claims of efficacy in subjective allegiance to particular approaches. Practitioners are often ambivalent about the legitimacy of these claims and confused by inconsistent use of terms in the literature.

This chapter therefore makes the following three contributions: (1) it provides a balanced and objective review of the IS quality literature (empirical observations and dispassionate practitioner accounts); (2) it assists with the assimilation of this literature by clarifying ambiguous terminology; and (3) it explicates the objectives and the applicability of alternative development practices in order to guide decision making about the selection of context-relevant approaches (or combination of methods) and methods to increase the probability of overcoming the pervasive problem of low-quality IS deployment.

In the following sections, I clarify the IS terminology used throughout and develop a definition of IS quality. Then I structure the discussion of IS approaches into potential quality-enhancing contributions from people-centered techniques, process management, and IS delivery methods. These sections are followed by the discussion and summary. The overarching thesis is that the confluence of several IS delivery strategies that blend people-centered principles, process management best practices, and pertinent systems delivery methods can successfully assail the essential difficulties of IS delivery and improve product quality. The analysis includes considerations of the contexts in which particular approaches may have relevance, known caveats associated with their use, and claimed benefits.

TOWARD A DEFINITION OF SYSTEMS DELIVERY TERMS AND IS QUALITY

The absence of a common vocabulary and inconsistent use of terms in the IS literature have curtailed the progress of cumulative IS research (Barki & Hartwick, 1994; Barki, Rivard, & Talbot, 1993) and presented difficulties for practitioners to decipher their meaning. For example, several terms such as software engineering, software development, systems development, and systems delivery are used in the literature to describe the process of establishing and deploying computer-based information systems. IS delivery is the preferred term in this chapter, used generically to incorporate all available means of obtaining IS such as in-house development, acquisition, or outsourcing. In this delivery process, stakeholders are supported by the adopted paradigms, methodologies, methods, and tools (Robey, Welke, & Turk, 2001) described in Table 1.

There is general agreement that the parameters that shape expectations about IS value are scope, schedule, cost, and quality (Friedlander, 1992). These interdependent factors may be traded off against each other but one cannot be adjusted independently without repercussive effects on the others. IS quality is widely recognized as a critical yet elusive organizational target (Kitchenham & Pfleeger, 1996); however, unlike the first three, there is considerable diversity of views about what it constitutes, what its determinants are, and how to assess it (Ravichandaran & Rai, 1994). Some researchers define IS quality in terms of inherent system attributes; others use usage parameters.

Garvin (1984) identified five views that have contributed to the definition of IS product quality: (1) the transcendental view of quality as recognizable but not definable; (2) the product-based view, which sees quality as identifiable in measurable characteristics of the deliverable; (3) the user-based view of quality that refers to the product's capability to satisfy stated or implied needs— its fitness for use; (4) the manufacturing-based view that measures quality by the degree of conformance to specification and requirements; and (5) the value-based view of quality as its economic worth to buyers.

ISO/IEC 9126-1 software quality model defines six discernible quality characteristics of a software product[2]—functionality, reliability, usability, efficiency, maintainability, portability (ISO/IEC 9126-1, 2001) that enables it to effectively satisfy implied user needs and goals. These characteristics, which are intended to cover the range of quality dimensions that are of interest to IS

Table 1. Classification of systems delivery approaches

Concept	Description	Examples
Systems delivery paradigm	Common distinguishing features of a family of life cycle approaches	Waterfall model; incremental/Iterative models; Reuse-based models
Systems development methodology	Comprehensive set of principles for structuring the delivery process that describes what, when, and how activities are performed and the supported methods and tools	Information Engineering; Method 1; Navigator, RUP
Systems delivery method	Set of principles and objectives for driving a specific development approach	Rapid application development; extreme programming; component-based development
Systems delivery tool	Specific implementation support for a variety of methods	CASE; data flow diagrams; use case

Figure 1. ISO 9126 characteristics and subcharacteristics

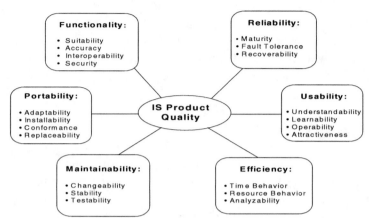

users, involve both internal and external attributes (each with several subattributes) that influence quality-in-use (Figure 1) and can be used to motivate design decisions during development. Internal attributes refer to the intrinsic properties of the software product that are implemented. They are the prerequisites of external attributes that reflect the manner in which the system interacts with a potential user.

It may be inferred from the combined indications of the various positions outlined above and the perspectives of other scholars (Erikkson & McFadden, 1993; Grady, 1993; Hanna, 1995; Hough, 1993; Palvia, Sharma, & Conrath, 2001) that IS quality is discernible in the features and characteristics that bear on the satisfaction of perceived needs and the delivery of expected benefits. A high-quality system should reliably produce required features that are easy to access and use with a high probability of correct response and consistently acceptable response times. Such a system should produce business value; it should be delivered on time so that the solution remains relevant beyond deployment, and the overall benefits should outstrip life-cycle cost of ownership. Defects discovered in field use should be easily isolated and corrected. The system should be scalable both with regard to functionality and usage, and should be portable to other operating platforms.

ANTECEDENTS OF IS QUALITY: PARTICIPATIVE AND USER-CENTERED APPROACHES

There has been significant focus on the quality-enhancing capability of participative approaches. These are rooted in socio-technical systems (STS) principles. STS concepts advocate the cogeneration of technical and social systems requirements and strong user association with IS delivery. It is acknowledged that user-centered approaches that encourage stakeholder involvement in IS delivery and incorporate elements of STS design principles are likely to produce better systems (Al-Mushayt et al., 2001; Barki & Hartwick, 1994, Doherty & King, 1998; Newman & Robey, 1992; Palvia et al., 2001; Robey et al., 2001).

The Social Processes of IS Delivery

Figure 2 provides a normative model of the social and technical interactions involved in the delivery and evolution of IS. It depicts that several organizational characteristics (such as business processes, organization structure and culture, IT infrastructure, etc.) bear on the IS delivery process. An organization plans IS delivery projects, sources them through in-house development, commercial off-the-shelf (COTS) purchase, or outsourcing and then deploys them. Users impact IS delivery initially through their involvement and eventually acceptance and use of the finished product. During the evolution of the system, they also identify errors to be corrected, assist systems developers adapt the system to business processes changes, and request new functionality.

According to Robey et al. (2001), IS delivery and use involve significant interactions among several stakeholders and technological components. Many organizations focus on the technical aspects and ignore important STS dimensions that reflect the symbiosis of man and machine in the accomplishment of IS objectives (Palvia et al., 2001). Consequently, several technically sound and successfully deployed systems remain unused (Newman & Robey, 1992).

Figure 2. IS delivery and evolution (adapted from Silver, Markus & Beath, 1995)

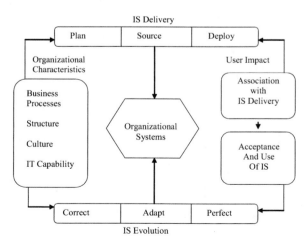

Systems success is not only determined by technical validity but also by affective and behavioral responses of the intended beneficiaries (Markus & Keil, 1994; Newman & Robey, 1992); effective employee involvement is also a prerequisite for eventual system use (Barki & Hartwick, 1994). This has prompted other scholars to include actual usage as a measure of software quality (Lyytinen, 1988; Markus & Keil, 1994).

Many IS problems in organizations originate in the complex social structures in which they are executed (Fox, 1995) where people organized into work units interact with technology to satisfy some instrumental (work-related) objective; equivalently, the technology embedded in the social (sub) systems may generate affective responses that contrive obstacles to system use (Shani & Sena, 1994). STS analysis therefore juxtaposes affective and instrumental elements of IS delivery to cogenerate social, and technical requirements and STS design principles seek to balance the human, organizational, and technical elements of the implementation environment (Al-Mushayt et al., 2001; Palvia et al., 2001). This practice allows the impact of different technical solutions to be assessed against potential social obstacles to system use and helps to preidentify ethical issues with technology implementation before critical incidents arise (Doherty & King, 1998); this influences systems quality (Fox, 1995; Shani & Sena, 1994).

User-Centered Approaches

STS objectives are incorporated in IS delivery by involving users throughout and employing user-centered approaches such as prototyping, joint application development (JAD), participatory design (PD), and quality function deployment (QFD) to facilitate effective user-developer interactions and promote other STS goals.

User Involvement in IS Delivery

The value of involving users in systems delivery has been well recognized (Barki & Hartwick, 1994). Involved users often endorse system goals, which increase their perception of the usefulness of the system (Carmel, George, & Nunamaker, 1995). This positive identification in turn produces a high level of commitment to system outcomes (Borovits, Ellis, & Yeheskel, 1990). However, empirical research results have not consistently confirmed this theory of positive correlation between user involvement and system success (Carmel et al., 1995). Barki and Hartwick (1994) attributed these inconclusive findings to inadequate definition of user-association constructs. For example, they distinguished between user participation—the intellectual occupation with the accomplishment of assigned tasks and user involvement—the psychological state that attaches significance to the affiliation with a systems delivery project. User ownership transcends user involvement and motivates pride of possession and a sense of responsibility for the success of the system. The quintessential state of association is user championship when user owners become "missionaries," promoting the system and encouraging others to use it (Dodd & Carr, 1994; Hough, 1993). These terms are often used interchangeably in the literature.

Prototyping

Prototyping involves close user-developer interaction to generate a series of progressively refined models of an intended system that demonstrates its appearance and behavior. This simulates usage experience and helps stakeholders isolate and discover design problems and obtain a more realistic sense of the proposed solution (Davis, 1994). This technique is recommended to reduce the risk of failure of complex systems, when system requirements cannot be rigorously prespecified (Weinberg, 1991), either because of intricate business relationships, divergent stakeholder interests, or highly politicized environments. An initial model is generated from partially defined requirements to obtain user reaction. Successive prototypes refine and expand the concept based on users' trial and feedback. The process then progresses iteratively toward the discovery of the requirements (Boar, 1984; Dekleva, 1992; Weinberg, 1991), then the prototype is either discarded and development continues with other technologies ("throwaway" model), or it is expanded to full functional form on the same design platform ("evolutionary" prototyping).

The close user-designer working relationship forged during prototyping and the effectiveness of communication about system features moderate both quality-related and usage failure factors (Baskerville & Stage, 1996). Prototyping also permits an early assessment of the impact of the system on the user environment, which may also facilitate more effective change management (Adamopoulos, Haramis, & Papandreou, 1998). However, users sometimes overemphasize aesthetic requirements, such as format of screens and reports, at the expense of other product quality attributes (Korac-Boisvert & Kouzmin, 1995). It can also lead to false expectations about the remaining effort required to convert the model into the final product (Weinberg, 1991), and some users have been known to press for the deployment of the unfinished prototype. The opportunity for repeated revisions may induce scope creep (Wetherbe, 1991) and over-analysis, which could become counterproductive.

Joint Application Development

JAD seeks to improve the effectiveness of communication and interaction among system users, developers, and sponsors to experience synergistic process gains (Liou & Chen, 1993-1994). It was first introduced by IBM in the 1970s as an alternative to the interviewing technique for eliciting system requirements. JAD consists of five phases[3] (Wood & Silver, 1995), which includes a series of face-to-face meetings (called workshops) where participants pool their knowledge, perspectives, and ideas under the guidance of a trained facilitator to determine appropriate information requirements. A typical JAD session runs for three to five days depending on the scope and complexity of the project.

JAD has proven to be more advantageous than conventional techniques. When applied successfully, it contributes to higher quality requirements—more accurate and consistent than those aggregated from several interviews (Dean et al., 1997-1998); reduced scope and feature creep and cycle time (from months and years to weeks) (Wood & Silver, 1995); and lower development costs (Davidson, 1999). The JAD workshop also provides a vehicle for strengthening user involvement, which typically leads to greater commitment to the decisions (Andrews, 1991; Wood & Silver, 1995).

However, JAD meetings are conducted under the freely interacting group structure, in which the affective (social and emotional) dynamics of group relationships often impede the instrumental (the accomplishment of task) (Duggan & Thachenkary, 2004). Facilitation excellence is therefore a pivotal requirement for overcoming potential group problems such as destructive dominance; free-loading—inadequate participation due to unnecessary acquiescence to powerful and influential group members, or simply by election because group members contribute of their own volition; groupthink—fixation on preserving group harmony; risky-shift behavior—groups shifting from the risk propensities of individual members; and the Abilene paradox—conflict avoidance that causes groups to arrive at decisions that do not reflect the desires of individual members (Kettelhut, 1993). Several prescriptions have been presented for overcoming these problems (Kettelhut, 1993; Wood & Silver, 1995).

Participatory Design

Participatory design (PD) is a user-centered participation scheme which originated, and is mostly practiced, in Scandinavia. Its objective is to empower workers to effectively participate in IS delivery projects. PD is rooted in the Scandinavian sociopolitical and cultural background and provides a basis for operationalizing user ownership. It is based on the philosophy of workplace democratization, which is supported by Codetermination Laws that mandate general worker engagement in organizational decision making that affects their work practices (Gill & Kreiger, 1999). PD stresses technical knowledge sharing to enhance social interactions (Carmel, Whitaker, & George, 1993). It forces systems developers to consider the sociology of the workplace to ensure mutual fit between technical and social systems (Kjaer & Madsen, 1995). PD also promotes organizational learning and synergy as users and developers help each other understand their respective domains.

This cross-fertilization of ideas, knowledge, and skills stimulates more informed decision making, broader user commitment, better systems fit to organizational needs, and, sometimes, longer term morale benefits (Mankin & Cohen, 1997). Effective system usage and the reduction of politically motivated abandonment after deployment are acknowledged advantages of PD. However, it is claimed that the Scandinavian cultural predisposition is a necessary, though not sufficient, condition for PD success and that it is not particularly useful outside of the specific climate fostered by their codetermination laws and the Scandinavian experience. This environment includes a relatively homogeneous workforce, a high level of unionization with strong national trade union federations and social democratic parties affiliated with these federations, and the trade unions' positive attitude to IT (Muller, Wildman, & White, 1993).

Quality Function Deployment

QFD is a customer-oriented approach that has been applied successfully in both manufacturing and service organizations to facilitate enterprise-wide quality control. It was first introduced in manufacturing environments to capture, quantify, and prioritize customer preferences, perceptions, expectations, and other quality requirements and monitor the delivery of these requirements throughout product design and fabrication (Erikkson & McFadden, 1993). Many supporting techniques are used to accomplish these objectives: the house of quality matrix; affinity diagrams; hierarchy trees for assimilating the interrelationships; and relations diagrams. Process decision program diagrams are sometimes used to study potential failure factors of proposed design solutions and the analytic hierarchy process (AHP) to incorporate qualitative factors in ranking the importance of proposed product features.

When QFD is used to track quality attributes throughout IS delivery, it is referred to as software QFD or SQFD (McDonald, 1995). Elboushi (1997) empirically demonstrated its effectiveness in producing robust and consistent requirements for customers with diverse needs in an object-oriented application. SQFD is time consuming, and successful use requires a quality-focused organization culture (Ho, Lai, & Chang, 1999). Excellent group decision-making techniques are necessary to resolve conflicting requirements and address other team relationship and behavior management problems (Martins & Aspinwall, 2001). These considerations may prejudice its wider adoption, especially in environments already encumbered with communication problems and pressured for rapid systems delivery.

ANTECEDENTS OF IS QUALITY: PROCESS IMPROVEMENT AND MANAGEMENT

Excellent process management does not automatically guarantee high-quality IS (Rae, Robert, & Haisen, 1995); however, they are positively correlated (Harter, Slaughter & Krishnan, 1998; Khalifa & Verner, 2000; Ravichandran & Rai, 1996, 2000), hence the extensive focus on IS process improvement and management (*CIO Magazine*, April 2001). The trend has been to employ formal process assessment instruments such as the capability maturity model (CMM) to gauge IS process competence and structured systems development methodologies to establish process repeatability and predictability so as to reduce reliance on individual and project group heroics for quality outcomes.

Capability Maturity Model

CMM is an instrument for assessing the maturity and the degree of discipline of an organization's IS delivery processes against a normative ideal (Paulk, 2001; Paulk et al., 1993). It was sponsored by the Department of Defense and developed by Software Engineering Institute (SEI) of Carnegie Mellon University. There are five maturity levels[4] that range from an immature process (ad hoc and chaotic) to an optimized process (one with unconscious, sustained competence). The introspection enabled by CMM assessment provides a baseline for improving process management capability. Other similar instruments include International Standards Organization's Software Process Improvement Capability Determination (SPICE) (Melo, El Emam, & Drouin, 1998) and Bootstrap (Kuvaja et al., 1994).

Some organizations have claimed CMM assessment benefits such as shorter development cycle, reduced rework, higher development productivity, and higher quality systems (*CIO Magazine*, April 2001). Other indirect benefits include more proactive IS groups; valuable, unsolicited end-user feedback about improvement opportunities; improvement in their capability to assess project risks; and cost-reduction opportunities enabled by more standardized software (Diaz & Sligo, 1997; Haley, 1996; Hollenbach et al., 1997). However, there are reports of difficulty in applying the CMM recommended sequence for successful process modification (Pfleeger, 1996; Ravichandran & Rai, 2000).

Systems Development Methodology

A systems development methodology (SDM) is a prerequisite for Level 3, CMM designation. It provides the blueprint for advancing through the systems development life cycle. It prescribes consistent, stable, repeatable protocols and procedures for IS delivery projects that cover what, when, and how activities are performed, the deliverables of each phase of the methodology and their quality standards, the roles of people, and the tools and techniques that are supported in each stage (Roberts, Gibson, & Fields, 1999). Although several commercial and proprietary systems development methodologies exist, it is recommended that a single organization adopts a single methodology. This is to accommodate process consistency across different projects, eliminate project start-up inertia, and help the project team focus more on the situational characteristics of the current project.

Organizations that make effective use of methodologies may dynamically deploy project participants across multiple projects and minimize the risk of project failures due to attrition. However, methodologies may also be burdensome. Some (particularly small) development efforts are frustrated by onerous process structures (Fitzgerald, 2000; Flatten, 1992), and the SDM learning curve is particularly steep (Dietrich, Walz, & Wynekoop, 1997). It is not unusual for a methodology to be altered either temporarily for a specific project but fully sanctioned by the organization, or permanently to achieve some desired improvement.

ANTECEDENTS OF IS DELIVERY: DELIVERY MEHODS

Traditional systems development life cycle (SDLC) models, embodied by the waterfall method, are characterized by the sequential execution of life cycle phases and the complete specification of information requirements up front. Robey et al. (2001) distinguished between two other IS delivery paradigms that have helped to improve systems quality by reducing the cognitive and technical complexity of the waterfall method. They identified the iterative/incremental paradigm and the software reuse paradigm. The waterfall model is well known, has longevity, and has been described ad infinitum; it will not be elaborated in this chapter.

Iterative/Incremental Delivery Methods

The iterative/incremental delivery paradigm describes a genre of systems delivery methods that produces manageable pieces of a system iteratively and/ or delivers usable functionality incrementally (Bandi, Vaishnavi, & Turk, 2003). These methods, such as rapid application development (RAD), the more aggressive agile development methods like extreme programming (XP)—one of many agile examples—and cleanroom software engineering (CSE), conform to Brooks' (1987) suggested approach of "growing" instead of building software. They substantiate a "less sooner" delivery philosophy to secure early buy-in and, to varying degrees, indulge user-centered approaches.

Rapid Application Development

RAD is based on the philosophy that the risk of IS failure increases with the duration of delivery (Hough, 1993). It embraces several user-centered design techniques: JAD (which is optional), structured analysis and design techniques for modeling and representing procedural logic and data relationships, and prototyping. These help to blend analysis, design, and construction into a single phase to accelerate systems delivery. CASE and fourth generation languages are typical but optional tools.

In RAD, requirements are not completely prespecified. The project is initiated with partial, high-level requirements (Hough, 1993). Then structured techniques are used to construct preliminary analysis models, from which a prototype is built. The software progresses toward finalization through several iterations of user-developer interactions involving feedback on the prototype, improvements to the model, and refinement of the prototype. The end result of this iterative process is a documented deployment-ready system (Hanna, 1995).

RAD seems to be appropriate for applications that are not computationally complex and with clearly defined user group, not large projects or distributed systems using corporate-wide databases (Beynon-Davies, 1998). It focuses more on quickly delivering functional modules with high business value (to reduce the likelihood of project abandonment) than on engineering excellence. RAD contributes to shorter development cycle times—from three to six month—which helps to reduce development costs while ensuring system-business fit (Hough, 1993). By limiting the project's exposure to change, it also helps to combat scope and feature creep and produces similar user-involvement benefits to those obtained from prototyping.

RAD, however, forces several trade-offs for the compressed development cycles, which is sometimes viewed as suboptimization on speed of development. Rework is sometimes necessary to address the integration of independently developed modules (Hanna, 1995). Quality may be sacrificed when users ignore rigor and robustness in favor of quick business value (Bourne, 1994), and project delays are sometimes avoided by reducing requirements rather than postponing and rescheduling deadlines. A fairly sophisticated development environment and familiarity with a variety of techniques are prerequisites for using RAD.

Cleanroon Software Engineering

CSE concepts were borrowed from the semi-conductor industry where contaminant-free environments (physical cleanrooms) were established to prevent defects during the production of silicon chips (Spangler, 1996). CSE's objective is to apply rigorous engineering and management practices to produce high-quality software with statistically certified reliability for failure-free performance in field use. A major CSE focus is the prevention, instead of the detection, of software defects. This IS delivery practice is based on mathematical foundations of referential transparency and function theory (Jerva, 2001).

Software is generated incrementally in small delivery units under statistical quality control with independent specification, development, and certification subteams. For larger projects, these small teams may engage in concurrent development of system modules. Peer reviews of incremental deliverables are conducted to increase the probability of error-free code. After construction, a subset of all possible uses of each module is sampled, and inferential statistical analysis is used to determine whether that module has defects. The test statistic may be errors per thousand lines of code (E/KLOC) or mean time to failure (MTTF). If the pre-established quality standards are not attained, the module is discarded and reconstructed.

Several authors have cited successful CSE applications that have improved software quality (Agrawal & Whittaker, 1993; Hausler, Linger, & Trammell, 1994; Head, 1994; Trammell et al., 1996) and significantly increased development productivity (Gibbs, 1994). Practitioners have also reported greatly reduced errors per line of cleanroom generated code (Jerva, 2001) of eight to ten times less than the average for other processes (Spangler, 1996). Indirect benefits that may accrue from the reduction of software failure in field-use include longer product life and the reduction of systems development resources devoted to maintenance activities. Opponents of the cleanroom technique have mainly focused on the method's philosophical aversion to traditional testing techniques (Beizer, 1997), mathematical complexity, and the high demand for human resources (Jerva, 2001), which may account for the relative sparseness of cleanroom applications.

Agile Development Methods

Agile development methods are a family of similar software development methods, which seek to minimize process impediments to early IS delivery and promote expeditious delivery of small increments of software functionality at regular intervals. Proponents have developed a manifesto[5] that outlines "agile principles." These methods are touted to be human-oriented (requiring extensive customer involvement), fast and efficient, small and nimble, and giving a higher priority to people than process. Agile methods embrace simplicity: Requirements determination is based initially on partial knowledge, system features are delivered in small releases, the development team is small and interacts closely with intended system users (interactive development), and testing is continuous (Beck, 2000).

XP, Adaptive Software Development, Feature Driven development, Crystal Clear Method, Dynamic Systems Development Method (DSDM), and Scrum are examples of agile methods. XP is probably the most popular of these methods and was therefore elected for further elaboration. It is typically used by small, co-located teams to quickly produce small-scale systems that are constructed by two-person programming teams (Beck, 2000). System builders (Development) and business domain experts (Business) engage in a "planning game" followed by "iteration planning game" that is played by Development alone; both involve a three-step process of exploration, commitment, and steering[6] (Hoffer et al., 2002).

Some systems development pundits are skeptical about this approach, claiming that some XP terminology are euphemisms for questionable systems practices—for example "refactoring," the XP concept of continuous design for "rework" (Glass, 2001). But proponents of the approach attest to its efficacy particularly in stabilizing systems quality and delivering applications rapidly in environments of high business processes volatility (Paulk, 2001). They also refute the claim that XP does not subscribe to modeling and documentation. While admitting that both are deliberately "light" (moderate) in XP, they say this is a deliberate strategy to disencumber the process (Paulk, 2001). XP supporters also concede its unsuitability for developing large multi-site (or global) applications with large development teams (Glass, 2001).

Reuse-Based Delivery Methods

The reuse paradigm seeks to produce small, manageable units of software functionality and develop modules (objects and components) that may be reused with or without modification. The concept is not new. Third-generation programming languages implemented reuse by providing subroutines for common functionality that are used in several programs. The primary target of these approaches was programming productivity, but object and component technologies have expanded this objective to also attack systems building quality directly by abstracting away scale-related complexities (Szyperski, 1998).

Object-Oriented Development

Object-orientated development (OOD) represents a paradigm shift from traditional systems-building approaches under which the independence of data and programs was almost sacrosanct. Object-oriented (OO) techniques embrace the exact opposite concept; IS are modeled and designed as a collection of interacting objects—"real world" entities about which organizations keep data. Objects encapsulate[7] (package and hide) attributes (data elements) and program procedures (also called behavior, methods, or operations) that are allowed to create, read, update, delete, and otherwise manipulate the attributes.

The close affinity of notional objects with physical objects helps to reduce conceptual complexity during analysis (Brown, 2002). The most important benefit of objects, however, is their reusability (with or without modification) in other applications (Schmidt & Fayad, 1997; Vessey & Conger, 1994). The focus on reuse may also enhance reliability resulting from more disciplined object design (Johnson, Hardgrove & Doke, 1999). Organizations who adopt the OO philosophy pursue this reuse benefit to establish more flexible systems that are easier to maintain (Agarwal et al., 2000) and thereby decrease information systems costs.

OO techniques have been available since the 1960s but have not been widely used until the 1990s (Brown, 2002). The slow acceptance has been attributed to the steep learning curve for developers trained under other paradigms and the initial inability to integrate object-based modules with legacy systems (Bordoloi & Lee, 1994; Johnson et al., 1999), which is now partially addressed by object wrappers. Initially also, analytical models and process methods were unavailable to assist OOD (Fichman & Kemerer, 1992). That has been remedied with the adoption of the unified modeling language (UML) as the de facto modeling and notations standard. UML and common object request broker architecture (CORBA), a protocol that facilitates object communication on a network, have been adopted as standards by the Object Management Group. Several OO process methodologies have also emerged, including rational objectory process (ROP) and rational unified process (RUP).

Component-Based Development

CBD refers to the delivery of information systems by acquiring and assembling independently prefabricated, platform-neutral "packages" of software functionality (components) that are reusable across multiple applications. The granularity of components may vary considerably from self-contained objects and subroutines to entire applications that deliver cohesive software services (Szyperski, 1998). CBD involves three steps—provisioning, inventorying, and assembling—in which software components are created by developers in compliance with standards, registered with component repositories, and made available for application assembly respectively. There are infrastructural components for providing commonly used and generic software services, domain components with specific and proprietary business application logic, and wrapped components to facilitate the interfacing of preexisting functionality provided in legacy systems.

Reuse is a large benefit of CBD. It contributes to delivery speed and eliminates repetitive development steps to produce infrastructure that all applications need. Reuse also reduces the delivered cost of software, which is amortizable over multiple applications (Szyperski, 1998). CBD assemblers need not be expert systems builders; systems may be assembled by solution providers who are also domain experts (Robey et al., 2001). Components are also replaceable, which enables evolutionary upgrade of specific outdated and/or inadequate pieces in the link instead of changing the entire system (Szyperski, 1998). It is claimed that the reuse benefit is often overrated, and that interface problems continue to plague "plug and play" capabilities, especially in the absence of agreed interoperability standards (Sparling, 2000). Perhaps the most immediate restriction, though, on the wider applicability of CBD is the lack of a critical mass of inventoried components.

SUMMARY AND CONCLUSION

Despite its best intentions, the IS community has failed persistently to establish successful organizational systems. The systems delivery process is complex, and there are no silver bullets. But perhaps the search for one has been the largest reason the problem endures. In this pursuit, each new technique, like the Pied Piper, attracts a following of dancers who sometimes abandon time-tested "waltzes." The dominant message of this chapter is that a well-considered amalgam of user-centered techniques, systems delivery methods, and process techniques, selected appropriately to match the context of the problem environ-ment, is required to overwhelm the creative complexity of the software delivery process. Instead of treating alternative methods as competitors, we should identify their boundary conditions—the perimeters of their applicability—and seek to exploit synergistic combinations of available approaches in flexible ways. No method is inherently better than another under all conditions.

Figure 3 illustrates that some development methods are associated with particular paradigms. However, process management techniques and the variety of IS delivery tools discussed may be used by any method and under any paradigm. It may be possible to combine IS delivery methods within and across paradigms to effect a more useful project-context fit and establish comprehen-sive systems delivery process support within a variety of development environ-ments. For example, some XP practices may be gainfully incorporated into RAD, or cleanroom techniques in OOD. The flexible integration of IS delivery approaches, called a "method mix," has fairly wide support among researchers (Broady, Walters & Hartley, 1994; Fitzgerald, 1998; Hocking, 1998; Jaakkola & Drake, 1991; Korac-Boisvert & Kouzmin, 1995; Lee & Xia, 2002; Meso &

Figure 3. Relationship among process methods and techniques

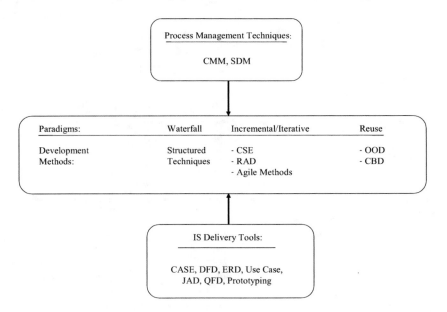

Medo, 2000; Saberwal & Robey, 1995; Vessey & Glass, 1998; Vlasblom, Rijsenbrij & Glastra, 1995).

Table 3 summarizes the salient features of the systems delivery approaches discussed. It provides synoptic statements about the primary objective, the condition most favoring the applicability of, and any major caveat associated with each approach. The approaches are by no means exhaustive. Typically, they are the precursor (and probably the best known) representatives of a family of similar approaches. They are still widely used and have extensive "name recognition." For example, rapid application development (RAD) was discussed in detail, but not dynamic systems development method (DSDM) its derivative, which is very popular in the UK, with claimed improvements over the original methods (Barrow & Mayhew, 2000; Beynon-Davies, Mackay & Tudhope, 2000). Similarly, the capability maturity model (CMM) is elaborated but not Capability Maturity Model Integrated (CMMI), its successor. However, space

Table 3. Summary of approaches

Approach	Objective	Applicability	Major caveat
Socio-Technical Features			
User Ownership	User responsibility for systems success	Where operational feasibility is threatened	Depends on the sophistication of users and developers
Prototyping	Simulate usage experience to discover problems	Difficult to discover requirements	Requires powerful development environment
JAD	Improve requirements & design through enhanced communication	Pooling of knowledge, heterogeneous stakeholders	Needs excellent facilitator to combat relational problems
PD	Technical knowledge sharing to enhance social interactions	Worker participation in decision making	Needs cultural predisposition
QFD	Capture user quality requirements	Intense customer focus	Time consuming; requires group structuring mechanism
Process Management			
CMM	Organizational assessment of systems delivery process	Improved process quality	No immediate impact; cost
SDM	Consistent, stable, repeatable process management	Multi-project environment	May be cumbersome if followed religiously; high learning curve
Methods			
RAD	Fast delivery of functional application (modules)	Expeditious solution implementation	Focus on development speed instead of quality
CSE	Failure-free software in field use	High-risk projects with low fault tolerance	Complexity; human resource requirement
XP	"Process-light" user-developer interaction with co-located teams	Small teams, small systems, quick value-added	Development rigor
OOD	Systems building with flexible, reusable, interacting "objects"	Complex projects; reductionism	Understanding the OO philosophy
CBD	Assembling systems from fully functional platform-neutral pieces	User-developer environment	Critical mass of available components; lack of interface standards

and time precluded the elaboration of second-generation techniques that are fairly similar to their "root" approaches.

There is no convergence of opinions about the effectiveness of many of the approaches; supporting claims of "goodness" and disputed declarations of ineffectiveness coexist in the literature. Some of them are also fairly "old" but were included (to accommodate the recommended method mix) as members of a possible candidate set of approaches with known strengths in particular contexts. If they are already well known by decision makers, older methods may serve as a baseline for the evaluation of other IS delivery options. However, the operational details of even longstanding approaches may not be sufficiently familiar to potential adopters and practitioners to allow them to decide whether they fit a particular development setting.

Research findings have supported the general propositions that (1) effective user involvement contributes to improvements in IS quality; (2) mature IS delivery processes are positively correlated with the quality of the resulting system; and (3) a variety of IS delivery methods that have been used establish excellent systems within well defined domains of applicability. These quality-enhancing approaches have mostly been used in isolation; however, there is a growing call for a method-mix. Further research is needed to legitimize this recommendation for a combination of methods, to identify the scope of the applicability of these approaches, and to empirically validate appropriate mappings of individual and combined approaches to particular development settings. This could eventually provide valuable insights into contingency considerations for the adoption of effective combinations of methods and approaches, and suitable criteria for grouping methods.

REFERENCES

Adamopoulos, D. X., Haramis, G., & Papandreou, C. A. (1998). Rapid prototyping of new telecommunications services: A procedural approach. *Computer Communications, 21*, 211-219.

Agrawal, K., & Whittaker, J. A. (1993). Experiences in applying statistical testing to a real-time, embedded software system. *Proceedings of the Pacific Northwest Software Quality Conference.*

Agarwal, R., De, P., Sinha, A. P., & Tanniru M. (2000). On the usability of OO representations. *Communications of the ACM, 43*(10), 83-89.

Al-Mushayt, O., Doherty, N., & King, M. (2001). An investigation into the relative success of alternative approaches to the treatment of organizational issues in systems development projects. *Organization Development Journal, 19*(1), 31-48.

Andrews, D. C. (1991). JAD: A crucial dimension for rapid applications development. *Journal of Systems Management, 42*(3), 23-27, 31.

Bandi, R. K., Vaishnavi, V. K., & Turk, D. E. (2003). Predicting maintenance performance using object-oriented design complexity metrics. IEEE *Transactions on Software Engineering, 29*(1), 77-87.

Banker, R. D., Davis, G. B., & Slaughter, S. A. (1998). Software development practices, software complexity, and software maintenance performance: A field study. *Management Science, 44*(4), 433-450.

Barki, H., & Hartwick, J. (1994). Measuring user participation, user involvement, and user attitude. *MIS Quarterly, 18*(1), 59-82.

Barki, H., Rivard, S., & Talbot, J. (1993). A keyword classification scheme for IS research literature: An update. *MIS Quarterly, 17*(2), 209-226.

Barrow, P. D., & Mayhew, P. J. (2000). Investigating principles of stakeholder evaluation in a modern IS development approach. *Journal of Systems and Software, 52*(2-3), 95-103.

Baskerville, R. L., & Stage, J. *(1996).* Controlling prototype development through risk analysis. *MIS Quarterly, 20*(4), 481-504.

Beck, K. (2000) *Extreme programming explained: Embrace change.* Boston: Addison-Wesley.

Beizer, B. (1997). Cleanroom process model: A critical examination. *IEEE Software, 14*(2), 14-16.

Beynon-Davies, P. (1998). *Information systems development: An introduction to information systems engineering.* London: Macmillan.

Beynon-Davies, P., Mackay, H., & Tudhope, D. (2000). It's lots of bits of paper and ticks and post-it notes and things: A case study of a rapid application development project. *Information Systems Journal, 10*(3), 195-216.

Beynon-Davies, P., Tudhope, D., & Mackay, H. (1999). Information systems prototyping in practice. *Journal of Information Technology, 14*(1), 107-120.

Boar, B. H. (1984). *Application prototyping.* New York: John Wiley & Sons.

Bordoloi, B., & Lee, M. (1994). An object-oriented view: Productivity comparison with structured development. *Information Systems Management, 11*(1), 22-30.

Borovits, I., Ellis, S., & Yeheskel, O. (1990). Group processes and the development of information systems. *Information & Management, 19*, 65-72.

Bourne, K. C. (1994). Putting the rigor back in RAD. *Database Programming & Design, 7*(8), 25-30.

Broady, J. E., Walters, S. A., & Hartley, R. J. (1994). A review of information systems development methodologies (ISDMS). *Library Management, 15*(6), 5-19.

Brooks, F. P., Jr. (1987). No silver bullet: Essence and accidents of software engineering. *IEEE Computer, 20*(4), 10-19.

Brown, D. W. (2002). *An introduction to object-oriented analysis*. New York: John Wiley & Sons.

Brynjolfssen, E. (1993). The productivity paradox of information technology. *Communications of the ACM, 36*(12), 67-77.

Carmel, E., George, J. F., & Nunamaker, J. F. (1995). Examining the process of electronic-JAD. *Journal of End User Computing, 7*(1), 13-22.

Carmel, E., Whitaker, R. D., & George, J. F. (1993). PD and joint application design: A transatlantic comparison. *Communications of the ACM, 36*(6), 40-48.

Cockburn, A. (2002). Agile software development joins the 'would-be crowd'. *Cutter IT Journal, 15*(1), 6-12.

Cox, B. J. (1995, November). No silver bullet revisited. *American Programmer Journal*. Retrieved from http://www.virtualschool.edu/cox/AMPROTTEF.html

Davidson, E. J. (1999). Joint application design (JAD) in practice. *The Journal of Systems and Software 45*(3), 215-223.

Davis, A. M. (1995). Software prototyping. *Advances in Computers, 40*, 39-63.

Dean, D. L., Lee, J. D., Pendergast, M. O., Hickey A. M., & Nunamaker, J. F. (1997-1998). Enabling the effective involvement of multiple users: Methods and tools for effective software engineering. *Journal of Management Information Systems 14*(3), 179-222.

Dekleva, S. M. (1992). The influence of the information systems development approach on maintenance. *MIS Quarterly, 16*(3), 355-372.

Diaz, M., & Sligo, J. (1997). How software process improvement helped Motorola. *IEEE Software, 14*(5), 1997, 75-81.

Dietrich, G., Walz, D., & Wynekoop, J. (1997). The failure of SDT diffusion: A case for mass customization. *IEEE Transactions on Engineering Management, 44*(4), 390-398.

Dodd, J. L., & Carr, H. H. (1994). Systems development led by end-users. *Journal of Systems Management, 45*(8), 34-40.

Doherty, N. F., & King, M. (1998). The consideration of organizational issues during the systems development process: An empirical analysis. *Behavior & Information Technology, 17*(1), 41-51.

Duggan, E. W., & Thachenkary, C. S. (2004). Integrating nominal group technique and joint application development for improved systems requirements determination. *Information and Management, 41*(4), 399-411.

Elboushi, M. I. (1997). Object-oriented software design utilizing quality function deployment. *The Journal of Systems and Software, 38*(2), 133-143.

Erikkson, I., & McFadden, F. (1993). Quality function deployment: A tool to improve software quality. *Information & Software Technology, 35*(9), 491-498.

Fichman, R. G., & Kemerer, C. F. (1992). Object-oriented and conventional analysis and design methodologies. *IEEE Computer, 25*(10), 22-39.

Fitzgerald, B. (1998). An empirical investigation into the adoption of systems development methodologies. *Information and Management, 34*(6), 317-328.

Fitzgerald, B. (2000). Systems development methodologies: The problem of tenses. *Information Technology & People, 13*(3), 174-182.

Flatten, P. O. (1992). Requirements for a life-cycle methodology for the 1990s. In W. W. Cotterman & J. A. Senn (Eds.), *Challenges and strategies for research in systems development* (pp. 221-234). New York: John Wiley & Sons.

Fox, W. M. (1995). Socio-technical system principles and guidelines: Past and present. *The Journal of Applied Behavioral Science, 31*(1), 91-105.

Friedlander, P. (1992). Ensuring software project success with project buyers. *Software Engineering Tools, Techniques, and Practices, 2*(6), 26-29.

Garvin, D. A. (1984). What does "product quality" really mean? *Sloan Management Review, 26*(1), 25-45.

Gibbs, W. W. (1994). Software's chronic crisis. *Scientific American, 271*(3), 86-95.

Gill, C., & Krieger, H. (1999). Direct and representative participation in Europe: Recent survey evidence. *International Journal of Human Resource Management, 10*, 72-591.

Glass, R. L. (2001). Extreme programming: The good, the bad, and the bottom line. *IEEE Software, 8*(6), 111-112.

Grady, R. B. (1993). Practical results from measuring software quality. *Communications of the ACM, 36*(11), 62-68.

Haley, T. J. (1996). Raytheon's experience in software process improvement. *IEEE Software, 13*(2), 33-41.

Hanna, M. (1995). Farewell to waterfalls? *Software Magazine, 15*(5), 38-46.

Harter, D. E., Slaughter, S. A., & Krishnan, M. S. (1998). The life cycle effects of software quality: A longitudinal analysis. *International Conference on Information Systems*, 346-351.

Hausler, P. A., Linger, R. C., & Trammell, C. J. (1994). Adopting cleanroom software engineering with a phased approach. *IBM Systems Journal, 33*(1), 89-109.

Head, G. E. (1994). Six-Sigma software using cleanroom software engineering techniques. *Hewlett-Packard Journal, 45*(3), 40-50.

Ho, E. S., Lai, Y. J., & Chang, S. I. (1999). An integrated group decision-making approach to quality function deployment. *IIE Transactions, 31*(6), 553-567.

Hocking, L. J. (1998). Developing a framework for examining systems development and its environmental context: The relationship between Gidden's structuration theory and Pettigrew's contextualist analysis. *Proceedings of the 4th Association for Information Systems Americas Conference* (pp. 835-837).

Hoffer, J., George, J., & Valacich, J. (2002). *Modern systems analysis and design.* New Jersey: Prentice Hall.

Hollenbach, C., Young, R., Pflugrad, A., & Smith, D. (1997). Combining quality and software process improvement. *Communications of the ACM, 40*(6), 41-45.

Hough, D. (1993). Rapid delivery: An evolutionary approach for application development. *IBM Systems Journal, 32*(3), 397-419.

ISO/IEC Standard 9126-1. (2001). *Software Engineering—Product Quality—Part 1: Quality Model.*

Jaakkola, J. E., & Drake, K. B. (1991). ASDM: The universal systems development methodology. *Journal of Systems Management, 42*(2), 6-11.

Jerva, M. (2001). Systems analysis and design methodologies: Practicalities and use in today's information systems development efforts. *Topics in Health Information Management, 21*(4), 13-20.

Johnson, R. A., Hardgrove, B. C., & Doke, E. R. (1999). An industry analysis of developer beliefs about object-oriented systems development. *The DATA BASE for Advances in Information Systems, 30*(1), 47-64.

Kettelhut, M. C. (1993). JAD methodology and group dynamics. *Information Systems Management, 14*(3), 46-53.

Khalifa, M., & Verner, J. M. (2000). Drivers for software development method usage. *IEEE Transactions on Engineering Management, 47*(3), 360-369.

Kitchenham, B., & Pfleeger, S. L. (1996). Software quality: The elusive target. *IEEE Software, 13*(1), 12-21.

Kjaer, A., & Madsen, K. H. (1995). Participatory analysis of flexibility. *Communications of the ACM, 38*(5), 53-60.

Korac-Boisvert, N., & Kouzmin, A. K. N. (1995). It development: Methodology overload or crisis. *Science Communication, 17*, 81-88.

Kuvaja, P., Similä, J., Kranik, L., Bicego, A., Saukkonen, S., & Koch, G. (1994). Software process assessment and improvement: The BOOTSTRAP approach. Cambridge, MA: Blackwell Publishers.

Lee, G., & Xia, W. (2002). Flexibility of information systems development projects: A conceptual framework. *Proceedings of the 8th Americas Conference on Information Systems*, (pp. 1390-1396).

Liou, Y. I., & Chen, M. (1993-1994). Using group support systems in joint application development for requirements specifications. *Journal of Management Information Systems, 8*(10), 805-815.

Lyytinen, K. (1988). Expectation failure concept and systems analysts' view of information system failures: Results of an exploratory study. *Information & Management, 14*(1), 45-56.

Mankin, D., & Cohen, S. G. (1997). Teams and technology: Tensions in participatory design. *Organizational Dynamics, 26*(1), 63-76.

Marakas, G. M., & Hornik, S. (1996). Passive resistance misuse: Overt support and covert recalcitrance in IS implementation. *European Journal of Information Systems, 5*, 208-219.

Markus, M. L., & Keil, M. (1994). If we build it they will come: Designing information systems that users want to use. *Sloan Management Review, 35*(4), 11-25.

Martins, A., & Aspinwall, E. M. (2001). Quality function deployment: An empirical study in the UK. *Total Quality Management, 12*(5), 575-588.

McDonald, M. P. (1995). Quality function deployment: Introducing product development into the systems development process. *Seventh Symposium on Quality Function Deployment*, Novi, Michigan.

Melo, W., El Emam, K., & Drouin, J. (1998). *SPICE: The theory and practice of software process improvement and capability determination.* Los Alamitos, CA: IEEE Computer Society Press.

Meso, P., & Madey, G. R. (2000). A complexity-based taxonomy of systems development methodologies. *Association for Information Systems 2000 Americas Conference*, 238-244.

Mousinho, G. (1990). Project management: Runaway! *Systems International, 6*, 35-40.

Muller, M. J., Wildman, D. M., & White, E. A. (1993). Taxonomy of PD practices: A brief practitioner's guide. *Communications of the ACM, 36*(4), 26-27.

Newman, M., & Robey, D. (1992). A social process model of user-analyst relationships. *MIS Quarterly, 16*(2), 249-266.

Niederman, F., Brancheau, J. C., & Wetherbe, J. C. (1991). Information systems management issues for the 1990s. *MIS Quarterly, 15*(4), 474-500.

Palvia, S. C., Sharma, R. S., & Conrath, D. W. (2001). A socio-technical framework for quality assessment of computer information systems. *Industrial Management & Data Systems, 101*(5), 237-251.

Paulk, M. C. (2001). Extreme programming from a CMM perspective. *IEEE Software, 8*(6), 19-26.

Paulk, M. C., Curtis, B., Chrissis, M. B., & Weber, C. V. (1993). The capability maturity model: version 1.1. *IEEE Software, 10*(4), 18-27.

Pfleeger, S. L. (1996). Realities and rewards of software process improvement. *IEEE Software, 13*(6), 99-101.

Rae, A., Robert, P., & Hausen, H. L. (1995). *Software evaluation for certification: Principles, practice and legal liability.* London: McGraw-Hill.

Ravichandran, T., & Rai, A. (1994). The dimensions and correlates of systems development quality. *Proceedings of the Annual SIG Computer Personnel Research Conference on Reinventing IS*, Virginia, (pp. 272-282).

Ravichandran, T., & Rai, A. (1996). Impact of process management on systems development quality: An empirical study. *Proceedings of the Americas Conference on Information Systems*.

Ravichandran, T., & Rai, A. (2000). Quality management in systems development: An organizational system perspective. *MIS Quarterly, 24*(3), 381-415.

Roberts, T. L., Gibson, M. L., & Fields, K. T. (1997). Systems development methodology implementation: Perceived aspects of importance. *Information Resources Management Journal, 10*(3), 27-38.

Robey, D., Welke, R., & Turk, D. (2001). Traditional, iterative, and component-based development: A social analysis of software of software development paradigms. *Information Technology and Management, 2*(1), 53-70.

Sabherwal, R., & Robey, D. (1995). An empirical taxonomy of implementation processes based on sequences of events in information systems development. In G. P. Huber & A. H. Van de Ven (Eds.), *Longitudinal field research methods: Studying processes of organizational change* (pp. 228-266). London: Sage.

Schmidt, D. C., & Fayad, M. E. (1997). Lessons learned building reusable OO frameworks for distributed software. *Communications of the ACM, 40*(10), 85-87.

Shani, A. B., & Sena, J. A. (1994). Information technology and the integration of change: Socio-technical system approach. *The Journal of Applied Behavioral Science, 30*(2), 247-270.

Silver, M. S., Markus, M. L., & Beath, C. M. (1995). The information technology interaction model: A foundation for the MBA core course. *MIS Quarterly, 19*(3), 361-390.

Spangler, A. (1996, October-November). Cleanroom software engineering: Plan your work and work your plan in small increments. *IEEE Potentials*, 29-32.

Sparling, M. (2000). Lessons learned through six years of component-based development. *Communications of the ACM, 43*(10), 47-53.

Szyperski, C. (1998). *Component software, beyond object-oriented programming.* New York: Addison-Wesley.

Trammell, C. J., Pleszkoch, M. G., Linger, R. C., & Hevner A. R. (1996). The incremental development process in cleanroom software engineering. *Decision Support Systems, 17*(1), 55-71.

Vessey, I., & Conger, S. A. (1994). Requirements specification: Learning object, process, and data methodologies. *Communications of the ACM, 37*(5), 102-112.

Vessey, I., & Glass, R. (1998). Stong vs. weak approaches to systems development. *Communications of the ACM, 41*(4), 99-102.

Vlasblom, G., Rijsenbrij, D., & Glastra, M. (1995). Flexibilization of the methodology of system development. *Information and Software Technology, 37*(11), 595-607.

Weinberg, R. S. (1991). Prototyping and the systems development life cycle. *Information Systems Management, 8*(2), 47-53.

Welke, R. J. (1994). The shifting software development paradigm. *Database, 25*(4), 9-16.

Wetherbe, J. C. (1991). Executive information requirements: Getting it right. *MIS Quarterly, 15*(1), 51-65.

Wood, J., & Silver, D. (1995). *Joint application development.* New York: John Wiley & Sons.

ENDNOTES

1. Examples of reports of the software crisis:
    -   Mousinho (1990), reported on runaway projects (two, three, or even four times over budget, at least 50% behind schedule, or both).
    -   Niederman, Brancheau, & Wetherbe (1991), identified the improvement of software development quality among the top ten issues of information systems management.
    -   KPMG Peat Marwick (Computerworld, April 25, 1994) reported the startling finding that 95% of all major computer projects slide into cost and time overruns; 65% of those become runaway projects.
    -   Charles B. Kreitzberg, President of Cognetics Corp., a software consulting firm in Princeton Junction, NJ, claim that CIOs estimate the failure rate for software projects at 60%; 25% are abandoned.
    -   In 1998, the Standish Group International Inc. indicated that although the picture is improving, only 24% of IS projects in Fortune 500 companies could be considered successful (up from 9% in 1994).
    -   June 2001 survey of MIS executives by *CIO Magazine*: Approximately 50% expressed dissatisfaction with the quality of their organization's business software.
2. ISO/IEC Quality Attributes
    -   **Functionality:** The extent to which functional and non-functional requirements and technical constraints are satisfied
    -   **Reliability:** The degree of failure-free usage
    -   **Usability:** How easy the system is to learn and understand and operate in terms of performance such as response and throughput

- **Efficiency:** Potential for correct performance with minimal waste of resources
- **Maintainability:** Potential for low cost error correction, adaptation, and enhancement
- **Portability:** Capability to reproduce operations and results on other technical platforms

3. JAD Phases:
    1. Project definition—facilitator works with system owners and sponsors to determine management perspectives and expectations regarding purpose, scope, and objectives.
    2. Background research by the facilitator into the current business processes and related computer systems in place.
    3. Extensive planning and preparation for the workshop, the logistics, and training of the scribe.
    4. The JAD workshop, where the interaction takes place, is the main event in this process. The facilitator assists in resolving conflicts, and encourages group participation and eventual consensus, and guides the session toward the accomplishment.
    5. Preparation of the final document containing the decisions and agreements.

4. CMM Levels:
    - Level 1, the "initial" stage is characterized by the absence of and formal procedures—a state of near chaos, where proper project planning and control are non-existent. Organizations may experience successful implementations but these depend on heroic individual effort.
    - Level 2 is called the "repeatable" stage, where basic project management capability exists. The organization can establish and track schedules and cost, and monitor and report on progress. But process management discipline does not exist and individual project leaders supply their own process management techniques. Project success depends greatly on the skill of the project group.
    - An organization at Level 3, the "defined" stage, uses a common, institutionalized process management method (systems development methodology), for all its IS projects. The process management discipline produces consistent, stable, and predictable outcomes. This allows dynamic redeployment of human resources and reduces attrition-related failure risks.
    - At Level 4, the "managed" stage, organizational learning is a key objective. Establishing a common methodology is not viewed as the end-all of process management. The organization collects detailed measures of process and product quality, which is used to refine the development process.

- An organization at Level 5 has "optimized" its process management capability. It uses the metrics from Level 4, acknowledged best practices, and benchmarks, and the results of controlled experiments and pilot studies to adjust the process to achieve continuous process improvement.

5. Agile manifesto

    The Manifesto for Agile Software Development, (http://www.agileAlliance.org), outlines 12 agile principles that were developed at a meeting of representatives of agile methods at Snowbird, UT in February 2001.

6. XP planning and iterative planning games

    1. **The planning game:** In exploration Business produces "story cards" of desired features, and Development estimates the implementation requirements. In commitment, Business prioritizes the story cards into essential, not essential but value adding, and nice-to-have features, and Development classifies them according to implementation risk. Based on the resulting matrix, Business selects the next feature(s) to be developed and deployed. In steering, Business and Development review progress and make adjustments as necessary.

    2. **The iterative planning game:** In exploration, story cards are converted to task cards that contain implementation details. During commitment, responsibilities are distributed and the workload balanced among pair-programming teams (dyads). In steering, the various dyads construct, test, integrate, and deploy new functionality into the overall system. Typically, the iteration planning game occurs in the interval between steering cycles of the planning game.

7. Key features of the OOD include:

    - Encapsulation, the idea of making an object self-sufficient by abstracting and isolating its attributes and procedures, as in a "capsule," and hiding them from other objects. The encapsulated procedures are the only instructions that can act on data within an object; both are protected from outside interference. Objects are protected from the need to keep track of the complications of (and the changes to) another object's internal structure. They interact by exchanging messages that request information or the activation of particular procedures.

    - Inheritance is accommodated by the fact that objects are modeled as classes (a generic grouping) or instances (specific concrete invocation of an example in application, i.e., with attribute values). Inheritance is enabled by defining special cases, subclasses or subassemblies, which share the common attributes, procedures, and relationships of a more general class (super class), but may have their own peculiar attributes and procedures. Existing objects may also be augmented with additional procedures to create new classes with enhanced functionality.

- Polymorphism exploits this hierarchy of object classification to apply the same named procedure in different ways depending on the characteristics of the object class in which it is invoked.

Chapter XIII

Testing and Extending Theory in Strategic Information Systems Planning Through Literature Analysis

Irwin T. J. Brown
University of Cape Town, South Africa

ABSTRACT

Strategic information systems planning (SISP) has been and continues to be a key concern to information systems managers, and much research effort has been devoted to studying it. SISP has been theorized in terms of an input-process-output model, with well-defined categories and a set of hypotheses to be tested. Based on this theoretical framework, a comprehensive analysis of academic literature published since 1991 is undertaken. The analysis reveals the extent to which the various categories and hypotheses within this framework have been researched, as well as identifying additional hypotheses that are suggested from the literature.

INTRODUCTION

Information systems planning (ISP) has been defined as the process of identifying "prioritised information systems (IS) that are efficient, effective and/ or strategic in nature together with the necessary resources (human, technical and financial), management of change considerations, control procedures and organisational structure needed to implement these" (Baker, 1995, p. 62). The focus of this research is on the strategic to tactical level of ISP, commonly referred to as strategic ISP (SISP) (O'Connor, 1993). This differs from lower levels of planning in that, in terms of scope, it is organizational, in perspective that of top management, in terms of level of abstraction, more conceptual than physical, and in time frame, medium to long (Segars, Grover & Teng, 1998).

SISP has long been a key issue for information systems managers (Luftman & McLean, 2004; Watson et al., 1997). This interest in SISP stems from the recognition that IS are a strategic resource for organizations, capable of providing strategic advantage, and improving overall business performance (Pant & Hsu, 1999). As such, they need to be managed strategically, planning being key to this endeavor. In the modern era, described variously as the information age or knowledge age, IS are furthermore ubiquitous in many organizations and play an increasingly important strategic role. E-business, for example, is the phrase coined to denote the use of Internet technologies to support both internal operations and processes within a firm, as well as those between firms (Pant & Ravichandran, 2001). These types of IS offer many potential benefits if adequately planned for and implemented (Pant & Ravichandran, 2001). In addition, IS continue to evolve and grow in complexity as technology, the competitive environment, and business strategies change (Benamati & Lederer, 2001). SISP helps organizations make sense of this complexity, as by adopting this practice, firms are able to analyze the environment, keep track of new developments, monitor how IT is being used by competitors, plan for adequate IT infrastructure, and establish how best IS can be used to both support and impact business strategies and objectives (Salmela & Spil, 2002; Segars et al., 1998). The efficacy of SISP has furthermore been demonstrated in several studies (Cohen, 2002; Premkumar & King, 1994).

The purpose of this chapter is to conduct an extensive analysis of academic research in order to test a theory of SISP proposed by Lederer and Salmela (1996) and, in so doing, to identify where further research is required. Extensions to theory may also be suggested from the analysis. In the following section, justification for using this theory as a basis will be provided by examining several other ways in which SISP has been studied and the limitations of these alternatives. The process by which data was collected will be described before the data is analyzed according to the theoretical framework. Results of this analysis are reported and discussed before implications for future research are outlined and the chapter concluded.

SISP RESEARCH TRENDS

According to Baker (1995), early research in SISP focused attention mainly on the derivation of methods and techniques for carrying out the process (e.g., Lederer & Putnam, 1986; McFarlan, McKenney & Pyburn, 1983; Porter & Millar, 1985; Shank, Boynton, & Zmud, 1985). Very often, however, these were developed in the absence of a sound theoretical underpinning for SISP, and as a result, there were reports of methodological problems and plan implementation failures (Lederer & Sethi, 1988). Suffice to say, methods and techniques continue to be prescribed but from a more informed understanding of SISP (Galliers, 1993; Min & Kim, 1999; Ormerod, 1996; Salmela & Spil, 2002; Van der Zee & De Jong, 1999).

Other streams of research have examined the state of planning practice (Conrath, Ang, & Mattay, 1992; Galliers, 1987; Pavri & Ang, 1995), success factors (Ang & Teo, 1997), problems (Lederer & Sethi, 1988; Teo & Ang, 2001), and prescriptions or guidelines for success (Galliers, 1991; Lederer & Sethi, 1996). In some cases, frameworks for carrying out SISP have been proposed (Pant & Hsu, 1999). While all these studies have made a valuable contribution to the body of knowledge, they lack the gestalt perspective necessary to outline a broad overview of SISP (Gottschalk, 1999a).

Earl (1993) identified, as a unit of analysis, an approach to SISP where this was defined as the interaction of method, process, and implementation. Segars and Grover (1999) identified alternative SISP profiles, differentiated by ratings for specified process characteristics and similarly compared the relative success of these alternative profiles. Doherty, Marples, and Suhaimi (1999) in like manner conducted a study in which they identified alternative approaches, based on a set of planning characteristics. These studies extended the scope of research beyond mere techniques and prescriptions for SISP to also look at planning characteristics and behaviors. However, the relationships between factors are not the prime focus of these studies, save for the relationship between approaches (a grouping of characteristics) and measures of planning success.

Some SISP studies have conceptualized SISP in terms of an input-process-model, or system. Lederer and Sethi (1988), for example, classified SISP problems as resource-related, process-related, or output-related. Premkumar and King (1991) provided empirical support for a general systems model of ISP, which included categories of input, process, output, outcomes, and context. Ang, Shaw, and Pavri (1995) also derived a similar model. A conceptual process model developed by Baker (1995) in addition included a plan implementation category and distinguished between the process (planning activities) and method (procedures and techniques) of SISP. This model also highlighted another element important to any system—feedback.

Lederer and Salmela (1996) extended this work by recommending that an input-process-output variance model form the basis for a theory of SISP, which includes the categories of external environment, internal environment, planning resources, planning process, information plan, plan implementation, and plan alignment (changed to Outcomes in this study, as alignment, although the most common outcome measure, is only one of several ways in which SISP outcomes have been measured) (see Figure 1). This theory provides a parsimonious way of viewing SISP, while also providing a clear set of hypotheses to be tested (see Table 1). It therefore serves as a useful basis for examining the literature in SISP, as it allows for simple classification of studies. It also embraces all the other conceptualizations encapsulating them into one or more planning categories or relationships. By determining to what extent the categories have been studied and operationalized and to what extent relationships (hypotheses) have been tested, areas for further research can be identified. As pointed out by Lederer and Salmela (1996), "the study of SISP is hampered by the absence of a theory that describes it" (p. 238), hence the reason for the formulation of their theory. Gottschalk (1999 a, b, c) explicitly tested the relationship between information plan and plan implementation, as suggested by the theory, but many other studies examining relationships between SISP categories make no specific mention of the Lederer and Salmela (1996) work (e.g., Reich & Benbasat, 2000; Segars et al., 1998). Given the limited explicit reference to this theory, it is thus opportune

Figure 1. A theory of SISP (amended from Lederer & Salmela, 1996)

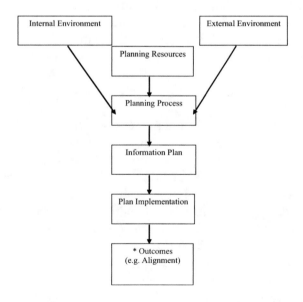

* Depicted as Alignment by Lederer and Salmela, but changed to Outcomes here to accommodate the other alternative outcome measures that have been used in SISP research.

to examine to what extent it is actually supported by existing work, further justifying this study.

Definitions for the categories in Figure 1 are provided below. These aim to be as broad as possible so as to enable inclusion of all likely factors into this framework:

- **External Environment:** This can be defined as the sum total of factors external to the organization(s) conducting SISP that may have an impact on the SISP system (modified from Lederer & Salmela, 1996). This category can be divided into two major subcategories – external business environment and external IT environment (Pant & Hsu, 1999). Environmental uncertainty is an example of a factor within this domain that has been examined in the context of SISP (Teo & King, 1997), with one study specifically looking at whether a comprehensive or incremental planning process is more effective in a turbulent environment (Salmela, Lederer, & Raponen, 2000).
- **Internal Environment:** This is defined as the sum total of factors within the organization(s) conducting SISP that may have an impact on the SISP system (modified from Lederer & Salmela, 1996). Once again this category can be divided into internal business environment and internal IS environment (Pant & Hsu, 1999). Examples of factors examined within this category include organization size, role of IS in the organization, and quality of strategic business planning, among others (Premkumar & King, 1994).
- **Planning resources:** Resources, of whatever nature (typically informational, human, financial, and technical), required for carrying out the planning process make up this category (modified from Lederer & Salmela, 1996). Examples of resources include top management input and involvement as well as user input and involvement (Basu et al., 2002; Premkumar & King, 1994).
- **Planning Process:** The planning process is defined by the set of steps for developing a strategic information plan, paying heed to the methods to be used, style of process (process characteristics), and implementation issues to be addressed (Doherty et al., 1999; Earl, 1993). The process is at the core of SISP, converting inputs into outputs (Baker, 1995). It is normally accomplished by employing a formal methodology that details the phases, stages, and activities to be carried out (Mentzas, 1997). However, just as important is the way in which the process is carried out, as the process characteristics have a major bearing on the ultimate success of SISP (Segars et al., 1998). For example, the extent to which the business planning and SISP processes are integrated (BP-ISP integration) is a key success factor (Teo & King, 1997).

- **Information Plan:** The tangible outputs of the SISP process are detailed in the information plan (Lederer & Salmela, 1996). The plan content will be, as expected, very closely related to the methodology employed in the process (Bergeron, Buteau, & Raymond, 1991). Nevertheless, a typical plan will contain, among other things, a portfolio of applications to be implemented together with priorities (Agarwal, Roberge, & Tannuri, 1994), as well as an overall information architecture for the organization (Periasamy & Feeny, 1997).

- **Plan Implementation:** The rate, extent, and performance of plan implementation is how this category has been operationalized (Gottschalk, 1999a). Its importance cannot be overstated, as without plan implementation, the whole planning exercise may be thrown into question.

- **Planning Outcomes (Primarily Alignment):** Planning outcomes have typically been operationalized as the extent to which key planning objectives have been fulfilled (Baker, 1995; Lederer & Sethi, 1996; Premkumar & King, 1991). *Alignment* of IS plans and objectives with business plans and objectives has often been the major objective of SISP and thus was illustrated as the ultimate outcome in the Lederer and Salmela theory. That it be represented as an outcome is supported by the work of Reich and Benbasat (2000). Segars and Grover (1999), however, identify the extent of *analysis*, level of *cooperation* achieved, and improvement in *capability* as key SISP objectives too. Thus, in order for this category to be inclusive of all possible outcome measures that have been used in SISP studies, it has been renamed in Figure 1 from Alignment to *Planning Outcomes*.

Table 1. SISP hypotheses (amended from Lederer & Salmela, 1996)

H1	A more stable external environment produces a more effective and efficient planning process. "The stability and predictability of industry, government, and economics appear to promote SISP" (Lederer & Salmela, 1996, p. 242)
H2	A simpler internal environment produces a more effective and efficient planning process. "Greater predictability and simplicity in the internal environment appear to promote SISP" (Lederer & Salmela, 1996, p. 244)
H3	More extensive and higher quality planning resources produce a more effective and efficient planning process. "Resources is the most significant variable to be associated with the two planning dimensions" (planning process quality and planning effectiveness respectively) (Premkumar & King, 1994, p. 96)
H4	A more comprehensive planning process produces a more useful information plan. "A planning process of higher quality produces a plan of higher quality" (Premkumar & King, 1991 in Lederer & Salmela, 1996, p. 246)
H5	A more useful information plan produces greater plan implementation. "There is a significant relationship between (plan) content characteristics and IT strategy implementation" (Gottschalk, 1999c, p. 115)
H6	Greater plan implementation produces more positive planning outcomes (e.g., better alignment). "By implementing projects according to comprehensive strategic plans, organisations validate the usefulness of the plan and should thus achieve better alignment" (Lederer & Salmela, 1996, p. 248)

Relationships between these categories were captured by Lederer and Salmela in the form of hypotheses as displayed in Table 1. It is recognized that there are other indirect and contingency effects that may also be studied, in addition to these hypotheses, and identification of these is probably the main contribution of this chapter. They will be discussed in further detail later.

DATA COLLECTION AND SAMPLE PROFILE

In order to collect data, a comprehensive search for articles on SISP was made on library and journal databases. Since the purpose of the study was to analyze SISP from a research perspective, only articles from peer-reviewed research journals were identified. Research papers describing studies of an empirical (qualitative or quantitative) nature were the specific target of selection. The scope of the study was further limited to SISP studies published after 1991. A quick review reveals that the many studies prior to 1991 were either conceptual in nature or focused on methods and techniques for carrying out SISP. Some major empirical studies done before 1991 were also reported in articles published in or after 1991 (e.g., Lederer & Sethi, 1991).

In total, 146 articles identified on SISP were found and formed the basis for further analysis. While not completely exhaustive, the articles identified were deemed to be sufficiently representative, as they were taken from 35 different research publications. The information systems and management journals, as expected, predominated given that SISP is a typical IS management concern, but articles were also found in other journals such as the *South African Computer Journal* (Cohen, 2002), the *Computer Journal* (Mehrez et al., 1993), and *Journal of Systems and Software* (Doukidis, Lybereas, & Galliers, 1996). Many studies in leading conference proceedings spawned related articles in journals (e.g., Finnegan, Galliers, & Powell, 1997, 1999; Kearns & Lederer, 1997, 2000; Periasamy, 1993; Periasamy & Feeny, 1997). Thus, conference proceedings were excluded from this analysis. Diversity of the sample was evidenced by the fact that the articles were also based on studies done in 20 different countries.

Sources of Data

The journals from which two or more articles were gathered and their ranking in terms of number of contributions are displayed in Table 2. They include reputable IS journals (e.g., *Information Resource Management Journal*), as well as some of the major management science journals (e.g., *Decision Sciences*).

Geographical Regions

As can be seen in Table 3, the articles examined emanate largely from studies done in North America, the US in particular (37% of total). There are also a sizeable number of articles based on studies in Europe and the Asia-Pacific region. The Middle East and Africa are the least represented in terms of publications. This may mirror the state of the global economy, whereby devel-

Table 2. Sources of articles—journals

Journal title	Frequency
Information & Management	26
International Journal of Information Management	18
Journal of Strategic Information Systems	13
Decision Sciences	10
European Journal of Information Systems	9
Journal of Management Information Systems	9
Long Range Planning	8
Information Systems Research	6
MIS Quarterly	6
Communications of the AIS	5
OMEGA--International Journal of Management Science	4
Journal of Information Systems	3
INFOR	2
Information Resources Management Journal	2
International Journal of Technology Management	2
Journal of the Operational Research Society	2
Logistics Information Management	2
Journal of End-User Computing	2

Table 3. Regions in which studies were conducted

Region	Country	Frequency
N. America	USA	49 (34%)
	Canada	4 (3%)
Europe	UK	24 (16%)
	Norway	3 (2%)
	Finland	3 (2%)
	UK/Ireland	1 (1%)
	Greece	2 (2%)
	Netherlands	2 (2%)
	Russia	1 (1%)
Asia-Pacific	Singapore	7 (5%)
	Australia	8 (5%)
	Taiwan	4 (3%)
	China	1 (1%)
	Hong Kong	1 (1%)
	South Korea	4 (3%)
	Japan	1 (1%)
Middle East	Kuwait	1 (1%)
	Israel	1 (1%)
	Arab Gulf	1 (1%)
	Bahrain	1 (1%)
Africa	South Africa	3 (2%)
Other	Multiple	5 (4%)
N/A	-	18 (12%)

oped countries dominate in most spheres, including that of research. In many developing countries too, there is a lack of skills, capacity, and funding to match research outputs of the developed countries, with the brain drain from developing to developed nations further hampering efforts at redress. The implications of this are that when research findings from the mainstream literature are applied, national context should also be considered (Aladwani, 2001). This is to ascertain whether the environment from which the research emanates is similar to the one in which it is being applied. If there are differences, the appropriateness of the findings to the new setting needs to be evaluated.

Study Purposes and Research Approaches

The purposes for which studies were conducted were classified as either:

- **Method:** Studies prescribing techniques, methods, and methodologies to be employed in SISP.
- **Conceptual:** Studies outlining conceptual models and frameworks on SISP.
- **Planning Practice:** Studies that examine the state of planning practice with regard to SISP.
- **Key Prescriptions and Success Factors:** Studies identifying prescriptions, guidelines, or critical success factors for SISP.
- **Problems:** Studies identifying problems encountered by organizations when carrying out SISP.
- **Construct/Concept Development:** Studies that aim to operationalize and measure constructs to be used in SISP or that identify important concepts.
- **Hypothesis Testing:** Studies that aim to test predefined hypotheses or propositions concerning SISP.

Some studies served one or more of these purposes (e.g., hypothesis testing studies that also aimed to develop and operationalize constructs as a first step). These were classified according to what their primary purpose was deemed to be. Table 4a shows that many studies sought to test some hypotheses or propositions. These are most useful in examining the relationships of the theory represented in Figure 1, but studies on planning practices (e.g., Ang & Quek, 1999) and prescriptions (Lederer & Sethi, 1996) also provide evidence of

Table 4a. Purpose of studies

Purpose	Frequency
Hypothesis testing	41
Methods	39
Planning practices	30
Construct/Concept development	13
Prescriptions, success factors	10
Problems	9
Conceptual	4

Table 4b. Research approaches

Research approach	Frequency
Survey	66 (45%)
Case study (Single)	29 (20%)
Case study (Multiple)	24 (16%)
Argumentative (Conceptual)	19 (13%)
Action research	4 (3%)
Simulation	1 (1%)
Laboratory experiment	1 (1%)
Field experiment	1 (1%)
Interviews	1 (1%)

relationships between categories. Studies that describe methods provide little input in this regard and are thus not as useful for this purpose.

Analysis of research approaches employed reveals also that survey research is the most popular, followed by case study and argumentative (conceptual) studies (Table 4b). Given the lack of theory in SISP (Lederer & Salmela, 1996), it may be appropriate for more theory-generating research to be conducted, employing qualitative, interpretive techniques such as the grounded theory method and action research approach.

DATA ANALYSIS

For each article, a full text review was in most cases necessary in order to gather the required data on the categories being examined and the relationships between categories. The criteria for determining whether an article addressed a specific category did not take into account the extent to which the category was addressed but simply assessed whether any aspect of the category was studied. While Lederer and Salmela (1996) undertook a similar analysis to come up with the theory in Figure 1 and Table 1, this analysis is different in several ways. First, it includes a different set of sample articles (inevitably there is some overlap), with many published after the Lederer and Salmela study. Second, it also investigates other relationships not specified by the theory in Table 1. Third, it offers a different interpretation of the literature, given it adopts more rigorous definitions for categories and is analyzed by a different author. Finally, this study quantifies the extent to which categories and relationships have been studied and also includes a meta-analysis in an attempt to quantify the strength of relationships found.

SISP Categories

The extent to which each category has been researched is depicted in Table 5. This extent is determined by counting the number of articles that address each of the categories depicted in Figure 1 and calculating this as a percentage of the

Tables 5. SISP categories researched

CATEGORY	Frequency
Planning process	120 (83%)
Planning resources	79 (54%)
Planning outcomes	71 (49%)
Internal environment	67 (46%)
Information plan	37 (26%)
External environment	28 (19%)
Plan implementation	12 (8%)

Table 6. SISP process—phases and stages (Brown, 2002 amended from Mentzas, 1997; Galliers, 1993)

SISP Phases	SISP Stages
Preparation	Planning for planning (preplanning).
Organization analysis	Analysis of internal business environment. Analysis of internal IS environment.
External environment analysis	Analysis of external business environment. Analysis of external IS environment.
Strategy conception	Scanning the future. Identification of alternative scenarios including information flows and requirements for each. Scenario elaboration.
Strategy formulation	Formulation of agreed organizational recommendations. Formulation of information architecture. Synthesis and prioritization of portfolio of information systems to be developed.
Strategy implementation planning	Definition of action plan elements. Elaboration of action plan. Definition of follow-up and control procedures.

total number of articles examined (146). Some articles address more than one of these categories and so may be counted several times.

Planning Process

The process is at the heart of SISP and thus forms part of the research in 83% of the studies. The process in this chapter has been defined very broadly to encompass formulation and implementation planning activities, planning characteristics, and methods and techniques for carrying out the process. This is reflected in the factors investigated within this category, which can be classified fairly easily as those examining planning activities (inclusive of methods and techniques), or planning characteristics. Planning approaches arise as a result of the co-alignment between planning characteristics (Segars et al., 1998), and so articles examining approaches can be classified together with those under planning characteristics. Mentzas (1997) provides a novel way of classifying the many process activities carried out in SISP, by organizing them at the highest level into phases. Phases can then be broken down into stages, which can be further broken down into modules of activities. Table 6 shows a set of process phases and stages amended from Mentzas (1997).

Various SISP process characteristics have furthermore been defined as shown in Table 7.

Planning Resources

Planning resources rank second, in terms of frequency of empirical research, and were examined in 54% of the sample articles. This category encompasses both the informational input required for planning (e.g., business plans and their quality) as well as the human, financial, and technical resources. Many of the studies focused on examining the human resource category specifically (Premkumar & King, 1994). The stakeholders of SISP are most often mentioned as being top management, IS management, user management, and end users (Hackney & Kawalek, 1999; Lederer & Sethi, 1996). Top management and IS management play an especially critical role (Reich & Benbasat, 2000). Attitude, communications, relationship, participation, involvement, responsibility, commitment, influence, competence, support, interaction, education, training, knowledge, motivations for planning, shared domain knowledge, and trust are some concepts mentioned within this domain (Allen & Wilson, 2003; Basu et al., 2002; Hann & Weber, 1996; Reich & Benbasat, 2000; Sabherwal & King, 1992; Sahraoui, 2003). Given the large number of such descriptors, development of higher order factors to describe this category would be useful. Additional stakeholders to consider in inter-organizations systems planning are external entities such as customers, suppliers, partners, and regulatory bodies (Finnegan et al., 1999).

Table 7. SISP process—characteristics (Doherty et al., 1999; Segars et al., 1998)

Characteristic	Definition
Comprehensiveness	The extent to which an organization attempts to be exhaustive or inclusive in making and integrating decisions.
Flow	The locus of authority or devolution of responsibilities for strategic planning (top-down, bottom-up, interactive)
Focus	The balance between creativity and control orientations inherent within the strategic planning system.
Formalization	The existence of structures, techniques, written procedures, and policies that guide the planning process.
Frequency	The frequency of planning activities or cycles and, relatedly, the frequency of evaluation/revision of strategic choices (occasional vs. continuous).
Participation	The breadth of involvement in strategic planning (narrow vs. wide).
Ownership	The locus of ownership for the planning process (business/IS group/mixed).
Alignment	The degree to which alignment between corporate and IS strategies is explicitly sought.
Implementation	Focus during the planning process on the implications for implementation.
Competitive focus	The range of benefits sought (primarily efficiency vs. wider benefits, including competitive advantage).
BP-ISP Integration	The level of integration between business planning and SISP (business-led, IT-led, reciprocal, or full integration) (Reich & Benbasat, 2000; Teo & King, 1997).
Alacrity	The speed of the SISP process (Lederer & Sethi, 1998).

Planning Outcomes

Evaluative research has focused on assessing the effectiveness and impact of SISP (49% of studies). Fulfillment of key planning objectives is the most often used measure for determining effectiveness (Baker, 1995; Lederer & Sethi, 1996; Premkumar & King, 1991; Segars & Grover, 1998). Alignment stands out as arguably the major goal for SISP and was therefore depicted by Lederer and Salmela (1996) as being the dependent variable in their theory. There is support for this representation of alignment as the outcome from Reich and Benbasat (2000), who note that in many studies there is a lack of distinction between factors causing alignment and alignment itself. They therefore conceptualize alignment as a state or an outcome and the determinants of alignment as process factors. An example of a process determinant is the level of integration between business planning and SISP processes (BP-ISP integration). This is also an example of a factor that is often confused with the alignment outcome. Reich & Benbasat (2000) furthermore distinguish between the intellectual dimension of alignment and the social dimension, the former concerned with the links and interrelationships between formal business and IS plans and the latter with the degree of mutual understanding of and commitment to business and IS plans and objectives by both business and IT executives.

While alignment is the most often researched outcome measure, other outcomes, such as planner/user satisfaction (Tang & Tang, 1996), extent of analysis, degree of cooperation achieved, improvement in capability over time (Segars & Grover, 1998), and the impact of SISP on IS functional performance (Cohen, 2002) and IS contribution to organizational performance (Premkumar & King, 1991; Sabherwal, 1999) have also been researched. Several studies have examined the interrelationship between outcome variables, such as between alignment and organizational performance, which have served to reinforce the efficacy of SISP (Chan & Huff, 1993).

Internal Environment

Various factors within the internal environment have been researched (46% of studies). There is typically a clear distinction between factors within the internal business environment—organizational size, complexity, type, structure, culture, management style, politics/power, sophistication, and strategy (Byrd, Sambamurthy, & Zmud, 1995; Flynn & Hepburn, 1994; McGrath, Dampney, & More, 1994; Premkumar & King, 1994; Sabherwal, 1999; Sillince & Frost, 1995)—and those within the internal IS environment—role of IS, applications portfolio, IT infrastructure, IS maturity, structure, formalization, and sophistication (Jiang & Klein, 1999; Premkumar & King, 1992; Ranganathan & Sethi, 2002; Sabherwal, 1999). Once again development of higher order factors would be useful to make sense of the multitude of variables identified.

Information Plan

The information plan has been researched in 26% of the sample articles. The reasons for this lower percentage in comparison to the other categories may be that the ultimate value of SISP is not in the plan documentation itself but in the plan implementation and ultimate impact on organizational performance. As well as this, many studies examining plan outputs may not be classified within the SISP domain. For example, one product of SISP is an information architecture, a whole area of research in itself (Periasamy & Feeny, 1997) and a separate issue in studies of key IS management concerns (Luftman & McLean, 2004, Watson et al., 1997).

External Environment

The external environment has been examined in only 19% of the sample. This may be due to the fact that the impacts of the external environment on SISP are primarily indirect through the internal environment. Nevertheless, the study of this category has been gaining ground recently as attention shifts to planning for inter-organizational systems, where suppliers, customers, and partners play a more significant role in terms of IS planning (Finnegan et al., 1999). Specific factors that have been mentioned within the general external business environment include government policies (socio-economic), regional policies (e.g., Gulf region, EU, etc.), marketplace volatility, type of industry, competitive forces, and environmental uncertainty (dynamism, heterogeneity, hostility) (Abdul-Gader, 1997; Aladwani, 2001; Sabherwal & King, 1995; Teo & King, 1997). Within the external IT environment, information intensity and the rate of IT change have been mentioned (Benamati & Lederer, 2001; Teo & King, 1997). There have been few studies that have attempted to operationalize constructs within the external environment, save for that of environmental uncertainty assessed in, for example, Sabherwal and King (1995), Teo and King (1997), and more recently Choe (2003). The external IT environment specifically has been operationalized by Ranganathan and Sethi (2000).

Plan Implementation

Plan implementation is researched in only 8% of the studies. This is perhaps surprising given that, without plan implementation, the whole planning process is thrown into question. Much research attention in SISP, however, has been on implementation planning (which is considered to be part of the process category according to the definition adopted in this study [Mentzas, 1997]) and on implementation predictors (considered part of the information plan [Gottschalk, 1999a]), rather than plan implementation per se, which has been assessed in terms of plan implementation rate, extent, and performance (Gottschalk, 1999a). The low percentage does, however, point to a need for more research in this domain.

Relationships between Categories

In order to ascertain what relationships have been identified between categories, the heuristic employed in the analysis was to specify a relationship as given if empirical evidence was provided for it, either between the defined categories or between several lower order variables within categories. By synthesis and generalization, a relationship was assumed if a sufficient number of lower order variables are related. Those identified are highlighted in Table 8. The major studies examining key relationships are mentioned in the discussion that follows.

The key relationships will be analyzed in turn to ascertain what hypotheses are either supported or suggested from the studies examining them.

Planning Process-Planning Outcomes

That this relationship is one of the most commonly assessed (see Table 8) is not surprising given that the planning outcome category is more often than not the dependent variable in SISP studies. Bajally (1998) showed that, where SISP is carried out comprehensively, there is more of a strategic IS orientation in the organization. It has been shown likewise that planning process quality (or the extent of planning activities or comprehensiveness) influences planning effectiveness (defined as the extent of fulfillment of key planning objectives), as well as IS functional performance and IS contribution to organizational performance (Premkumar & King, 1991, 1994). Wang and Tai (2003) furthermore demonstrate that a more extensive environmental assessment leads to greater improvement in planning capability and subsequently more effective SISP. Tang and Tang (1996) found that the extent of SISP was positively associated with user satisfaction with IS. Lederer and Sethi (1996, 1998) demonstrated that planning practices that emphasize alacrity (planning quickly) and identify business value in the plan are associated with planning effectiveness. It has been confirmed too in several studies that an organizational approach (also called rational-adaptive) is the most successful. Rationality is reflected in a highly formalized, top-down approach that is comprehensive in the making of decisions and focused on control. Adaptation is reflected in frequent planning cycles and broad participation profiles (Doherty et al., 1999; Segars et al., 1998). In contrast, where there

Table 8. Relationships researched

	IntEnv	ExtEnv	Resource	Process	Plan	Implem.	Outcome
IntEnv	-	-	10	27	4	1	9
ExtEnv	2	-	-	7	2	1	1
Resource	-	-	-	16	4	4	13
Process	1	-	-	-	8	4	25
Plan	-	-	-	-	-	3	5
Implem.	-	-	-	-	-	-	2
Outcome	-	-	-	1	-	-	-

is a highly political as opposed to rational planning process, non-alignment is common and may be deliberately engineered to serve vested interests (Sillince & Frost, 1995). The level of integration between business planning and SISP (BP-ISP integration) has been found to have a positive impact on the social dimension of alignment between business and IS (Reich & Benbasat, 2000), IT infrastructure capability (Broadbent, Weill, & Neo, 1999), and IS contribution to organizational performance (King & Teo, 2000; Teo & King, 1996). Cohen (2002) confirmed that the emphasis placed on planning activities and SISP integration mechanisms that aim to increase interaction between business and IS have a positive impact on IS functional performance. There is thus compelling evidence provided for the following hypothesis:

- A more comprehensive, sophisticated (rational-adaptive, high BP-ISP integration) planning process results in more positive planning outcomes.

These studies show that the planning process category can be examined from two perspectives—planning activities and their comprehensiveness, and planning characteristics—which can be classified as rational, adaptive, and integrative (e.g., BP-ISP integration).

Evidence is presented from studies in the public sector (Bajally, 1998; Sillince & Frost, 1995), as well as the corporate (Premkumar & King, 1991; Segars & Grover, 1998) and from a variety of countries including the U.S. (King & Teo, 2000), Canada (Reich & Benbasat, 2000), Taiwan (Tang & Tang, 1996), UK (Doherty et al., 1999), and South Africa (Cohen, 2002), further confirming the efficacy of SISP in different contexts.

The relationship is not indicated in the framework in Figure 1, as this effect may be assumed to take place through the information plan and plan implementation categories. However, the benefits of SISP process are sometimes intangible and are not reflected in tangible plan outputs (Baker, 1995). These are factors such as improved coordination and communications with top management and users (Premkumar & King, 1994; Segars & Grover, 1998), increased top management commitment to IT (Lederer & Sethi, 1996), increased IS understanding of the business (Hackney & McBride, 2002), and increased top management understanding of the strategic potential of IS (Segars & Grover, 1998). This justifies, therefore, that a direct relationship is important and should be represented in any theory of SISP.

Internal Environment—Planning Process

Relationships between various lower order factors within the internal environment and within the planning process have been examined in several of the studies. Conrath et al. (1992) showed that organizational size (annual revenue and number of employees) and IS function size (IS budget, number of

IS employees) distinguished those who did carry out SISP from those who did not, a finding supported by Teo, Ang, and Pavri (1997). Lederer and Sethi (1992) showed that for those that do carry out SISP, failure to adequately analyze and take into account the internal environment leads to an excessively lengthy and costly planning exercise. Byrd et al. (1995) found complexity (number of stakeholders) to impact negatively on the level of agreement within the SISP process, while Flynn and Goleniewska (1993) showed that business-planning horizon determined the SISP horizon. Dufner, Holley, and Reed (2002, 2003) demonstrate that organization type (public vs. private) impacts the characteristics of the SISP process, such as setting of strategic objectives and planning horizon.

In terms of the internal IS environment, Jiang and Klein (1999) showed that IS maturity (the extent to which IS plays a strategic role) determined the IS project evaluation criteria used, and Sabherwal and King (1992) show IS maturity (number of functions supplied by IT, IT penetration, functional impact, competencies) to have an influence on the extent of analysis in IS decision-making processes. Ranganathan and Sethi (2002) demonstrate also that rationality in IS decision making is influenced by the degree of formalization of the IT unit structure.

Premkumar and King (1991, 1992, 1994), in a comprehensive study, showed that better quality strategic business planning and a more strategic role for IS in the organization impacted on the quality (comprehensiveness) of the planning process. Wang and Tai (2003) too demonstrate that, where the future role of IS is strategic, environmental assessment in SISP is carried out more comprehensively. Sabherwal (1999) show that SISP process sophistication (business plans considered, degree of formalization) is influenced by better integration between strategic business units and on the organizational IT capability. Sabherwal and King (1995) explore the concept of fit between the internal environment, external environment, and IS decision-making process characteristics in determining the best approach to identifying strategic IS.

No studies have therefore specifically examined the simplicity of the internal environment and its impact on SISP process efficiency and effectiveness as suggested by hypothesis H2. There is some support from Byrd et al. (1995) who found organizational complexity (number of stakeholders) to negatively impact on the level of agreement in SISP. However, the measure of complexity and the scope of impact in the SISP process are too narrow to show strong support for this hypothesis. Thus, more studies are needed to investigate it further.

Analysis and synthesis of the articles lead to two major propositions:

1.   Where the internal environment has higher levels of sophistication (e.g., quality in strategic business planning, strategic role for IS), planning processes tend to be more comprehensive and rational.

2.   The environmental context in which SISP is taking place should be carefully considered to ensure that there is a fit between environment and SISP process characteristics.

As a result, the following additional hypotheses are identified:

*   The more sophisticated the internal environment, the more comprehensive and sophisticated (rational) the planning process.
*   The better the fit between environmental (internal and external) characteristics and planning characteristics, the more positive the planning outcomes.

External Environment—Planning Process

Few empirical studies have examined this relationship. Of the studies that have, findings have been mixed with one study showing a weak relationship between environmental uncertainty and BP-ISP integration (Teo & King, 1997). Sabherwal and King (1992), however, show that the extent of analysis in the decision-making process is impacted negatively by environmental dynamism and positively by heterogeneity, while environmental hostility leads to a more political process. Sabherwal and King (1995) demonstrate the need for a fit between the external environment and process characteristics. Choe (2003) demonstrates that environmental uncertainty has an indirect impact on the level of IS strategic applications through the facilitators of IS strategic alignment. Choe (2003) furthermore demonstrates that in an uncertain external environment, a high level of strategic applications, and well-defined alignment facilitators result in improved organizational performance. Thus, the hypothesis H1, which suggests the need to examine the stability of the external environment and its impact on process efficiency and effectiveness has not explicitly been examined. Instability or uncertainty have, however, been shown to have an impact, but their negative influences may possibly be offset by appropriate alignment facilitators (Choe, 2003). An additional hypothesis that is suggested is:

*   The better the fit between environment characteristics and planning process characteristics, the more positive the planning outcomes.

Planning Resources—Planning Process

Hann and Weber (1996) demonstrate that top management competence in IS and the degree to which they depend on IS management will determine who controls the SISP process, while Allen and Wilson (2003) show that trust relationships between key stakeholders influence the process of SISP. Shared domain knowledge between business and IS management was shown to influence rationality in the decision-making process (Ranganathan & Sethi, 2002), and top management perceptions of IT and business competence of IS were found to affect levels of BP-ISP integration (Teo & King, 1997). Broad participation profiles are furthermore an important characteristic of an organizational approach to SISP, demonstrated to be the most successful (Doherty et al., 1999; Earl, 1993; Segars & Grover, 1999), while top management IS knowledge, IS management business knowledge, and top management involvement are considered to be representative of a sophisticated planning process (Sabherwal, 1999). Dufner et al. (2002, 2003) found there to be little top management involvement in SISP in the public sector, and thus SISP was deemed to be more tactical than strategic as a result. One key study examined a hypothesis similar to hypothesis H3 (Table 1) and showed that there is a strong relationship between planning resource extensiveness/quality (top management and user involvement, adequacy of IS planners and financial resources, and quality of input) and planning process quality (comprehensiveness) (Premkumar & King, 1994). Wang and Tai (2003) similarly show that appropriate co-alignment between resource commitment planning acceptance and mechanisms to assist stakeholders in integrating and implementing plans results in more extensive environmental assessment. In all, therefore, this relationship is well tested. However, rather than the efficiency and effectiveness of the process being the dependent variable as suggested by hypothesis H3, it has been either comprehensiveness of planning activities or planning characteristics, such as BP-ISP integration and rationality. Thus, the hypothesis identified is:

• More extensive and higher quality planning resources produce a more comprehensive and sophisticated (rational, high BP-ISP integration) planning process.

Planning Process—Information Plan

Bergeron et al. (1991) demonstrate that choice of methodology impacts the applications portfolio (a category of the information plan) resulting from the process, thus the need to match methodology with desired objectives. It has been shown also that planning process problems lead to problems with the plan output (Lederer & Sethi, 1992). Where the focus of SISP is on the business rather than IT, the quality of plan output is better (Byrd et al., 1995). This is somewhat confirmed by Hann and Weber (1996), who show that if top management control the SISP process, their goals are present in the IS plan, and thus the plans are more useful. Whereas if IS management are in control, it is their goals that are evident, leading to a less useful plan for the organization as a whole. A major study showed that greater BP-ISP integration results in fewer plan output problems (Teo & King, 1996). Strong support is provided for hypothesis H4 specifically by Premkumar and King (1991) who demonstrate a relationship between planning process quality (comprehensiveness) and information plan quality.

Empirical research suggests that, once again, the SISP process should not be viewed only in terms of the extent of planning activities but also in terms of planning characteristics such as BP-ISP integration. Thus, hypothesis H4 can be expanded to read:

- A more comprehensive and sophisticated (high BP-ISP integration) planning process produces a more comprehensive and useful information plan.

Information Plan—Plan Implementation

The articles that report on this relationship examined specifically hypothesis H5 (Table 1) and provided some support for it (Gottschalk, 1999 a, b, c). The variables examined, however, explained only a small percentage of the variation in plan implementation, thus indicating that there are other factors that influence plan implementation that were not considered. The two key predictors of plan implementation were description of responsibility for implementation and description of user involvement in implementation, items that relate to the resources category.

Plan Implementation—Planning Outcomes

Two articles in the sample allude to a relationship between plan implementation and planning outcomes, but rather than referring to the extent of plan implementation, the independent variables were quality of implementation mechanisms, such as top management monitoring of implementation (Premkumar & King, 1994), or tracking of implementation (Broadbent et al., 1999). Thus, hypothesis H6 has not been fully tested within the context of SISP.

Internal Environment—Planning Resources

No hypothesis is suggested for this relationship in Figure 1, but it has been shown that there are relationships between lower order factors in the internal environment and planning resources category. Dufner et al. (2002, 2003) demonstrate that, in the public sector, the breadth and extent of stakeholder involvement differs from that in the private sector, with involvement of top management in particular less prevalent in the public sector. Sahraoui (2003) shows that, where there is a planning culture in organizations, knowledge workers feel more empowered. Premkumar and King (1992) demonstrate that, where the role of IS is strategic in a firm, planning resource quality is better. Ranganathan and Sethi (2002) also demonstrate that the greater the level of formalization within the IT unit structure, the greater the levels of shared domain knowledge between business and IS executives, but greater centralization of the IT unit structure has a negative impact on shared domain knowledge. IS maturity (inclusive of business competence of IS staff and IS competence of business staff) was found to be related to the influence wielded by top management and

IS management in strategic IS decision-making processes (Sabherwal & King, 1992). The following hypothesis may hold true:

* A more sophisticated internal environment results in more extensive and better quality planning resources.

Internal environment—Information plan: Hackney and McBride (2002) demonstrate that political and managerial changes within an organization may render plans obsolete even before implementation. Byrd et al. (1995) show a relationship between the fit between organizational size and IT infrastructure sophistication and the quality of IT plan produced. Lederer and Sethi (1991) show that when business planning is strategic, rather than tactical or financial, there are fewer problems with hardware plans. This relationship may be indirect, as these factors have been shown to influence the planning process, which in turn influences the information plan. Nevertheless, the following hypothesis is suggested:

* A more sophisticated internal environment results in a more extensive and more useful information plan.

Internal Environment—Planning Outcomes

This relationship is not shown in the SISP theory in Figure 1 but has recently been the focus of some empirical studies (Lee & Pai, 2003). Lee and Pai (2003) found a negative relationship between organization centralization and IS planning alignment, while Wang and Tai (2003) found that centralization negatively impacted on planning capability improvement. A positive relationship between IS function maturity and dimensions of SISP success (alignment, effectiveness, and capability improvement) was however demonstrated by Lee and Pai (2003), while Wang and Tai (2003) showed organizational formalization to have a positive impact on planning capability. Ang and Quek (1999) showed that there is a relationship between internal environment factors (e.g., organizational structure, IS sophistication, and IT configuration) and organizational performance indicators (improved competitiveness, operational efficiency, and resource management). This may possibly be due to SISP, where as a result of implementing plans, appropriate organizational structures, IS procedures, and IT configurations are established, having a positive impact on organizational performance. Chan et al. (1997) show furthermore that realized business strategic orientation, IS strategic alignment, and IS effectiveness have an impact on organizational performance. Given these are expected outcomes of SISP, this further demonstrates its efficacy. Sabherwal (1999) show also that IT capability impacts on IS success (contribution to organizational performance) and suggest that it may therefore be possible to achieve IS success without carrying out SISP but through building IT capabilities. The successes that result from this will then lead to justification for a strategic role for IS in the firm and, consequently, SISP leading to further IS success. Premkumar and King (1992) provide support for this argument by demonstrating that the more strategic the role of IS in a firm, the more effective SISP is and the better the IS function performance and contribution of IS to organizational performance.

In summary, therefore, three possibilities are suggested by the studies examining the relationship between the internal environment and planning outcomes:

1.   The relationships found between internal environment and planning out-
      comes may simply be due to the fact that, as SISP plans are implemented,
      they result in improvements to the internal environment, which ultimately
      reflect in IS function and organizational performance because these are
      measures of SISP performance. This demonstrates the cyclical and
      longitudinal nature of SISP, whereby the impacts of one planning cycle
      need to be assessed over time, as plans are implemented and result in
      changes to the internal environment.
2.   The impact of the internal environment on planning outcomes may be
      indirect through the planning process. For example, where there is a
      strategic role for IS in a firm, SISP is recognized as important, thus planning
      processes are more comprehensive and sophisticated, leading to positive
      planning outcomes.
3.   It may be possible to achieve the intended outcomes of SISP (e.g., improved
      IS contribution to organizational performance) through other means in the
      short term, such as through enhanced IT capabilities (Sabherwal, 1999).

Findings thus support the following hypothesis:

•   A more sophisticated internal environment leads to more positive planning
     outcomes.

Planning Resources—Information Plan

It has been found that problems with resources (such as inadequate user involvement or lack of top management commitment) lead to plans being perceived as not useful (Lederer & Sethi, 1992). Byrd et al. (1995) show also that conversely top management support for SISP leads to better quality IT plans. Lack of agreement between stakeholders, however, negatively impacts the IT plan quality. This provides some support for the following hypothesis:

•   More extensive and better quality planning resources result in a more
     extensive and useful information plan.

The nature of this relationship may be indirect, however, through the planning process itself, thus limited research attention.

Planning Resources—Plan Implementation

Gottschalk (1999a), in a study examining aspects of the information plan that may lead to implementation, found that the two key predictors of plan implementation were description of responsibility for implementation and description of user involvement in implementation. Both items relate to the resources category, providing indirect support for a relationship between resource quality and plan implementation. Premkumar and King (1994) furthermore show a strong relationship between planning resource quality and the quality of plan implementation mechanisms. These mechanisms incidentally include resource-related concerns such as mobilization of resources for implementation, top management monitoring of implementation, and user involvement in implementation. Hartono et al. (2003) demonstrate that top management monitoring and control of SISP have a major influence on the extent of plan implementation. Thus, it can be hypothesised that:

•   More extensive and better quality planning resources result in greater plan implementation.

Planning Resources—Planning Outcome

Several studies examined relationships between lower order factors within these categories. Shared domain knowledge between business and IS executives has been shown to be associated with a greater degree of long-term social alignment (Reich & Benbasat, 2000). This is confirmed by Lee and Pai (2003) who demonstrate that the relationship between business and IS executives has a positive influence on both planning effectiveness and alignment. Informed IT management, organizational commitment, top management involvement, and empowered knowledge workers are also shown to be associated with planning effectiveness (Aladwani, 2001; Basu et al., 2002; Sahraoui, 2003), as is planning resource quality (Premkumar & King, 1994) and effective task coordination (Lee & Pai, 2003). Organizational commitment has been shown to impact IS functional performance (Cohen, 2002). Choe (2003) refers to the above factors as facilitators of IS strategic alignment and demonstrates their impact on the level of strategic applications realized in organizations. Wang and Tai (2003) show that the co-alignment between resource commitment, planning acceptance, integration mechanisms, and implementation mechanisms positively influences planning capability improvements. The direct relationship between planning resources and planning outcomes is not shown in the theory of SISP in Figure 1. The strong relationships shown in the studies analyzed, however, do point to the importance of extensive and quality resources in order to achieve positive planning outcomes, thus the hypothesis:

- More extensive and better quality planning resources result in more positive planning outcomes.

Planning Process—Plan Implementation

Premkumar and King (1994) demonstrated a relationship between planning process quality and implementation mechanism quality, while Lederer and Sethi (1992) found organizational and cost problems during SISP lead ultimately to implementation problems. Higher levels of BP-ISP integration were found to alleviate these problems however (Teo & King, 1996). Hartono et al. (2003) found that deliberately planning for implementation during the SISP process increased the rate and extent of implementation, and Tang and Tang (1996) found that more extensive planning was associated with greater plan implementation. Hartono et al. (2003) demonstrated, however, that if too much effort is spent analyzing and documenting current needs, this may divert attention from plan implementation. Thus, the hypothesis supported would be:

- An integrated planning process that comprehensively addresses implementation issues leads to greater plan implementation.

Information Plan—Planning Outcomes

Few studies have specifically focused on this relationship, and it is not shown in the theory in Figure 1. Its limited attention may be due to the fact that planning outcomes arise either from carrying out the planning process or implementing the information plans, rather than the plans themselves. Nevertheless, some studies suggest a relationship. Hann and Weber (1996) show that, where top management goals are reflected in the plan, they are more useful. Premkumar and King (1991) demonstrate that output plan quality is associated with positive planning outcomes, and Lederer and Sethi (1996) show that several prescriptions relating to information plan output are strongly associated with planning effectiveness (e.g., preparation of migration plan, documentation of existing systems). Thus, there is some support for the following hypothesis:

- A more extensive and useful information plan results in more positive planning outcomes.

Planning Outcomes—Planning Process

Sabherwal (1999) demonstrate a relationship between IS success and SISP sophistication (Sabherwal, 1999). The finding highlights the fact that, where the efficacy of SISP is proven, there is greater organizational commitment to carry on the process and even improve it. This argument is supported by Reich and Benbasat (2000), who found that IT implementation success leads to better communications between business and IS, which in turn improves the level of social alignment. The finding also highlights the importance of feedback mechanisms, whereby planning outcomes are evaluated and these results used to either improve the process that was used or confirm its utility (Baker, 1995). Thus, the hypothesis suggested is:

• The more positive the planning outcomes, the more comprehensive and sophisticated the planning process becomes.

This analysis has revealed several other hypotheses that can be formulated, in addition to those postulated in Table 1. These are summarized in Table 9, together with the original set and are further illustrated in Figure 2. A quantitative meta-analysis was conducted in order to assess the strength of relationships found. This is discussed in the next section.

Meta-Analysis

In order to assess the strength of relationships described above, a quantitative meta-analysis is useful. As stated by Legris, Ingham, and Collerette (2003):

[a] meta-analysis aims at integrating a large number of results to determine if they are homogeneous. Statistical methods are applied to summary statistics. The focus is not on statistical significance, but on the size of treatment effects. The objective is a detailed review that supports making a sound judgement on the average of the findings computed, and on the reasons for inconsistencies. (p. 197)

Sixty-seven articles that provided statistical support for relationships were examined using meta-analysis. The meta-analytic technique employed was to identify coefficients between relationships (correlation, regression, path, etc.) and then to aggregate these (weighted by sample size in each case) to obtain an overall mean effect size. This was done as described by Hwang, Windsor, and Pryor (2000). For each instance of a relationship, sample size (N_i) was multiplied by the coefficient (r_i). For each relationship, these products were then aggregated. The total sample sizes were also aggregated. The mean size effect was then obtained by dividing the summed products by the summed sample sizes, as shown in Table 9.

The equation used for each relationship was therefore:

Mean effect size = $\sum (N_i * r_i) / \sum N_i$

Table 9. Extended set of hypotheses*

	Hypotheses	Effect	Support
H1	A more (un)stable external environment produces a more (in) effective and (in) efficient planning process.	-0.04	WEAK
H2	A simpler internal environment produces a more effective and efficient planning process.	-	QUAL
H2b	The more sophisticated the internal environment, the more comprehensive and sophisticated (rational) is the planning process.	0.19	SOME
H2c	A more sophisticated internal environment results in more extensive and better quality planning resources.	0.22	SOME
H2d	The better the fit between environmental (internal and/or external) characteristics and planning characteristics, the more positive the planning outcomes.	-	SOME
H2e	A more sophisticated internal environment results in a more extensive and more useful information plan.	-	SOME
H2f	A more sophisticated internal environment leads to more positive planning outcomes.	0.18	SOME
H3	More extensive and higher quality planning resources produce a more comprehensive and sophisticated (rational, high BP-ISP integration) planning process.	0.22	SOME
H3b	More extensive and better quality planning resources result in a more extensive and useful information plan.	-	SOME
H3c	More extensive and better quality planning resources result in more positive planning outcomes (e.g., better alignment).	0.38	MEDIUM
H3d	More extensive and better quality planning resources result in better plan implementation.	0.47	STRONG
H4	A more comprehensive and sophisticated (high BP-ISP integration) planning process produces a more comprehensive and useful information plan.	0.47	STRONG
H4b	A more comprehensive and sophisticated planning process leads to greater plan implementation.	0.54	STRONG
H4c	A more comprehensive, sophisticated (rational-adaptive, high BP-ISP integration) planning process results in more positive planning outcomes.	0.35	MEDIUM
H5	A more useful information plan produces greater plan implementation.	0.27	MEDIUM
H5b	A more extensive and useful information plan results in more positive planning outcomes.	0.33	MEDIUM
H6	Greater plan implementation produces more positive planning outcomes.	0.26	MEDIUM
H7	The more positive the planning outcomes, the more comprehensive and sophisticated the planning process becomes.	0.5	STRONG

* Hypotheses were derived by combining the initial Lederer and Salmela hypotheses in Table 1 with those emerging from the analyses in section above.

In order to compare the strength of relationships, the following heuristic was employed. A strong relationship is implied where the mean effect size between dimensions is estimated at above 0.45 (STRONG). A medium-strength relationship is indicated by a value between 0.25 and 0.45 (MEDIUM), and some evidence of a relationship is where the effect size is between 0.05 and 0.25 (SOME) (e.g., Hwang et al., 2000). Included in the SOME category are quantitative studies where coefficients were not reported and could not be determined but where support was shown. If any mean effect is less than 0.05, the relationship is defined as WEAK. Where no coefficients are reported, as with qualitative and conceptual research, a relationship is specified as being supported by qualitative evidence (QUAL). The findings are displayed in Table 9 and illustrated in Figure 2.

The limitation of the above approach was that the technique required coefficients be reported on, mitigating against incorporating qualitative findings into the meta-analysis. Furthermore, although correlation coefficients were used where available; when not reported, regression or path coefficients were used. Another limitation was when aggregating factors together, no account was taken of the granularity of each factor, nor of relative importance. So, for example, in the relationship between resource quality and process quality, Premkumar and King (1994) specifically assessed this relationship and found a coefficient of 0.44. Ranganathan and Sethi (2002), in examining the relationship between level of shared domain knowledge (a resource factor) and level of rationality in the decision-making process (considered to be a process factor), found a coefficient

Figure 2. SISP theory—An extended set of hypotheses (amended from Lederer & Salmela, 1996)*

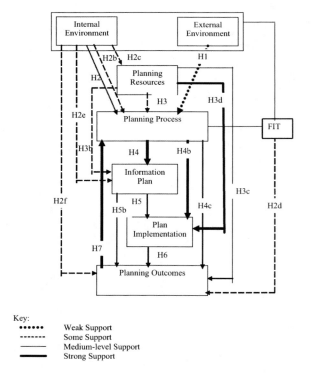

Key:
•••••• Weak Support
------- Some Support
——— Medium-level Support
▬▬▬ Strong Support

* The above illustration represents pictorially the information displayed in Table 9.

of 0.34. In aggregating these and other results together to get the mean size effect, no account was taken of the differences in scope of factors (overall planning process quality much broader than rationality in decision making), nor of their relative importance. The analysis was deemed sufficient, however, as its purpose was to get a rough estimate of strength of relationships.

DISCUSSION AND IMPLICATIONS FOR FURTHER RESEARCH

The analysis reveals that much research emanates from North America and Europe, with Asia-Pacific countries such as Singapore also contributing significantly. Research on SISP in the Middle Eastern and African regions has been minimal. This is perhaps not surprising, given that this is simply a reflection of the developed vs. developing countries divide, as well as the differences in overall size of countries, in terms of both population and economy. In terms of theoretical contribution, however, there needs to be recognition that the context in which much of the mainstream SISP research is generated (e.g., Fortune 500 companies) may not be the same as where it may be applied (e.g., developing African countries context). In some cases, it may not be appropriate, as some of the assumptions may not hold (e.g., cultural differences [Aladwani, 2001]). More work therefore needs to be done in these under-represented regions, as they also form part of the global village and possibly have a different perspective to offer that may generate further insight into the field.

The SISP theory proposed by Lederer and Salmela (1996) has not always been referred to in subsequent empirical research. The analysis does show, nevertheless, that many studies examine aspects of the relationships illustrated, even if the exact hypotheses have not been tested. The extended model in Figure 2 suggests that systems ideas ought to play a greater role in conceptualization of SISP theory, as suggested by Baker (1995) and Brown (2002). The dynamics of the SISP process could, for example, be examined through the use of systems dynamics techniques (Brown & Quaddus, 1996).

The categories most often referred to have been the planning process, planning resources, internal environment, and planning outcomes (the dependent variable). A large number of factors have been considered within the internal environment and resources categories, but there is still a need for studies that will more clearly organize these into higher order factors, as is the case for the planning process and planning outcomes categories. The external environment, information plan, and plan implementation have received little attention too. The apparent lack of attention to the information plan may be because aspects of this are the domain of other subject areas, such as information architecture (Periasamy & Feeny, 1997). Plan implementation, too, appears not to have been given adequate attention, possibly because of the definition adopted in this study (implementation rate and extent). There has been much research attention on implementation planning (Lederer & Sethi, 1998), considered to be rather a major phase of the overall planning process (Hartono et al., 2003; Mentzas, 1997).

Table 9 and Figure 2 classify the relationships and subsequent hypotheses generated as either strongly supported by empirical evidence, medium level support provided, some support provided, weak support, or only qualitative evidence. These distinctions were made by performing a meta-analysis on the sample articles. The meta-analysis provided only a rough estimate of relationship strengths, however, and should therefore be interpreted keeping this in mind.

Relationships which are strongly supported are those between resource quality and plan implementation (H3d), planning process and information plan (H4), planning process and plan implementation (H4b), and outcomes and planning process (H7). However, this strong support needs to be viewed in the light of the number of studies that examined each relationship. H7, for example, has been examined empirically in only one study in our sample, and thus further work in possibly different environmental contexts would serve to confirm findings. Refinement of measures to better conform with the definitions provided in this chapter may also add value.

Those relationships with medium-level support include resource quality to planning outcomes (H3c), planning process sophistication to outcomes (H4c), plan usefulness to plan implementation (H5), plan usefulness to outcomes (H5b), and plan implementation to outcomes (H6). It is interesting to note that most of the relationships in this category have planning outcomes as the dependent variable. It would therefore be opportune to investigate why there is only medium level support for many of these hypotheses and not strong support.

Some support is provided for relationships between internal environment sophistication and various categories of the planning system, namely, planning process quality (H2b), resource quality (H2c), plan usefulness (H2e), and planning outcomes (H2f) respectively. There is also some support for the relationship from fit between environmental characteristics/planning process and planning outcomes (H2d), between resource quality and planning process (H3), and between resource quality and plan usefulness (H3b). Of interest in this category is the frequent appearance of internal environment and resources. Further investigation is needed to examine why there is only some support, given the importance of context and resources to planning systems (Premkumar & King, 1994).

Weak support was found for the relationship between external environment and planning process (H1), thus it also merits further research. This weak relationship may be due to the fact that, while environmental conditions may have an impact on SISP, at the same time, organizations adopt coping mechanisms to deal with these (Choe, 2003). The negative impacts of environmental factors therefore become difficult to isolate.

The relationship between internal environment simplicity (or complexity) and planning process (H2) is supported by qualitative findings only, based on the sample articles gathered. It would therefore benefit from quantitative analysis, although it is possible that such analysis may have been done, since the articles identified in this study are not entirely exhaustive. That no such study was easily found nevertheless shows that not much research has been done in this area, and it therefore warrants further attention.

LIMITATIONS OF THE STUDY

The study has been restricted to examining most, but not all, research articles from reputable academic journals since 1991. Refereed conference proceedings were not explicitly included, as it was found that many studies reported in conferences lead to publications in journals, thus there would have been duplication in these cases. Earlier studies done prior to 1991 were also not included in the detailed analysis.

Some assumptions with regards to the theory will have to be re-examined in the light of current trends. For inter-organizational systems planning, which cuts across organizational boundaries in order to electronically link suppliers, customers, and partners, the scope of SISP is no longer limited to the organization alone. This has implications on, for example, who should be participating in the SISP process from among stakeholders outside the organization. Traditional SISP methodologies may also not be appropriate in this environment (Finnegan et al., 1999).

CONCLUSION

Lederer and Salmela (1996) proposed a theory of SISP based on the idea of an input-process-model. The theory identifies seven major categories and six hypotheses. This study has attempted to assess the extent to which this theory has been empirically tested and to uncover other relationships that have been examined by SISP research, thus extending the theory. The study reveals that the process category is the most often researched, followed by resources, planning outcome, internal environment, the information plan, the external environment, and plan implementation respectively. As a result of this examination, several additional hypotheses also become apparent in addition to the major six. The direct effect of the planning process on outcomes, for example, is a glaring omission, as many of the benefits of SISP are intangible and achieved through carrying out the process, rather than producing the tangible plan output (Baker, 1995). The fact that SISP practice in an organization is contingent on the internal and external environment (Sabherwal & King, 1995) is also represented in the extended theory. The robustness and usefulness of the original theory is nevertheless demonstrated as a clearer picture of the state of SISP research emerges. The findings are of benefit to researchers working in this domain, indicating clearly what work has been done so far and where further work is needed in the context of this theory. Practitioners, too, may benefit by using the additional hypotheses to examine whether they are taken into consideration in their SISP systems.

REFERENCES

Abdul-Gader, A. (1997). Information systems strategies for multinational companies in Arab Gulf countries. *International Journal of Information Management, 17*(1), 3-12.

Agarwal, R., Roberge, L., & Tanniru, M. (1994). MIS planning: A methodology for systems prioritisation. *Information & Management, 27*, 261-274.

Aladwani, A. (2001). IT Planning effectiveness in a developing country. *Journal of Global Information Technology Management, 4*(3), 51-65.

Allen, D., & Wilson, T. (2003). Vertical trust/mistrust during information strategy formation. *International Journal of Information Management, 23*, 223–237.

Ang, J., & Quek, S. (1999). Modeling IS planning benefits using ACE. *Decision Sciences, 30*(2), 533-562.

Ang, J., Shaw, N., & Pavri, F. (1995). Identifying strategic management information systems planning parameters using case studies. *International Journal of Information Management, 15*(6), 463-474.

Ang, J., & Teo, T. (1997). CSFs and sources of assistance and expertise in strategic IS planning: A Singapore perspective. *European Journal of Information Systems, 6*(3), 164-171.

Bajally, S. (1998). Strategic information systems planning in the public sector. *American Review of Public Administration, 28*(1), 75-85.

Baker, B. (1995). The role of feedback in assessing information systems planning effectiveness. *Journal of Strategic Information Systems, 4*(1), 61-80.

Basu, V., Hartono, V., Lederer, A., & Sethi, V. (2002). The impact of organisational commitment, senior management involvement and team involvement on strategic information systems planning. *Information & Management, 39*, 513-524.

Benamati, J., & Lederer, A. (2001). Rapid information technology change, coping mechanisms and the emerging technologies group. *Journal of Management Information Systems, 17*(4), 183-202.

Bergeron, F., Buteau, C., & Raymond, L. (1991). Identification of strategic information systems opportunities: Applying and comparing two methodologies. *MIS Quarterly, 15*(1), 99-103.

Broadbent, M., Weill, P., & Neo, B. (1999). Strategic context and patterns of IT infrastructure capability. *Journal of Strategic Information Systems, 8*, 157-187.

Brown, I. (2002). Systems thinking in the theory and practice of strategic information systems planning. In G. Ragsdell, D. West, & J. Wilby (Eds.), *Systems theory and practice in the knowledge age.* New York: Kluwer Academic/Plenum Publishers.

Brown, I., & Quaddus, M. (1996). Cognitive maps in the analysis of information systems planning success: Tales from two cases. *Australian Systems Thinking Conference*, Monash University, Brown 1–Brown 10.

Byrd, T., Sambamurthy, R., & Zmud, R. (1995). An examination of IT planning in a large, diversified public organisation. *Decision Sciences, 26*(1), 49-74.

Chan, Y., & Huff, S. (1993). Strategic information systems alignment. *Business Quarterly, 58*(1), 51-55.

Chan, Y., Huff, S., Barclay, D., & Copeland, D. (1997). Business strategic orientation, information systems strategic orientation and strategic alignment. *Information Systems Research, 8*(2), 125-150.

Choe, J. (2003). The effect of environmental uncertainty and strategic applications of IS on a firm's performance. *Information & Management, 40*, 257–268.

Cohen, J. (2002). Information systems strategic planning and IS function performance: An empirical study. *South African Computer Journal, 28*, 44-53.

Conrath, D., Ang, J., & Mattay, S. (1992). Strategic planning for information systems: A survey of Canadian organisations. *INFOR, 30*(4), 364-378.

Doherty, N., Marples, C., & Suhaimi, A. (1999). The relative success of alternative approaches to strategic information systems planning: An empirical analysis. *Journal of Strategic Information Systems, 8*, 263-283.

Doukidis, G., Lybereas, P., & Galliers, R. (1996). Information systems planning in small business: A stages of growth analysis. *Journal of Systems and Software, 33*(2), 189-201.

Dufner, D., Holley, L., & Reed, B. (2002). Can private sector strategic information systems planning techniques work for the public sector? *Communications of the Association for Information Systems, 8*(28), 1–35.

Dufner, D., Holley, L., & Reed, B. (2003). Strategic information systems planning and U.S. county government. *Communications of the Association for Information Systems, 11*, 219–244.

Earl, M. (1993). Experiences in strategic information systems planning. *MIS Quarterly, 17*(1), 1-21.

Finnegan, P., Galliers, R., & Powell, P. (1997). Investigating inter-organisational systems planning practices in Ireland and the UK. *Proceedings of the 5th European Conference on Information Systems* (pp. 281-294).

Finnegan, P., Galliers, R., & Powell, P. (1999). Inter-organizational systems planning: Learning from current practices. *International Journal of Technology Management, 17*(1), 129-144.

Flynn, D., & Goleniewska, E. (1993). A survey of the use of strategic information systems planning approaches in UK organisations. *Journal of Strategic Information Systems, 2*(4), 292-319.

Flynn, D., & Hepburn, P. (1994). Strategic planning for information systems - a case study of a UK metropolitan council. *European Journal of Information Systems, 3*(3), 207-217.

Galliers, R. (1987). Information systems planning in the United Kingdom and Australia - a comparison of current practice. *Oxford Surveys in Information Technology, 4*, 223-255.

Galliers, R. (1991). Strategic information systems planning: Myths, realities and guidelines for successful implementation. *European Journal of Information Systems, 1*(1), 55-64.

Galliers, R. (1993). Towards a flexible information architecture: Integrating business strategies, information strategies and business process redesign. *Journal of Information Systems, 3*, 199-213.

Gottschalk, P. (1999a). Implementation predictors of strategic information systems plans. *Information & Management, 36*, 77-91.

Gottschalk, P. (1999b). Implementation of formal plans: The case of information technology strategy. *Long Range Planning, 32*(3), 362-372.

Gottschalk, P. (1999c). Strategic information systems planning: The IT strategy implementation matrix. *European Journal of Information Systems, 8*(2), 107-118.

Hackney, R., & Kawalek, J. (1999). Strategic information systems planning: Perspectives on the role of the "end-user" revisited. *Journal of End User Computing, 11*(2), 3-12.

Hackney, R., & McBride, N. (2002). Non-implementation of an IS strategy within a UK hospital: Observations from a longitudinal case study. *Communications of the Association for Information Systems, 8*, 130–140.

Hann, J., & Weber, R. (1996). Information systems planning: A model and empirical tests. *Management Science, 42*(7), 1043-1064.

Hartono, E., Lederer, A., Sethi, V., & Zhuang, Y. (2003). Key predictors of the implementation of strategic information systems plans. *The DATA BASE for Advances in Information Systems, 34*(3), 41–53.

Hwang, M., Windsor, J., & Pryor, A. (2000). Building a knowledge base for MIS research: A meta-analysis of a systems success model. *Information Resources Management Journal, 2,* 26–32.

Jiang, J., & Klein, G. (1999). Project selection criteria by strategic orientation. *Information & Management, 36*(2), 63-75.

Kearns, G., & Lederer, A. (1997). Alignment of information systems plans with business plans: The impact on competitive advantage. *Proceedings of the 2nd AIS Conference,* Indianapolis, Indiana, 840-842.

Kearns, G., & Lederer, A. (2000). The effect of strategic alignment on the use of IS-based resources for competitive advantage. *Journal of Strategic Information Systems, 9,* 265-293.

King, W., & Teo, T. (2000). Assessing the impact of proactive versus reactive modes of strategic information systems planning. *OMEGA—International Journal of Management Science, 28*(6), 667-679.

Lederer, A., & Putnam, P. (1986). Connecting systems objectives to business strategy with BSP. *Information Strategy: The Executive's Journal, 2*(2), 12-18.

Lederer, A., & Salmela, H. (1996). Toward a theory of strategic information systems planning. *Journal of Strategic Information Systems, 5,* 237-253.

Lederer, A., & Sethi, V. (1988). The implementation of strategic information systems planning methodologies. *MIS Quarterly, 12*(3), 445-461.

Lederer, A., & Sethi, V. (1991). Critical dimensions of strategic information systems planning. *Decision Sciences, 22*(1), 104-119.

Lederer, A., & Sethi, V. (1992). Root causes of strategic information systems planning problems. *Journal of Management Information Systems, 9*(1), 25-45.

Lederer, A., & Sethi, V. (1996). Key prescriptions for strategic information systems planning. *Journal of Management Information Systems, 13*(1), 35-62.

Lederer, A., & Sethi, V. (1998). Seven guidelines for strategic information systems planning. *Information Strategy: The Executive's Journal, 15*(1), 23-29.

Lee, G., & Pai, C. (2003). Effects of organisational context and inter-group behaviour on the success of strategic information systems planning: An empirical study. *Behaviour & Information Technology, 22*(4), 263–280.

Legris, P., Ingham, J., & Collerette, P. (2003). Why do people use information technology? A critical review of the technology acceptance model. *Information & Management, 40,* 191–204.

Luftman, J., & McLean, E. (2004). Key issues for IT executives. *MIS Quarterly Executive, 3*(2), 89–104.

McFarlan, F., McKenney, J., & Pyburn, P. (1983). The information archipelago — plotting a course. *Harvard Business Review, 61*(1), 145-156.

McGrath, G., Dampney, C., & More, E. (1994). Planning for information systems integration: Some key challenges. *Journal of Information Science, 20*(3), 149-160.

Mehrez, A., Howard, G., Lugasi, Y., & Shoval, P. (1993). Information systems planning and selection: A multi-attribute theoretic approach. *Computer Journal, 36*(6), 525-541.

Mentzas, G. (1997). Implementing an IS strategy—A team approach. *Long Range Planning, 30*(1), 84-95.

Min, S., & Kim, S. (1999). An integrated approach toward strategic information systems planning. *Journal of Strategic Information Systems, 8*, 373-394.

O'Connor, A. (1993). Successful strategic information systems planning. *Journal of Information Systems, 3*, 71-83.

Ormerod, R. (1996). Putting soft OR methods to work: Information systems strategy development at Richard's Bay. *Journal of the Operational Research Society, 47*(9), 1083-1097.

Pant, S., & Hsu, C. (1999). An integrated framework for strategic information systems planning and development. *Information Resources Management Journal, 12*(1), 15-25.

Pant, S., & Ravichandran, T. (2001). A framework for information systems planning for e-business. *Logistics Information Management, 14*(1), 85-98.

Pant, S., Sim, H., & Hsu, C. (2001). A framework for developing web information systems plans: Illustration with Samsung Heavy Industries Co., Ltd. *Information & Management, 38*, 385-408.

Pavri, F., & Ang, J. (1995). A study of the strategic planning practices in Singapore. *Information & Management, 28*(1), 33-47.

Periasamy, K. (1993). The state and status of information architecture: An empirical investigation. *Proceedings of the 14th International Conference on Information Systems*, Orlando, Florida, (pp. 255-270).

Periasamy, K., & Feeny, D. (1997). Information architecture practice: Research-based recommendations for the practitioner. *Journal of Information Technology, 12*(3), 197-205.

Porter, M., & Millar, V. (1985). How information gives you competitive advantage. *Harvard Business Review, 63*(4), 149-160.

Premkumar, G., & King, W. (1991). Assessing strategic information systems planning. *Long Range Planning, 24*(5), 41-58.

Premkumar, G., & King, W. (1992). An empirical assessment of information systems planning and the role of information systems in organisations. *Journal of Management Information Systems, 9*(2), 99-125.

Premkumar, G., & King, W. (1994). Organisational characteristics and information systems planning: An empirical study. *Information Systems Research, 5*(2), 75-109.

Ranganathan, C., & Sethi, V. (2000). External IT environment: Dimensionality and measurement. *Proceedings of the 21st International Conference on Information Systems,* Brisbane, Australia, 594-600.

Ranganathan, C., & Sethi, V. (2002). Rationality in strategic information technology decisions: The impact of shared domain knowledge and IT unit structure. *Decision Sciences, 33*(1), 59-86.

Reich, B., & Benbasat, I. (2000). Factors that influence the social dimension of alignment between business and information technology objectives. *MIS Quarterly, 24*(1), 81-113.

Sabherwal, R. (1999). The relationship between information system planning sophistication and information system success. *Decision Sciences, 30*(1), 137-167.

Sabherwal, R., & King, W. (1992). Decision processes for developing strategic applications of information systems: A contingency approach. *Decision Sciences, 23*(4), 917-943.

Sabherwal, R., & King, W. (1995). An empirical taxonomy of the decision-making processes concerning strategic applications of information systems. *Journal of Management Information Systems, 11*(1), 177-214.

Sahraoui, S. (2003). Learning through planning: Conceptual definition, and empirical validation of a planning culture construct. *Journal of End-User Computing, 15*(2), 37–53.

Salmela, H., Lederer, A., & Reponen, T. (2000). Information systems planning in a turbulent environment. *European Journal of Information Systems, 9*(1), 3-15.

Salmela, H., & Spil, T. (2002). Dynamic and emergent information systems strategy formulation and implementation. *International Journal of Information Management, 22*, 441-460.

Segars, A., & Grover, V. (1998). Strategic information systems planning success: An investigation of the construct and its measurement. *MIS Quarterly, 23*(2), 139-163.

Segars, A., & Grover, V. (1999). Profiles of strategic information systems planning. *Information Systems Research, 10*(3), 199-232.

Segars, A., Grover, V., & Teng, J. (1998). Strategic information systems planning: Planning system dimensions, internal co alignment, and implications for planning effectiveness. *Decision Sciences, 29*(2), 303-344.

Shank, M., Boynton, A., & Zmud, R. (1985). Critical success factor analysis as a methodology for MIS planning. *MIS Quarterly, 9*(2), 121-129.

Sillince, J., & Frost, C. (1995). Operational, environmental, and managerial factors in non-alignment of business strategies and IS strategies for the Police Service in England and Wales. *European Journal of Information Systems, 4*(2), 103-115.

Tang, J., & Tang, M. (1996). A study of information systems planning and its effectiveness in Taiwan. *International Journal of Information Management, 16*(6), 429-436.

Teo, T., & Ang, J. (2001). An examination of major IS planning problems. *International Journal of Information Management, 21*, 457-470.

Teo, T., Ang, J., & Pavri, F. (1997). The state of strategic IS planning practices in Singapore. *Information & Management, 33*, 13-23.

Teo, T., & King, W. (1996). Assessing the impact of integrating business planning and IS planning. *Information & Management, 30*(6), 309-321.

Teo, T., & King, W. (1997). Integration between business planning and information systems planning: An evolutionary-contingency perspective. *Journal of Management Information Systems, 14*(1), 185-214.

Van Der Zee, J., & De Jong, B. (1999). Alignment is not enough: Integrating business and information technology management with the balanced business scorecard. *Journal of Management Information Systems, 6*(2), 137-157.

Wang, E., & Tai, J. (2003). Factors affecting information systems planning effectiveness: Organisational contexts and planning systems dimensions. *Information & Management, 40*, 287–303.

Watson, R., Kelly, G., Galliers, R., & Brancheau, J. (1997). Key issues in information systems management: An international perspective. *Journal of Management Information Systems, 13*(4), 91-115.

Chapter XIV

Business Process Reengineering:
The Role of Organizational Enablers and the Impact of Information Technology

Hamid Reza Ahadi
Iran University of Science and Technology in Tehran, Iran

ABSTRACT

This study examines organizational factors that affect the implementation of business process reengineering (BPR) when applying two specific information technologies (i.e., Electronic Data Interchange and/or Internet technology). This research uses a survey methodology to gather information about how organizational enablers and information technology affect BPR implementation. By determining the factors that affect BPR implementation, these factors can be managed in the best interest of customers, employees, and organizations. From the nine hypotheses tested in this study, six factors were found to be positively associated with successful implementation of BPR. These factors are top management supports, change management, centralization of decision making, formalization of procedure, organizational culture, and customer involvement. No significant relationship was found between employee resistance and integration of jobs with successful implementation of BPR. In this research, we found that the lack of resources is negatively associated with successful implementation of BPR. We also found that different information technologies such as those examined in this chapter—EDI and Internet—provide different capabilities and can be useful in different ways and for different purposes. The findings of this research can help practitioners to better understand the role of critical success and failure factors in BPR as well as the impact of different information technologies on BPR. By determining the factors that affect BPR implementation, these factors can be managed in the best interest of customers, employees, and organizations.

INTRODUCTION

The concept of BPR was first introduced by Hammer in 1990. Since initiation, it has become a popular management tool for dealing with rapid technological and business change in today's competitive environment. BPR evolved from the experiences of a few US-based companies in the late 1980s (Martinsons & Hempel, 1998). They radically changed their work process by applying modern information technology. Report of their dramatically improved performance helped to make reengineering the American management phenomenon of the early 1990s and its international diffusion.

Traditional organizations have different departments such as sales, marketing, finance, purchasing, production, and each department is responsible for undertaking one part of a large whole. This chain of linked departments allows for specialization where the overall task is broken down, and people with specific expertise can be applied as required. Such specialization of labor, whether on the manufacturing shop floor or within offices, has been a normal way of working for a long time. Levels of seniority evolve within these functions to form the organizational hierarchy. This model is so widely established that it is rarely questioned. That is all changing now. Business process reengineering is questioning this functional way of thinking and is making processes a main focus for organizations (Peppard & Rowland, 1995).

Figure 1 illustrates the shift from functional organization to process organization. Figure 1a depicts that the organization is actually made up of a number of suborganizations known as functions, each of which has its own management hierarchy. Figure 1b shows that management focus has traditionally been on the functional hierarchy. Figure 1c shows that BPR emphasizes a "process" view, which cuts across the functional hierarchies to reach the customer.

Figure 1. Shift from functional organization to process organization

Figure 1(a). Traditional organizations with functional departments

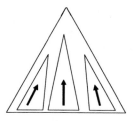

Figure 1(b). Functional departments

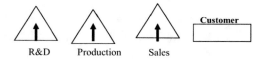

Figure 1(c). Process organization

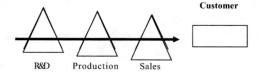

Organizations adopting a process approach find that many steps in their order cycle have nothing to do with delivering the required outcomes. It is something difficult to identify why some steps exist at all. It is for no reason other than that they always have been! Getting rid of all these unnecessary steps means quicker customer service at considerably lower cost. This is all very well, but doing this usually cuts across the functional departments (Peppard & Rowland, 1995).

BPR has been defined and conceptualized in many different ways. The following sample definitions of BPR illustrate the slightly varying views of many researchers and practitioners.

Use the power of modern Information Technology to radically redesign business processes in order to achieve dramatic improvements in performance. (Hammer, 1990)

Total transformation of a business; an unconstrained reshaping of all business processes, technologies and management systems, as well as organizational structure and values, to achieve quantum leaps in performance throughout the business. (Goll, 1992)

The process of fundamentally changing the way work is performed in order to achieve radical performance improvements in speed, cost, and quality (CSC Index, 1994)

From the practitioner definitions, there are five elements that stand out to form the critical issues that define BPR: (1) BPR consists of radical or at least significant change; (2) BPR's unit of analysis is the business process, not the department or functional area; (3) BPR tries to achieve major goals or dramatic performance improvements; (4) IT is a critical enabler of BPR; and (5) organizational changes are a critical enabler of BPR and must be managed accordingly.

Numerous organizations have reported success from their BPR efforts by containing costs and achieving breakthrough performance in a variety of parameters like delivery times, customer service, and quality. For example, Bell Atlantic reduced the time to install new telecommunication circuits from 15 to 3 days and cut labor cost from U.S. $88 million to $6 million (Stewart, 1993). Ford Motor reduced its account payable staff by 75% with BPR. Motorola, when faced with higher defect percentages and longer cycle times, redesigned its parts and tooling process, simultaneously upgrading its manufacturing equipment; this decreased the total production cost by U.S. $1 billion per year and cut cycle time in half (Harrison & Pratt, 1993). Other often cited examples of successful BPR programs include AT&T, Eastman Kodak, Hallmark Cards Inc., and IBM Credit and are discussed in some recent works (Aggarawal, 1997; Ascari, Rock, & Dutta, 1995). However, not all companies that undertake BPR achieve their intended results. Hammer and Champy (1993) reveal that as many as 50% to 70% of organizations that make an effort to employ BPR do not achieve the dramatic results they seek. These mixed results make issues of BPR implementation especially important. BPR has great potential for increasing productivity through reduced process time and cost, improved quality and greater customer satisfaction, but to do so it must be implemented and managed in the best interest of customers, employees, and organizations.

PURPOSE OF THE STUDY

Despite the importance of BPR, research on this subject is not yet firmly established or well structured. Most studies on this subject are either conceptual or case studies. Those case studies usually describe the success of BPR efforts in situations where variables are not defined. Therefore, it is difficult to say what the critical success and failure factors of BPR are. Furthermore, the role and impact of information technology in BPR in most of the literature is neglected.

This study will propose that successful BPR using information technology is related to different organizational enablers. In other words, this study will attempt to identify the managerial and organizational issues and structures (organizational enablers) associated with a successful BPR project using information technology (IT enabler). Although there has been some empirical investigation of BPR, no research to date has examined BPR when EDI (Electronic Data Interchange) and Internet technology are used during implementation.

BPR AND ORGANIZATIONAL ENABLERS

BPR projects have been evaluated from a number of perspectives in attempting to measure their degree of success. As in any new field, different researchers have identified different factors in BPR success. Davenport and Short (1990) identify four objectives of BPR. Their set of objectives include cost reduction, time reduction, output quality, and quality of work life (QWL)/learning/empowerment. Morris and Brandon (1993) suggest six basic goals of BPR: (1) streamline the operation; (2) reduce costs; (3) improve quality; (4) increase revenue; (5) improve customer orientation; and (6) merge acquired operations. Stow (1993) reports that the objectives of BPR can be identified as improving an organization's effectiveness, efficiency, competitiveness, and profitability. He especially argues that a reengineering project should be conducted by its objectives, and the key to a successful BPR project is defining objectives first.

REVIEW OF BPR SUCCESS FACTORS

There have been numerous studies from different perspectives that identify success factors of BPR. The success factors of BPR can be divided into two groups. One group of factors involves process redesign, and the other group of factors is related to change management.

In process redesign, three categories of success factors exist: (1) success factors of process, (2) success factors of project team management, and (3) IT-related factors. For change management issues, three categories of success factors can be reported: (1) people-oriented factors, (2) managerial/administrative factors, and (3) organizational factors.

Numerous researchers and practitioners believe that top management commitment is the most important factor for a successful BPR effort (Davenport, 1993; Janson, 1993). They argue that BPR never happens bottom-up, and a reengineered process alone will not change the way people work. Champy and Arnoudse (1992) identify the role, attitude, vision, and skill or knowledge of leaders as necessary for successful BPR. Especially, they state that BPR must be more top-down driven than a quality improvement plan because of its radical change requirement. Since BPR focuses on processes that are inherently cross-functional, leadership by those who have comprehensive perspectives and the authority to coordinate different interest groups is essential.

Hammer and Champy (1993) also emphasize the importance of measurement and rewards for reengineered process performance. They argue that paying employees based on their position is inconsistent with the principles of BPR. They must be paid based on their performance and ability. Measuring the performance of a process and people is important for evaluating BPR, but the way of measuring is sometimes inadequate. To get employees to operate productively in teams, share information, take initiative, and display other behaviors that are now important, top management must devise new rewards and management processes.

Bashein, Markus, and Riley (1994) suggest more concrete factors of successful BPR projects. They argue that sound financial conditions, an appropriate number of BPR projects under way, and IS and human resource specialist involvement are critical to BPR success. Clear, honest, and frequent communication is also important for successful BPR implementation. Sharing information and empathizing with employee concerns can help minimize resistance (Janson, 1993).

Katzenbach and Smith (1993) propose that it is important for a BPR project team to have people from different interest groups. They identified that the size of a BPR project team, its members level of skill, a shared goal, and mutual accountability among team members are important factors for successful project team management. Stow (1993) argues that BPR efforts must be conducted by objectives. Defining objectives establishes a road map for the BPR efforts, and BPR objectives must be selected based on company strategy and vision.

Davenport and Short (1990) identify that selecting the right processes for BPR is an important success factor. Although total redesign is the ultimate objective, companies should select a few key processes for their initial efforts. They suggest two approaches to selecting processes for BPR. The exhaustive approach attempts to identify all processes within a company and then prioritize them in order of redesign urgency. The "big-impact" approach attempts to identify only the most important processes or those most in conflict with the business vision and process objective.

Harrison and Pratt (1993) state that providing the baseline and benchmark of the existing business process, constructing the vision of the future process, and designing the improvement are other important factors of process redesign. Stanton, Hammer, and Power (1992) propose that project duration is another important success factor of BPR. The carefully reengineered process and its supporting infrastructure might be obsolete if a project takes too much time. To avoid this outcome, they suggest a method of process design that consists of decomposition, integration, and validation of processes.

REVIEW OF BPR FAILURE FACTORS

In almost every case, BPR brings about major changes in organizations that make them more competitive and more responsive to the market. However, its implementation is never easy. According to the 1991 report of CSC Consulting, one quarter of nearly 300 North American companies involved in BPR reported they were not meeting their goals (Stanton, Hammer & Power, 1992). Hammer and Champy report that more than 75% of BPR projects have been unsuccessful. One reason for the high failure rate is the scope of BPR: It often involves large numbers of people and may extend over a period of years. Another reason is that it always demands radically new behaviors, and that can provoke strong resistance within organizations (Janson, 1993). The following are major reasons for BPR failure.

Resistance to Change

The primary reason for BPR failure is resistance from key persons who would be affected by a BPR effort (Stanton et al., 1992). By giving employees the tools and expertise to take on multiple tasks, BPR breaks down the longstanding walls that separate departments and functional units. Managers may lose their power as a result of BPR since it flattens management layers, shifts responsibility, and disrupts the status quo. Therefore, resistance by managers generally is caused by altered status, job security, and loss of control and position (Davenport, 1993; Hammer & Champ, 1993; Stanton et al., 1992). Others may be afraid of losing their job since BPR eliminates unnecessary jobs and tasks. Resistance by workers is also caused by the team-oriented approach, lack of ability to adjust to new technologies and processes, and vested interests and territorial disputes.

Other sources of resistance are fear and skepticism about BPR results. Feeling discomfort is another important source of resistance. Since a reengineered process often requires skills for operating advanced IT, some people may feel discomfort (Davenport, 1993). Thus, failure to accommodate those key persons influenced by BPR can cause failure. A functional unit's parochial interests are another barrier to successful BPR projects. When a BPR project does not have top management commitment or is initiated from the bottom-up, the BPR effort can be stymied by functional managers defending their parochial interests (Stanton et al., 1992). Since BPR focuses on processes that are inherently cross-functional, leadership by those who have a comprehensive perspective and the authority to coordinate different interest groups is essential for a successful BPR effort.

Lack of Resources

A company that is financially unhealthy is unlikely to succeed at BPR. A company may have too many disparate businesses or be too leveraged to be able to commit the significant financial resources required by BPR (Bashein et al., 1994). A company that lacks competent technical/managerial skill is unlikely to succeed. A BPR project requires technical as well as managerial skill to redesign and implement the reengineered process (Johansson et al., 1993).

Unrealistic Expectations

Misconceptions and misunderstandings about BPR are allegedly common among stakeholders (Hall, Rosenthal, & Wade, 1993). Top management expectations may not be realistic. They may want concrete evidence of success within a few months, when the design and implementation of a project may take more than a year. If misconceptions and unrealistic expectations exist among stakeholders, attracting their commitment throughout the project duration is impossible. Without their commitment, a BPR project can hardly be successfully conducted.

Too Many Improvement Projects Under Way

BPR may be viewed as just another program in an organization with too many improvement projects already under way. Diverse projects may be poorly planned, badly integrated, and mutually self-defeating. When multiple projects are undertaken at the same time, their effectiveness may be diluted. Too many projects may compete for scarce organization resources such as human, technical, and financial resources. Management commitment may not be sustained throughout the project duration.

Narrowly Defined Process

Many BPR efforts fail because of insufficient process breadth. Hall and her associates (1993) state that narrowly defined process redesign may cause BPR failure since redesigned processes cannot mesh with related processes. As a result of a carefully redesigned process, a company can achieve dramatic improvements individual processes only to watch overall performance decline. They propose that the process to be redesigned must be broadly defined in terms of cost or customer value in order to improve performance across the entire business unit. However, other BPR efforts fail because of a too broad, indiscriminate approach.

Incomplete Restructuring of an Organization

The successful BPR effort requires a complete restructuring of the key drivers of organizational behavior (Hall et al., 1993). Hall et al. propose six key drivers of organizational behavior—roles and responsibilities, measurements and incentives, organizational structure, IT, shared value, and skills—have to change as a result of BPR. Their investigation of BPR cases find that companies that manipulate all six depth levers to bring about behavioral change show the most dramatic process cost reduction.

BPR AND IT ENABLERS

IT plays an enabling role in BPR. An enabler is an agent that allows organizations to break their old rules and create new reengineered processes (Hammer & Champy, 1993). IT should be considered as more than an automating or augmenting force. It can fundamentally reshape, or enable, the way business processes are done. IT can include any enabling technology that an organization uses to support its business. This includes its systems for manufacturing, information management, control, measurement, design, and engineering. IT obviously has great potential, but it is difficult to use effectively. BPR addresses these difficulties by directly designing the effective use of IT into reengineered business processes. Although IT is not the solution, the use of IT to improve processes is essential in BPR projects. During BPR's examination of existing business processes, new and improved uses of IT are often discovered. It is BPR that can relate the use of IT directly to business processes. In addition to enabling productivity improvement, IT can also enable radical alterations of the cost structure of jobs. However, to actually change jobs takes a combination of management leadership and employee participation. IT is also an enabler of social and organizational transformation, making it an integral part of an organization's strategy (Parker, 1996).

Some categories of information technologies that are commonly used in BPR programs are as follows:

* Databases and related technologies;
* Networking and communication;
* Electronic data interchange (EDI);
* Workflow automation and groupware;

- Internet Web-based technology;
- Enterprise system and enterprise resource planning (ERP); and
- Multimedia and interactive computing.

Of course, this list is neither exhaustive nor mutually exclusive. However, a firm needs to make independent decisions about each (Ranganathan & Dhaliwal, 2001).

IT enables BPR by providing tools necessary to analyze, communicate, and redesign business processes. IT in this study refers specifically to Electronic Data Interchange and Internet technology. Different information technologies provide different capabilities and can be useful in different ways.

EDI AS AN IT ENABLER

The idea of doing business in the networks developed in the 1960s when Electronic Data Interchange (EDI) and Electronic Fund Transfer (EFT) were first introduced to banks and financial institutes and gradually expanded to many other applications for exchanging data among private networks (Ahadi, 2002). The United Nations Electronic Data Interchange for Administration, Commerce, and Transportation (UN/EDIFACT) defines EDI as interchange of standard formatted data between computer application systems of trading partners with minimal manual intervention (Kalakota & Whinston, 1996). EDI is a rapidly growing technology. The number of registered EDI users, according to EDI yellow pages international, has shown impressive gains in the past several years, well in excess of a 50% annual growth rate (Lim & Palvia, 2001).

Of course, routine communications over the Internet are widely accepted, and even EDI over the Internet is increasing because of its lower costs. However, issues of security, accuracy, and the size of files may hold up Internet usage for production and business transactions (Brunell, 2000). EDI enables BPR through faster processing speed, greater accuracy, reduced costs, competitive advantages, improved operation, security, tracking and control, intra- and inter-company communications, and customer service (Lim & Palvia, 2001).

INTERNET AS AN IT ENABLER

Internet is the most recent information technology used in BPR. Internet is widely used and the fastest growing technology. According to estimates, the number of Internet users surpassed 888 million or about 14% of the world's population by the year 2005 (http://www.internetworldstats.com/stats.htm). Since initiation, it took only 5 years for this new phenomenon to reach 10 million users (Zeff & Aronson, 1997).

Figure 2 illustrates the diffusion of Web-based Internet technology compared to other technologies.

The Internet can be used as an IT enabler by allowing organizations to create easily accessible communication networks (Parker, 1996). Internet technology enables BPR projects through three benefits: (1) cost; (2) availability; and (3) compatibility. The cost benefit of Internet technology includes the cost of Internet technology itself as well as cost savings incurred through its use.

Internet technology has saved costs by allowing faster and easier access to more accurate company information. Internet technology enables BPR through the availability of the technology itself as well as making information more easily and quickly available. Productivity increases from Internet technology arise from more rapid and easier exchange of information. Internet technology allows both structured and unstructured information to be easily accessed from data storage throughout an organization. Cross-functional teams can proactively share information about issues such as: (1) employee policies; (2) daily announcements; (3) company mission and objectives; and (4) project information. For example, Ford Motor Company used Internet technology to facilitate the global exchange of information to create 24 hours a day, 7 days a week organizational productivity. Design centers in Asia, Europe, and the United States were connected through Internet technology to engineer the 1996 Ford Taurus (McGrath & Schneider, 1997).

METHODOLOGY AND HYPOTHESES GENERATION

Through review of the literature, four groups of factors critical to BPR implementation were identified: (1) management commitment, (2) organizational

Figure 2. Number of years for different technologies to reach 10 million consumers

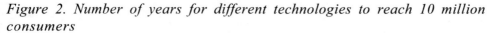

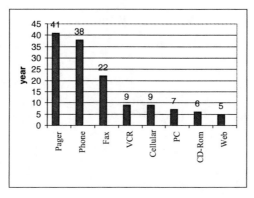

culture, (3) organizational structure, and (4) customers. These groups of factors can be further divided as depicted in Figure 3. To examine the role of organizational enablers to BPR, nine hypotheses were generated. Related questions to each factor were addressed in our survey questionnaire to measure the extent of these factors for a successful implementation of BPR.

Top Management Support

Top management support is an important ingredient of an innovative organizational environment (Van De Ven, 1986). Top management represents decision makers, visionary leaders, political actors, and teachers (Smith & Willcocks, 1995). Top management support must be obtained and sustained to successfully implement BPR. We designed appropriate questions in our survey questionnaire to measure the extent of top management support for successfully implementing the reengineered process. Therefore, we developed the related hypothesis:

- **H1:** Top management support is positively associated with successful implementation of BPR.

Change Management

Another essential element of developing an innovative organizational environment for successful BPR implementation is change management (Hammer, 1990). Change management commitment includes (1) employee empowerment; (2) performance measurement; (3) reward systems; (4) training and education; (5) communication; and (6) organizational structure (Hall et al., 1993). We developed the second hypothesis:

- **H2:** Effective change management is positively associated with successful implementation of BPR.

Figure 3. Factors affecting BPR implementation

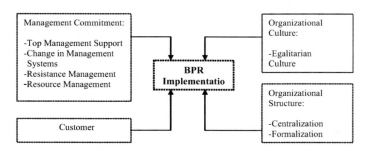

Employee Resistance

Employee resistance can prevent BPR projects from succeeding. Employee resistance can be caused by (1) the danger of losing job security (Hammer & Stanton, 1994; Venkatraman, 1994); (2) loss of power (Hammer & Stanton, 1994); (3) skill or knowledge requirement (Morris & Brandon, 1993); (4) skepticism about results (Hammer & Stanton, 1994); (5) functional unit's interests (Hall et al., 1993; Hammer & Stanton, 1994); and (6) resistance of customers (Hammer & Stanton, 1994; Venkatraman, 1994).

• **H3:** Employee resistance is negatively associated with successful implementation of BPR.

Lack of Resources

Organizations use resource management to develop an innovative organizational environment for successful BPR implementation. A lack of resources can prevent BPR projects from succeeding (Bashein et al., 1994; Venkatraman, 1994). Resource management involves the following four resources: (1) financial (Johansson et al., 1993; Marchand & Stanford, 1995); (2) technical (Davenport & Short, 1990; Marchand & Stanford, 1995; Parker, 1996); (3) human (Marchand & Stanford, 1995; Smith & Willcocks, 1995); and (4) time (Marchand & Stanford, 1995; Smith & Willcocks, 1995).

• **H4:** Lack of resources is negatively associated with successful implementation of BPR.

Centralization of Decision Making

Centralization of decision making involves the degree of participation of employees in the organization in the decision-making process. In centralized organizations, most of the important decisions are made by upper level management. Researchers have found that centralized decision making is positively associated with creating an innovative organizational environment (Beyer & Trice, 1978). In decentralized organizations, lower level employees are allowed to make many decisions. Researchers have also found that decentralized decision making is positively associated with creating an innovative organizational environment (Moch & Morse, 1977). One reason for conflicting findings is that innovation is promoted from the top down during the initialization phase of a BPR project and from the bottom up during the implementation of a BPR project (Zaltman, 1973). Even though research findings may be conflicting, it is generally thought that centralized decision making reduces input from multiple sources. Thus, a strong initiative and drive for BPR implementation can be possible. One the other hand, this reduction of input hinders the creation of an innovative organizational environment (Zaltman, 1973). Therefore, this study will hypothesize that centralization of decision making has a negative impact on BPR implementation.

- **H5:** Centralization of decision making is negatively associated with successful implementation of BPR.

Integration of Jobs

Job integration attempts to incorporate work into a process to more effectively manage a complete business. The integration of jobs is used to design work that is performed along process lines rather than functional lines. Most BPR projects cross functional or department lines in an organization (Grover, Teng, & Fiedler, 1995; Hammer & Champy, 1993; Scheer, 1998). Thus, job integration is a common characteristic of a reengineered process. However, there can be negative consequences to job integration. Employees may develop lower job satisfaction or deterioration in the quality of their work life. The relationship between job integration and BPR is still unclear.

- **H6:** Integration of jobs is positively associated with successful implementation of BPR.

Formalization of Procedures

Formalization of procedures is the extent to which job responsibilities are expressed in written rules and regulations, and employees are evaluated based on the written procedures (Beyer & Trice, 1978). A formalized organization has a comprehensive set of written rules and regulations developed to handle decision making and business processes. It was found that the degree of formalization was negatively associated with the adoption and implementation of innovations in organizations.

- **H7:** Formalization of procedures is negatively associated with successful implementation of BPR.

Egalitarian Culture

Organizational culture is an important factor in developing an innovative organizational environment for successful BPR implementation. Cooperation, coordination, and empowerment of employees are the standard characteristics of an innovative organizational environment. Egalitarian culture supports these attitudes. Egalitarian culture is characterized by (1) shared organizational vision and information; (2) open communication; (3) strong leadership style; and (4) employee participation in decision making (Grover et al., 1995).

- **H8:** An egalitarian culture is positively associated with successful implementation of BPR.

Customer Involvement

An innovative organizational environment requires customer involvement during BPR (Zirger & Maidique, 1990). Customer involvement includes (1) customers involved throughout the BPR project; (2) information gathered from customers drives the BPR project; (3) the BPR project satisfies customers' needs; and (4) gathering requirements from customers before the BPR project begins.

- **H9:** Customer involvement is positively associated with successful implementation of BPR.

SUCCESS

In addition to the variables discussed above, BPR implementation success was measured over the six dimensions: (1) process time reduction; (2) process cost reduction; (3) user learning; (4) output quality; (5) quality of work life; and (6) responsiveness to customer needs (Davenport, 1993; Morris & Brandon, 1993).

DATA COLLECTION

The exploratory nature of the research lends itself to using informants and respondents to gather information. The questionnaire was prepared using information gleaned from prior literature in the area. It was pilot tested with three faculty member in management information systems and a consulting firm specialist in BPR. Based on their feedback, appropriate changes were made to the questionnaire. We chose two methods of soliciting respondents: Web- and paper-based.

1. In November 2001, our finalized questionnaires were transmitted via email to 190 selected companies for two specific industries: automotive parts and electronics.
2. In January 2002, finalized questionnaires were distributed to 155 selected companies, attended on first international conference on intellectual property and e-business. This event was used to examine the benefits offered by the convergence of major industries engaged with information technology.

A total of 345 questionnaires were distributed, and 77 were returned for a response rate of 22%. Five of the returned questionnaires were deemed invalid because too many values were missing or incomplete. Thus, 72 companies are examined in this study. The demographic of respondent organizations are shown in Figures 4 through 7.

STATISTICAL ANALYSIS

As the first step of measurement validation, the reliability of collected data was examined using Cronbach s coefficient alpha. The Cronbach s alpha value is 0.7417, which is relatively high and falls within the acceptable range. The Pearson correlation coefficient was chosen to reveal the magnitude and direction of the hypothesized relationships. T-tests with alpha level set at 0.05 were used to determine significance of the Pearson correlation coefficients. In information systems research, it is common for correlation coefficients of 0.20 and above to be considered meaningful when using correlation analysis in an exploratory study (Griffith & Northcraft, 1996).

Findings

The collected data revealed that 74% (53 firms) of our respondent firms had completed some BPR projects in the past 18 months, and 26% (19 firms) had some BPR projects currently under implementation.

Figure 4. Participating organizations

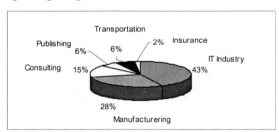

Figure 5. Sample demographic revenue $U.S.

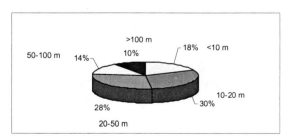

Figure 6. BPR implementation statistics

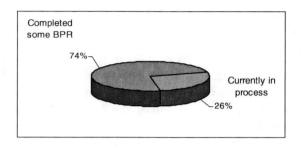

Figure 7. Type of IT used in BPR projects

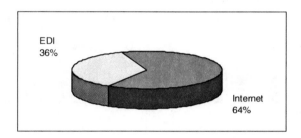

All of the BPR projects in this research used either EDI or Internet technology. Any questionnaires returned that did not use EDI or Internet technology were not included in the analysis. As depicted in Figure 7, 64% of our respondent firms cited the Internet as an IT enabler for their BPR efforts.

There are two basic approaches to BPR (Klein, 1994). One group of researchers relies on an intuitive approach. They believe that too much attention to current practices gets in the way of innovative thinking. Hammer and Champy (1993) belong to this group.

The other group of researchers and practitioners, so-called methodists, believe that a structured methodology is a good way of facilitating training, providing check points for an on-going project, and building expertise on different aspects of BPR. Davenport, Short, Harrison, Pratt, and Johansson belong to this group. In this study, 75% of the participant organizations sought some type of expertise from external consultants. From the high percentage of organizations that reported using some type of methodology, it seems obvious that organizations have seen the benefits of utilizing a BPR methodology when using either EDI or Internet to reengineer processes.

EDI vs. INTERNET

We tried to assess the functional areas that have been targeted for BPR efforts by participant organizations. The statistics are presented in Table 2. From Table 2, it is evident that participant organizations have essentially focused on their customer service followed by order management, inventory management, and purchasing management for either EDI or Internet applications. Our results are different from the results of the CSC/Index survey which reported that accounting and finance were the functions that were reengineered by most North American companies, followed by marketing and sales. We also found that the frequency of selected information technology is different within the selected process for reengineering. For example, human resources management, new product development, and marketing management rank 5, 6, 7 for Internet application and ranks 10, 13, 12 for EDI application to BPR respectively. BPR programs may be undertaken for a variety of reasons. Our survey indicated significant difference among the objectives for BPR when two different

Table 1. Summary of correlation analysis

Hypotheses	Variable	Correlation Coefficient	T-test value	Result
H1	Top Management Support	0.680	.0000	Accepted
H2	Change Management	0.708	.0000	Accepted
H3	Employee Resistance	0.186	.117	Rejected
H4	Lack of Resources	- 0.522	.0000	Accepted
H5	Centralization of Decision Making	0.480	.0000	Rejected
H6	Integration of Jobs	0.079	.508	Rejected
H7	Formalization of Procedures	0.530	.0000	Rejected
H8	Egalitarian Culture	0.437	.0000	Accepted
H9	Customer Involvement	0.451	.0000	Accepted

Table 2. Comparison of selected process for reengineering by using EDI or Internet technology

Type of Business	Rank in Internet	Rank in EDI
Customer service	1	1
Order management	2	2
Inventory management	3	3
Purchasing	4	4
Human resources	5	7
New product development	6	10
Marketing	7	13
Research and development	8	12
Sales	9	15
Production	10	14
Receiving	11	16
Shipping	12	17
Billing	13	6
Invoicing	14	5
Accounts receivable	15	8

information technologies—EDI or Internet—were applied to BPR. Easier access to information, electronic commerce, and cost reduction are the main motives for undertaking BPR by applying Internet technology.

Efficient connection of organizational resources, exchange information, and increase productivity seem to be the most important reasons for applying EDI to BPR. The results of our survey support the CSC/Index survey of North American firms in which cost cutting was ranked as the second most important objective, next to improving the speed of business processes.

Another survey of 80 American corporations identified cost cutting as a major goal for BPR programs (Maglitta, 1995). A study of European organizations also found that BPR projects in Europe are mostly concerned with saving of cost and time (Coulson & Colin, 1997). As indicated in Table 3, there is a different relationship between selected information technology—EDI or Internet—with the objectives of BPR. For example, for objectives such as easier access to information, electronic commerce, and cost reduction, it seems that Internet technology is more preferred IT for reengineering than EDI, ranks 1, 2, 3 compared to 15, 6, 7. For objectives such as efficient connection of organizational resources, exchange information, and increase productivity, EDI ranks 1, 2, 3, and Internet application ranks 15, 16, 14 respectively.

SUCCESS OF BPR EFFORTS

We tried to assess BPR efforts from different perspectives. A series of analysis of variance was performed to further investigate the responses by the participant organizations to the selected variables.

Table 3. Comparison of reasons for using EDI or Internet technology for BPR

Reasons for Using Internet or EDI	Rank in Internet	Rank in EDI
Easier access to information	1	15
Electronic commerce	2	6
Cost reduction	3	7
Reduce geographic distance	4	17
Faster processing speed	5	8
Reduce administration	6	4
Reduce distribution costs	7	12
Easily accessible communication network	8	14
Faster access to information	9	13
Reduce paper flow	10	11
Access to more accurate information	11	9
Communication between employees	12	16
Global exchange of information	13	18
Increase productivity	14	3
Efficient connection of organizational resources	15	1
Exchange information	16	2

Perceived Success of BPR Across Different Kinds of Organizations

We performed ANOVA to investigate the perceived success scores across three main participant organizations, including IT related business, manufacturing, and consulting firms.

It was found that the mean scores were significantly different across different organization types (F-value = 13.2, P < 0.05). While the mean for perceived success score was lowest among the consulting firms, it was highest among the IT industries. See Table 4 for more statistics.

Perceived Success of BPR Between EDI and Internet Applications

We performed ANOVA to see if there are any significant differences among the perceived success scores across selected technologies for BPR. It was found that the mean scores were significantly different between EDI and Internet applications with a mean score of 3.25 for EDI and 3.55 for Internet (F-value = 8.97, P < 0.05). The results are presented in Table 5.

Perceived Success of BPR Across Different Kinds of Methodology

ANOVA was performed to investigate the perceived success scores across three main methodologies that are commonly use in BPR programs: outside consulting methodology, internal methodology, and joint methodology (internal

Table 4. ANOVA: Perceived success of BPR across different kinds of organizations*

Participant Organizations	Mean	S.D.	F-value
IT Industries	3.65	0.29	
Manufacturing	3.34	0.19	13.2
Consulting	3.32	0.26	

*1: Low, 5: High

Table 5. ANOVA: Perceived success of BPR across different kinds of information technology

Selected technology	Mean	S.D.	F-value
EDI	3.25	0.45	
Internet	3.55	0.37	8.97

and external). It was found that the mean scores were significantly different across different kinds of methodology (F-value = 6.84, P < 0.05).

While the mean for perceived success score was lowest among the organizations using their own methodology, it was highest among the organizations using a joint methodology with conjunction of internal and external expertise. The detailed statistics are presented in Table 6.

PROBLEMS IN BPR

Through review of the literature (Clemons, Thatcher, & Row, 1995; Grover et al., 1995; Grover, Jeong, & Teng, 1998; Hammer & Champy, 1993), we compiled a list of four main problems commonly encountered in BPR efforts and included them in the questionnaire. The severity of the problems was again measured on a Likert scale of 1 to 5. Financial problems, technical ability, human resources, and time limitation are the greatest problems when firms engage in BPR. In order to determine whether there were any significant differences in the severity of problems in BPR efforts among three main participant organizations, ANOVA test was performed. Two of the four problems including human resources and technical ability were significantly different among different organizations. The results are presented in Table 7.

Table 6. ANOVA: Perceived success of BPR across different kinds of methodology

Participant Organizations	Mean	S.D.	F-value
External methodology	3.52	0.27	
Internal methodology	3.33	0.17	6.84
Joint methodology	3.69	0.23	

Table 7. ANOVA: Problems in BPR across different kinds of organizations

Problems in BPR	Mean			S.D.			F-value
	I	M	C	I	M	C	
Financial Problems	3.54	3.52	3.36	0.29	0.32	0.32	1.45
Technical abilities	3.32	3.70	3.46	0.20	0.28	0.33	12.80
Human resources	3.34	3.69	3.70	0.21	0.23	0.33	15.81
Time schedule	3.54	3.48	3.40	0.29	0.33	0.32	0.85

I: IT Industries; M: Manufacturing; C: Consulting firms

DISCUSSION AND CONCLUSION

This research used nine hypotheses to investigate the relationship between managerial and organizational factors and successful BPR implementation using EDI or Internet technology. Although all hypotheses were not accepted, recommendations can be made from the accepted and rejected hypotheses as well as comparison results of selected technology for BPR. The following is a discussion of the recommendations to organizations based on these research findings.

The BPR project should be conducted using a specific BPR methodology that is strictly adhered to and well documented from beginning to end of the process. Procedures for the new process should also be specifically defined and quantitatively measured. When properly constructed, a BPR methodology is designed to steer the reengineering of business processes toward success. This allows a BPR methodology to guide analytic thinking without bias toward one right answer or implementing a rigid set of rules that must be followed in an inflexible order. Without a methodology, BPR projects can flounder and be unsuccessful. According to our findings from 72 participant organizations in this research, only two respondents reported not using any type of BPR methodology. From the high percentage of organizations that reported using some type of methodology, it seems obvious that organizations have seen the benefits of utilizing a BPR methodology when using either EDI or Internet technology.

Despite popularity of BPR, many organizations have lack of experience in conducting BPR projects. To relax this problem, outside consultants can be used to provide expertise to BPR projects. However, consultants may lack the business expertise needed to develop a new cross-functional process for a specific organization. A good solution for utilizing outside BPR expertise is conjunction and collaboration of in-house expertise with outside BPR consultants for additional assistance. The finding of this study supports the joint collaboration of internal and external expertise for BPR efforts. We found that the mean for perceived success score was highest among the organizations using a joint methodology for BPR while it was lowest among the organizations using their own methodology without assistance of external expertise.

One of the first issues a BPR project should address is obtaining top management's support. Top management should serve as the BPR project's champion from the beginning all the way through the project's implementation. This champion should be well informed about the BPR project's objectives and its potential effects on the organization. This allows the champion to effectively communicate with employees affected by the BPR project. Most of the important decisions about the BPR should be made by top management and the BPR project team. Therefore, top management support must be obtained and sustained to successfully implement BPR.

We found a positive and strong correlation between egalitarian culture and centralization of decision making with successful implementation of BPR.

Organizational culture is an important factor in developing an innovative organizational environment for successful BPR implementation. Cooperation, coordination, and empowerment of employees are the standard characteristics of an innovative organizational environment. Therefore, open communication with strong leadership should be encouraged during the BPR project.

Customers of the BPR project should be involved throughout the BPR methodology s analysis, design, and implementation phases. The satisfaction of their requirements and needs should be one of the primary goals of the BPR project.

It is important for organizations to create an innovative environment to increase the chances of successfully implementing a BPR project that uses information technology. In order to do so, organizations must use a strong leadership style to create an environment where employees affected by the BPR project understand its objectives and are involved throughout the BPR process.

Radical changes may occur as a result of BPR and must be understood by all affected employees. Training and reward programs should be implemented to assist employees during their transition. These initiatives are easily implemented, especially when applying Internet technology because employees find Internet technology easy to work with and do not feel threatened by the technology.

This research found that financial problems, technical ability, human resources, and time limitation are the greatest problems when firms engage in BPR. It is also found that two of the four problems, including human resources and technical ability, were significantly different among different organizations. Understanding the expected problems and severity of them can help organizations to face these problems properly and increase the possibility of a successful implementation of BPR.

In this study, we found significant differences between selected information technology for BPR. We found that the perceived success score for participant organizations that applied Internet technology for BPR is significantly higher than those that applied EDI (3.55 vs. 3.25). This higher success result is perhaps due to ease of use of Internet technology. We also found significant differences across different kinds of organizations when applying information technology for their BPR programs, for instance, 3.65, 3.34, and 3.32 for IT industries, manufacturing, and consulting companies, respectively. Lack of attention to these relationships may be one reason for unacceptably high implementation failure rates in the previous BPR efforts.

REFERENCES

Aggarwal, S. (1997). Re-engineering a breakthrough or little new. *International Journal of Technology Management, 13*(3), 326-344.

Ahadi, H. R. (2002, June 8-9). Potential of IT application to business process reengineering. *Proceedings of the 2002 Asian Forum on Business Education Conference,* Beijing, China.

Ascari, A., Rock, M., & Dutta, S. (1995). Reengineering and organizational change: Lesson from a comparative analysis of company experiences. *European Management Journal, 13*(1), 1-30.

Bashein, B., Markus, L., & Riley, P. (1994). Precondition for BPR success. *Information Systems Management, 11*(2), 7-13.

Beyer, J., & Trice, H. (1978). *Implementing change: Alcoholism policies in work organizations.* New York: Free Press.

Brunell, T. (2000). Net's impact on SCM is still unclear. *Electronic Buyers' News.* Retrieved August 2, 2005, from http://www.ebnonline.com/supplychain/columns/story/OEG20000907S0041

Champy, J., & Arnoudse, D. (1992). The leadership challenge of reengineering. *Insights Quarterly: The Executive Journal of Business Reengineering, 4*(2), 17-25.

Clemons, K., Thatcher, M. E., & Row, M. C. (1995). Identifying sources of reengineering failures: A study of the behavioral factors contributing to reengineering risks. *Journal of Management Information Systems, 12*(2), 9-36.

Coulson, T., & Colin, J. (1997). The future of organization's achieving excellence through business transactions. *Management Services, 41*(12), 16-18.

CSC Index. (1994). *State of reengineering report.* Author. Retrieved December 18, 2001, from http://search.csc.com/query.html?st=121@charset=iso-8859-1&nh=20&col=csc&qt=%221994

Davenport, T. H. (1993). *Process innovation: Reengineering work through information technology.* Boston: Harvard Business School Press.

Davenport, T., & Short, J. (1990). The new industrial engineering: Information technology and business process redesign. *Sloan Management Review, 31*(4), 11-27.

Goll, E. O. (1992, December). Let's debunk the myths and misconceptions about reengineering. *APICS The Performance Advantage,* pp. 29-32.

Griffith, T., & Northcraft, G. (1996, March). Cognitive elements in the implementation of new technology: Can less information provide more benefits. *MIS Quarterly,* pp. 99-110.

Grover, V., Jeong, S. R., & Teng, J. T. C. (1998). Survey of reengineering challenges. *Information System Management, 15*(2), 53-59.

Grover, V., Teng, J., & Fiedler, K. (1995). The implementation of business process reengineering. *Journal of Management Information Systems, 12*(1), 109-144.

Hall, G., Rosenthal, J., & Wade, J. (1993). How the reengineering really work. *Harvard Business Review, 71*(6), 119-131.

Hammer, M., & Stanton, S. (1994). *The reengineering revolution.* New York: Harper Business.

Hammer, M., & Champy, J. (1993). *Reengineering the corporation: A manifesto for business revolution.* London: HarperCollins.

Hammer, M. (1990). Reengineering work: Don't automate, obliterate. *Harvard Business Review, 68*(4), 104-112.

Harrison, D. B., & Pratt, M. D. (1993). A methodology for reengineering business. *Planning Review, 21*(2), 6-11.

Janson, R. (1993). How reengineering transforms organizations to satisfy customers? *National Productivity Review, 12*(1), 45-53.

Johansson, H., McHugh, P., Pendlebury, J., & Wheeler, W. (1993). *Business process reengineering: Break point strategies for market dominance.* West Sussex, UK: John Wiley & Sons.

Kalakota, R., & Whinston, A. (1996). *Frontiers of electronic commerce.* Reading, MA: Addison-Wesley.

Katzenbach, J. R., & Smith, D. K. (1993). The rules for managing cross-functional reengineering teams. *Planning Review, 21*(2), 12-13.

Klein, M. M. (1994). Reengineering methodologies and tools: A prescription for enhancing success. *Information Systems Management, 11*(2), 30-35.

Lim, D., & Palvia, P. C. (2001). EDI in strategic supply chain: Impact on customer service. *International Journal of Information Management, 21*, 193-211.

Maglitta, J. (1995). IS seen as reengineering blockade. *Computer World, 29*(24), 20.

Marchand, D., & Stanford, M. (1995). Business process redesign: A framework for harmonizing people, information and technology. In V. Grover & W. J. Kettinger (Eds.), *Business process change: Concepts, methods and technologies.* Hershey, PA: Idea Group Publishing.

Martinsons, M. G., & Hempel, P. S. (1998). Chinese business process re-engineering. *International Journal of Information Management, 18*(6), 393-407.

McGrath, G., & Schneider, A. (1997, June-July). Measuring intranet return on investment. *Intranet Communicator, 1*, 10-15.

Moch, M., & Morse, J. (1977). Ambiguity and choice in organizations. *Administration Science Quarterly, 22*(2), 351-362.

Morris, D., & Brandon, J. (1993). *Re-engineering your business.* New York: McGraw-Hill.

Parker, M. M. P. (1996). *Strategic transformation and information technology: Paradigms for performing while transforming.* Upper Saddle River, NJ: Prentice Hall.

Peppard, J., & Rowland, P. (1995). *The essence of business process reengineering.* Upper Saddle River, NJ: Prentice Hall.

Ranganathan, C., & Dhaliwal, S. (2001). A survey of business process reengineering practices in Singapore. *Information and Management, 39,* 125-134.

Scheer, A. W. (1998). *Business process engineering: Reference model for industrial enterprises.* Springer.

Smith, G., & Willcocks, L. (1995). *Business process reengineering, politics and management: From methodologies to processes.* Harrisburg, PA: Idea Group Publishing.

Stewart, T. A. (1993). Reengineering: The hot new management tool. *Fortune,* 41-48.

Stow, R. P. (1993). Reengineering by objectives. *Planning Review, 21*(3), 14-16.

Stanton, S., Hammer, M., & Power, B. (1992). From resistance to results: Mastering the organizational issues of reengineering. *Insights Quarterly: The Executive Journal of Business Reengineering, 4*(2), 6-16.

Van De Ven, A. H. (1986). Central problems in the management of innovation. *Management Science, 32,* 590-607.

Venkatraman, N. (1994). IT-enabled business transformation: From automation to business scope redefinition. *Sloan Management Review, 35*(2), 73-87.

Zaltman, G., (1973). Note on an international invisible college for information exchange. *Journal of American Information, 25*(2), 74.

Zeff, R., & Aronson, B. (1997). Advertising on the Internet. *Wiley Computer Publishing,* pp.7-27.

Zirger, B., & Maidique, M. (1990). A model of new product development: An empirical test. *Management Science, 36,* 867-883.

About the Authors

Mehdi Khosrow-Pour, DBA, is executive director of the Information Resources Management Association (IRMA) and senior academic technology editor for Idea Group Inc. Previously, he served on the faculty of the Pennsylvania State University as a professor of information systems for 20 years. He has written or edited more than 30 books in information technology management. Khosrow-Pour is also editor-in-chief of the *Information Resources Management Journal, Journal of Electronic Commerce in Organizations, Journal of Cases on Information Technology*, and *International Journal of Cases on Electronic Commerce.*

*   *   *

Hamid Reza Ahadi (ahadi@imi.ir; ahadi@iust.ac.ir) earned his PhD in management science from Tsinghua University in Beijing, China (2002) and his master's and bachelor's degrees from Tehran and Shiraz University in Iran, respectively. Currently, he is an assistant professor at the Iran University of Science and Technology in Tehran. He is also a member of the advisory board at the Industrial Management Institute of Iran. His research interests include IT application to business process reengineering, management information technology, and electronic commerce.

Hayward P. Andres is a management information systems professor with an interest in the impact of information technology on organizational processes, organizational and social factors that impact software project success, enterprise-wide information systems, computer-mediated communication, team processes, and multimedia systems. Dr. Andres received his PhD in management information systems from Florida State University. Currently, Dr. Andres is an assistant professor of information systems at North Carolina A&T State University, USA. Dr. Andres has published in the *Journal of Management Information Systems*, *Information Resources Management Journal*, *Journal of Educational Technology Systems*, and the *Team Performance Management Journal*.

Catherine M. Beise is an associate professor in information systems in the Perdue School of Business at Salisbury University in Salisbury. Her previous experience includes work in industry as a consultant, systems analyst, and programmer, and as a GSS facilitator for the U.S. Army. She holds a PhD from the College of Business at Georgia State University and an MS in information and computer science from the Georgia Institute of Technology. Her current research interests include project management, team technology support, and diversity in IT project teams. Her previous publications have appeared in *MIS Quarterly* and *Communications of AIS* and other outlets, and she is a member of the Association for Information Systems, ACM, and the Project Management Institute.

Irwin T. J. Brown is a senior lecturer in information systems at the University of Cape Town, South Africa and holds a Master of Information Systems from Curtin University of Technology, Perth, Australia. His research interests include IT in developing countries, technology adoption, and strategic information systems planning. He has recently had papers accepted in the *International Journal of Information Management*, the *Journal of Global Information Management*, *Journal of Global Information Technology Management*, and *Electronic Journal of Information Systems in Developing Countries*.

Terry Anthony Byrd is a professor of MIS in the Department of Management, College of Business, Auburn University, USA. He holds a BS in electrical engineering from the University of Massachusetts at Amherst and a PhD in management information systems from the University of South Carolina. His research has appeared in *MIS Quarterly*, *Journal of Management Information Systems*, *Decision Sciences*, *OMEGA*, *Interfaces*, and other leading journals. His current research interests include the strategic management of information technology, information technology architecture and infrastructure, electronic commerce, and information technology implementation.

C. Clay Dibrell is an assistant professor of strategic management in the College of Business at Oregon State University (USA). He earned his PhD from the

University of Memphis, where he majored in strategic management and minored in international business. His areas of research interest include a strong focus on strategic planning, the influence of information technology and temporal strategies on firm processes within both a domestic and international context, and the issues of legitimacy surrounding entrepreneurial start-ups.

Evan W. Duggan is an associate professor of MIS in the Culverhouse College of Commerce & Business Administration, University of Alabama (USA). He earned a PhD and MBA from Georgia State University and a BSc from the University of the West Indies, Jamaica. He has more than 25 years of IT experience in industry. His research interests involve the management of information systems (IS) in corporations with reference to IS success factors and quality, socio-technical issues, and systems development and project management methodologies. He has publications (or articles forthcoming) in the *International Journal of Industrial Engineering, Journal of International Technology and Information Management, Information Technology & Management, Journal of End User Computing, Information Resources Management Journal, Human-Computer Interactions, Information & Management, Electronic Journal of Information Systems in Developing Countries*, and *Communications of the Association of Information Systems*. Dr. Duggan has taught MIS and decision sciences courses at the graduate and undergraduate levels, including executive MBA programs, in several U.S. and international institutions.

Aryya Gangopadhyay (gangopad@umbc.edu) is an associate professor of information systems at the University of Maryland, Baltimore County (UMBC). He has a PhD in computer information systems from Rutgers University. His research interests include decision support using data warehousing and mining, database applications in geographic information systems, and health care informatics. He has co-authored and edited three books, several book chapters, and numerous papers in journals.

Michael S. Gates received his MS in information technology from the University of North Texas and received his BS from Texas Tech University. He is currently pursing doctorate studies in business computer information systems at the University of North Texas (USA). He has worked in information technology for IBM, Verizon, and BEA Systems. His research interests include information system metrics and database design, implementation, and management. He has taught in the public school system in Texas and at Texas Tech University.

Zhensen Huang (zhuang@umbc.edu) is a senior system architect at a government agency. He earned a PhD from the University of Maryland, Baltimore

County, USA. His research interests include supply chain management, decision support systems, and human computer interaction. He has published several papers in journals such as the *Information Resources Management Journal* and *Journal of Global Information Management*. Also, he has presented his research at national and international conferences such as the annual meetings of the Decision Sciences Institute (DSI) and Information Resources Management Association (IRMA). His research also appeared as book chapters in *Advanced Topics in Global Information Management* and *Human Computer Interaction Development and Management*.

Grover S. Kearns is an assistant professor at the College of Business, University of South Florida, St. Petersburg (USA). He holds a PhD in decision sciences and information systems from the University of Kentucky, an MBA from the University of Texas at Austin, BA degrees in both management and accounting, and is a licensed CPA. Prior to his current position, he was director of planning for an electric utility. His research focuses on the strategic aspects of information systems and electronic commerce, particularly investment evaluation, project management, and alignment. He has published his research in the *Information Resources Management Journal, Decision Sciences, Information and Management, Journal of Strategic Information Systems*, and elsewhere.

Bruce R. Lewis is an assistant professor of information systems and director of the IS program in the Wayne Calloway School of Business and Accountancy at Wake Forest University (USA). He spent 25 years as a practicing IT professional, including serving as executive director of computing at Auburn University and as a member of the board of the Alabama Supercomputer Authority. He holds a BS in mathematics and an MS in statistics; he received his PhD in MIS from Auburn University. His research interests include issues relating to the management of information technology and business intelligence systems. He has published in the *Journal of Management Information Systems, Communications of the AIS*, the *Journal of Computer Information Systems, Information Systems Management*, and *Expert Systems with Applications*.

Herb Mattord completed 24 years of IT industry experience before becoming a full-time academic. His experiences as an application developer, database administrator, project manager, and information security practitioner were a valuable background to his current role, a tenure-track instructor at Kennesaw State University in Georgia (USA). During his career as an IT practitioner, he has been an adjunct professor at Kennesaw State University in Kennesaw Georgia, Southern Polytechnic State University in Marietta, Georgia, Austin

Community College in Austin, Texas, and Texas State University-San Marcos. He currently teaches undergraduate courses in information systems and information security and assurance. He was formerly the manager of corporate information technology security at Georgia-Pacific Corporation, where his practical knowledge of information security implementation and management was acquired. He is the co-author of *Principles of Information Security*, with Dr. Michael Whitman. Their new textbook, *Management of Information Security*, is in press.

Fiona Fui-Hoon Nah is an associate professor of information systems at the University of Nebraska - Lincoln (USA). She received her PhD in MIS from the University of British Columbia. Her research interests include the use of knowledge-based systems to support group decision making, HCI in individual and group settings, and ERP. She is an associate editor for the *Journal of Electronic Commerce Research* and an editorial board member of seven other major journals.

Stefan G. Nicovich is currently an assistant professor in the Whittemore School of Business and Economics at the University of New Hampshire (USA). He holds a PhD from the University of Memphis. His research interests include computer-mediated communication and the effect of presence in mediated environments.

Fred Niederman serves as the Shaughnessy endowed professor of MIS at Saint Louis University, USA. His doctoral degree is from the University of Minnesota in 1990. His primary research areas pertain to using information technology to support teams and groups; global information technology; and information technology personnel. He has published more than 30 refereed journal articles include several in top MIS journals including *MIS Quarterly*, *Communications of the ACM*, and *Decision Sciences*; has presented papers at several major conferences; and serves as associate editor of the *Journal of Global Information Systems*.

Sherry D. Ryan is an assistant professor of business computer information systems at the University of North Texas (USA). She received her PhD in MIS from the University of Texas at Arlington and her MBA from the University of Southern California. Prior to returning to academia, she worked for IBM, teaching courses and speaking at national conferences. Her research interests include knowledge management, database design, IT training and human resource issues, and IT investment decisions. Her work has appeared in several journals including *Journal of Management Information Systems, Information* *and Management, DATA BASE*, and *Information Resources Management Journal*.

Toru Sakaguchi is assistant professor of information systems in the College of Business at Northern Kentucky University (USA). He completed his PhD in management information systems at the University of Memphis. His research interests are in interorganizational systems, electronic commerce, and global information technology management.

Mary Sumner is serving as associate dean for executive education for the School of Business at Southern Illinois University, Edwardsville (USA). In this role, she organizes business/university partnerships and executive education programs, including the Technology and Commerce Roundtable, the Construction Leadership Institute, the High-Tech Bootcamp, and the e-Business initiative. Dr. Sumner is a professor of computer management information systems and also serves as director of the undergraduate program in computer management information systems (BS, CMIS). She has written seven textbooks and has published more than 40 research papers on computer-supported collaborative work, the management of information technology personnel, ERP project implementation, and electronic commerce. Her research has appeared in *Database, Journal of Systems Management, Information and Management, Journal of Computer Information Systems*, and *Information Resource Management Journal*. Her academic background includes a bachelor's degree from Syracuse University, a master's from the University of Chicago, a master's from Columbia University, and a doctorate from Rutgers University.

Xin Tan is a PhD candidate in the Department of Management at the University of Nebraska - Lincoln (USA). He obtained a BE from Shanghai Jiao Tong University and an MBA from Miami University. His current research interests include end users' acceptance of advanced information technology and enterprise systems, conceptual and data modeling methods, and using cognitive mapping techniques to improve requirements determination.

W. A. Taylor is associate dean for research and chair of operations and information systems at the Bradford School of Management, University of Bradford, UK. He holds a BSc in electronics and information systems, an MSc in industrial engineering, and a PhD in intelligent knowledge based systems, all from the Queen's University in Belfast. Before embarking on his academic career, Taylor worked in aerospace, public utilities, and government organizations, latterly advising private firms on the implementation of new technologies. His current research interests include knowledge management and IT in health care, alliances, and partnerships. He is also an adviser to government on matters of information resource management, performance and governance. He has published widely and has authored more than 100 papers and monographs.

Soon Hing Teh completed his master's degree in MIS at the University of Nebraska - Lincoln. His industry experience includes various aspects of testing associated with ERP, ABAP programming, and help desk support. He is now an analyst programmer at Singapore Power Ltd.

Douglas E. Turner is an assistant professor in management and business systems at the State University of West Georgia (USA). He earned a master's degree in operations management and a PhD in management information systems from Auburn University. He has published in *Journal of Management Information Systems*, *Decision Sciences*, *Information & Management*, and other leading journals. His current research focuses on information infrastructures and competitive advantage.

G. H. Wright is executive director of research and chair of strategic marketing at the Business School at Manchester Metropolitan University, Business School, UK. Professor Wright obtained a BA in business studies from Middlesex University and a PhD from the University of Bradford. Her research is concerned with the effective management of quality and customer focus, with a particular emphasis on the health care sector. This focus builds on 10 years of research experience in market focused service delivery. Her professional background is in market research in the pharmaceutical industry and market analysis in electronics. Her research on quality in customer focused service management has been widely published, and she has been a visiting fellow of the Nuffield Institute for Health since 1995.

Index

A

Abilene paradox 261
agile development methods 266
analytic hierarchy process (AHP) 262

B

behavioral intention 148
BPR failure factors 325
business process reengineering (BPR)
    319

C

capability maturity model (CMM) 263
centralization of decision making 331
change management 330
cleanroom software engineering (CSE)
    264
cleanroon software engineering (CSE)
    265
commercial off-the-shelf (COTS) 258
compatibility 152
component-based development (CBD)
    268
confirmatory factor analysis (CFA) 154
customer involvement 333

D

data collection 288
design techniques 264

E

EDI as an IT enabler 328
Egalitarian culture 332
employee resistance 331
enterprise resource planning (ERP) 143
external environment 286
extreme programming (XP) 264

F

formalization of procedures 332

I

information plan 287
information quality 243
information systems planning (ISP) 283
integration of jobs 332
internal environment 286
Internet as an IT enabler 328
iterative/incremental delivery paradigm
    264